BONHOEFFER AND CHRISTOLOGY

T&T Clark New Studies in Bonhoeffer's Theology and Ethics

Series editors
Jennifer McBride
Michael Mawson
Philip G. Ziegler

BONHOEFFER AND CHRISTOLOGY

Revisiting Chalcedon

Edited by
Matthias Grebe, Nadine Hamilton and
Christian Schlenker

LONDON • NEW YORK • OXFORD • NEW DELHI • SYDNEY

T&T CLARK

Bloomsbury Publishing Plc

50 Bedford Square, London, WC1B 3DP, UK
1385 Broadway, New York, NY 10018, USA
29 Earlsfort Terrace, Dublin 2, Ireland

BLOOMSBURY, T&T CLARK and the T&T Clark logo are trademarks of Bloomsbury Publishing Plc

First published in Great Britain 2023
Paperback edition published 2025

Copyright © Matthias Grebe, Nadine Hamilton and Christian Schlenker, 2023

Matthias Grebe, Nadine Hamilton and Christian Schlenker have asserted their rights under the Copyright, Designs and Patents Act, 1988, to be identified as Editors of this work.

Cover image: Dietrich Bonhoeffer (1906–1945) photographed in the late 1930s.
Photo by ullstein bild via Getty Images

All rights reserved. No part of this publication may be reproduced or transmitted in any form or by any means, electronic or mechanical, including photocopying, recording, or any information storage or retrieval system, without prior permission in writing from the publishers.

Bloomsbury Publishing Plc does not have any control over, or responsibility for, any third-party websites referred to or in this book. All internet addresses given in this book were correct at the time of going to press. The author and publisher regret any inconvenience caused if addresses have changed or sites have ceased to exist, but can accept no responsibility for any such changes.

A catalogue record for this book is available from the British Library.

A catalog record for this book is available from the Library of Congress.

ISBN: HB: 978-0-5677-0841-0
       PB: 978-0-5677-0846-5
       ePDF: 978-0-5677-0842-7
       eBook: 978-0-5677-0845-8

Series: T&T Clark New Studies in Bonhoeffer's Theology and Ethics

Typeset by Integra Software Services Pvt. Ltd.

To find out more about our authors and books visit www.bloomsbury.com and sign up for our newsletters.

In memory of Prof. Dr. Christoph Schwöbel (1955–2021)

CONTENTS

List of contributors ix
List of abbreviations xi
Preface xiv

Introduction 1

Part I
RECOVERING CHALCEDONIAN LOGIC WITH BONHOEFFER

Chapter 1
THE CHALLENGE OF DIETRICH BONHOEFFER'S CHRISTOLOGY AND
THE CONTEMPORARY DEBATES ON CHALCEDON
  Christoph Schwöbel 11

Chapter 2
ONTOLOGY AND SALVATION: WHY CHALCEDON MATTERS FOR
BONHOEFFER
  Rowan Williams 21

Chapter 3
KIERKEGAARD'S AND BONHOEFFER'S PARADOX CHRISTOLOGY
  Lea Weber 36

Chapter 4
BONHOEFFER'S UNDERSTANDING OF CHALCEDON IN DIALOGUE
WITH CONTEMPORARY CATHOLIC CHRISTOLOGY
  Jacob Phillips 55

Chapter 5
'TO CARRY ON IN THIS CHALCEDONIAN SENSE': CHRISTOLOGY IN
LETTERS AND PAPERS FROM PRISON
  Philip G. Ziegler 75

Part II
JESUS CHRIST: VERE HOMO, VERE DEUS

Chapter 6
BEING HUMAN IN LIGHT OF CHALCEDON: THE NECESSARY POSSIBILITY
OF BEING ONE
  Nadine Hamilton 93

Chapter 7
BONHOEFFER'S ECCE HOMO!: CHRISTOLOGY FROM THE CENTRE AND THE FULLNESS OF LIFE
    Christian Schlenker   113

Chapter 8
THE SUFFERING GOD: BONHOEFFER AND CHALCEDONIAN CHRISTOLOGY
    Matthias Grebe   137

Chapter 9
HOW GOD SUFFERS: BONHOEFFER, MOLTMANN AND THEOLOGICAL LANGUAGE
    Michael Mawson   154

Part III
THE WORLD AND THE CHURCH

Chapter 10
CHRISTOLOGY'S COUNTERPOINT: BONHOEFFER ON KNOWING THE CHRIST WHO CALLS
    Koert Verhagen   173

Chapter 11
'PREPARING THE WAY' FOR GOD'S WORD: A CENTRAL MOTIF OF BONHOEFFER'S ETHICS AND ITS IMPLICATIONS FOR PUBLIC THEOLOGY
    Hannah Bleher   187

Chapter 12
'GOING AHEAD' AS REAL HUMAN BEINGS IN THE *GEMEINDE*: BONHOEFFER'S CHRISTOLOGICAL FORM AND FORMATION IN SUFFERING AND DYING
    Samuel Efrain Murillo Torres   209

Chapter 13
JESUS CHRIST: THE CENTRE OF THE CHURCH
    David Emerton   236

Cumulative bibliography   256
Index   271

CONTRIBUTORS

Hannah Bleher is doctoral researcher at the Chair of Social Ethics & Ethics of Technology at the University of Bonn, Germany. Her publications include 'Diffused Responsibility: Attributions of Responsibility in the Use of AI-driven Clinical Decision Support Systems' in *AI & Ethics* (2022). Bleher is pursuing a PhD on political science approaches to public discourse, its forms, structures and potentials from a theological–ethical perspective.

David Emerton is Director of St Mellitus College, East Midlands (UK). He is the author of *God's Church-Community: The Ecclesiology of Dietrich Bonhoeffer* (2020). Emerton's current research is focused on contemporary approaches to ecclesiology. He is working on his second monograph, a study entitled *Types of Ecclesiology*.

Matthias Grebe is Lecturer in Theology at St Mellitus College, London. His first monograph was published as *Election, Atonement, and the Holy Spirit: Through and Beyond Barth's Interpretation of Scripture* (foreword by David F. Ford, 2014). He is currently working on his *Habilitation* on Bonhoeffer and theodicy, and is one of the editors of the forthcoming *T&T Clark Handbook of Suffering and the Problem of Evil*.

Nadine Hamilton is Akademische Rätin and teaches Systematic Theology at the Friedrich-Alexander Universität Erlangen-Nürnberg, Germany. She is the author of *Dietrich Bonhoeffers Hermeneutik der Responsivität: Ein Kapitel Schriftlehre im Anschluss an 'Schöpfung und Fall'* (2016). Hamilton's *Habilitation* is entitled *Eine Ontologie des Namens Gottes. Zur Wiedergewinnung christologischer Grundgedanken*.

Michael Mawson is the Maclaurin Goodfellow Associate Professor of Theological and Religious Studies at the University of Auckland and Research Fellow at the University of the Free State, South Africa. He is the author of *Christ Existing as Community: Bonhoeffer's Ecclesiology* (2018) and co-editor (with Philip Ziegler) of the *Oxford Handbook of Dietrich Bonhoeffer* (2019).

Samuel Efrain Murillo Torres is lecturer at Comunidad Teológica de México, currently, teaching assistant and PhD candidate in Systematic Theology at the University of Aberdeen. His research is on 'Aesthetic Public Theology from the Margins: Engaging Bonhoeffer's Public Theology with Searching Efforts of Families Experiencing Enforced Disappearances in Mexico,' as part of the national process for peace and ecumenical accompaniment in search of disappeared people in Mexico: ¡Hasta Encontrarles!

Jacob Phillips is Associate Professor of Theology at St Mary's University, Twickenham, UK, and Director of the Institute of Theology and Liberal Arts. He works across a diverse range of sub-disciplinary areas, mostly within systematic and philosophical theology. His recent publications include *Human Subjectivity in the Theology of Dietrich Bonhoeffer* (2019) and *Obedience Is Freedom* (2022), and *John Henry Newman and the English Sensibility* (forthcoming 2023).

Christian Schlenker is a research assistant and teaches Systematic Theology and Ethics at the Faculty of Protestant Theology at the University of Tübingen. His publications include 'Dietrich Bonhoeffer. Seine theologische Ethik und ihre Relevanz für die Friedensethik heute' (2018). Schlenker just finished a PhD on *'Dasein für Andere. Subjektivitätskritik, Transzendenz und Verantwortung in Bonhoeffers "Ethik" in Auseinandersetzung mit Heideggers "Sein und Zeit"'*.

Christoph Schwöbel was Professor at St Andrews University and held the Chair of Divinity from 2018 until his death in 2021. His vast variety of publications includes *Gott in Beziehung: Studien zur Dogmatik* (2002) and *Gott im Gespräch: Studien zur theologischen Gegenwartsdeutung* (2011). One of his last essays engages with Chalcedon 'The Generosity of the Triune God and the Humility of the Son' (2022).

Koert Verhagen is Assistant Professor of Philosophy and Religion at Taylor University (USA). He holds a PhD from the University of St Andrews and is the author of *Being and Action* Coram Deo: *Bonhoeffer and the Retrieval of Justification's Social Import* (2021). He is currently working on a monograph-length theology of gratitude.

Lea Weber is a PhD candidate at the University of Tübingen. She studied theology at Tübingen, Greifswald, and Duke University, USA. Her dissertation focuses on the significance of the Incarnation in the thought of Søren Kierkegaard and Dietrich Bonhoeffer.

Rowan Williams is a former Archbishop of Canterbury and recently retired as Master of Magdalene College, Cambridge. The author of many books on patristic and systematic theology, he published in 2018 *Christ the Heart of Creation*, which included a discussion of Bonhoeffer's Christology, and has more recently (2021) published *Looking East in Winter*, essays on the significance of Eastern Christian thought for contemporary theological debates.

Philip G. Ziegler is Professor of Christian Dogmatics at the University of Aberdeen, Scotland. He is the author of *Doing Theology when God Is Forgotten: The Theological Achievement of Wolf Krötke* (2007) and *Militant Grace: The Apocalyptic Turn and the Future of Theology* (2018). Together with Michael Mawson he co-edited the *Oxford Handbook of Dietrich Bonhoeffer* (2019).

ABBREVIATIONS

DBWE 1   *Sanctorum Communio: A Theological Study of the Sociology of the Church*. In *Dietrich Bonhoeffer Works*, English Edition, vol. 1. Edited by Clifford Green and translated by Reinhard Krauss and Nancy Lukens. Minneapolis, MN: Fortress Press, 1998.

DBW 1   *Sanctorum Communio: Eine dogmatische Untersuchung zur Soziologie der Kirche*. In *Dietrich Bonhoeffer Werke*, Bd. 1. Edited by Joachim von Soosten. Gütersloh: Gütersloher Verlagshaus, 1986.

DBWE 2   *Act and Being: Transcendental Philosophy and Ontology in Systematic Theology*. In *Dietrich Bonhoeffer Works*, English Edition, vol. 2. Edited by Wayne Whitson Floyd, Jr, and translated by H. R. Rumscheidt. Minneapolis, MN: Fortress Press, 1996.

DBW 2   *Akt und Sein: Transzendentalphilosophie und Ontologie in der systematischen Theologie*. In *Dietrich Bonhoeffer Werke*, Bd. 2. Edited by Hans-Richard Reuter Gütersloh: Gütersloher Verlagshaus, 1988.

DBWE 3   *Creation and Fall: A Theological Exposition of Genesis 1–3*. In *Dietrich Bonhoeffer Works*, English Edition, vol. 3. Edited by John W. de Gruchy and translated by Douglas Stephen Bax. Minneapolis, MN: Fortress Press, 2004.

DBW 3   *Schöpfung und Fall*. In *Dietrich Bonhoeffer Werke*, Bd. 3. Edited by Martin Rüter and Ilse Tödt. Gütersloh: Gütersloher Verlagshaus, 1989.

DBWE 4   *Discipleship*. In *Dietrich Bonhoeffer Works*, English Edition, vol. 4. Edited by Geoffrey Kelly and John D. Godsey and translated by Barbara Green and Reinhard Krauss. Minneapolis, MN: Fortress Press, 2001.

DBW 4   *Nachfolge*. In *Dietrich Bonhoeffer Werke*, Bd. 4. Edited by Martin Kuske and Ilse Tödt (Gütersloh: Gütersloher Verlagshaus, 1989).

DBWE 5   *Life Together/Prayerbook of the Bible*. In *Dietrich Bonhoeffer Works*, English Edition, vol. 5. Edited by Geoffrey Kelly and translated by Daniel Bloesch and James Burtness. Minneapolis, MN: Fortress Press, 1996.

DBW 5   *Gemeinsames Leben/Das Gebetbuch der Bibel*. In *Dietrich Bonhoeffer Werke*, Bd. 5. Edited by Gerhard Ludwig Müller and Albrecht Schönherr. Gütersloh: Gütersloher Verlagshaus, 1987.

DBWE 6   *Ethics*. In *Dietrich Bonhoeffer Works*, English Edition, vol. 6. Edited by Clifford Green and translated by Reinhard Krauss, Charles West and Douglas W. Stott. Minneapolis, MN: Fortress Press, 2006.

DBW 6	*Ethik*. In *Dietrich Bonhoeffer Werke*, Bd. 6. Edited by Ilse Tödt, Heinz Eduard Tödt, Ernst Feil and Clifford Green. Gütersloh: Gütersloher Verlagshaus, 1992.
DBWE 7	*Fiction from Tegel Prison*. In *Dietrich Bonhoeffer Works*, English Edition, vol. 7. Edited by Clifford Green and translated by Nancy Lukens. Minneapolis, MN: Fortress Press, 2000.
DBW 7	*Fragmente aus Tegel*. In *Dietrich Bonhoeffer Werke*, Bd. 7. Edited by Renate Bethge and Ilse Tödt. Gütersloh: Gütersloher Verlagshaus, 1994.
DBWE 8	*Letters and Papers from Prison*. In *Dietrich Bonhoeffer Works*, English Edition, vol. 8. Edited by John W. de Gruchy and translated by Isabel Best, Lisa E. Dahill, Reinhard Krauss, Nancy Lukens, H. Martin Rumscheidt and Douglas W. Stott. Minneapolis, MN: Fortress Press, 2010.
DBW 8	*Widerstand und Ergebung: Briefe und Aufzeichnungen aus der Haft*. In *Dietrich Bonhoeffer Werke*, Bd. 8. Edited by Christian Gremmels, Eberhard Bethge and Renate Bethge in Zusammenarbeit mit Ilse Tödt. Gütersloh: Gütersloher Verlagshaus, 1998.
DBWE 9	*The Young Bonhoeffer: 1918–1927*. In *Dietrich Bonhoeffer Works*, English Edition, vol. 9. Edited by Paul Duane Matheny, Clifford J. Green and Marshall D. Johnson and translated by Mary C. Nebelsick and Douglas W. Stott. Minneapolis, MN: Fortress Press, 2003.
DBW 9	*Jugend und Studium: 1918–1927*. In *Dietrich Bonhoeffer Werke*, Bd. 9. Edited by Hans Pfeifer in Zusammenarbeit mit Clifford Green and Carl-Jürgen Kaltenborn. Gütersloh: Gütersloher Verlagshaus, 1986.
DBWE 10	*Barcelona, Berlin, New York: 1928–1931*. In *Dietrich Bonhoeffer Works*, English Edition, vol. 10. Edited by Clifford Green and translated by Douglas W. Stott. Minneapolis, MN: Fortress Press, 2007.
DBW 10	*Barcelona, Berlin, Amerika: 1928–1931*. In *Dietrich Bonhoeffer Werke*, Bd. 10. Edited by Reinhart Staats and Hans Christoph von Hase in Zusammenarbeit mit Holger Roggelin and Matthias Wünsche. Gütersloh: Gütersloher Verlagshaus, 1992.
DBWE 11	*Ecumenical, Academic, and Pastoral Work: 1931–1932*. In *Dietrich Bonhoeffer Works*, English Edition, vol. 11. Edited by Victoria J. Barnett, Mark S. Brocker and Michael Lukens and translated by Anne Schmidt-Lange, Isabel Best, Nicolas Humphrey, Marion Pauck and Douglas W. Stott. Minneapolis, MN: Fortress Press, 2012.
DBW 11	*Ökumene, Universität, Pfarramt 1931–1932*. In *Dietrich Bonhoeffer Werke*, Bd. 11. Edited by Eberhard Amelung and Christoph Strohm. Gütersloh: Gütersloher Verlagshaus, 1994.

DBWE 12	*Berlin: 1932–1933*. In *Dietrich Bonhoeffer Works*, English Edition, vol. 12. Edited by Larry Rasmussen and translated by Isabelle Best and David Higgins. Minneapolis, MN: Fortress Press, 2009.
DBW 12	*Berlin 1932–1933*. In *Dietrich Bonhoeffer Werke*, Bd. 12. Edited by Carsten Nicolaisen and Ernst-Albert Scharffenorth. Gütersloh: Gütersloher Verlagshaus, 1997.
DBWE 13	*London: 1933–1935*. In *Dietrich Bonhoeffer Works*, English Edition, vol. 13. Edited by Keith Clements and translated by Isabel Best and Douglas W. Stott. Minneapolis, MN: Fortress, 2007.
DBW 13	*London 1933–1935*. In *Dietrich Bonhoeffer Werke*, Bd. 13. Edited by Hans Goedeking, Martin Heimbucherm and Hans-Walter Schleicher. Gütersloh: Gütersloher Verlagshaus, 1994.
DBWE 14	*Theological Education at Finkenwalde: 1935–1937*. In *Dietrich Bonhoeffer Works*, English Edition, vol. 14. Edited by H. Gaylon Barker and Mark S. Brocker and translated by Douglas W. Stott. Minneapolis, MN: Fortress Press, 2013.
DBW 14	*Illegale Theologenausbildung: Finkenwalde 1935–1937*. In *Dietrich Bonhoeffer Werke*, Bd. 14. Edited by Otto Dudzus and Jürgen Henkys in Zusammenarbeit mit Sabine Bobert-Stützel, Dirk Schulz and Ilse Tödt. Gütersloh: Gütersloher Verlagshaus, 1996.
DBWE 15	*Theological Education Underground: 1937–1940*. In *Dietrich Bonhoeffer Works*, English Edition, vol. 15. Edited by Victoria J. Barnett and translated by Victoria J. Barnett, Claudia D. Bergmann, Peter Frick and Scott A. Moore. Minneapolis, MN: Fortress Press, 2012.
DBW 15	*Illegale Theologenausbildung: Sammelvikariate 1937–1940*. In *Dietrich Bonhoeffer Werke*, Bd. 15. Edited by Dirk Schulz. Gütersloh: Gütersloher Verlagshaus, 1998.
DBWE 16	*Conspiracy and Imprisonment: 1940–1945*. In *Dietrich Bonhoeffer Works*, English Edition, vol. 16. Edited by Mark S. Brocker and translated by Lisa E. Dahill and Douglas W. Stott. Minneapolis, MN: Fortress Press, 2006.
DBW 16	*Konspiration und Haft 1940–1945*. In *Dietrich Bonhoeffer Werke*, Bd. 16. Edited by Jørgen Glenthøj, Ulrich Kabitz and Wolf Krötke. Gütersloh: Gütersloher Verlagshaus, 1996.
DBWE 17	*Index and Supplementary Materials*. In *Dietrich Bonhoeffer Works*, English Edition, vol. 17. Edited by Victoria J. Barnett and Barbara Wojhoski. Minneapolis, MN: Fortress Press, 2014.
DBW 17	*Register und Ergänzungen*. In *Dietrich Bonhoeffer Werke*, Bd. 17. Edited by Herbert Anzinger and Hans Pfeifer unter Mitarbeit von Waltraud Anzinger and Ilse Tödt mit einem Nachwort von Wolfgang Huber. Gütersloh: Gütersloher Verlagshaus, 1999.

PREFACE

This anthology considers Bonhoeffer's engagement with Chalcedonian Christology. His theology offers the retrieval of a Christology that reflects the entangledness of the beliefs of the Church Fathers and Mothers with our contemporary concerns. Bonhoeffer characterizes his enterprise as follows: 'What keeps gnawing at me is the question, what is Christianity, or who is Christ actually for us today.'[1] Accordingly, the key question this volume addresses is: *how does Bonhoeffer's thought help Christian theology re(dis)cover the doctrine of Christ's two natures and one person, and revive its significance for a modern post-metaphysical and secular world?* The volume partly comprises the proceedings of an international and interdisciplinary workshop organised by Nadine Hamilton and Christian Schlenker entitled 'On the Recovery of Chalcedonian Christology. Dietrich Bonhoeffer's Theology as Focal Point for Contemporary Christology', which took place at Tübingen University from 23 to 27 August 2021. The workshop was supported by the Federal Ministry of Education and Research (BMBF) and the Baden-Württemberg Ministry of Science as part of the Excellence Strategy of the German Federal and State Governments. Many of the essays are based on contributions presented here, with a few added for publication. We would also like to express our gratitude to the International Bonhoeffer Society, German Language Section (ibg), for their financial support towards the publication.

The workshop sought to engage with ma/patristic literature and the work of Bonhoeffer. Sarah Coakley's essay on Chalcedon[2] provided a helpful introduction to Chalcedonian Christology. Nevertheless, it was the common reading and discussion of the ma/patristic sources in an ecumenical context that proved essential in highlighting the relevance of the doctrine, its terminological distinctions and contextual differentiations. We were and are especially grateful for the discussion we were able to have on these core issues of Christology and wider dogmatic reflection with Prof. Dr. Christoph Schwöbel, who sadly passed away a few weeks after the workshop. This volume includes the theses he presented on Bonhoeffer's Christology today, and we are greatly indebted to his wife Katrin Bosse for her assistance here. We are also grateful to our series editors at T&T Clark for including the volume in their Bonhoeffer series and to Anna Turton for her help in bringing the work to publication.

Matthias Grebe,[3] Nadine Hamilton and Christian Schlenker (August 2022)

1. DBWE 8:362 (DBW 8:402).
2. Sarah Coakley, 'What Does Chalcedon Solve and What Does It Not? Some Reflections on the Status and Meaning of the Chalcedonian "Definition"', in *The Incarnation: An Interdisciplinary Symposium on the Incarnation of the Son of God*, ed. Stephen T. Davis, Daniel Kendall SJ and Gerald O'Collins (Oxford: Oxford University Press, 2018), 143–63.
3. Thanks are due to the *Deutsche Forschungsgemeinschaft* (DFG) for supporting Matthias' research fellowship on theodicy and the problem of evil.

INTRODUCTION

Christian Schlenker, Nadine Hamilton, Matthias Grebe

The origins of the current debate in Christology date back to the nineteenth century. It was at this point that the plausibility of the doctrine of two natures – which expresses the paradoxical unity of Jesus Christ as truly human and truly God – laid down in the confession of Chalcedon (451 CE) was first systematically called into question by academic theology and ultimately in some cases rejected. However, even when rejected as a counterpart, the doctrine of two natures still provides *the* referential framework for the Christological discussion in both the Western and almost all Eastern churches. In contrast to this doctrine, the modern approach has been to begin from the human being Jesus, as distinct from the 'Christ of faith'. Similarly, recent Christological approaches have spoken of Christ's divinity as characterized by his ideal humanity. Methodological and practical problems arise in this context, however: not only is the inner-Christian debate restricted when the dogma of Chalcedon is condemned as an empty dogmatic formula but, in recent times, we have also observed an increasing interest in Chalcedonian Christology. Much of this discussion aims to articulate why the metaphysical construction of Chalcedon is not absurd or paradoxical but, in fact, coherent. This in turn points to the old, though still controversial, question at the centre of this volume: how can the two natures be understood as an unmingled unity in such a way that the paradox in their relationship is no longer insurmountable?

The work of Dietrich Bonhoeffer centres on Christology. In his remarkable study *Christ, the Heart of Creation*, Rowan Williams highlights that Bonhoeffer takes the ma/patristic 'grammar' of Christology seriously, while rearticulating it for his own time.[1] One key concern of this anthology is to explore and thereby regain Christology's potential to offer a precise articulation of the Chalcedonian doctrine through an examination of the theology of Bonhoeffer or, more precisely, his reflections on Christology.

---

1. For a detailed theological engagement with Bonhoeffer and Chalcedon, see Rowan Williams, *Christ the Heart of Creation* (London: Bloomsbury, 2018), 169–219. For a comprehensive study on the importance Bonhoeffer placed on Chalcedon in articulating his ethical insights, see Ulrik Nissen, *The Polity of Christ: Studies on Dietrich Bonhoeffer's Chalcedonian Christology and Ethics* (T&T Clark Enquiries in Theological Ethics, 2021).

Unusually at the time, Bonhoeffer chose to emphasize the importance of Chalcedonian Christology for the academy, the Church and the wider world: an articulation of faith for the field of dogmatics, for ecumenism and for a 'world come of age'. While scholars have acknowledged Bonhoeffer's placing a strong emphasis on Christology, comprehensive systematic analyses of the Chalcedonian core of his Christocentric approach are widely – but not entirely – absent from scholarly discussion. Ulrik Nissen shows how Chalcedonian thinking is profoundly embedded in Bonhoeffer's thinking of social ethics.[2] While the Chalcedonian doctrine of the two natures of Christ is important for Bonhoeffer's Ethics, more importantly, it represents the very foundation of his theology and faith.[3] Bonhoeffer was concerned to tackle the question of how apparently antiquated Creeds could relate to life and faith in the here and now, as well as how to take these traditions seriously, regarding them as neither absolute nor merely relativistic. It is only from this theological perspective that Bonhoeffer's Christology and its enduring significance for today can fully be grasped.

It is for this reason that this volume focuses on Bonhoeffer's particular treatment of Chalcedonian Christology. Bonhoeffer doesn't simply translate or uncritically employ the Creed in the present but *asks how the grammar of the Creed can articulate how we are translated into the presence of Christ*.[4] What emerges throughout this volume is that Bonhoeffer does not simply allow the contemporary understanding of Christology to shape the meaning and relevance of the Chalcedonian Creed. Instead, he allows the Creed to speak for itself, critically examining and re-evaluating its theological assumptions and allowing it to inform and challenge his own time and context. Because of this concern, Bonhoeffer investigates Chalcedon through different philosophical approaches, of both ma/patristic and modern origin. Accordingly, Bonhoeffer connects the questions and answers of the early Church with his own time and its necessities.

This applies especially to Christology, which is the core of Christian theology and must therefore always be reflected upon in the light of contemporary circumstances concerning its underlying *Credo* and the respective contexts of meaning. This calls for an ability to articulate one's own existential knowledge of faith, which manages to constitutively incorporate openness for constructive dialogue. Especially in recent decades, however, Western theology has come to exhibit a loss of theological articulation in this respect. Bonhoeffer's engagement with the Chalcedonian Creed represents an example of how we might engage with these past articulations of faith. The ethical-theological demands which unfold

---

2. In his study on the significance of an explicitly Chalcedonian Christology in Bonhoeffer's ethics, Nissen notes that while most studies "demonstrate the inevitability of Christological motifs in an understanding of Bonhoeffer's ethics, we do not find a focused attempt to demonstrate the Chalcedonian theme and an elaboration of its potential in Christian social ethics," Nissen, *The Polity of Christ*, 11.

3. See ibid., 39–48.

4. See DBWE 2:133–4 (DBW 2:110–1); DBWE 3:63–4 (DBW 3:59–60); DBWE 6:65–6 (DBW 6:52–3).

through this engagement, even today, may lead us to challenge ethical positions previously understood to be settled.

This volume follows a similar approach: each essay approaches Bonhoeffer and his Christology from different questions, perspectives, disciplines and denominations. The result is a multi-perspective examination of Bonhoeffer's Christology and his treatment of the early Church teaching of two natures and its ethical implications.[5] The volume is structured in three parts, building on each other. Part I deals with the influences, relevance and contemporary significance of Bonhoeffer's Chalcedonian thought. Part II then takes a closer look at the implications Bonhoeffer offers for the statement that Jesus Christ is fully human and fully God, exploring the inner workings of Bonhoeffer's Chalcedonian adaption further. Finally, Part III considers the worldly relevance of these insights and examines the connection between Bonhoeffer's Christology, ethics, and ecclesiology.

I. Recovering Chalcedonian Logic with Bonhoeffer

Christoph Schwöbel: The Challenge of Dietrich Bonhoeffer's Christology and the Contemporary Debates on Chalcedon

The last decades have witnessed a radical change in Christological discussion. While in the second half of the twentieth century there was a general exploration of approaches to finding new ways of Christological expression, appropriate to the sensibilities of modernity, the advent of the post-modernity debates has led to a radical questioning of the received – but rarely questioned – standards of modernity in their significance for Christian theology. While Chalcedon was viewed as a milestone in the history of dogma that had little lasting significance for modern Christological reflection, it has at the beginning of the twenty-first century become the main measuring gauge for the orthodoxy of Christological proposals. Is there a way of interpreting Chalcedon in such a way that it is neither relegated to the archives of the history of Christology nor employed as a standard of formal doctrinal orthodoxy that seems removed from the substantive questions the council attempted to reflect? This chapter 'invites' Bonhoeffer, in keeping with his own views on personal communication, to become a dialogue partner who interrupts, challenges and contradicts our theological reflection and challenges us to respond critically and constructively to his suggestions.

Rowan Williams: Ontology and Salvation: Why Chalcedon Matters for Bonhoeffer

This chapter explores the development in Bonhoeffer's thinking, beginning with his *Habilitationsschrift* 'Akt und Sein', which emerges as crucial for his understanding of the Chalcedonian doctrine: how and as what are the limits of

---

5. On this consideration of Bonhoeffer's social ethics, see also Nissen, *The Polity of Christ*, passim.

the finite world understood? What constitutes finitude, viewed from a theological angle? It suggests that, with the help of the Patristic distinctions but remaining in a Harnackian framework, Bonhoeffer develops a new grammar of what finitude, limit and therefore the difference between creator and creation means.

Lea Weber: *Kierkegaard's and Bonhoeffer's Paradox Christology*

This chapter looks at how Bonhoeffer draws on Kierkegaard's paradoxical thinking to define a new grammar for Chalcedonian thinking. This influence enables him to incorporate Chalcedon into post-metaphysical thinking employing the categories of paradoxical thinking – the absolute paradox, the veiling in incognito, as well as vexation. The direction of Kierkegaardian thought for Bonhoeffer's Christology, which especially develops in the 1930s, is crucial for the enduringly relevant character of Chalcedon's formula even in a secular world. As a first step, this chapter shows how Bonhoeffer adapts Kierkegaard's arguments on the relationship between Christological reflection and human reason. In a second, the discussion turns to the character of God's revelation in Christ and the response of faith or offence, especially pertaining to the notion of the God-human's hiddenness. Finally, it focuses on the theologians' common intention in Christology, which may have led Bonhoeffer to rely so heavily on Kierkegaard.

Jacob Phillips: *Bonhoeffer's Understanding of Chalcedon in Dialogue with Contemporary Catholic Christology*

This chapter brings Bonhoeffer's understanding of the Chalcedonian Definition into dialogue with contemporary Catholic Christology. There are clear synergies between Bonhoeffer's 'limit' Christology and twentieth-century Catholic Christologies. Contemporary Catholic Christology is undergoing a turn to 'metaphysical realism', with increased confidence in the descriptive content of terms like *ousia/hypostasis*. This chapter seeks to understand how Bonhoeffer's 'limit' Christology might actually be complemented by today's heightened metaphysical realism, and to situate this against the background of plurality, assessing the ramifications and consequences of seeking answers to the question 'Who?' that are meaningful and communicable to those with no explicit confessional allegiance.

Philip G. Ziegler: *'To Carry On in this Chalcedonian Sense': Christology in Letters and Papers from Prison*

Bonhoeffer's *Letters and Papers from Prison* include several compressed and potentially explosive Christological remarks, culminating in what Eberhard Bethge considered nothing less than a new Christological definition: 'Jesus, the man for others'. This chapter revisits the question of the nature and work of Christ in the context of Bonhoeffer's 'new theology' limned in the prison letters, asking specifically about its relation to the other hallmark themes of these late writings, as well as to Bonhoeffer's earlier Christological and soteriological thinking.

II. Jesus Christ: Vere Homo, Vere Deus

Nadine Hamilton: Being Human in Light of Chalcedon: The Necessary Possibility of Being One

The Chalcedonian doctrine of Jesus Christ's two natures can be viewed as dogmatic Christology's foundational moment. This chapter argues that Dietrich Bonhoeffer's Christology lectures are a key text in the productive contemporary retrieval of the doctrine of two natures. Bonhoeffer argues that substance-ontological interpretations of the concepts 'nature' and 'person' misrepresent the intentions of the Church Fathers and are an obstacle to a constructive reflection of the doctrine today. Instead, Bonhoeffer suggests a narrative reading, in which the concepts 'nature' and 'person' do not denote two static entities, but instead an accentuation of biblical stories and hence a summary of God's story with humanity. His change of perspective characterizes a constructive approach to dogmatic Christology, beginning in a 'who': in a retelling of the life of Jesus Christ. Bonhoeffer, therefore, rejects all abstract conceptions of a God-Man, as well as all attempts to construct the two in the sense of fixed entities. A Christology linked to the who-question, in contrast, requires the two 'natures' not to be understood in isolation but instead to be tied back to their origins in the biblical narrative to illuminate this narrative itself. Therefore, the doctrine of two natures is not an isolated truth-claim to be debated: rather, it should be understood as a tracing of two paths, of God and humanity.

Christian Schlenker: Bonhoeffer's Ecce Homo!: Christology from the Centre and the Fullness of Life

In discussion with Bonhoeffer's teachers Karl Holl and Adolf von Harnack, this chapter looks at how Bonhoeffer questions in a remarkable way the 'Hellenization thesis' that, among other things, the Chalcedonian formulation of the two natures doctrine is an inheritance not of revelation but of Greek metaphysics. In doing so, Bonhoeffer interprets the statement that Jesus Christ was 'a perfect human' as meaning that Jesus Christ was perfectly human, rather than a perfect human: he was vulnerable, weak, suffering and exposed to cruel finiteness. The chapter then shows how this means a shift of emphasis on what finitude means concerning the *assumptio carnis* that is explored in the discussion with Karl Barth. For God to have accepted the finitude of his creation in Christ, he must have been there for his creation in the midst of this finite creation. Bonhoeffer underlines this as an assumption of life rather than flesh. Thus, the chapter shows, Bonhoeffer's articulation of the humanity of Jesus Christ is directly related to his understanding of Christ's existence for a fallen secular world that cannot rely on metaphysical assumptions but only on the assumption of this human life by the Divine.

Matthias Grebe: The Suffering God: Bonhoeffer and Chalcedonian Christology

For the early Church, the doctrine of God's impassibility was central to Christian theology. By the end of the nineteenth century, however, we see the beginnings of a shift emerging and many theologians now hold that God is in fact passible and can suffer. Bonhoeffer famously said that only a God who suffers can help people in the midst of their own suffering. In his *Lectures on Christology*, Bonhoeffer challenges his reader to think differently about the Chalcedonian formula and argues that we cannot think about the two natures in isolation. In this way, Bonhoeffer's theology prompts a new engagement with the person and work of Christ, Christology, and soteriology, and their proper relationship. Ultimately, it casts new light on the age-old question of what it means for an indivisible God-human to suffer at all.

Michael Mawson: How God Suffers: Bonhoeffer, Moltmann and Theological Language

In the last fifty years, many theologians have moved away from traditional doctrinal emphases on the impassibility and immutability of God, and have instead sought to understand and speak of a God who suffers in and with creation. In light of this shift and the ensuing debate, this chapter shows how Bonhoeffer in particular uses the language of the suffering God. Moltmann and other advocates of divine passibility have therefore drawn on and appealed to Bonhoeffer in support of their position, and this chapter underlines the subtle yet important differences between how Bonhoeffer and Moltmann are using this language.

III. The World and the Church

Koert Verhagen: Christology's Counterpoint: Bonhoeffer on Knowing the Christ Who Calls

This chapter considers the resonances and overlap between how Bonhoeffer begins his Christology lectures and how he describes the call to discipleship. More specifically, it explores his basic assumption that both the task of Christology and a life of discipleship begin with death. In other words, knowing the person of the risen Christ necessarily involves disciples not only existentially, but also as embodied, whole persons, a relationship that, it is argued, sheds light on Bonhoeffer's understanding of the task of theology more broadly.

Hannah Bleher: 'Preparing the Way' for God's Word: A Central Motif of Bonhoeffer's Ethics and Its Implications for Public Theology

Besides the prominent distinction between the ultimate and penultimate things, 'preparing the way' (*Wegbereitung*) as a *leitmotif* of Bonhoeffer's ethics and concept of responsibility remains relatively neglected. Especially in political–ethical discourses about public theology, the motif remains underdetermined, even though it addresses a political–ethical dimension. This chapter first examines the relation between Bonhoeffer's Christology and ethics; the motif of 'preparing the way' is outlined more closely in this contribution. In a second step, the chapter will focus on the Christological justification and, above all, the related consequences for Bonhoeffer's ethical conception of responsibility. The chapter concludes with a look at the challenges and chances for the discourse on public theology, with a consideration of the political–ethical potential of 'paving the way'.

Samuel Efrain Murillo Torres: 'Going Ahead' as Real Human Beings in the Gemeinde: *Bonhoeffer's Christological Form and Formation in Suffering and Dying*

This chapter complements the previous one with a focus on the role of *form* [*Gestalt*] and *formation* [*Gestaltung*] in Bonhoeffer's *Ethics* with recourse to the *Lectures on Christology*. Employing these categories, it is shown how Bonhoeffer describes the public sphere as an aesthetic–ontological–dynamic process. Samuel Murillo Torres investigates how Bonhoeffer's Christology can yield fruitful insights to explore an Aesthetic Public Theology. The dynamic relation of *form* and *formation* describes how the public sphere can be conceptualized and what it means to be a real human being, considering his Christology. This aesthetic–ontological–dynamic process is the reality between Easter and Ascension. On this path, we can *go ahead* in the likeness of Christ; this is being called to be formed by Christ.

David Emerton: Jesus Christ: the Centre of the Church

This chapter considers what is taken to be the *leitmotif* of Bonhoeffer's ecclesial thinking: 'in der Kirche ist "Christus als Gemeinde existierend"' ('in the church is "Christ existing as church-community"'). In its consideration of this, it explores the co-inherence between Christ and the church that Bonhoeffer articulates, and does so by asking how this co-inherence exists for Bonhoeffer. To articulate a response to this question, the chapter turns to Bonhoeffer's understanding of the person and work of the Holy Spirit as the Holy Spirit relates to the church-community existing as Christ: 'through the Holy Spirit, the crucified and risen Christ exists as the church-community.'[6] From here, and in light of this pneumatological indexation, the extent to which Christology really is the centre of Bonhoeffer's ecclesial thinking is explored, with the chapter positing that, while Christology might well be its central dogmatic res, its foundational dogmatic res is pneumatology.

The contributions can either be read individually, or the volume as a whole can be understood as an invitation to approach Bonhoeffer's Christology from many angles. Naturally, the conversations and reflections that emerged in the workshop cannot be reproduced in these pages in their entirety. We hope, however, that this volume might play a part in illuminating the relevance of Dietrich Bonhoeffer's theology in contemporary Christological discussion. In this way, this volume goes further than filling a lacuna in Bonhoeffer studies – important though this is. It also poses a fresh challenge to modern Christology, asking how theological traditions and truths are to be understood in a pluralistic 'world come of age'.

6. DBWE 4, 220 (DBW 4, 234).

Part I

RECOVERING CHALCEDONIAN LOGIC
WITH BONHOEFFER

Chapter 1

THE CHALLENGE OF DIETRICH BONHOEFFER'S CHRISTOLOGY AND THE CONTEMPORARY DEBATES ON CHALCEDON

Christoph Schwöbel

I. Bonhoeffer's Christology in the Changing Climate of Christological Debate

1. The last decades have seen a radical change in Christological discussion. While the second half of the twentieth century explored ways of finding new possibilities of Christological expression, appropriate to the sensibilities of modernity, the advent of the debates on post-modernity has led to a radical questioning of the received, but rarely questioned, standards of modernity in their significance for Christian theology. The strange gift of post-modernity's Pandora's box has been that the strictures 'modernity' seemed to have placed on theological reflection have lost their plausibility. The event of modernity or 'the Enlightenment' is no longer seen – to borrow Lessing's metaphor – as an 'ugly, broad ditch' that separates our present from pre-modern times. Contemporary theological and philosophical reflection seems to be carried out in the conviction that the 'ditch' can be bridged in many ways, that even the perception of the existence of such a 'ditch' depends on the way in which one explains the genesis of modernity and the dissolution of its normative significance. For Christological debates the effect is astonishing. Rather than seeing discourse of God incarnate as a mythological expression that

---

Christoph Schwöbel presented the following twelve theses in Tübingen in August 2021, in a style with which those who knew him were deeply familiar. Schwöbel's characteristic 'thesis'-style paper is reproduced here in its 'barest', pre-publication form, and his particularly engaging style continues to shine through. Footnotes have been added to speak to some of the additional comments Schwöbel made during and after the presentation, and their inclusion not only points to the presentation's great scope, but also gives us an indication of what a revised paper would have looked like.

has to be transcended,[1] recent Christological debates have concentrated on the ways in which Christology continues to be shaped by the debates of the early Church and the conciliar decisions, culminating in the Definition of Chalcedon. While Chalcedon was viewed as a milestone in the history of dogma that had little lasting significance for modern Christological reflection, it has, at the beginning of the twenty-first century, become the main benchmark for the orthodoxy of Christological proposals. Is there a way of interpreting Chalcedon in such a way that it is neither relegated to the archives of the history of Christology nor employed as a standard of formal doctrinal orthodoxy that seems removed from the substantive questions the council attempted to reflect?[2]

2. The perception of Dietrich Bonhoeffer's theology has changed with the changing climate of the theological and the not-so-theological *Zeitgeist*. Was Bonhoeffer in the second half of the twentieth century, mainly on the basis of *Letters and Papers from Prison* (1951), seen as a paragon of radical theology, trying to spell out effects of the 'coming of age' of humanity in the West, he is at the beginning of the twenty-first century invoked as the advocate of orthodox Christian theology over against revisionary forms of Christian theology. Any engagement with Bonhoeffer's theology in general and his Christology in particular should be wary not too eagerly to enlist Bonhoeffer's support for one's own Christological endeavours, developed many years later in different settings, but to reconstruct the formative insights of his Christology in order to challenge, inspire and contradict our attempts to find orientation in Christology. As so often, Bonhoeffer's theological ideas appear incisive, provocative, passionately presented, but also fragmented and experimental, due to the circumstances in which they were developed and due to the literary form in which they were preserved. This suggests that we should invite Bonhoeffer – in keeping with his own views on personal communication – as our dialogue partner who interrupts, challenges and contradicts our theological reflection and urges us to respond critically and constructively to his suggestions.

---

1. See the debates around *The Myth of God Incarnate*, ed. John Hick (London: SCM Press, 1977). Hick's book initiated an extensive and wide-ranging provocation for Christological thought in the late 1970s, even beyond the boundaries of the academic theological world. A similar theological discussion occurred in Germany as part of Rudolf Bultmann's program of de-mythologization.

2. Taking the Definition of Chalcedon as the benchmark for orthodoxy challenges both broad-brush and more superficial assessments of what constitutes 'orthodox' Christology. For a balanced account of approaching the Definition of Chalcedon critically and with awareness for its historical contexts, see Bruce L. McCormack, *The Humility of the Eternal Son: Reformed Kenoticism and the Repair of Chalcedon* (Cambridge: Cambridge University Press, 2021).

II. 'Who is Jesus Christ for Us Today?'[3]

3. The Logos and the Counter-Logos

Bonhoeffer prefaces his lectures on Christology with an extended reflection on the Logos in Christology. This Logos is not identical with our own logos, the human logos, but challenges our human logos in the most radical way. It cannot be integrated in the already-established classification schemes of our human rationality which focus on the question of 'how' and on the question of 'whether' in search of causal explanations and factual evidence for Christological claims.[4] Bonhoeffer portrays the conflict between the logos of sinful humanity and the counter-logos, the Logos of God, in a most dramatic way as a battle of life and death. 'Because the human logos does not want to die itself, the Logos of God, which is death to the human logos, must die instead. The Word become human must be hung on the cross by the human logos.'[5] However, the resurrection of the one who died on the cross ensures that the question that the Logos raised, the question asked of Christ 'Who are you?' and the question this confronts the human with, the question 'but who are you (i.e. the human person)?', continue to challenge humanity. This dramatic scenario draws together three strands: the question of transcendence, the question of existence and the question of ultimate salvation. All three questions are contained in the who-question asked of Christ. Bonhoeffer asserts that these questions can only be raised and answered from the perspective of faith in the community of the church. They

---

3. The following section considers those important aspects of Bonhoeffer's Christology which might be seen to challenge our approaches in discussing Christology and which were evident at the core even of Bonhoeffer's earliest theological endeavours. The section focuses on Bonhoeffer's lectures on Christology and refers mainly to the older German edition, edited by Eberhard Bethge, which Christoph Schwöbel translated into English. See Dietrich Bonhoeffer, *Gesammelte Schriften: Band III, Theologie - Gemeinde (Vorlesungen - Briefe - Gespräche, 1927-1944)*, ed. Eberhard Bethge (München: Chr. Kaiser Verlag, 1966), hereafter *GS* III.

4. Christology as interpreted as the *Logos* of Christ cannot be fitted into an extant scheme of classification; rather, it is the person of Christ who reshapes our perception of conceptuality. This implies a need to acknowledge the finitude of all human (creaturely) reflection, which highlights the soteriological importance of all Christological inquiry. It follows that human rationality and creaturely reflection can never be neutral. Quite the contrary: questions about 'the good,' salvation and fulfilment in the eschaton are present in all questions of human rationality. Rationality is not abstract, but always relative to an existential commitment, to the basic orientation of human life. According to Bonhoeffer's preface, Christology relativizes all claims of human rationality, which has to be recognized as embodied, social, historical rationality bound to faith traditions and to ultimate commitment.

5. DBWE 12:305 (DBW 12:285).

are relative to a particular form of basic orientation and its social embodiment in the church. We can try to spell out the implications of this approach by attending to the different elements of the Christological question: Who is Jesus Christ for us today?

4. 'Who?' – The Significance of the 'Who'-Question over against the Questions of 'How' and 'Whether'

Bonhoeffer gives the question 'who are you?' priority over against the question of 'how', seeking causal explanation, and of 'whether' ('Dass-Frage'), searching for factual evidence. This has far-reaching epistemological and ontological implications. Epistemologically, the who-question, the significance of which Bonhoeffer grasped from engagement with Emil Brunner's *Der Mittler* (1927), secures that we do not understand the reality of Christ as the realization of an idea, but are confronted primarily with the 'otherness of the other'. Both the idealistic identification of the Logos of God and the human logos and the Catholic interpretation of their relationship by analogy must be resisted.[6] The question 'who are you?' confronts us with the transcendence of the other and so draws the boundaries of our own existence. In their conjunction, the question of transcendence and the question of existence is the question of the person. Knowledge of the other cannot be deduced by metaphysical speculation nor inferred from the other's works. It can only be given in self-disclosure.[7] For Bonhoeffer, the who-question necessitates both a relational ontology, where identity is constituted through the encounter with the other, and a communicative ontology, where the ontological relation is established in a relationship between address and response, and as such a phenomenological ontology based on revelation. The who-question cannot be answered by giving the how-question or the question 'whether?' priority. Bonhoeffer bluntly asserts: 'The early Church foundered on the "how question," modern theology since the Enlightenment on the "that question." Luther, Paul, and the New Testament stayed on track through the middle.'[8]

---

6. 'Dabei bleibt aber zu beachten, daß der Gotteslogos nicht mit dem menschlichen identifiziert werden darf wie im deutschen Idealismus, und daß er ebensowenig mit ihm analogisiert werden darf wie im Katholizismus. Denn das käme auf Selbsterlösung hinaus und der menschliche Logos entzöge sich dem Gericht durch den Christuslogos.' (*GS* III, 184–5).

7. By insisting on the priority of the who-question, Bonhoeffer emphasizes the character of knowledge as (to use Bertrand Russell's expression) *knowledge by acquaintance* – that is, knowledge bound to the second-person-perspective rather than knowledge by metaphysical speculation or empirical hypotheses. This is exemplified in Simon Peter's confession of faith in Matthew 16.

8. DBWE 12:304 (DBW 12:285).

5. 'Is' – The Shape of an Ontology of Faith Based on the Structure of the Person of Christ

Bonhoeffer states clearly: 'So the Christological question is in its essence an ontological question.'[9] This implies that the structure of the person of Christ is the judgement and the relative justification of the 'old logos'. If we want to characterize this ontology, we can already say that at the time of the *Lectures on Christology* Bonhoeffer is already committed to a social ontology, developed in *Sanctorum Communio*, culminating in the formula of Christ existing as communion, and to an ontology which it expresses in the unity of act and being in his *Habilitationsschrift*. Christ's being is in Christ's act. The way in which Bonhoeffer tries to navigate the *Scylla* of essentialism and *Charybdis* of actualism is perhaps most clearly developed in *Creation and Fall* as an ontology of communicative relations. To this we must add that Bonhoeffer's ontology is from then on further developed in terms of a Christological ontology where the new creation envelops and comprehends the old creation in judgement and grace. This ontology has both a critical and constructive potential. Critically, it serves to reject Docetism both in its ancient and modern forms where Christ is seen as the embodiment of particular essences, ideas and values. It also remains critical with regard to Ebionitism insofar as, for all its insistence on the monotheistic principle, it shies away from the identity of being between God and Christ.

It is in this context that we must see Bonhoeffer's assessment of Chalcedon. It is the climax of all critical (or negative) Christology. For Bonhoeffer, the main point of the Chalcedonian Definition is a critical one. Over against the Monophysite and the Nestorian positions the Definition maintains '*that all options of thinking all this* [i.e. the two natures in the one person] *together ... are represented as impossible ... options*'.[10] It is no longer allowed, Bonhoeffer states, to talk about divinity and humanity in a 'reified way and to distinguish them as things' ('über Gottheit und Menschheit dinglich zu reden und sie als Dinge voneinander abzugrenzen'[11]). The theologian who does Christology must 'stay within the conceptual tension of this negative formula and must endure it' ('muß sich ... innerhalb der begrifflichen Spannung dieser negative Formel aufhalten und sie aushalten'[12]). Even stronger: 'it takes the concept of substance which underlies the relationship of the natures to its highest level and sublates it'.[13] Chalcedon is maintained as a negative and critical horizon of Christological statements while at the same time excluding, in Bonhoeffer's interpretation, a continuation of the substance metaphysics which underlies the concept of nature. Bonhoeffer states that Chalcedon attempted

---

9. DBWE 12:304 (DBW 12:284).
10. DBWE 12:342 (DBW 12:329), emphasis in the original.
11. *GS* III, 218.
12. *GS* III, 218.
13. *GS* III, 218: 'Es treibt den dem Naturenverhältnis zugrundeliegenden Substanzbegriff auf die Höhe und hebt ihn auf.'

to answer the 'how'-question, but, in trying to answer it, the question itself is surmounted:

> 'In its negative retaining of contradictory opposites it [i.e. the Chalcedonian Definition] has surmounted the two-natures-doctrine and says in reality, that the matter of Jesus Christ cannot be conceived with the concept of nature and cannot be brought to a descriptive (anschaulich) unity.'[14]

The way in which Bonhoeffer continues the narrative of Christological developments can be read as a radical Lutheran Christology, a Christology of radical personal union of God and humanity in Christ. Bonhoeffer keeps to Luther's Christology and criticizes Lutheran Christology for falling back into the conceptuality of natures.

Reformed Christology is criticized for postulating an existence of the Logos *extra carnem*. The Lutheran doctrines of the ubiquity of the person of Christ and of the presence of Christ in the union of God and Jesus (Ubivolipräsenz) are rejected by Bonhoeffer as consequences of trying to answer the Reformed question within a Lutheran framework. They separate Christ's presence and Christ's presence for me as a communicative act. Ubiquity presents Christ's presence without revelation, and Ubivolipresence makes Christ's presence a contingent attribute of his person. In both cases, Christ's presence is not seen as Christ's mode of existence.

6. Jesus Christ – In Word, Sacrament and Community 'in the Middle' of Human Existence, History and Nature

The positive development of Bonhoeffer's Christology rests on the way in which he sees the relationship to believers today (the 'pro me') as part of the ontology of the person of Christ. The set of relations which defines the person of Christ includes the believer as a form of personal presence for the believing community. 'Der Personkern selbst ist das pro me.'[15] Trying to reflect on Christ in himself is godless. Divine action and divine presence remain constitutively con-joint. Christ's being-there for me is Christ's active presence and Christ's present activity.

Christ's being must be understood as communicative being, as being which freely gives Christ's person in relation. The three forms in which Christ is given are the word of preaching as address and the call to responsibility, the sacraments

---

14. *GS* III, 227: 'In seinem negativen Festhalten an kontradiktorischen Gegensätzen hat es die Zweinaturenlehre selbst überwunden und sagt in Wirklichkeit, daß die Sache Jesus Christus nicht mit dem Begriff der Natur zu erfassen und zu einer anschaulichen Einheit zu bringen ist.'

15. *GS* III, 182.

as the embodied word in which God addresses humanity within the fallen world as the restored creation of our existence. These modes of presence as modes of the presence of the person of Christ as Christ create the community, the reality of restored relationships in Christ, redeemed sociality which restores created sociality.

Bonhoeffer's reflection of Christ as being 'in the middle' (not being the centre) of human existence, history and nature try to formulate the way in which in Christ transcendence and existence come together. If Christ is the middle of existence, history and nature, existence, history and nature have no immanent centre of being and meaning. Christ is both the boundary of existence, history and nature, marking its limits as a reality without an immanent centre, and the border in which transcendent meaning and being are realized in the midst of existence, history and nature.

7. 'For Us' – 'Being-there-for' as the Ontology of Persons and the Reality of Saving Representation ('Stellvertretung')

According to Bonhoeffer, the soteriological import of Christ's personal presence cannot be developed by focusing on Christ's work. Bonhoeffer would have rejected Paul Tillich's maxim: 'Christology is a function of soteriology.' Luther's slogan that good works do not make a good person, but that a good person does good works, is here applied to the relationship of Christology and soteriology. Christ in his person is his own work. Bonhoeffer tries to avoid a number of common ways of developing the 'for us' of salvation, that is, to see it as an external effect of Christ, a transaction once achieved that has now become effective, a representation that represents something that is absent, and a transformation that does not address the real state of condemnation and misery in which the sinner exists. The 'for us'/'for me' is not an external, but an internal relation.

The negative criteria of Chalcedon establish for Bonhoeffer to talk of the unity of the person of Christ in the radical way introduced by Luther's theology: 'This man is God', and so appropriate statements can be phrased in such a way:

> God who became human is the God of glory; God glorifies himself in becoming human. This is the ultimate mystery of the Trinity. From 'now unto eternity', God regards himself as the God who became human. God's self-glorification in the human is thus the glorification of the human, which shall have eternal life with God the Three in One.[16]

Against the backdrop of this strong statement of the Incarnation, Bonhoeffer attempts a renewal of the Lutheran doctrine of the states of Christ. He is adamant that the Incarnation is not the act of humiliation, but that the God-human is the one who is the humiliated one and, at the same time, the one who is exalted. In

---

16. DBWE 12:355 (DBW 12:342).

these last remaining sections of the Christology lectures Bonhoeffer heaps paradox upon paradox. The point seems to be to make clear that once the Chalcedonian emphasis on 'one and the same Son, Christ, Only-Begotten' is established, once the radical unity of the person of Christ is secured, there is no way in which Christ's humility detracts from Christ's divinity and no way in which Christ's exaltation diminishes Christ's humanity. It would be too much to claim that this establishes a Christological theory. Rather, it seems to establish a Christological perspective: The reality of Christ comprehends all spheres of reality within itself, even the abject situation of sin and the exalted vista of God's glory. There are no non-Christological limits that can be imposed on the activity and presence of God in the world, even the seemingly most godless places can be the space where faith grasps the self-disclosure of God in Christ.

8. 'Today' – The Mode of Christ's Presence and Our Present

Once this Christological perspective is established, the mode of Christ's presence can be specified. For Bonhoeffer, the approach to Christology 'from above' or 'from below', from the Jesus of history or the Christ of faith does no longer offer viable ways for doing Christology. The only possible perspective that can do justice to the reality of Christ is a Christology 'of today', a Christology of the 'present Christ'. Bonhoeffer approaches the problem of the presence of Christ through the pro-me structure of Christ's being. There is a difference between something's being there and a person's being there for me. Christ's presence must in this sense be understood as communicative and revelatory presence in an ontological sense. The act of being present for me is the constitutive aspect of Christ's being present. Christ's being is ontologically relational so that it includes the church-community. The relation to the church-community is integral to Christ's being, and as such he is (a) 'the beginning, ... the firstborn within a large family'[17] and this is the historicity of the historical Jesus; (b) the new humanity as Christ stands before God in the place of the new humanity and therefore Christ is (c) insofar as he acts as the new humanity, also in the new humanity which is judged and pardoned in him. All these specifications assume that the mode of Christ's presence transcends both metaphysical atemporality and temporal limitation: 'God in his timeless eternity is *not* God. Jesus in his humanity, limited in time, is *not* Jesus Christ.'[18] Only the mode of presence of the God-human, the one who in his humiliation is also the exalted one, can make Christ present for us.

17. DBWE 12:315 (DBW 12:296).
18. DBWE 12:313 (DBW 12:294).

III. Provocations and Inspirations of Bonhoeffer's Christology for Interpreting Chalcedon: Recovery or Repair?

9. The provocation of Bonhoeffer's Christology for the contemporary discussions on Chalcedonian Christology must be seen in the fact that in recovering Chalcedon, Bonhoeffer also seems to suggest to repair the consequences of Chalcedon by insisting that Chalcedon itself has surmounted the language in which it is expressed. In order to make the Chalcedonian point about the unity of 'one and the same Son', Chalcedon had to use the language of two natures in order to show that it has only a critical, negative function and in its reifying ('dinglich') tendency cannot be employed to make the point positively that Chalcedon makes critically. Does faithfulness to Chalcedon mean *not* to employ the language Chalcedon uses to make its critical point in our constructive attempts at developing an adequate Christology? Is the recovery of Chalcedon the first step in trying to repair its fateful consequences?

10. Furthermore, Bonhoeffer seems to contradict the attempt at trying to develop the significance of the atonement by elaborating various models of Christ's atoning work, from penal substitution to vicarious representation or vicarious repentance. Every attempt of speaking of the work of Christ must for Bonhoeffer be rooted in the ontological structure of the person of Christ as pro me and in this sense involves a real (ontological) changing of places between Christ and us. Bonhoeffer's criticism would be that none of the conventional models really meets the logic of the patristic statement: He became what we are so that we become what he is. Bonhoeffer's Christology must be seen as an attempt to provide the ontological foundation for this claim.

IV. Tentative Steps Forward: Towards a Trinitarian Framework for Christology

11. If we invite Bonhoeffer's Christology to question the contemporary Christological discussion critically, would it also be a way of taking Bonhoeffer's Christology seriously that we raise critical questions with regard to Bonhoeffer's own Christology? Of course, we have Bonhoeffer's Christology only in fragments. The whole planned third main part of the Christology Lectures of 1933 on 'the eternal Christ' does not exist, because the semester had come to an end. Nevertheless, one of the questions that springs immediately to my mind is whether taking up the inspirations of Bonhoeffer's Christology would not lead to a fuller development of the role of the Holy Spirit in the Christological account that is being offered. And would such a reflection on the constitutive role of Jesus' relationship to God the Father in the Spirit and of God the Father in Jesus through the Spirit not require a more consistently developed trinitarian framework for Christology. After all, the Christological debates that led to

the Definition of Chalcedon were triggered by the trinitarian teaching of the Councils of Nicaea, Constantinople and Ephesus. Or more systematically: Does the relational Christology that Bonhoeffer suggests need a trinitarian foundation? At least Bonhoeffer's phrase of being-there-for-others (*Dasein für andere*)[19] as the core of the person cries out for a trinitarian elaboration.[20]

12. Bonhoeffer's Christology calls for a Christological revision of the traditional divine attributes. He is consistently critical of applying a preconceived notion of the being of God to the questions of Christology. Would such a revision of the teaching of the perfections of God have to take a trinitarian modulation into account which does full justice to Bonhoeffer's insistence that revelation – and that is the self-revelation of the triune God – is the only source for Christology, indeed for Christian theology as a whole? This seems to me most required where Bonhoeffer's insistence on the passibility of God does not appear as an expression of a mutable God, but as an expression of the immutability of God being pro me in Christ. Bonhoeffer's quote '[o]nly a suffering God can help' is probably one of the most frequently quoted sentences of the twentieth century. It is important to acknowledge that it is God's passibility by which God remains faithful to Godself. Becoming the passible God in Jesus Christ is God's realization of God's immutability.

---

19. See Dietrich Bonhoeffer, 'Outline for a Book', in *The Bonhoeffer Reader*, ed. Clifford J. Green and Michael P. DeJonge (Minneapolis: Fortress, 2013), 813.

20. This is of crucial importance with regard to the discussion of the question of God's 'need for humanity'. If we want to keep a Bonhoeffer-type Christology and avoid the problems of Open and Relational Theology (where, following Alfred North Whitehead's notion that 'God creates the world *as* the world creates God' [*Process and Reality: An Essay in Cosmology* (New York: Macmillan Co., 1929/1969), 405], humanity has a need for God in order to be complete) then we need to ensure that the pro-me relation is ontologically rooted in the triune relationship of Father, Son, and Spirit, and thus constitutes part of God's very being. It is part of God's fullness and therefore the relationship between God and humanity remains one of not of deficiency but of abundance – emphasizing a trinitarian 'ontology of communicative relations,' see Christoph Schwöbel, 'The Generosity of the Triune God and the Humility of the Son', in *Kenosis: The Self-Emptying of Christ in Scripture and Theology*, ed. Paul T. Nimmo and Keith L. Johnson (Grand Rapids: Eerdmans, 2022), 288.

Chapter 2

ONTOLOGY AND SALVATION: WHY CHALCEDON MATTERS FOR BONHOEFFER

Rowan Williams

Dietrich Bonhoeffer's *Habilitationsschrift*, *Act and Being*, first published in 1931,[1] is still one of the less well-explored of his works – not too surprisingly, given that (even by the standards of his early writings) it is both intensely compressed, almost telegraphic, and unapologetically expansive in its scope. It is conceived as a map of modern philosophical thought in which two basic orientations are charted – an idealist configuring of reality as ultimately generated in the operation of the transcendental ego and an 'ontological' concern to recover and recognize what exceeds or evades the ego. To accept the idea of revelation in any really intelligible sense requires the theologian to lean towards ontological thinking; yet 'transcendentalism' lays down a proper warning about the kind of descriptive metaphysics which screens out the truth that the human subject exists always 'in reference to' what the subject thinks and knows, and so must always acknowledge itself to be *located*. Of particular interest in the first section of the discussion are Bonhoeffer's critical accounts of Heidegger[2] and Erich Przywara[3] as philosophers defending the ontological, thinking through the priority of world to subject. Heidegger's *Dasein* offers a conceptuality which seeks to balance the recognition that our existence is always responding to what it has not chosen with the imperative of taking responsibility, manifesting *Sorge*, 'care', in seeking 'its most authentic possibility' by affirming its being towards death, its implication in the inexorably temporal world into which it has been 'thrown'.[4] Przywara's version of Thomism understands finite reality as being the way it is because it is dependent on, inflected by, and participating in infinite reality. Crucially, this means that finite reality cannot be self-enclosed (as with Heidegger's *Dasein*); but the problem of Przywara's statement of this is that it implies a steady foundation

---

1. DBWE 2 (DBW 2). The *Habilitationsschrift* was accepted in 1930.
2. DBWE 2:67–73 (DBW 2:61–7).
3. DBWE 2:73–6 (DBW 2:67–71).
4. DBWE 2:69–70 (DBW 2:63–5).

of being-in the divine life that is the same whether we are 'in Adam' or 'in Christ'.[5] And this is either unhelpfully abstract and formalist or else it is theologically corrosive because it posits a divine 'is' which is indifferent to the reality of sin and righteousness: 'God "is" the righteous one; God "is" the holy one; God "is" love. The ontological foundation for theological concepts of being must remain precisely the realization that this "is" can in no way be detached from the concrete definition.'[6] An abstract account of human participation in/analogy with the divine life produces an abstract notion of God; and this lands us back where we must as Christians never find ourselves – in the illusion that we can in some way know God from a starting-point of 'nowhere in particular.'[7] The definitions of God and the human are detached from the actuality of what each in fact does. And this means that no truly *theological* language can be generated from this kind of metaphysic, since it precludes an appropriate account of God, the God who is never 'at hand' (*zur Hand*) in or among a plurality of determinate objects.

So ends the first section of *Act and Being*. On the adequacy of Bonhoeffer's summaries of various thinkers there would be quite a bit to say; certainly as regards Przywara, this is very much a prosecutorial brief (though in some ways a more penetrating and interesting one than Barth's critique of the great Jesuit).[8] But the insistence on knowing God only from within one kind of solidarity or another is a significant clue to reading what Bonhoeffer has to say about Christology in general and Chalcedon in particular. In the second part of *Act and Being,* Bonhoeffer pursues the point made at the end of the first, the emphatic denial that the subject can 'place itself into truth' – that is, the denial that the subject can from its own resources locate itself in relation to a prior and greater reality: unless we accept the presupposition that vitiates the systems of 'transcendentalism' – that is, unless we

---

5. DBWE 2:74, 80 and see 136–57 (DBW 2:68–9, 74 and see 135–57).

6. DBWE 2:75 (DBW 2:69).

7. DBWE 2:79–80 (DBW 2:72–4).

8. Bonhoeffer to some extent reproduces Barth's fundamental misunderstanding of Przywara's use of the *analogia entis*, as if this were an ontological assimilation of divine being to finite being. Przywara's emphatic insistence on the *maxima dissimilitudo* between God and creation, as implied in the model of 'in-and-beyond' which dominates Przywara's metaphysics, is ignored. See the Translator's Introduction by John R. Betz to his and David Bentley Hart's English translation of Przywara's major work (Erich Przywara, *Analogia Entis: Metaphysics: Original Structure and Universal Rhythm* [Grand Rapids: Eerdmans, 2014], especially 72–6), and Rowan Williams, 'Dialectic and Analogy: A Theological Legacy', in *The Impact of Idealism: The Legacy of Post-Kantian German Thought. Volume IV: Religion*, ed. Nicholas Boyle, Liz Disley and Nicholas Adams (Cambridge: Cambridge University Press, 2013), especially 287–8. But the interesting question Bonhoeffer raises is whether there can be a properly theological account of finite dependence on God that presupposes a kind of timeless or continuous and essential relation between God and humanity, irrespective of the history of fallenness; if so, as we have noted, something holds true of God (God 'is' in a certain way) which is unconnected with God's reality as righteous or merciful.

accept the collapse of reality into the subject – we must see that the subject's place is always already conditioned. The subject is acted upon before it acts. This means that the subject is itself only as it encounters *limit*: but if that limit is conceived only as the mutual or complementary limitations of finite substances, we are still left in a conceptual territory in which we can manage or negotiate our place. The limit posed by the finite other simply allows us to construct a system of interacting agencies on the same level, and this does not generate any awareness of *absolute* limit, a boundary beyond which we cannot project any imaginative or analogical patterns. We are not here confronted with a limit which is over and above *all* finite difference.[9] But it is this kind of limit alone with which theology is concerned, since this alone makes sense of both history and theology.[10] Theology has to acknowledge that it is responding to something that is not 'available' to it, not 'at hand' as something belonging in a world that is open to scrutiny and ultimately to some sort of 'capture' by knowledge. Revelation is the impact upon humanity of this 'unavailable' reality which will always establish itself as beyond possession even in the act of imparting itself. It is supremely *act*, in the sense of being initiated outside my human consciousness, but as the act of infinite reality it is inexhaustible for the human subject; it is ontologically grounded outside finite selfhood. And my knowledge of revealed truth is always *aufhebt* through its relation with what it knows. Bonhoeffer's use of this term is as taxing and elusive as any other German writer's: to be *aufhebt* is to be subverted, 'translated' and transcended. My knowledge is transfigured by way of the unceasingly rediscovered priority of what is known over the knowing subject; my knowledge is reconstituted as a participation in the prior knowing actuality of that which reveals. For this to make full sense, we must always understand our knowing self as already 'implicated', already acted upon, and so as already part of a complex network of agency rather than a solitary and self-sufficient consciousness. And so if we are to speak about revelation we must equally speak about solidarity: we shall not be able to talk coherently about revelation unless we let go of any vestige of the isolated ego.[11]

'Revelation happens in the community of faith; it requires primarily a specific Christian sociology.'[12] This is not a claim that revealed truth is a kind of knowing restricted to those who opt for membership in a religious community; it is to say that the *fact* of the community that is the Church is what allows us to speak as we do about revelation. Bonhoeffer is struggling here to clarify a central insight for which familiar theological categories do not quite fit. His goal is to show that

---

9. DBWE 2:87–90 (DBW 2:81–5).

10. DBWE 2:88 (DBW 2:82); it makes sense of history, presumably, as preventing us from ignoring the continuing emergence of unprecedented perspective and possibility in temporal existence, which can never be reduced to a fixed calculus of stimulus and response, reduced to some plain oppositional alterity/alternation.

11. DBWE 2:103–9 (DBW 2:99–106); this is a notably dense and complex section of the argument.

12. DBWE 2:113 (DBW 2:109).

the tension he has been exploring between transcendental idealism and ontology, between the priority of act and the priority of being, is transformed by the existence of the Church. To paraphrase his argument slightly, he is pointing to the fact that here is a community, a visible social reality, whose defining claim is that it does not exist by contract or consensus between individuals: it arises from, and unbrokenly depends on, an event in which a certain relation is created by an initiative from beyond the entire ensemble of finite interaction. The Church has not – we could say – been *devised* by human agency or human agreement. It looks to an ontologically independent reality as its ground, a reality acting upon us; and the paradox is that while we cannot in any way at all abstract this action from its community-creating effect – its here-and-now *pro nobis* character – the very freedom and efficacy of that act demonstrate that its *being* is not exhausted in or conditioned by its presence for and with us. So we can never speak as though God were simply and neutrally 'there': there is, says Bonhoeffer succinctly, no *es gibt* where God is concerned. God's being is not a contingent fact among others, and we cannot speak of his being except as it impacts upon us. And equally, there is no *es gibt* where human nature is concerned either: we cannot speak of humanity outside its relation with the divine act of judgement and grace.[13] To speak about humanity in sin and humanity in grace, in Adam and in Christ, is not to speak about any phenomenon 'at hand' in the world, as if we could describe in third person terms what it is that would constitute a state of sin or of grace. We even have to say about the entire material world around us, from the point of view of faith and ecclesial identity, that it has no *es gibt* existence: my entire capacity to see and relate to the world is now conditioned by being in Christ. I am a *person* in the strict theological sense only because of this basic locatedness in Christ.[14]

This is in outline the theological epistemology which, for Bonhoeffer, takes us beyond the misleading binaries of 'act' and 'being' as philosophically conceived – or at least as conceived in his schematic summaries. The third section of the *Habilitationsschrift* proceeds to lay out something of the theological agenda that arises from this recognition – though with tantalizing brevity (less than thirty pages). 'Being in Adam' is being in the untruthfulness of self-referentiality; and since this is where we in fact are as human beings, we cannot construct a doctrine of creation and a theological perspective on unfallen humanity, a Thomist picture of *integra natura*, without abandoning theology itself, because this would be to claim a perspective independent of the first person position (as *actually* confronted by truth or God) that we cannot but occupy. As Bonhoeffer puts it more than once,[15] borrowing a Heideggerian vocabulary, our *Dasein* is wholly enclosed in the *Wiesein* of sin, and we cannot understand our creatureliness except in this context. Being in sin is living in the illusion that we 'possess full power over the self',[16] that

---

13. DBWE 2:115, 122–3 (DBW 2:112, 119–21).
14. DBWE 2:127, 134–5 (DBW 2:124–5, 132–4).
15. DBWE 2:144, 147, 152 (DBW 2:142, 145, 151).
16. DBWE 2:144 (DBW 2:142).

we – and the world, and its maker – are 'at hand' for understanding; it is both our condition and our action (and so our responsibility). It is this essential aloneness and self-referentiality from which being in Christ delivers us; and it is only being in Christ that permits us to see what we are as creatures. Our being in Adam prevents us seeing this because we confuse ourselves with the Creator; only when, in Christ, we allow the illusory selfhood of Adam-humanity to be destroyed are we free to be creatures for the first time.[17] And living in Christ is being defined by the future – by the ultimate 'outsideness' of what is still to come. It is, as Bonhoeffer strikingly puts it, living as a *child*.[18] The child's locatedness and horizons, the child's possibilities, have nothing to do with consciousness, decision or achievement – and Bonhoeffer does not miss the chance to trail his coat on the subject of infant baptism at this point. Being in Christ is being *dispossessed* of any claim or ambition to be able to construct the world we inhabit or the selves that we are; and this is not to commend passivity or stasis but to insist that it is only the gift of a relatedness we could not generate for ourselves that will break through the ingrained fiction that we are the makers of our meaning.

The themes of *Act and Being* develop the earlier ecclesiological speculations in *Sanctorum Communio*, and are echoed in aspects of *Creation and Fall*; but it is perhaps the Christology lectures[19] that most clearly read as a next chapter of *Act and Being*. And it is the account of what a theological ontology requires that casts most light on how Bonhoeffer deals in those lectures with patristic Christology and especially with the Definition of Chalcedon. The lectures are once again tantalizing, all the more so as we do not have Bonhoeffer's own written text, but they very clearly develop at least three major aspects of *Act and Being*: the 'locatedness' of theology in Adam or in Christ, the annihilating effect of Christ on the human *logos*, and the fact that what Christ does is not conditional on any prior human act or disposition – so that the universal efficacy of Christ's work cannot be in doubt for the believer. Towards the beginning of the lectures, we are told that the question of Christology is: 'by virtue of what personal ontological structure is Christ present to the church?'[20] and we are told that the being of Christ *pro me* 'is not a historical, factual, or ontic statement, but rather an

---

17. DBWE 2:151–3 (DBW 2:149–53).

18. DBWE 2:157–61 (DBW 2:156–61); see DBWE 2:158n57 (DBW 2:159n63), on other treatments of the subject in Bonhoeffer's early works.

19. The work was reconstructed from notes taken by auditors of the lecture course in Berlin in 1933. The latest text appears as 'Lectures on Christology', in DBWE 12:299–360 (DBW 12:279–348). The earlier German edition (Dietrich Bonhoeffer, *Theologie – Gemeinde: Vorlesungen, Briefe, Gespräche: 1927–1944*, Gesammelte Schriften, vol. 3, ed. Eberhard Bethge [München: Chr. Kaiser, 1960]) was translated by John Bowden (Dietrich Bonhoeffer, *Christology*, trans. John Bowden [London: Collins, 1966]); it was based on a more limited selection of student notes, but offers a fuller and more intelligible rendering of certain passages.

20. DBWE 12:314 (DBW 12:295).

ontological one'.[21] That is to say: talking about Christ must entail clarity about the kind of being we are talking of – which in this case can never be a passive object manipulated in our thinking. Jesus Christ is *only* for me, in relation to me, and any other sort of discourse misconstrues the grammar of theology itself (i.e. it is an ontological error, a category mistake).

This picks up and sharpens a point that becomes crucial in the immediately following section of the lectures, which deals with 'The Form of Christ'. Liberal Christologies attempt to move from work to person: they begin with the supposed effects of Christ's historical presence and deduce truths about who he is from this. But, says Bonhoeffer, this opens a gap between who Jesus is and what he does. In such a structure of argument, there is a Jesus who is not identical with the Christ – a sort of historical residue of identity unconnected with the Church and so unconnected with myself as believer and theologian, a Jesus with whom my relation cannot be one of indwelling. And in taking such a presupposition as a starting point, we focus on the wrong place simply in epistemological terms: we are beginning by trusting a human consciousness which is equipped to perceive and assess a phenomenon that is 'available'. For Bonhoeffer there can be no such thing. He draws a contrast between 'person' and 'personality'[22] in this context, suggesting that the error of liberal theology is to confuse the two, so that the merely *psychological* category of personality obscures the ontological reality of the person. The 'person' is who or what we are before God, and that is our real centre; it is not in any way identical with our conscious subjectivity, but is that which most deeply conditions and determines that subjectivity – so that we cannot truthfully refer to or inhabit or trust our subjectivity without asking about its ontological hinterland. Our personal being is a matter of *where* we are (in Adam or in Christ); thus for the human being in Adam, the centre of personal being is the place where we are confronted with the absolute limit that is the reality of the Creator, the reality we deny by our self-referentiality. But once we are confronted by and related to Christ *pro nobis*, this limit, which denies and annihilates our efforts to make meaning for ourselves – the human *logos* which Bonhoeffer has discussed earlier in the introduction to the lectures[23] – is recognizable as the centre of our humanity and our history. More specifically, it is the cross that effects and manifests this transformation of the 'limit': the cross as the ultimate declaration, the ultimate exposure, of the human desire to create meaning at the expense of the Word from outside, the cross as the ultimate embodiment of being in Adam, shows that the messianic historical story we want to tell about ourselves can only be told where God is silenced. There is thus no hope left in history (we might recall here the importance in *Act and Being* of the future as the ultimate 'outside' for the human self). 'History finds its meaning in the humiliation of Christ. Here every other claim that history might make

---

21. DBWE 12:314 (DBW 12:295).
22. DBWE 12:324 (DBW 12:306).
23. DBWE 12:300–9 (DBW 12:280–91).

is finished.'²⁴ The alternatives are the truth-excluding (God-excluding) claims of the self-in-Adam and the re-establishment of human being in Christ. And these are not alternatives presented to some judicious finite subjectivity; they are, so to speak, the superimposed realities which we come to know from the point of view of our being in Christ.

Concern with a 'pre-Christological' Jesus, a 'Jesus of history' who is not ontologically *pro me*, is a symptom of the refusal of human *logos* to die in the presence of the Word. What would be of supposedly salvific importance for us in such a picture could only be something we were able to conceive of – the 'idea' of Jesus, the 'mission' of Jesus or whatever; but the Word that addresses us is not an *idea*, any more than the effect of the person of Jesus is the impact of the set of contingent particulars we call a personality. The idea is 'available', the person is not, because the person appears only in the fact of encounter; truth is irreducibly a relational discovery.²⁵ To say that the historical Jesus is wholly identical with the Word of truth cannot therefore be a judgement at which we arrive when we have accumulated the appropriate amount of evidence (so that much of the debate about how much we know of the 'Jesus of history' becomes irrelevant[26]); but the opposite error, the Bultmannian dissolution of the historical Jesus into a proclaimed Word, must also be identified and ruled out. Jesus Christ as known in the Church, as known 'from within', is the actual historical person who is present as resurrected and exalted.²⁷ As Bonhoeffer has earlier put it, rather epigrammatically, Jesus can be present with us only because he is human, (since he belongs in the same world as we do); but equally, he can be present with us only because he is divine (since no historically conditioned person could be present outside their own historical context).²⁸ If there is One who is present here and now as limit, centre, judgement, promise, it can only be as *der Gottmenschlicher*, the divine-human. As God, Jesus is free to be contemporary with every single human subject and human society; as human, Jesus is connatural with every single human subject and society. To make this contemporaneity dependent on a judgement of the interest or pertinence of Jesus' ideas or mission is to make the extent of the transformation Jesus can bring about a local and contingent matter; at worst it can limit the relevance of Jesus to a human subgroup capable of grasping the ideas involved, or, worse still (with the theology of the Third Reich's apologists very much in mind), it can limit his

---

24. DBWE 12:325–6 (DBW 12:307–10).

25. DBWE 12:316–8 (DBW 12:297–301).

26. DBWE 12:330–1 (DBW 12:313–5); Hans Frei's classic study of *The Identity of Jesus Christ: The Hermeneutical Bases of Dogmatic Theology* (Philadelphia: Fortress Press, 1975), can be read as taking off from Bonhoeffer's rather gnomic reflections on this.

27. The *Lectures on Christology* do not engage directly with Bultmannian Christology, though there are passages, though the target of some statements, such as those just discussed, is fairly clear. It helps to read *LC* alongside the critique of Bultmann in *AB*, DBWE 2:94–103 (DBW 2:89–100).

28. DBWE 12:312–13 (DBW 12:293–5).

human connaturality to a racial subgroup. The resilient human *logos* yet again seeks to evade its necessary death at the hands of the Word of God.[29]

There are many other important themes in these early sections of the Christology lectures, but these are the most pertinent for our present enquiry, since these are the ones most obviously taking forward the argument of Act and Being about the centrality of ontology; and it is this which should clarify for us why exactly the Chalcedonian Definition is accorded such significance by Bonhoeffer. It is above all an ontological statement; and it functions, in Bonhoeffer's terminology, as a 'negative' theological exercise, an example of 'critical Christology' – that is, as an example of where conceptual analysis can take us and where it cannot, as a prohibition of certain strategies which will vitiate the whole theological enterprise. This is a slightly chaotic section of the lectures; and its accounts of patristic theology, while shot through with unexpected and original observations, need a lot of cautionary notes. Thus the discussion of Docetism[30] moves rapidly from a rather cursory summary of early Christian debate to the general proposal that Docetism is essentially the attempt 'to bring the history of Jesus into harmony with the idea of God'[31] – in which sense Ritschl and Hegel can be identified as docetists. Any theology that makes the specific flesh and blood of Jesus an *instrument*, a vehicle for a divine communication that would be intelligible in principle without that flesh and blood, will be essentially anti-theological. Hegel is responsible for 'the most brilliant exposition of docetism'[32] through his assimilation of idea and historical appearance to one another; the problem with his system is not that he wants to discard the historical particularity but that this particularity is reconceived as *necessity*. God cannot but be incarnate – which means that we cannot understand God without the incarnation; but having understood God, we then understand the incarnation as entailed by what is said about God's being, and this dissolves the impossibility or unthinkability of the incarnation itself and lands us back with the ambition of the self-in-Adam to possess meaning by its own labour.

The opposite error, which Bonhoeffer calls the 'Ebionite' view – once again with a slightly cavalier attitude to historical precision – is to read the narrative of Jesus as the story of how a historical human being 'becomes' God. As errors go, it is

---

29. DBWE 12:307 (DBW 12:287), 'the human being must either die or kill Jesus'. This must not be misunderstood as a contest between the created subject and the infinite, as if only one could occupy a place in the world: the point is that the aspiration of human *logos* is precisely to be *free from the world*, not to be part of a created (wholly dependent) order, and so cannot live alongside the truth, the realization of the actual relation between creator and creation, which is revealed in Jesus.

30. DBWE 12:332–8 (DBW 12:315–23).

31. DBWE 12:336 (DBW 12:320); it should be noted that here and elsewhere Bonhoeffer repeats what was in his day the common misunderstanding of the Byzantine theological concept of *enhypostasia* as evacuating the specificity of Jesus' human nature.

32. DBWE 12:337 (DBW 12:321).

preferable to Docetism because it does not seek to dissolve the historicity of the saviour; but in purporting to trace a *process* by which the divine and the human come together, it assumes a doctrine of human perfectibility as an abstract given[33] outside of the Adam/Christ polarity and thus allows us to occupy a place from which we may observe God and ourselves independently of sin and grace.

A perfunctory and none too accurate summary of Monophysite and Nestorian theories[34] brings us at last to the Chalcedonian formula. Both Monophysitism and Nestorianism have to be rejected. The former is distorted by its interest in the transfiguration of human *nature* in the incarnation: the divine person takes on human nature so as to make it something other than human – which yet again posits a human nature that can be conceived independently of being in Adam and being in Christ, and then compounds the problem by effectively eradicating this human nature in the event of salvation. The latter starts with exactly the same problem of reifying divine and human nature, but declares that this must mean that any union between the two is external, a unity of will or disposition. Hence the primary significance of Chalcedon is simply that the Definition rules out absolutely any language that treats divine and human nature as self-contained objects for observation and analysis. *'All options for thinking of all this together and in juxtaposition are represented as impossible and forbidden options.'*[35] We cannot isolate divine and human nature as items which must be brought together by some process such that there is a before and after in their relationship. Whether their unity is imagined as an absorption of one by the other or a juxtaposition of one with the other, any kind of unity that is *produced* is ruled out. And so, Bonhoeffer insists paradoxically, 'Chalcedon cancels itself out'[36]: it refines and focuses what is meant by divine and human 'substance' only to conclude that all talk of Christology in 'substance' terms has to cease. To put it slightly differently, Bonhoeffer is arguing that Christology is not and absolutely cannot be any sort of *narrative* about how two prior substances arrive at a state of union. The language of Lutheran orthodoxy about the different 'states' or different *genera* in which Jesus can be spoken of represents an attempt to move beyond the bare statement of divine-human alterity and inseparability in the Chalcedonian text,[37] but it does not succeed in breaking the hold of substance language and so risks slipping back into the abstract question of how we 'reconcile' the divine and the human in Christ – what moves we can make in order to show that these conceptualities can be put together. Out of this problematic comes eventually the family of

---

33. Flagged in the earlier version of the text, (Bonhoeffer, Christology, 86) in Bowden's translation; the point is lacking in the DBWE version.

34. DBWE 12:340–2 (DBW 12:324–8).

35. DBWE 12:342 (DBW 12:327), italics in original.

36. DBWE 12:343 (DBW 12:328).

37. DBWE 12:343 (DBW 12:328); once again, the point is better represented in Bonhoeffer, *Christology*, 92.

'kenotic' theologies in the seventeenth century. But Chalcedon posits an absolute simultaneity of divinity and humanity in Jesus Christ, and this should warn us against kenoticism, whether in its seventeenth-century forms or in its later avatars. Kenotic theory leaves us with an incarnate God who must become *less* than God in order to become incarnate, contradicting the fundamental theological principle that God is always present in the entirety of Godhead; and it also adjusts what can be said of the humanity of Jesus to make it somehow 'special', a kind of humanity that is ultimately different from ours. It tries to 'even out' the 'contradictory, mutually exclusive opposites'[38] of divinity and humanity, constructing definitions of each that can be fitted to one another. 'The recognition of the real Jesus Christ was turned into a construction.'[39] From the beginning of the lectures, Bonhoeffer has insisted that we stop asking the 'how' question about the incarnation and concentrate on the 'who': the Chalcedonian Definition sounds like an answer to 'how?' but in fact Chalcedon's use of the categories of *ousia* and *hypostasis* serves only to demonstrate that these terms are of no explanatory use – and that in any event *explanation* is precisely what Christology does not set out to do.[40]

So critical or 'negative' Christology finds its climax at Chalcedon; the Definition has the effect of 'letting the fact of the God-human stand as the presupposition'[41] for theology. The reality of the Church is the reality of the denied and dethroned *logos*, of the community living from the encounter with its limit; that limit is historical and specific in the life and death of Jesus, in the evacuation of humanly constructed meaning that takes place in these events; and this limit is present and active as the centre of a new humanity, free with a transcendent freedom in virtue of the resurrection of the historical person of Jesus. All of this is what Bonhoeffer means by 'the fact of the God-human'. But not even the resurrection itself is an 'available' reality; it is simply that which grounds the present encounter of the believing community with its limit and its centre, the source of its life. God in Christ acts without the 'visible authentication' of some sort of public demonstration of power; and so the Church shares that divine 'humiliation' – present and visible in the world yet incapable of demonstrating its divine origin. It cannot turn its humiliation into a principle, let alone a strategy, because it is a simple *fact*.[42] 'Positive' Christology – as opposed to the critical/negative Christology of Chalcedon – amounts only to this affirmation of the identity of the human being whose life is narrated in the gospels with God, the identity of this human life with God's judgement upon it[43]: the historically humiliated individual whose history is thus narrated is no more and no less than God's act of 'doing justice' to the divine identity in the active presence of the human Jesus, a presence which,

38. DBW 12:349 (DBW 12:335).
39. DBWE 12:349 (DBW 12:335).
40. DBWE 12:350 (DBW 12:336).
41. DBWE 12:354 (DBW 12:340).
42. DBWE 12:355–60 (DBW 12:342–8).
43. DBWE 12:353–5 (DBW 12:339–43).

because it is God's act of doing justice, continues unchanged today in, for and as the *communion sanctorum*.

Bonhoeffer's reading of Chalcedon is distinctive enough in our own day, but it was even more surprising in the 1930s. The Harnackian consensus that Chalcedon represented the surrender of Christian discourse to 'Hellenic' ways of thinking, combined with the Bultmannian absorption of Christological confession into the bare event of preaching the Crucified as the trigger for existential decision, had between them left the Chalcedonian formula as no more than a legacy of outmoded and inappropriate metaphysical ambition in the eyes of a substantial number of Protestant theologians. In contrast, Bonhoeffer emphatically repudiates the notion that the formula is 'Greek',[44] just as he emphatically repudiates the idea that Christology can dispense with ontology – the question of what kind of existence we ascribe to Jesus, what is the appropriate 'grammar' of our speech about him. At the same time, he is clear that the actual conceptual toolkit of Chalcedon is no longer useable: the way Chalcedon deploys the language of *ousia*, substance, simply makes it plain that any future 'positive' Christology cannot echo these idioms. In this brief concluding comment, my aim is to summarize the points of lasting significance in Bonhoeffer's use of Chalcedon, but also to suggest some areas in which he takes a few conceptual short-cuts, so as to bring out the potential for further Christological development here.

We have seen that one of the main points in his exposition is his powerfully consistent emphasis on the fact that we cannot understand the incarnate Christ as the product of a process in which two previously self-contained entities are brought together – which means that we cannot understand *Christology* as an attempt to explain such a process through the analysis of those entities. This is not just a matter either of intellectual fastidiousness or of a sub-Barthian emphasis on the utter givenness of revelation in Christ. Read against the backdrop of Bonhoeffer's entire work, there are other themes that come into view. The problem for any Christology that works by appealing to a recognition of Jesus' human excellence is that it makes the transformation effected by Jesus dependent on existing standards of human excellence – presupposing a reliable model of humanity with which we can work. This, I think, is part of what Bonhoeffer means by saying[45] that the Christology of a Paul of Samosata, say, offers an inadequate account of the universal scope of salvation as compared with the alternative tradition which was more ready to make use of the terminology of substance: this latter is fraught with problems and ultimately unsuitable, but it does not make salvation conditional on *being a certain kind of human* – the kind who can recognize a specific pattern of excellence and be inspired by it. Substance language at least allow us to say – with all appropriate qualifications in

---

44. DBWE 12:352 (DBW 12:338): 'nothing is further from being a product of Greek thinking'.

45. DBWE 12:352-3 (DBW 12:338-40); see Bonhoeffer, *Christology*, 104 which makes the point a bit more clearly.

the context of Christology – that whatever humanity is, its wholeness is involved, addressed, embraced and transfigured in the reality of Jesus. As noted earlier in this chapter, the spectre that haunts Bonhoeffer's thinking is surely that of a selective humanism, implicitly or explicitly disenfranchising certain classes of human agents,[46] not an academic question in Berlin in 1933.

Similarly, he is insistent on clarity about *where we are speaking from* as theologians. Whatever may be the case in other intellectual disciplines, the theologian is speaking either as someone determined to *create* meaning in the 'Adamic' mode or as someone who is *being drawn* into a meaning irreducibly beyond their agenda or capacity, someone alive in Christ. It is precisely this duality that will, a couple of years after the delivery of the Christology lectures, allow Bonhoeffer to formulate his harshest statements about the *Deutsche Christen*: to stand outside the Confessing Church is to stand 'in Adam', and so to refuse salvation – not because the Confessing Church is making a superior doctrinal claim but because the Confessing Church alone refuses to limit the grace of being in the Church to a defined category of humans. The denial of this is quite simply the denial of the very notion of Church, of being in Christ.[47] A theoretical anthropology which begins from distinctions between human beings that have nothing to do with the Adam/Christ polarity can have no place in theology. And the Chalcedonian affirmation of what we have called the absolute 'simultaneity' of divine and human in Jesus Christ, by refusing any idea that God's presence in Jesus is some sort of response to specific features, qualities or achievements of the humanity of Jesus, denies us any grasp on a humanity that we are able to understand and evaluate independently of the reality of grace and belonging in Christ.

These crucial points help us to see how Bonhoeffer's apparently very abstract discussion in *Act and Being* connects with the immediate practical concerns that faced him in the mid-1930s; and also how the Christology lectures form an indispensable bridge between the two. The connections with the deeply Christological concerns of the *Ethics* fragments is also clear.[48] But perhaps one element in the *Ethics* discussion represents a significant refinement of the arguments we have examined here. *Act and Being* and the Christology lectures posit a single oppositional pattern of human belonging, Adam or Christ, an unsparingly theological topography. *Ethics* continues to assume that where we speak from is

---

46. It is worth emphasising that Bonhoeffer is not here undertaking a discussion of 'universalism' as such. Unlike Barth, he does not have a fully worked theological commitment to universal salvation, and I suspect that he would not have wanted to develop one.

47. On these questions, the various texts collected in Clifford J. Green and Michael P. DeJonge (eds), *Theology and Third Reich. The Bonhoeffer Reader*, vol. 4 (Philadelphia: Fortress Press, 2013) contain the essential arguments. See especially 384, 387–8, 433–7, 448–51.

48. This is explored at greater length in Rowan Williams, *Christ the Heart of Creation* (London: Continuum, 2016), 185–217.

an essential question for the theologian and the believer, and it reiterates in strong terms the significance of Christ's embrace of all humanity, and the foundation of all our renewed thought and action in our acceptance of the No to our self-constructed world which Christ utters and effects.[49] But it also foregrounds other sorts of belonging – in family, labour and state or society. We do not grow into our full and Christlike maturity as individuals but as *responsible* persons, persons, that is, who are answerable for those whose lives are connected with theirs. This is the realm of the 'mandates' which Bonhoeffer explores at various points in the *Ethics* drafts:[50] these networks of relational imperatives are certainly not (as some of Bonhoeffer's *Deutsche Christen* opponents would have maintained) independently accessible sources of insight about God and God's will to be set alongside the data of revelation. But they are undoubtedly the specific forms of human togetherness which we are always already embedded in. Being in Adam or in Christ will in fact be a matter of how we live out our solidarities in society, family and so on. Being in Christ does not lift us out of those solidarities, as if being in Christ were a sort of 'supplemental' belonging alongside the others; but it shows us where those other belongings are oriented, how we are to discern and probe their requirements so that they do not destroy the ultimately determining solidarity of life in Christ. And in this light, we might conclude – though this is to go beyond what Bonhoeffer himself says – that to ask for theological clarity about where someone speaks from requires attention to these historical forms of belonging as well as to the overarching theological categories. Being in Adam (though Bonhoeffer in fact does not make use of this phrase in the *Ethics*) and being in Christ are not discernible except as ways of being responsible (or failing to be responsible) in the specific solidarities we actually inhabit. And to work honestly as a theologian means attending to this – so that, for example, our complicity in *particular* sinful solidarities, of inherited racial or gendered privilege, say, needs to be seen simply as the form taken here and now by 'being in Adam' and must be named as such. It is a kind of theological *Ideologiekritik*, a practised alertness to what self-oriented human *logos* looks like in our specific circumstances. To the extent that the Chalcedonian formula (in its plain statement of God's active presence in Jesus in and for humanity as such) disallows any appeal to an already-evaluated calculus of human excellence or normativity, it is a key element in this critical task.

So to a final point. The insistence on ontology which the Christology lectures take on from the discussion in *Act and Being* clearly works as a vehicle to challenge any system that imagines meaning as self-created. Why then is Bonhoeffer so wary of saying anything positive about substance language, insisting that it functions at Chalcedon only to subvert itself? He seems to assume that any use of substance terminology in the cause of a 'positive' Christology must entail an Adamic confidence about our ability to construct a full account of what constitutes a particular substance. But what he underrates is the concern in patristic theology

---

49. See, for example, DBWE 6:223–4, 249–53 (DBW 6:221–3, 248–53).
50. E.g. DBWE 6:68–75 (DBW 6:54–61).

to deny precisely this: the mid-fourth century debates about trinitarian theology, especially as reflected in – say – Gregory of Nyssa's writings, show very plainly that language about the divine *ousia* was regarded as at best heuristic. There is a programmatic denial that it could make assertions about the content of divine life. What is more, Gregory will also argue that we are equally incapable of forming a definitive concept of our own human subjectivity, a picture of our humanity that would reduce it to a simple set of conditions to be satisfied, thus eroding any grasp of its freedom and God-relatedness.[51] In other words, the problem in Christological debate in the fourth and fifth centuries is not exactly one of how to reconcile two pre-existing and competing essential definitions. It is that we know that, in order to speak recognizably of God, certain things cannot be said (e.g. that God is passive, mutable and so on); and in order to speak recognizably of humanity we know likewise that certain things cannot be said (anything that would deny embodiment and physical vulnerability for example, or anything that would isolate humanity from its dependence on God's gift and its character as reflecting the divine image). Discourse about 'substance' here is a way precisely of noting the risks of over-ambitious definition and conceptual closure, rather than a matter of enshrining an illegitimate speculative confidence at the heart of theology; it is arguably just to do with seeing the ontological imperative for what it is, and so congruent with Bonhoeffer's fundamental concerns. We cannot simply say what we choose; we are always already involved in meanings we have learned rather than created, and our Christological language cannot sidestep the question of what will *count* as speaking about God.

Bonhoeffer most definitely presupposes this in his quite proper concern that we should not abandon theological discourse entirely by minimizing the radical difference of God from finite existence. Similarly, he is consistently anxious not to be speaking of Jesus' humanity in a way that makes it less than human; and, perhaps more importantly in this context, he is clear that 'being in Adam' is a distorted way of being human because it fails to reckon with the central truth about human nature, its inescapable dependence. The proclamation of the God-man is an affirmation of the proper grammar of both the divine and the human, of a divinity that escapes our power of thought and a humanity that lives out its dependence in a unique radicality. But this *is* in effect the language of substance, and Chalcedon does not require us to go further in stipulating a capacity in the human mind for some exhaustive definition of conditions that have to be met for divinity or humanity. When he says that we cannot and must not think of the

---

51. Gregory of Nyssa, *de hominis opificio* 11 (Greek text in *Patrologia Graeca* 44, ed. Claude Blume [Paris: Classiques Garnier Numérique, 2006]); for detailed commentary, see recently Ilaria Ramelli, 'Gregorio di Nissa, de hominis opificio 1–13: la natura magnifica della creatura', in *Stylos*, no. 22 (2013): 187–224; English translation of Gregory's text in *Nicene and Post-Nicene Fathers. Second Series Volume V Gregory of Nyssa: Dogmatic Treatises* ed. Philip Schaff and Rev. Henry Wallace (New York: Cosimo Classics, 2007).

divine nature in relation to Jesus as 'all-powerful and ever-present',[52] he does *not* mean that we should think of God as having a different kind of 'grammar' which would allow us to say that he was limited in power or presence; this would be to make nonsense of Bonhoeffer's entire insistence on the transcendent priority of divine reality. He is rightly warning against any version of Christology that sees the tension of crucified divinity in terms of how one individual with one set of properties can become the subject of a contradictory set of properties, diverting our attention to an imagined God who is other than the infinite action that is real here and now *in* and *as* the crucified, and yet is still unlimited in its reaching out towards us. But when Bonhoeffer attempts to discuss the inadequacies of substance terminology, he is, in this respect at least, still awkwardly wedded to a Harnackian assumption about how metaphysical terminology works in the patristic (or for that matter, mediaeval) context.

The Christology lectures, though, remain one of the major theological achievements of the twentieth century, even more so when read as a continuation of his earlier work. As *Act and Being* in effect concludes, only a Christological focus can provide a sustainable foundation for Christian theology: the relation between finite and infinite is as it is in the incarnate Creator, and in no other way. To think of God outside this is not to think of the Christian God at all. This is neither (as Bonhoeffer makes abundantly clear[53]) a triumphalist claim for the demonstrable superiority of Christianity within the world of 'faiths' – a context completely alien to Bonhoeffer's thinking – nor a prescriptive demand that all theology should formally begin with Christological discussion (his own practice shows that this cannot be what he has in mind). It is closer to the conviction of the early Luther that theology begins in a deliverance from Hell; it begins when we are able to recognize that we were never free to change ourselves or love ourselves before we acknowledged the presence of the new creation within our world. In Bonhoeffer's eyes, Chalcedon, by refusing to conceive the incarnation as a process in which independent rival realities are somehow brought into alignment, is a crucially important ally in the theologian's liberation from 'how' questions. It leaves us with the challenge which echoes throughout the lectures, and indeed the rest of Bonhoeffer's work: 'Who is this human being who is said to be God?'[54]

---

52. DBWE 12:354 (DBW 12:340).
53. DBWE 12:325–7 (DBW 12:307–11).
54. DBWE 12:350 (DBW 12:336).

Chapter 3

KIERKEGAARD'S AND BONHOEFFER'S PARADOX CHRISTOLOGY

Lea Weber

'[A]ll Christian theology finds its origin in the miracle of miracles, that God became human,'[1] Dietrich Bonhoeffer wrote in his Christmas meditation from December 1939, composed for the monthly letter of the Confessing Church's *Council of Brethren*. The head of the underground seminary of Finkenwalde hereby promoted a Christological focus that can be called characteristic of his theological thinking as a whole.[2] As researchers have pointed out numerous times, the question of 'who is Jesus Christ, for us, today'[3] is the central issue governing Bonhoeffer's work, from his ecclesial theory in *Sanctorum Communio* and the problem of perceiving God's revelation in *Act and Being*, all throughout his reflections of discipleship and Christian community, to the letters and fragments from prison. For Bonhoeffer, Christ is the ultimate revelation of God's love being unremittingly directed towards others. In his incarnation, life, crucifixion and resurrection, Christ – and subsequently the Church as the body of Christ – anticipated the goal of new creation that God intends for all of humankind (substitutionary representation [*Stellvertretung*]). He is the mediator through which his followers relate to God, each other and the world.

Due to scholars like Geffrey B. Kelly, Friederike Barth and Matthew Kirkpatrick it has been well established in recent years that Bonhoeffer was considerably influenced by the nineteenth-century Danish writer Søren Kierkegaard. Bonhoeffer must have become acquainted with Kierkegaard around the year of 1927, possibly

---

My doctoral research is made possible by a scholarship of the Hanns-Seidel-Stiftung, München. This chapter is dedicated to Professor Amy Laura Hall, who inspired my passion for Kierkegaard's theology and embodies his maxim to lovingly engage others through her teaching and writing.

1. DBWE 15:528 (DBW 15:537–8).
2. See Hans-Jürgen Abromeit, *Das Geheimnis Christi: Dietrich Bonhoeffers erfahrungsbezogene Christologie* (Neukirchen-Vluyn: Neukirchener Verlag, 1991), 17.
3. DBWE 8:362 (DBW 8:402).

through an essay by Heinrich Barth that was published the year before.[4] Although the explicit references to Kierkegaard in his published works are sparse and all of them are confined to the time prior to 1933, Bonhoeffer referred or alluded to Kierkegaard throughout his entire career: Bonhoeffer's cousin Hans Christian von Hase remembers discussing Kierkegaard's *Sickness Unto Death* and further literature with the young Dietrich.[5] In 1935, Bonhoeffer seems to have given *Either/Or* as a gift to Eberhard Bethge.[6] He also recommended reading Kierkegaard to his fiancée, Maria von Wedemeyer, in the spring of 1944 and mentioned him in several other letters from prison.[7] External indicators alone therefore already point to an ongoing involvement with Kierkegaard's thought. More importantly yet, Bonhoeffer's published writings show an extensive knowledge of and substantial engagement with the Danish writer. Many of the crucial areas of his theology suggest profound parallels to Kierkegaard. The two theologians share an interest in the shape of Christianity in today's world as well as the personal appropriation of faith.[8] Kierkegaard and Bonhoeffer criticize a purely philosophical approach to Christianity and making use of grace without committing to the demands of discipleship. Being conformed to the image of Christ is central for them and they both assume suffering on the part of believers is inevitable. Yet, aside from a chapter in Kirkpatrick's profound study and some rather scattered hints, the relationship

---

4. Heinrich Barth, 'Kierkegaard, der Denker: Vier Vorlesungen', *ZZ* 4 (1926): 194-234.

5. See DBWE 10:596 (DBW 10:593). Through a comparison with Jutta Koslowski (ed.), *Aus dem Leben der Familie Bonhoeffer: Die Aufzeichnungen von Dietrich Bonhoeffers jüngster Schwester Susanne Dreß* (Gütersloh: Gütersloher Verlagshaus, 2018), 147, those conversations at the Bonhoeffers' house can be pinpointed to the period between Dietrich's return to Berlin on 27 February 1929 and his departure for America on 6 September 1930, possibly even before Dreß's wedding on 14 November 1929. Bonhoeffer thus became familiar with *The Sickness unto Death* (Søren Kierkegaard, *The Sickness unto Death* [*SUD*], KW 19, ed. Howard V. Hong and Edna H. Hong [Princeton: Princeton University Press, 1980]) earlier than Kirkpatrick (Matthew D. Kirkpatrick, *Attacks on Christendom in a World Come of Age: Kierkegaard, Bonhoeffer, and the Question of 'Religionless Christianity'* [Eugene: Pickwick Publications, 2011], 214) has been able to show so far.

6. See ibid., 12.

7. See Dietrich Bonhoeffer, *Love Letters from Cell 92: The Correspondence between Dietrich Bonhoeffer and Maria von Wedemeyer 1943–45*, ed. Ruth-Alice von Bismarck and Ulrich Kabitz (Nashville: Abingdon Press, 1992), 185-6 and DBWE 8:123, 193, 374 (DBW 8:179, 291, 548-9).

8. Kierkegaard's influence to that effect is especially graspable in Bonhoeffer's *Discipleship*, in which concepts like 'cheap grace', 'simple obedience' or 'the extraordinary' were inspired by him. See Geffrey B. Kelly, 'Kierkegaard as "Antidote" and as Impact on Dietrich Bonhoeffer's Concept of Christian Discipleship', in *Bonhoeffer's Intellectual Formation: Theology and Philosophy in His Thought*, ed. Peter Frick (Tübingen: Mohr Siebeck, 2008), 145-56.

between their Christological thinking has been neglected up until now. It is thus the purpose of the this chapter to trace similarities and differences in their understanding of (paradoxical) Christology. First, I shall survey how Bonhoeffer adapts Kierkegaard regarding the relationship between Christological reflection and human reason. The discussion will then turn towards the character of God's revelation in Christ and the response of faith or offence, especially pertaining to the notion of the God-human's hiddenness. The third section of the chapter focuses on the theologians' common intention concerning Christology, which shows how it is not overstating the case to consider them kindred spirits.

I. Collision with the Paradox – Christology and Human Understanding

The first intersection between Kierkegaard and Bonhoeffer regarding Christology can be found in the latter's lecture on *Jesus Christ and the Essence of Christianity* from his time as a vicar in Barcelona. According to Ernst Feil, this lecture can be seen as a prelude to Bonhoeffer's later theology, since it already addresses some of the topics that will prove to be most important to him in the future.[9] In that sense, *Jesus Christ and the Essence of Christianity* also prefigures vital strands of Bonhoeffer's engagement with Kierkegaard. Generally, the lecture voices criticism of turning Christianity into a religion, thereby distracting from its true substance, which is Jesus' assertion to be the Christ of God.[10] He lays claim to the individual's life beyond being venerated as a religious genius or hero. A proper understanding does not tie God's revelation to Christ's outward looks or personality, nor does it exhaust itself in ethics. Rather, Christ's divinity is hidden (see II.), and it is the sheer authority of his word that is calling for a decision on the individual's part to give in to God's will. Only understanding it this way does justice to the earnestness 'that it is God who is speaking here, and if it is only in Christ that God's word once became a present reality, then Christ possesses for me not only a merely relative but also absolutely urgent significance.'[11] In the course of this, history should not be considered as something past, put in its place by applying the system of idealistic philosophy to it, thus diminishing its decisive meaning. Instead, Bonhoeffer attaches importance to listening to Jesus as if one were a contemporary, hearing the words of the man from Nazareth as God's own word addressed to oneself personally. The goal of it would be to become 'inwardly completely poor',[12] acknowledging that there is no human way to God, only God's way to humankind in Jesus Christ.

---

9. See Ernst Feil, *Die Theologie Dietrich Bonhoeffers: Hermeneutik, Christologie, Weltverständnis* (München: Kaiser, 1971), 157.

10. See DBWE 10:343, 347 (DBW 10:303, 308). In this, Bonhoeffer was clearly influenced by Karl Barth.

11. DBWE 10:343 (DBW 10:303).

12. DBWE 10:352 (DBW 10:314).

These notions of the God-human as the core of Christianity, him being hidden but demanding an immediate reaction and the conceptualization of history as something concerning each person in an existential way are central to Kierkegaard's Christology, too. They play a significant role in *Philosophical Fragments, Concluding Unscientific Postscript* as well as in *Practice in Christianity*[13] and touch on the more general question of human understanding. For Kierkegaard, the Incarnation is anything but self-evident. Instead, it is *'the wonder'*,[14] something that reason could not have imagined and that it cannot fully grasp either. He fleshes this out in *Fragments* by contrasting the philosopher Socrates and a divine teacher. The pseudonym Johannes Climacus opens his thought project by asking in what way the truth could be learned.[15] For Socrates, who eventually exemplifies the non-Christian, truth is inherent to the human being. It is something not to discover on the outside, but to recover in oneself through remembrance (*anamnesis*). He thus presents himself as a midwife who helps others rediscover the truth which is buried in them. It can be gained by the passionate search of the individual. In consequence, '[i]n the Socratic view, every human being is himself the midpoint, and the whole world focuses only on him because his self-knowledge is God-knowledge.'[16] As an alternative standpoint, Johannes Climacus develops the figure of the divine teacher. Presuming a different anthropology, he regards the individual being as in self-deceit over their capabilities of gaining the truth. The divine teacher must first convey the learner's stance as untruth and prepare them for receiving the desired good. In that regard, Christ embodies

> in every aspect of his existence what is being communicated: he is entirely and without remainder an act of communication, an incarnate word. […] Jesus does not remind us of what we have forgotten but creates the conditions for knowing him. He *is* what he teaches.[17]

---

13. See Søren Kierkegaard, *Concluding Unscientific Postscript to Philosophical Fragments* [*CUP*]. *Kierkegaard's Writings* [*KW*] 12.1, ed. Howard V. Hong and Edna H. Hong (Princeton: Princeton University Press, 1992), 96–8. 343–9, 598–601 (*AUN-1*: 89–91; *AUN-2*, 47–54, 312–4). The German translation of Kierkegaard's works is referenced according to the edition by Emanuel Hirsch et al.: Søren Kierkegaard, *Gesammelte Werke*, ed. Emanuel Hirsch et al. (Düsseldorf: Eugen Diederichs Verlag, 2.1986–96).

14. See Søren Kierkegaard, *Philosophical Fragments* [*PF*], *KW* 7, ed. Howard V. Hong and Edna H. Hong (Princeton: Princeton University Press, 1985), 36, emphasis in the original (*PB*, 34).

15. The Danish 'hvorvidt' can mean both 'whether' and 'how' and is best reproduced by the German 'inwiefern'.

16. *PF*, 11 / *PB*, 9.

17. Rowan Williams, *Christ the Heart of Creation* (London: Bloomsbury, 2018), 188.

Any autonomous grasping of the truth will prove to be fruitless. Only by abstaining from construing reality from its own viewpoint does the person concerned actually learn it.

The parallel with Bonhoeffer is evident. The introduction to his *Lectures on Christology* from 1933 seeks to express the very same notion. The truth of Christ goes beyond the boundaries of the immanent logos of human beings: it is not something to simply be recovered or even be grasped through dedicated striving. That would make Christ an object to be discussed and judged among others. But Christ is not part of the domain of things. Instead, he is the very ground of reality and in this, ultimately different from any created being. The truth about the world is its utmost dependence on God, the sheer opposite of autonomy. The Socratic view as introduced by Climacus is misguided in failing to recognize precisely this: Christ himself is the middle;[18] knowing *him* is God-knowledge. Christ can therefore be neither the object of natural sciences nor of arts and humanities, because both represent an order based on the self-referentiality of human reason. He rather serves as the 'counter Logos'[19] to human reason that is absolutizing itself, taking away every possibility of understanding God in a scientific way without acknowledging God's God-ness. Bonhoeffer expresses this distinction by differentiating between the 'how' and the 'who question'. When encountering the God-human, any query about the 'how', meaning the possibility or thinkability of Christ, must die away. 'The fact that the Logos became flesh, a human being, is the prerequisite, not the proof.'[20] Otherwise, human reason too desperately holds on to its own authority and remains enclosed in itself. According to Bonhoeffer, the only appropriate question is that of 'who are you?', entailing a limitation of the inquirer's being: after the resurrection, it is turned around to the query of 'who are you, that you ask this question?'[21]

So for Bonhoeffer, in common with Kierkegaard, Christology has existential bearings on the inquirer.[22] The who question plainly shows how in Christ the believer deals with a person, not an object, entailing a stance of responsivity instead of distanced observation. She is claimed along with her whole existence to position herself in relation to the God-human. The promise of this process is the potential breakup of human self-referentiality. Through being the middle, Jesus Christ simultaneously functions as a boundary of the individual's existence and hereby restores what was lost in the Fall. By trusting that it could find a way to serve God better apart from God's commandment, humanity had moved away from perceiving of God and the other person as a boundary offering grace and freedom. It had raised itself to the position of being the middle, thus becoming

18. See DBWE 12:324 (DBW 12:307).
19. See DBWE 12:302 (DBW 12:282).
20. DBWE 12:301 (DBW 12:281). See already earlier in Dietrich Bonhoeffer, 'Concerning the Christian Idea of God [CCIG]', *JR* 12 (1932): 177–8.
21. DBWE 12:304 (DBW 12:286).
22. See *CCIG*, 177–85, 178–9 (DBW 10:426), DBWE 4:51 (DBW 4:38), and DBWE 12:303 (DBW 12:283).

sicut deus, but breaking bonds with God and the neighbour. Entering into fallen humanity's state, Christ re-establishes God as boundary and middle. However, that amounts to the death of the immanent logos. By asking the who question, it loses any right to subsume the Logos made flesh under its own classification system. Instead, it is itself surmounted by the revelation of God in Christ.

This also finds expression in Kierkegaard's concept of the 'paradox'. In confrontation with the human mind, the God-human Jesus Christ becomes something 'thought itself cannot think'.[23] According to Climacus, human reason desires mastery, always seeking to test whether there are limits to its understanding. The incarnation, however, resists the desire to dominate or control. It cannot be fit into the categories of the immanent logos and eventually proves to be a boundary to seemingly limitless thought. In Christ, the eternal not only relates to the existing, but comes into existence itself and therefore serves as the 'absolute paradox'. God appears as an individual human being in time. As a result, two options emerge: either the understanding is unhappy, so that reason takes offence, or it accepts its creaturely limitedness, subordinating in faith to the mystery of God becoming human. In the second case, the individual is led to the realization of God's ultimate otherness and acquires the consciousness of sin. This constitutes the paradoxical redoubling of their existence. Self-referential human thinking is shown to be in the untruth and incapable of apprehending God. It requires revelation, that is an encounter with the godly teacher Jesus Christ, to gain the condition for being able to understand the truth. In this, the paradox ultimately has a positive function. Kierkegaard is neither aiming at conceiving of the incarnation as logically contradictory nor does he support a dialectical notion. The paradox rather 'maintains the simultaneity of the one and the other, and [...] orients us beyond ourselves toward faith in the truth of God, which is God's relation to us'.[24]

Although Bonhoeffer does not use the term 'paradox' to specifically describe Christ,[25] it is clear that he shares Kierkegaard's criticism. Humanity's false autonomy is deluded and misguided. Only collision with the paradox of Godself in Christ provides the key to true transcendence, since for Bonhoeffer personality is inextricably bound to facing a counterpart.[26] The God-human is given in the sense

---

23. *PF*, 37 / *PB*, 35. Kierkegaard's position also leads to a rejection of proving God's existence.

24. Tim Boniface, *Jesus, Transcendence, and Generosity: Christology and Transcendence in Hans Frei and Dietrich Bonhoeffer* (Lanham: Lexington Books / Fortress Academic, 2018), 135.

25. By 'paradox', Bonhoeffer refers to the contrast of the transcendent God seeking sinners (see DBWE 10:352; *CCIG*, 183, 185 [DBW 10:314, 430, 433]), the crucifixion (see DBWE 10:357 [DBW 10:320]) or the impossibility of winning assertion from history (see DBWE 12:329 [DBW 12:313]).

26. See DBWE 12:305 (DBW 12:286). See also Christiane Tietz-Steiding, *Bonhoeffers Kritik der verkrümmten Vernunft: Eine erkenntnistheoretische Untersuchung* (Tübingen: Mohr Siebeck, 1999), 116–21.

of an answer preceding and enabling the question in the first place. He ultimately judges the immanent logos, which could not move beyond being incurved in itself by its own power. Just like for Kierkegaard, precisely the seizure of power by reason is problematic. However, Kierkegaard does not only view human rationality as limited in terms of the divine, but he also takes a certain kind of cognitive knowledge for the wrong way to approach Christianity in general. As opposed to a focus on doctrine (*Lære*), Christianity is 'existence-communication'[27] for him. In the course of this, thinking itself is not the problem, but *merely thinking* faith instead of existing in it is. For Kierkegaard, 'Christianity is not a series of propositions, but a relationship to a *person*'.[28] The individual is to become a self before God, venturing a life of discipleship. Logic cannot execute the movement of existence though. Therefrom results a refusal of idealism, which Kierkegaard accuses of forgetting to exist. Here, he finds the wrong orientation of reason brought to its extreme, leading to most speculative thought. It disregards how rationality is posited; reason cannot overhaul its own foundation of God-given freedom. Kierkegaard especially criticizes objectivization at the cost of subjectivity, which he considers essential to Christianity: true conviction enacts or expresses existingly what it believes.[29] There is no access to actuality apart from personal involvement. Therefore, world-historical thinking in the sense of creating a 'system' is incompatible with Christian religious existence. Bonhoeffer echoes this criticism of carrying out theology as a system in his essay *Concerning the Christian Idea of God* from 1932. He accuses idealism of subordinating God and the other person to thinking, contradictory to their 'objectivity' in existence. Once more, this evidences the autocracy and self-glorification of human reason. It has been cut off from reality, trying to reach transcendence through its own effort, but remaining within the realms of possibility: '[t]hinking always means system and the system excludes the reality.'[30] God, by contrast, *is*. Revelation posits a new reality that resists a predomination of thought at the expense of existence. Nevertheless, Bonhoeffer does not stop at a negative evaluation of human thinking per se either. For him, Christology is the centre not only of theological science, but any science at all.[31] Christ functions as the key to properly understand God, oneself and the world.

---

27. *CUP*, 383, 570 / *AUN-2*, 87, 282. See also Søren Kierkegaard, *Judge For Yourself* [*JFY*], KW 21, ed. Howard V. Hong and Edna H. Hong (Princeton: Princeton University Press, 1990), 191 / *US*, 219.

28. David R. Law, *Kierkegaard's Kenotic Christology* (Oxford: Oxford University Press, 2013), 10, emphasis in the original.

29. See *CUP*, 406 / *AUN-2*, 112.

30. *CCIG*, 178 (DBW 10:424), see *PF*, 80 / *PB*, 77 and see also Kirkpatrick, *Attacks*, 88. Compare Bonhoeffer's *extra nobis* of existence (*CCIG*, 179 [DBW 10:426]) to Kierkegaard's definition of a self-resting 'transparently in the power that established it' (*SUD*, 14 [*KzT*, 10]).

31. See DBWE 12:305 (DBW 12:285). See also DBWE 6:341 (DBW 6:344). The English translation 'knowledge' does not reproduce the German 'Wissenschaft' quite correctly in this case.

Closely related to the opposition to idealism and theology as a system, Bonhoeffer also shares Kierkegaard's aversion to conceiving of Christianity as doctrine. Needless to say, Bonhoeffer's *Lectures on Christology* are in itself a doctrinal undertaking, and his writings correspond much more to the character of systematic theology in the strict sense than Kierkegaard's. But what he distances himself from is searching for truth without any existential appropriation. In opposition to idealistic philosophy, he does not differentiate between mediated insight and the immediate understanding or assertion of faith.[32] Rather, knowledge is constitutively linked to the individual, so that there is no absolute truth independent from one's personal relation to it. Knowledge becomes doing.[33] Again however, faith relies on the antecedent revelation of God. It is an *a posteriori* existence or a 'direct act', as Bonhoeffer frames it in *Concerning the Christian Idea of God*.[34] Only in setting forth what is already posited, can theological thinking account for the reality of God. In this, it is inextricably tied to Christ's person. He is to be received as a gift, God coming near, instead of a general truth.[35] For Kierkegaard, the straightforward consequence of this concentration on the paradoxical God-human would be the possibility of offence, which is a constitutive part of Christian existence. Bonhoeffer, however, does not extensively discuss offence in this context. He has a passing mention of it in *Act and Being* and includes it in his *Lectures on Christology* (see II.) a few years later, but it 'does not bear all the hallmarks of Kierkegaard's deeper analysis'.[36] Bonhoeffer puts the emphasis on the problem that if revelation were to be regarded as doctrine, God would exhaust Godself in a system constructed by humans.[37] His account of – Christologically qualified – truth thus ultimately flows into his criticism of idealism.

Bonhoeffer's conflict with philosophy plays out further in his challenge of the idealistic category of necessity applied to the incarnation. Just like Kierkegaard, he identifies Hegel as the ultimate originator of this thought. The Dane had first

---

32. See Friederike Barth, *Die Wirklichkeit des Guten: Dietrich Bonhoeffers 'Ethik' und ihr philosophischer Hintergrund* (Tübingen: Mohr Siebeck, 2011), 98–100, 106–8.

33. Compare *JFY*, 115 / *US*, 145; Søren Kierkegaard, *Practice in Christianity* [*PC*], *KW* 20, ed. Howard V. Hong and Edna H. Hong (Princeton: Princeton University Press, 1991), 196 (*EC*, 196) to DBWE 4:77 (DBW 4:69) and DBWE 6:317–8, 327–9, 378–9 (DBW 6:320, 330–2, 382). For Kierkegaard's influence on the category of 'Einfalt' in Bonhoeffer, which is again only limitedly translated by the term 'simple obedience', see also Kelly, Antidote, 152–3.

34. See *CCIG*, 179 (DBW 10:425) and DBWE 6:317 (DBW 6:320). Bonhoeffer had already developed the concept of *actus directus* in *Act and Being*, DBWE 2:28, 128–9, 133, 158–161 (DBW 2:23, 126, 131, 158–61).

35. See DBWE 12:319 (DBW 12:301).

36. Kirkpatrick, *Attacks*, 151. See DBWE 2:104 (DBW 2:100) and DBWE 12:313. 319. 357–60 (DBW 12:295. 302. 345–7). Due to the almost sole occurrence of 'offence' in the *Lectures on Christology* it can be suspected that Bonhoeffer mainly drew on Kierkegaard here, instead of offence being a category that sprung from his own thinking.

37. See Tietz-Steiding, *Kritik*, 233. See also DBWE 2:103–4 (DBW 2:100–101).

and foremost treated the problem in the light of the *Fragments*' opening question regarding the relationship between history and faith, claiming that historical phenomena are never necessary.[38] Otherwise, they would always *be*, losing the contingent nature of history, which could also have come to pass in a different way. But for both, Kierkegaard and Bonhoeffer, the modality of becoming is based on the free agency of a subject, the opposite of necessity. Transferred to the incarnation, this means that the epiphany of God in Jesus Christ must invariably be considered a free resolve on the part of God. Anything else would amount to a docetic Christology for Bonhoeffer. What is more, exactly God's having come into existence amounts to the paradox. God *is* and still *became*, the *eternal* has gained *history*, *creator* and *creature* became one in the God-human Jesus Christ. 'God's becoming a human being is that which is impossible, incomprehensible, God's coming into history in a way that cannot be deduced from God. God and humanity cannot be drawn together [in this relationship] as a necessity.'[39] The paradoxical nature of the incarnation shall be further examined in the next section, tracing how the Kierkegaardian concept concretely plays out in Bonhoeffer's Chalcedonian Christology.

II. Affirming the Paradox – Christ's Revelation in Hiddenness

The parallels of Kierkegaard's and Bonhoeffer's Christology are plainest in Bonhoeffer's *Lectures* from the summer semester of 1933. As some of the student transcripts reveal, he already references Kierkegaard in his starting remark that Christology begins with silence as opposed to expressing the inexpressible,[40] thereby echoing the Kierkegaardian paradox. Bonhoeffer then relates to Kierkegaard more extensively when he discusses the mantling of Christ in his humiliation. Christ's lowliness had been one of the core topics of Kierkegaard's *Practice in Christianity*, a work that Bonhoeffer shows familiarity with at the time of his *Lectures on Christology*. In his idealism-critical exposition of 'offence', Kierkegaard had distinguished between three possible forms of it: offence relating to Christ's collision with the established order, offence springing from Christ's claim to be God, and offence with the lowliness and suffering of the God-human. Only the third form of offence constitutes the true umbrage for Kierkegaard. It ignites itself at the servant form of Christ, his 'incognito'.[41] This concept is to

---

38. See *CUP*, 53 (*AUN-1*, 50).

39. DBWE 12:337 (DBW 12:322). See also *PF*, 87 (*PB*, 84).

40. Dietrich Bonhoeffer: *Gesammelte Schriften* [*GS*] vol. *III: Theologie – Gemeinde: Vorlesungen, Briefe, Gespräche: 1927 bis 1944*, ed. Eberhard Bethge, (München: Chr. Kaiser, 1966), 167. See also Kirkpatrick, *Attacks*, 148. Neither the *DBW* nor the *DBWE* attest to this variant because they use only one of the preserved transcripts as the basis for their reconstruction of Bonhoeffer's lecture, respectively.

41. See *PC*, 75–144 (*EC*, 79–148). See *GS III*, 238 for a distinct reference to Kierkegaard regarding the category of 'incognito' in Bonhoeffer.

be understood as a specific dimension of the paradox. While Climacus had mainly used the latter to express the collision between human reason and God's incarnation in general as well as the revelation of God in history, Anti-Climacus argues more decidedly Christian. The incognito particularly relates to the abasement of Christ, that is the hiddenness of his divinity in his worldly lowliness. From the latter, Kierkegaard draws two conclusions. The first conclusion pertains to the epistemological challenge of coming to believe in the God-human Jesus Christ: it is impossible to immediately know that he is the Son of God when looking at the single individual Jesus of Nazareth.[42] Christ's divinity is only accessible through faith (see above). The second conclusion Kierkegaard arrives at is that Christ's incognito demands an existential re-enactment of humiliation by the believer, since their life in God also happens covertly. For this reason, being a Christian is characterized by conflict, mockery and voluntary suffering in relation to the world.[43]

The Kierkegaardian incognito has had specific impact on Bonhoeffer. Following Kierkegaard, he rejects any immediate recognizability of Christ's divinity. The God-human has indeed drawn attention to himself by his sheer existence, but even his miracles do not jeopardize his incognito. Faith cannot get around the 'ambiguity of [his] history'[44] and the need of a personal decision (see III.), represented by the question of who. By using Kierkegaard, Bonhoeffer aims at showing once more that the central problem when confronted with the paradox of the God-human is not judgement regarding his deeds, but reaction to his person. He thus distances himself from liberal theologies of his time that are stressing Christ's character as role model instead of saviour. At the same time, Bonhoeffer differs from his Berlin teachers in holding on to the paradox in contrast with proceeding to explain the person of Christ more closely. As Hans-Jürgen Abromeit has shown, both Adolf von Harnack and Reinhold Seeberg refused to hinge faith's assertion on anything paradoxical. They would have liked to see the relation between the human and the divine nature of Christ more deeply explained. But according to Bonhoeffer, they were therein giving short shrift to Christ's divine nature or the paradoxical mystery of the God-human, respectively.[45] Once more, the danger would consist in trying to grasp the truth, ruining its very character of being given from outside. On the whole, Bonhoeffer thus mostly subscribes to Kierkegaard's

---

42. Technically, *The Concept of Irony* needs to be exempted from this claim on Kierkegaard's stance, because the concept of 'incognito' had not emerged in his magister thesis yet. But since *Concept*, he continually held on to the hiddenness of Christ.

43. See *PC*, 133–6, 105–13 (*EC*, 135–9, 108–16). See Florian Schmitz, *'Nachfolge': Zur Theologie Dietrich Bonhoeffers* (Göttingen: Vandenhoeck & Ruprecht, 2013), 207–28 for Christoform suffering in *Discipleship*.

44. DBWE 12:309 (DBW 12:291). See also DBWE 12:307, 359 (DBW 12:287, 346) and *PC*, 26–7, 96–7 (*EC*, 31–3, 98–9).

45. See Abromeit, *Geheimnis*, 80–1. See also DBWE 12:352 (DBW 12:339).

notion of paradox and incognito. Yet, one subtle difference consists in their stance towards the 'unsubstitutability'[46] of the God-human. For Kierkegaard, the concrete circumstances of Christ's life stand back in comparison with his eternal significance. Both in *Philosophical Fragments* and *Practice in Christianity* he is God having become human, but his particularity as a Jewish man in first-century Middle East seems practically irrelevant. The world-historical *nota bene* gets at the heart of it: 'Even if the contemporary generation had not left anything behind except these words, "We have believed that in such and such a year the god appeared in the humble form of a servant, lived and taught among us, and then died" – this is more than enough.'[47]

Bonhoeffer is more cautious in that regard. He always bears Christ's whole existence in mind. Kierkegaard's tendency to abstract God's revelation from the specific human being Jesus of Nazareth is foreign to him. Another nuanced difference consists in the judgement regarding the states of Christ (*status exinanitionis, status exaltationis*). While Kierkegaard in a sense conflates the elevated into the humiliated Christ so that the incognito mainly covers the hidden deity and suffering of Christ, Bonhoeffer holds on to a clearer distinction between the latter (see below).[48] For him, this is the only way to preserve the possibility of offence even at the risen Christ, which is the basis for the category of promeity. By '*pro me*', Bonhoeffer refers to the essentia[l] relatedness' of Christ to me.[49] On the one hand, he thereby stresses the existential character of faith and theology; on the other hand, and more importantly, he understands the incarnation as well as the subsequent presence of Christ in Church, history, and nature as the free and willful binding of Godself to humankind. Christ's being consists in being for others. In this vein, the relationality of Bonhoeffer's theology, as a whole, turns out to be grounded in the revelation of God. Both the abased and elevated Christ is present to the believer in a salvific way, exemplifying the meaning of 'mediator' or that Christ's person 'is, in fact, its own work'.[50] This feature of Bonhoeffer's theology is a clear alignment with Martin Luther. For the Reformer too, Christ is true God and true human *in the fact* that he redeems.

> He is not somehow, primarily, first of all, someone who in his nature as subject or substance as God and man is a substantative being, a 'God-man', and only

---

46. Boniface, *Jesus*, 136.
47. *PF*, 104 (*PB*, 101).
48. See DBWE 12:359 (DBW 12:347). See also Schmitz, *Nachfolge*, 88. Nevertheless, this does not mean that Bonhoeffer separates the two states. Just like for Kierkegaard, 'this means that the presence of the God-human as the Resurrected One, that is the Exalted One, is at the same time the presence of the humiliated Christ' (DBWE 12:314 [DBW 12:295]).
49. DBWE 12:314 (DBW 12:295).
50. DBWE 12:324 (DBW 12:307) and DBWE 12:312 (DBW 12:293).

secondarily – materially, logically, temporarily, or in whatever manner – treated as redeemer as well [...]. No, his nature is actually his work and his work is his nature.[51]

Christ virtually *is* the sacrament. For both Bonhoeffer and Luther it is idle, and even impossible to inquire after God in and of Godself, because God can only be known in promeity, which also means that God fully embarks on the self-determination towards creation. There is no arbitrary side of God withheld from the commitment in Jesus Christ. Still, the presence of Christ can never be had without the possibility of offence since the nature of faith is not seeing but believing. Otherwise, the Church would be taking on a life of its own and separating its knowledge of God from the actual encounter with God's revelation, that is Christ incarnate in his life, death and resurrection. The difference from Kierkegaard now lies in the question of the state in which Christ relates to believers today. The 'for me' of Christ had not been irrelevant to Kierkegaard either, but he had located it differently: 'Christ can be said to be essentially *pro nobis*, and the specific form of his being-for-us is above all else, we might say, his being-contemporary-for-us.'[52] Contemporaneity with the God-human, however, is to be understood as contemporaneity with the humiliated Christ in his worldly lowliness. Even as the Risen and Exalted One, he 'still continues to be the abased one', 'he does not exist in any other way, for only in this way has he existed. That he will come in glory is anticipated, but can be anticipated and believed only by the person who has adhered and adheres to him as he has existed.'[53] Therefore, it is nothing amiss for Kierkegaard in mainly relating the incognito to the hidden deity and suffering of Christ. He is the whole Christ that is present. While Bonhoeffer echoes Kierkegaard in saying that 'we can have the Exalted One only as the Crucified One',[54] he also states: 'The Humiliated One is pro nobis only as the Exalted One.'[55] Although it must be acknowledged that Kierkegaard and Bonhoeffer share a reworking of 'the classic doctrine of the Incarnation so as to bring out the fundamental decision with which the paradox of the God-human confronts each and every human being',[56] Bonhoeffer nevertheless differentiates both between the *status exinanitionis* and *exaltationis* in a more traditional way and carries out the reworking more consistently. Together with the broad absence of the resurrection from his account of Christian faith, it becomes

---

51. Oswald Bayer, *Martin Luther's Theology: A Contemporary Interpretation* (Grand Rapids: W.B. Eerdmans, 2008), 232.
52. Philip Ziegler, 'Christ for Us Today: Promeity in the Christologies of Bonhoeffer and Kierkegaard', *IJST* 15 (2013): 25–41, 36.
53. Both *PC*, 24 (*EC*, 29–30). See also *PC*, 36, 166, 172 (*EC*, 43, 167, 173).
54. DBWE 12:359 (DBW 12:347). See *PC*, 154. 160 (*EC*, 154, 160).
55. DBWE 12:359 (DBW 12:347).
56. David R. Law, 'The Existential Chalcedonian Christology of Kierkegaard's *Practice in Christianity*', *KSY* (2010): 129–52, 152.

clear that Kierkegaard did not consider it necessary to reflect upon the elevated Christ. Bonhoeffer can hence be said to have a more balanced Christology than Kierkegaard. This might be due to the fact that Bonhoeffer's Christology is more elaborated and dogmatical in the strict sense, which also finds expression in his distinction between the incarnation and the lowliness of Christ in general.

Kierkegaard once more does not carry out the differentiation as clearly and grounds Christ's abasement in his social background as well as his suffering[57] so that the incognito consists in the hiddenness of his *divinity*, whereas Bonhoeffer resists any separation of the natures: 'God is not concealed in Christ as a human being but rather is revealed as God-human. But this God-human is veiled in his existence as the Humiliated One. In Christ's being humiliated, we are talking about neither divinity nor humanity, but rather the ὁμοίωμα σαρκός.'[58] The appearance of Christ's sinfulness is then one more sign of the incognito for Bonhoeffer: 'He is a human like us and is tempted as we are, even more than we are. In his σάρξ too there was a law, which was opposed to the will of God. It was a constant struggle for him. He also did things that appeared to be sins.'[59] Nevertheless, Christ did not sin, he was at the same time the sinless and holy One. As a consequence of the unity in the person of the Incarnate, those distinctions cannot be recognized from the outside. The whole God-human is hidden. Ultimately, this plays out in Bonhoeffer's insistence that the depth of Christ's incognito is not even broken on the cross: 'In his death, Jesus does not reveal any of his divine attributes.'[60] Here, Bonhoeffer seems to share appreciation for 1 Corinthians with Kierkegaard: 'It is precisely this, which is the *foolishness* of the Christian idea of God, which has been witnessed to by all genuine Christian thinking from Paul, Augustine, Luther, to Kierkegaard and Barth.'[61] Bonhoeffer then goes on to transfer this to the justification, speaking of the paradox that 'God is where death and sin are, not where righteousness is.'[62] God's revelation is different from what the human mind would expect, showing its promeity in the place of judgement, giving life to creation through the death of Godself.

Altogether, Kierkegaard's and Bonhoeffer's rejection of speculative thought, their confession of the lowliness of God and the willing acknowledgement of the limitedness of human beings display central characteristics of a Lutheran *theologia crucis*.[63] Both agree that any knowledge of God must stem from God's revelation in

---

57. See *PC*, 37, 102–3 (*EC*, 44, 105–6).
58. DBWE 12:356 (DBW 12:343). See DBWE 12:313 (DBW 12:295).
59. DBWE 12:356–7 (DBW 12:344). See Schmitz, *Nachfolge*, 86–7.
60. DBWE 12:355 (DBW 12:343).
61. *CCIG*, 184 (DBW 10:432), emphasis LW.
62. *CCIG*, 184 (DBW 10:432).
63. H. Gaylon Barker has compiled a helpful list of characteristics in *The Cross of Reality. Luther's Theologia Crucis and Bonhoeffer's Christology* (Minneapolis: Fortress Press, 2015), 104–8.

Jesus Christ. But this revelation is a revelation in hiddenness. Eventually, God is to be found in the place least expected, that is as a suffering creature.

> It is God up close and personal, God not distant or removed from the world but intimately involved with the world. The incarnation displays the extent to which God is willing to go, the risks God is willing to bear to become like us, not for the mere fact of identification, but in order to save us. That is the scandal – the stumbling block – of Christianity, but at the same time, is its distinguishing mark.[64]

Kierkegaard and Bonhoeffer deeply appreciated Martin Luther's thought. Their emphasis on the lowliness of Christ can be seen as a spelling out of what Luther had set forth in §19 of the *Heidelberg Disputation*: God's glory is found in the ugliness of Christ abased. For the Reformer, it requires faith to recognize God at work in the midst of it. At the same time, the possibility of offence is always present. Human reason alone cannot gain access to the paradoxical revelation. That is why the *theologia crucis* is a method or mode of doing theology as opposed to a mere understanding of the cross. Together with the *pro me*, it connects Christology, soteriology as well as the life of the believer.[65] This conjunction of an ultimately 'existential Christology' is typical of Kierkegaard and Bonhoeffer, too. However, they consider it to be precisely not humanity opening a way to God, but the grateful acknowledgement of God's way to humanity. Everything is dependent on the *person* of Christ.

Bonhoeffer's essay *Concerning the Christian Idea of God* had already prepared the notion of the paradox epiphany of God in an idealism-critical context years before he presupposed that a personal God could only reveal Godself in history: '[R]evelation in history means revelation in hiddenness; revelation in ideas [...] means revelation in openness.'[66] For Bonhoeffer, Christ's abasement does not make him any more human and thus less God. On the contrary, the emphasis of the lowliness of Christ is part of Bonhoeffer's programme of Chalcedonian Christology, that is precisely the spelling out of the unconfused and unchangeable, indivisible and inseparable character of Christ's natures. Through the *communicatio idiomatum*, the abasement of Christ cannot be attributed to one nature alone. For Bonhoeffer, it is always the whole God-human who is hidden so that 'the "stumbling-block" is not [God's] humanity but *this* kind of humanity'.[67] In his *Lectures on Christology*, Bonhoeffer identifies the decisions of the councils throughout church history as the only places which have stayed true to the task of theology, namely 'to let stand that which we cannot comprehend' or to reinstate 'the holy mystery, which

---

64. Barker, *Cross*, 104.
65. See Barker, *Cross*, 98.
66. *CCIG*, 182 (DBW 10:429). See also DBWE 15:537 (DBW 15:548) and *PC*, 198 (*EC*, 198).
67. Williams, *Christ*, 189.

theology was instituted to protect and preserve'[68] of God incarnate. Their 'negative Christology' has refrained from a specific allocation of the human and the divine natures in Christ, an undertaking that would have corresponded to Bonhoeffer's question of how. Instead,

> [t]he Chalcedonian formula is an objective, living assertion about Christ that goes beyond all conceptual forms. Everything is encompassed in its very clear yet paradoxical agility.[69] – The Chalcedonian formula is an answer to the 'how' question, but it is an answer in which the 'how' question has already been surmounted. In the Chalcedonian formulation, the doctrine of the two natures has itself been surmounted.[70]

Søren Kierkegaard has both been suspected to align with the Chalcedonian Creed and to undermine it. Him speaking of the 'God-human' could be taken for agreeing with the formula; stressing the 'paradox' could be seen as an overemphasis of the unconfusedness of Christ's natures over their indivisibleness. Since Kierkegaard does not explicitly address the topic anywhere, it seems fairest to say that he disregarded dogmatic 'fine tuning' by virtue of his existential focus of *appropriating* a belief in Jesus Christ. Still, it makes sense to consider him a Chalcedonian theologian in the widest sense. Like Bonhoeffer, he is keen to express the self-disposition of God towards the world, which uncloses a new reality. He too could be said to object to treating the divinity of Christ as a piece of information that would justify a response of belief.[71] Christ always remains the lowly God-human. Anything else would amount to a *theologia gloriae*. If it were true that Kierkegaard subscribed to the doctrine of *enhypostasia*,[72] however – which is impossible to determine without overstraining his statements – Bonhoeffer would depart from him there. The Berlin theologian deems those doctrinal controversies of Lutheran orthodoxy misguided. For him, they fall under the verdict of answering the question of how, not who: 'Since the Chalcedonian formula, we can no longer say, how shall we think about the difference of the two natures and the unity of the person.'[73] Instead, the way to carry on with the Chalcedonian objective is to speak

---

68. DBWE 12:331/ DBW 12:315. In a Christmas meditation from 1940, Bonhoeffer admonished: 'In Mary's child, Jesus, dwells almighty God. Pause here a moment! Do not speak, do not analyze further. Grow still before this Word. God has become a child!' (DBWE 16:614 (DBW 16:636)). See also DBWE 15:529 (DBW 15:538) and Abromeit, *Geheimnis*, 191–9. Adolf von Harnack, by contrast, had criticized the Chalcedonian formula, see DBWE 12:342 (DBW 12:327).

69. DBWE 12:343 (DBW 12:328).

70. DBWE 12:350 (DBW 12:336).

71. Williams, *Christ*, 269.

72. See Law, 'Existential Christology', 139–40.

73. DBWE 12:350 (DBW 12:336). See also DBWE 12:336 (DBW 12:320).

of the statuses of the God-human. Bonhoeffer phrases it in the manner that God can never be understood differently than as 'der Menschgewordene'[74] anymore, encompassing both the lowliness and loftiness of Christ. These categories are the key to bringing out how the glorification of God happens in human flesh – thus being connected to the glorification of humankind – but not in a visible way.

The true paradox consists in the revelation of God in a place God would never be expected in: *tectum sub contrario* – in the form of a lowly creature, so generous with God's love as to not avoid suffering or death for the sake of the beloved. Faith as the corresponding equivalent to revelation on humankind's part then must also never mean glory in openness. It is for that reason that Kierkegaard and Bonhoeffer so adamantly insist on the incognito of the God-human Jesus Christ. They can both be said to be refusing a *theologia gloriae*, seeking to theologically honour the hiddenness of God's revelation by letting the paradox stand: 'That the eternal once came into existence in time is not a truth that must stand up to the test of time, is not something that *must be tested by human beings* but is the paradox *by which human beings must be tested*.'[75]

III. Going beyond the Paradox – The Aim of Encountering Christ

It has become clear so far that Bonhoeffer draws on Kierkegaard for quite many areas of his Christology and that the two theologians share a certain fundamental grasp on what a human answer to God's revelation looks like. For both men, paradox and incognito play a key part in their account of Christianity, highlighting that faith encompasses possible offence and the moment of decision. The latter is sparked by confrontation with the God-human Jesus Christ, his person in the truest sense of the word being the decisive factor. Here, Bonhoeffer has again learned from Kierkegaard. The Dane had criticized modern theology for making Christ's teaching the centre of faith, whereas in reality, 'the teacher is more important than the teaching. [...] But in our day everything is made abstract and everything personal is abolished: We take Christ's teaching – and abolish Christ.'[76] It is obvious that this topic relates to Kierkegaard's dismissal of Christianity as doctrine and his program of subjectivity. Bonhoeffer adopted it in parts, but not to its full existentialist extent and he also gave it a decidedly Christological foundation that goes beyond Kierkegaard. Nevertheless, Bonhoeffer shares the opposition to any concentration on the teaching of Christ instead of his person. This Christocentricity can be well studied in *Discipleship* and finds expression

---

74. DBW 12:329 (DBWE 12:344) translates as 'the one who has become human' and is therefore not able to convey the nuanced difference of 'Menschwerdung' and 'Menschgewordener' in DBW 12:341.

75. Kierkegaard, *The Book on Adler*, KW 24, ed. Howard V. Hong and Edna H. Hong (Princeton: Princeton University Press, 1998), 37–8 (*BüA*, 50).

76. See *PC*, 123–4 (*EC*, 125). See also Law, 'Existential Christology', 131.

in his ethics of responsibility. For him, the commitment to Christ is 'completely breaking through anything preprogrammed, idealistic, or legalistic. No further content is possible because Jesus is the only content. [...] He himself is it.'[77] This close relationship even has a bodily aspect in the sense that commitment to Christ is commitment to Christ incarnate, present in the community of his body, the Church.[78] Other authorities gain their entitlements solely through the reality of Christ (f. i. the mandates). In any event, good and evil lose their validity as principles for Christian ethics. Even the possibility of knowing good and evil in and as of themselves, that is outside of commitment to Christ, is impossible. That way, humankind would deem itself absolute, finding the source of good and evil within itself instead of within the relationship to God. But what is to be aspired to, is union with God. Precisely this union is recovered in the God-human Jesus Christ[79] and is not based on his teachings but his being.

The centrality of Christ's person is also reflected in the question what can essentially be known about him from history. Do Christ's life and his deeds make him meaningful? Does the range of his influence reveal that he is the God-human? For Kierkegaard, Christ's divinity is not something that could ever be proven from the past in the shape of the success of Christianity or the results of Christ's life. That would be a μετάβασις εἰς ἄλλο γένος since there is an absolute difference between creator and creature. Syllogisms are unemployable in differing realms, which is precisely the reason to speak of Christ as the paradox.[80] Furthermore, the results of a person's life are only an appropriate standard when speaking of humans: 'that God has lived here on earth as an individual human being is infinitely extraordinary. Even if it had had no results whatever [...] it remains just as extraordinary, infinitely extraordinary, infinitely more extraordinary than all the results.'[81] There is no way around finding Christ's divinity than in his person alone, but it is not visible from the outside or demonstrable from the results his appearance provoked in history. One can find remarkably similar remarks in Bonhoeffer's *Lectures on Christology*. In distancing himself from Melanchthon's *hoc est Christum cognoscere beneficia eius cognoscere*, the Berlin theologian advises against concluding Christ's *who* from his deeds or from history. Taking a similar line in relation to liberal theology, Bonhoeffer also refuses deriving Christ's divinity from his impact on others. In the flesh, even the doings of someone like Christ remain arbitrary.[82] Both Kierkegaard and Bonhoeffer thus advocate becoming contemporary with the God-human, and, in the course of this, perceiving the claims that history makes (that is to be of absolute significance) and reacting to them, either in acceptance or refusal. The

---

77. DBWE 4:59 (DBW 4:47).
78. See Schmitz, *Nachfolge*, 61–2. See DBWE 4:58–9, 215 (DBW 4:47, 229).
79. See DBWE 6:299–338 (DBW 6:301–41).
80. See *PC*, 26–32 (*EC*, 32–8).
81. *PC*, 31 (*EC*, 37). See also DBWE 12:310–311 (DBW 12:292–3).
82. DBWE 12:308–9, 328 (DBW 12:289–91, 311).

term 'contemporaneity' alone once more suggests a direct influence of Kierkegaard on Bonhoeffer. Kierkegaard had introduced it in *Philosophical Fragments*, arguing that each generation is as close to Christ as any other, including the one during his life on earth.[83] Each individual must enter into faith through offence, which never becomes less difficult or offensive over time. Since the *Fragments*, contemporaneity has remained Kierkegaard's 'signature category' in Christological discourse, containing his existential objective in a nutshell. Bonhoeffer uses the concept as early as his Barcelona lectures, emphasizing how in giving in to history's claims the believer gains contemporaneity with the historical.[84] In the summer of 1933, he had advanced the category, linking it with the ecclesiologically tied presence of Christ (*pro me*), at the same time also turning it into a dig at the doctrine of Christ's ubiquity.[85] Different from Kierkegaard, contemporaneity is made possible through the resurrection for Bonhoeffer. Still, their intention is similar. Both theologians argue against historicist, rationalist and speculative Christologies. They consider neither the image of an individual from the past that is only ever approached with methodical distance, nor that of a mere teacher, nor the appearance of a divine idea in abstract union with human nature as the appropriate way to speak of Christ. None of those Christologies do justice to who Christ really is, namely the paradoxical God-human.

Doing Christology in Kierkegaard's footsteps allows Bonhoeffer to say as much as possible and as little as necessary about the person of Christ, that is to articulate the mystery of the incarnation without explaining it and pressing for personal as well as contextual appropriation while not losing sight of the free self-revelation of God.[86] To put it straight, in Kierkegaard he finds an ally fostering the same thrust of Christology that he aims at, which seems to be the underlying commonality of categories such as contemporaneity, offence, *pro me* as well as Bonhoeffer's perception of existence and truth: 'encounter' ('Begegnung').[87] For Bonhoeffer, Christology never is a theological discipline entertained for its own sake. Instead, he seeks to take seriously the event of the self-revelation of God in Jesus Christ in its constitutive relation to human beings, or as Wolf Krötke has phrased it quite fittingly: 'The particularity of God's mystery as it is come across in the human Jesus does not consist in it withdrawing itself from humanity, but

---

83. See *PF*, 58 (*PB*, 55).

84. See DBWE 10:346 (DBW 10:307).

85. See DBWE 12:312 (DBW 12:294), translated as 'the ability to be simultaneously present to all' instead of 'Gleichzeitigkeit und Anwesenheit Christi'. DBWE 12:321, 330 (DBW 12:304, 314), translated as 'simultaneously'. *GS III*, 203 points to an explicit mention of Kierkegaard again.

86. These ideas are perfectly summed up in the question of 'who is Jesus Christ, for us, today?'.

87. See DBWE 12:306 (DBW 12:287).

in coming *ever closer*.'[88] In an ideal situation, through happy concurrence with the responsive individual, Christ's paradoxity is accepted as impenetrable barrier, but thereby losing its offensive character and prying open incurvate immanence. This way, Christ would be truly apprehended for who he is, namely a person for others: God's being-there comes together with God's being-there-for-*you*.[89] In this, the Kierkegaardian paradox, already being an 'encounter-category' in itself by speaking of the confrontation of the human individual with the God-human Jesus Christ, captures the notion that is indispensable for any productive encounter between two subjects, which is that the counterpart retains some alienness, and in God's case remaining the wholly other.

---

88. Wolf Krötke, 'Der begegnende Gott und der Glaube: Zum theologischen Schwerpunkt der Christologievorlesung D. Bonhoeffers', in *Bonhoeffer-Studien: Beiträge zur Theologie und Wirkungsgeschichte Dietrich Bonhoeffers*, ed. Albrecht Schönherr and Wolf Krötke (München: Chr. Kaiser, 1985), 25–35, 27: 'Die Besonderheit von *Gottes "Geheimnis"*, so wie es im Menschen Jesus begegnet, besteht nicht darin, daß es sich dem Menschen entzieht, sondern daß es dem Menschen *immer näher* kommt.'

89. See DBWE 12:315 (DBW 12:296).

Chapter 4

BONHOEFFER'S UNDERSTANDING OF CHALCEDON IN DIALOGUE WITH CONTEMPORARY CATHOLIC CHRISTOLOGY

Jacob Phillips

I. Introduction

Dietrich Bonhoeffer is not always included in courses on Christology, at least in the UK. The reasons are partly practical. While Christology permeates all of Bonhoeffer's book-length writings, he did not present a specific Christological treatise, as such. The notes from the Christology lectures of 1933 do not result in a finished text. When Bonhoeffer does appear in the canon of twentieth-century Christologies, however, he is often inserted somewhere before Jürgen Moltmann and/or Liberation Christologies like that of Jon Sobrino. He seems to fit neatly in place here, along a developing trajectory of the increasingly practical and political foci for understanding Jesus in the second half of the twentieth century. In the background are the societal changes of the 1960s, which were being reflected in more overtly 'worldly' approaches to theology more generally. Along with Moltmann and Sobrino, Bonhoeffer situates Christ in the embodied world of human struggles and tensions. Johannes Zachhuber's Oxford lectures on twentieth-century Christology show the general scheme. The topics are: the Historical Jesus, Dialectical Theology, Bultmann, Tillich, the mature Barth, John Hick and *The Myth of God Incarnate*, then two examples of 'ethical Christology': namely, Bonhoeffer and Liberation Theology, before finishing with insights from René Girard.[1]

On one hand, this situating of Bonhoeffer in the 1960s makes perfect sense. In the English-speaking world, this was when the first wave of interest in his work followed the first translation of the Tegel writings.[2] More substantially, the *Letters*

---

1. Johannes Zachhuber, 'God, Christ, and Salvation; Topics in 20th Century Christology', lectures delivered at Oxford University, 2009, (accessed 17 August 2022.)

2. *Widerstand und Ergebung* was first published in English translation in 1954, but gained popularity in the 1960s after the publication of John Robinson, *Honest to God* (London: SCM Press, 1963), 64–6 and 75–6.

and Papers described Christ as the 'man for others',[3] which resonates powerfully with early Liberation Theology texts. The same is true of one of the very well-known letters, where Bonhoeffer writes that one only learns to have faith by 'living fully in the midst of life's tasks, questions, successes and failures, experiences, and perplexities'.[4] This broadly aligns with Jon Sobrino's criticisms of those who are comfortable with their dogmatic understanding of Christ, but have 'absolutized' Jesus to such a degree that he is disconnected from life, from what he calls 'the non-absolutes of history'.[5] There are also important epistemological aspects to Sobrino which warrant considerable critical discussion with Bonhoeffer. Sobrino argues that 'Christ has been reduced to a sublime abstraction', and as such, one can give an intellectual assent without that having much impact on life itself.[6] That is, for Sobrino, Christology should proceed not from Christological formulae, but rather 'from within the context of praxis'. People who 'understand and appreciate the Jesus who sends the Spirit', says Sobrino, 'only if they live a life in accordance with that Spirit'.[7]

In this chapter I want to do two things. In the first place, describe why I suspect Bonhoeffer will feature even less in courses on Christology in the coming years. This is particularly true for Catholic contexts. He has always been a bit of an outlier in Catholic Christology anyway. A recent textbook by Gerald O'Collins, for example, has a chapter entitled 'The Last 50 Years', which follows the trajectory of Tillich, Barth, Bultmann, Moltmann, Rahner, Kaspar, Sobrino *et al*, and then Jacque Dupuis.[8] Unlike Karl Barth, Bonhoeffer has not been cited as central influence on canonically Catholic theologians like Hans Urs von Balthasar and Joseph Ratzinger.[9] But Bonhoeffer's inclusion in courses on Christology in Catholic contexts seems even less likely at the current time, because important works in Catholic Christology have recently appeared which I would group loosely as pertaining to a general 'metaphysical turn', or perhaps a 'turn to metaphysical realism'. The two examples I will discuss here are Aaron

---

3. DBWE 8:501 (DBW 8:558), translation altered.

4. DBWE 8:486 (DBW 8:542).

5. Jon Sobrino, *Christology at the Crossroads: A Latin American Approach*, trans. John Drury (London: SCM Press, 1978), xviii.

6. Ibid.

7. Ibid., xxv. Another less overtly Christological factor here is Bonhoeffer's engagement with the African American community of Harlem, making him an admirable and very rare example of a canonical twentieth-century theologian who began asking the sorts of questions that would eventually lead to Black Liberation Theology.

8. There are many others listed whose tenets aren't discussed, see Gerald O'Collins, *Christology: Origins, Developments, Debates* (Waco: Baylor Press, 2015), 5–15.

9. The Pope Emeritus states 'I was a sort of Barthian … He was one of the fathers of theology with whom I had grown up' in Pope Benedict XVI and Peter Seewald, *Last Testament: In His Own Words*, trans. Jacob Phillips (London: Bloomsbury, 2016), 152.

Riches' *Ecce Homo* and Thomas Joseph White OP's *The Incarnate Lord*, although other works should certainly be included.[10]

Before going into the detail of these two books, the main point to bear in mind is that the general direction of travel in contemporary Catholic Christology is to claim that most twentieth-century Christology went quite severely wrong. The outcome of this wrong turn, we read, is that many of the Christological thinkers listed above are guilty of practising a modern variant of the ancient heresy of Nestorianism. The reasons given for this usually centre on the argument that the traditionally metaphysical (as in scholastic, patristic, or dogmatic) components of Christological doctrine were downgraded or reconfigured in the post-Kantian era, with gravely detrimental consequences. Bonhoeffer appears to be situated right in the middle of those listed as typical of this tendency. His Christology is one in which an analysis of the meaning of terms like nature, person, or hypostatic union is almost entirely absent, and Jesus is instead presented as the 'man for others' who meets us in life's struggles. Proponents of this 'metaphysical turn', however, would argue that starting with such a human Christ, and leaving to one side his metaphysical uniqueness, invariably leads into Nestorian modes of thinking. So Bonhoeffer seems even less like to appear in twenty-first century courses on Catholic Christology than he was in the twentieth century.

My second task in this chapter is to evaluate whether or not this should be the case. That is, to ask whether there is more to Bonhoeffer's Christology than a sort of proto-Liberation Theology born of the *Kirchenkampf* and its aftermath. Or, put differently, to ask what position Bonhoeffer might take if read sympathetically in a more robustly metaphysical scene than that of recent decades. The key focus here will be Bonhoeffer's distinct approach to the Chalcedonian Definition in his Christology lectures, notwithstanding its stilted and fragmentary prose. There, Bonhoeffer certainly seems a long way from any metaphysical realism, but the question of his falling into the allegedly Nestorian tenor of many of his contemporaries is much more ambiguous. In what follows I will look firstly at Riches' *Ecce Homo*, then at White's *The Incarnate Lord*, after which I can bring Bonhoeffer into dialogue with the critical questions each of these books pose to his Christology. From there, the ground will be clear to argue that Bonhoeffer's sidestepping of metaphysics has certain qualities which mean that many of the fears of contemporary writers are unfounded in his case. That is, that he has a great deal to offer to Christology today, despite appearances to the contrary.

---

10. Others that can be included in this list would be Simon Gaine O.P, *Did the Saviour see the Father?* (London: Bloomsbury, 2015), and Matthew Levering, *Did Jesus Rise from the Dead?* (Oxford: Oxford University Press, 2019).

II. Aaron Riches, *Ecce Homo: On the Divine Unity of Christ*

Riches' book is primarily a study of patristic Christology, particularly that which preceded and followed the formulation of the Chalcedonian Definition of 451. But it is not restricted to this period only, and is much more than a work of historical theology. To draw this out, it is helpful to touch on Riches' work as essentially 'postliberal'. He argues that 'modern theology' has proved itself complicit with prevailing 'Nestorian logic of *separatio*'.[11] He holds that there is a 'deep correspondence between Nestorian logic and some of the constitutive false dualisms of modernity', and that 'modernity is broadly "Nestorian", if we take the term Nestorian as descriptive of the normative mode of conceiving the relation of unity and difference, transcendence and immanence, God and the world'.[12] In modernity, Riches claims this logic holds God and the world apart, and he cites David L. Schindler's rooting of this tendency in Descartes, from whom it is presupposed that 'if X is truly distinct from Y, X must just so far share nothing in common with Y'.[13] This means, for Riches, that 'as with Nestorian logic, so with modernity, the difference of X and Y is only safeguarded by separation, a strict autonomy that ensures no intimacy crosses the basic parallelism whereby each thing remains distinct from its opposite'.[14] This is postliberal because of the proposed 'basic metaphysical compatibility of modernity and Nestorian logic'.[15] It resonates with insights commonly associated with John Milbank's *Beyond Secular Reason*, and rooted ultimately in the work of Hans Frei, George Lindbeck and the 'Yale School'. In this context, postliberalism is an instinct for eschewing the 'correlationist habits of modern theology', insofar as one side of the correlation ('the world', 'immanence', 'humanity', 'society', 'reason', etc.) purportedly has some epistemological and ontological stability apart from the other ('God', 'transcendence', 'divinity', 'faith', etc.).[16] The 'Liberal' of postliberalism is the secular realm so conceived, separated from the realm of faith, as some neutral and foundational space of pure reason.

To bring this back to Christology, I think Riches would agree that much twentieth-century is broadly 'correlationist' in its specifics. That is, 'humanity' or 'human nature' is understood in a more-or-less secular way, through the historical–critical

---

11. Aaron Riches, *Ecce Homo: On the Divine Unity in Christ* (Michigan: Eerdmans, 2016), 6.

12. Ibid., 11.

13. Ibid., see David L. Schindler, 'The Embodied Person as Gift and the Cultural Task in America: Status Quaestionis', in *Communio: International Catholic Review* 35, (2008): 397–431., 411.

14. Riches, *Ecce Homo*, 11–12.

15. Ibid., 12.

16. See Daniel M. Bell 'Postliberalism and Radical Orthodoxy', in *Cambridge Companion to Political Theology*, ed. Craig Hovery and Elizabeth Phillips (Cambridge: Cambridge University Press, 2015).

method, via political ideologies like Marxism, or intimate subjectivities as with the many descendants of Schleiermacher. From there, it tends then to be *correlated* with Christ's 'divinity' or 'divine nature'. For Riches this correlation can never be successful, because the inescapable starting-point for any genuinely Chalcedonian Christology is the hypostatic union, which by definition cannot be considered correlative of divinity and humanity, or to use his word, as a 'parallelism'. Riches doesn't give us a sweep of all the types of Christology just mentioned, although he does cite Philip McCosker's observation that the twentieth century involved a 'preference for functional over metaphysical/ontological Christologies' and the 'belief that the two can be separated'.[17]

Riches' book is, for the most part, a close reading of patristic texts, secondary commentaries, and historical research, with the overarching goal of correcting popular misconceptions about purported dangers in the writings of Cyril of Alexandria in distinction to the revisionary thinking about Nestorius he sees as gaining currency in the modern era. He roots Nestorius' thinking in the work of his predecessor Theodore of Mopsuesta, who considered 'the unity of Christ in terms of an "indwelling" (*evoikesis*) in an "assumed" (*lambano*) human being'.[18] The great appeal, and great danger, of this *homo assumptus* approach is the resulting separation of 'characteristics' pertaining to the divine and human aspects of Christ. That is, it answers to the classically Greek concern about God's impassibility by holding the divinity apart, very subtly, from a more-or-less full or autonomous humanity, which then becomes the exclusive site of Jesus' suffering.

This *assumptus* line of thinking was then developed further by Nestorius, who focused on a third conceptuality added to the key terms nature (*physis*) and person (*hypostasis*), namely, *prosopon*. Anyone familiar with basic Christology knows the story well, of course. Nestorius held there to be two hypostases, but Christ was eventually defined as bearing the union of two natures in one hypostasis, viz. the hypostatic union. What thus makes the case of Jesus completely different to any other case is – *contra* Nestorius – that his human nature did not have a human hypostasis. Riches focuses our attention, however, on a less mentioned aspect of Nestorius' error. This is that he did not just posit two hypostases to Christ, but also two prosopa. Riches argues that Nestorius held that every instantiation of nature must, by definition, have a hypostatic emergence, and a corresponding prosopon. All this requires some elementary definition of terms. Hypostasis is a metaphysical category, to bear a hypostasis is to be a 'unique being' of a certain genus or nature.[19] Prosopon, by Riches' interpretation at least, is not so much metaphysical as empirical. He calls it 'an "observable character" through which

---

17. Riches, *Ecce Homo*, 6; 'Philip McCosker review of Communicatio idiomatum; lo scambio delle proprietá: storia, status quaestionis e prospettive', in *Modern Theology* 23 (2007), 298–301, 300.

18. Riches, *Ecce Homo*, 27.

19. Thomas Joseph White, *The Incarnate Lord: A Thomistic Study in Christology* (Washington: CUA Press, 2017), 62–3.

the properties of [an] hypostasis are phenomenally manifested in reality'. It is thus 'more empirical or phenomenal than ontological', an earthly counterpart, if you will, to the undergirding hypostatic reality: 'not so much an ontological constituent of being as … the external aspect by which it is subject to outside observation and scrutiny'.[20]

Cyril's work of course constituted a counterpoint to his enemy Nestorius. This is rightly centred on the final decision of Chalcedon to opt for the union of two natures in one hypostasis, thus departing with the prior philosophical position that every physis must have a corresponding hypostasis. This allows, says Riches, for the '*descensus de caelis* of Nicaea' to make proper sense, because it is then not just the divine Logos that 'descends', but also 'the mode of being human he brings down in bringing himself': that is, *homo factus est*.[21] Thus, the fact probably most well-known about Nestorius applies here; his refusal to accept the term *Theotokos* as applied to the Blessed Virgin, in favour of his preferred term *Christotokos*. For Nestorius, the divinity is separable, however subtly, from Christ's humanity, so much so that the process of earthly gestation and birth cannot fully apply to God himself, the Logos, but only to the hypostasis and prosopon of Christ's humanity. If these are not to be found in Christ, then God himself is born of the Virgin Mary, for there is one divine subject, the Logos of God.

While many modules on Christology will include all this when it comes to covering Nestorius and arriving finally at Chalcedon, Riches' interpretation implies there has been a significant neglect regarding the place of the conceptuality of prosopon in the way the Christological controversies are presented. That is, any student of Christology can recite the formula of the hypostatic union (two natures united in one hypostasis), but they often neglect to distinguish the terms 'hypostasis' and 'prosopon' like the Definition does, for it states: 'the properties of each Nature being preserved, and (both) concurring into one person [prosopon] and one hypostasis'. Students of modern Christology thus need to be alert to the subtle ways in which Jesus of Nazareth is sometimes presented in such a way that there is, surreptitiously, an 'external aspect' of human personhood at play, 'subject to outside observation and scrutiny', which the metaphysics of Chalcedon, the hypostatic union, forbids. As well as this, there is a second tendency at play, says Riches. This is that Cyril is often presented as evincing tendencies towards monophysitism – an inclination to deny or underemphasize the full humanity of Jesus in favour of an overarching divine nature. Connected to this is Cyril's oft-mentioned use of the term 'one nature' (*mia physis*) in reference to Christ. One of Riches' key arguments is that this term, as used by Cyril, primarily meant that there was only one divine hypostasis, not one nature. This is indeed confusing, so perhaps modern-day Christological interpreters can be forgiven for presenting Chalcedon as some sort of balance, or 'compromise formula', between two opposed theological tendencies, Nestorianism and Monophysitism. This is a grave error,

---

20. Riches, *Ecce Homo*, 31.
21. Ibid., 37.

4. Bonhoeffer's Understanding of Chalcedon   61

says Riches, for it leads to an approach to Chalcedon as a means of navigating between opposing tendencies, yet devoid of meaningful descriptive content. The difference at stake here is like the difference between a mere compass which keeps people on the right path, rather than the views of the landscape those people see along the way.

This last point will prove important when we finally get to Bonhoeffer, for Riches connects it with Karl Rahner's hugely influential reading of Chalcedon. For Riches, Rahner is a deeply problematic figure, for he is emblematic of the problems of modern Christology. In the first place, there is the neglect of the full ramifications of Chalcedon's specification of one hypostasis *and* one prosopon. This is such that, unwittingly it seems, Rahner's concentration on ensuring the full humanity of Jesus was such that Jesus is implicitly treated as if there is indeed a human prosopon at play; a distinctly human 'observable character' by which he was 'phenomenally manifested in reality' *apart from* the divine nature.[22] Riches draws our attention to Rahner's comment that 'if it is possible to be an orthodox Nestorian or an orthodox Monophysite … I would prefer to be an orthodox Nestorian'.[23] The background to this is of course Rahner's primary Christological concern, to tackle the monophysitist tenor of pre-conciliar piety, in which Jesus is at worst an ethereally divine figure who floats down from heaven to save the universe, but has little or nothing to contribute to those struggles of life which were so pressing for Bonhoeffer. Riches points out that this is not unique to Rahner, by any means. He sees it as indicative of 'the persistent temptation of Christology as leaning in a more or less Nestorian or *homo assumptus* direction', and cites J. A. Jungmann, Karl Adam and F. X. Arnold as indicative of the same tendency.[24]

The main essay of Rahner's with which Riches is concerned is the 'Chalcedon: End or Beginning?' piece from 1954, written to mark the 1500th anniversary of Chalcedon itself.[25] In this essay Rahner 'programmatically proposed that, in matters Christological, the *Definitio fidei* of Chalcedon … must become "not only our end but our beginning"'.[26] Riches does not discuss why this proved so important in the decades following its publication. I'd suggest a key factor here was the popularity of the later 'regulative' approach to doctrine of the 1980s. It suggests doctrine is not about final answers to specific questions, that is, authoritative descriptive content, but more about defining the rules of engagement with perennial

---

22. Riches' condemnation of Rahner is, to my mind, over-reliant on certain texts, and the allegation of a neglect of prosopon could be amended somewhat by giving more attention to the essay 'Dogmatic Reflections on the Knowledge and Self-Consciousness of Christ' from 1961, in Karl Rahner, *Theological Investigations V* (Baltimore: Helicon, 1966), 193–215.

23. Riches, *Ecce Homo*, 9n17.

24. Ibid.

25. Also titled 'Current Problems in Christology', which does not do justice to the original German title, in Karl Rahner, *Theological Investigations I* (Baltimore: Helicon, 1961), 149–200.

26. Riches, *Ecce Homo*, 11.

theological questions. For Riches however, Rahner's essay is important because this 'beginning not end' approach to Chalcedon was used to critique what Rahner termed 'an existential current of monophysite tendency'.[27] It was not explicitly questioning Chalcedon, of course, but saying there are *de facto* misapprehensions of the Chalcedonian Christ in the lived witness of piety. This led him to seek 'to recover the credibility of Jesus' finite humanity, which he took to be sublated by the "straightforward descending Christology" of the Magisterium'.[28] The upshot seems to be, then, if Chalcedon merely sets boundaries over which one may not trespass, ample space is then left to explore what descriptive content of Christ's personhood might be most fitting for today's world. Against the background of existentialism, for Rahner this meant filling the space with explorations of Christ's human consciousness.

Space will not permit me to assess whether Rahner's explorations of Christ's human consciousness do indeed include the surreptitious return of a human prosopon.[29] The key point for this discussion is that Riches maintains that Rahner presents Chalcedon as something that 'is less a recapitulation of the apostolic proclamation and more essentially a "compromise formula" that resolves the great theological clash between two opposing "factions"', namely the Nestorian and Monophysite groups. He evinces a 'presupposition that the aim and key achievement of the *Definitio* was to carefully balance Nestorian "separation" against Cyrillian "union" and thus achieve an unbeknownst balance that negatively avoids the error of each'.[30]

For Riches this is deeply problematic because he says Chalcedon does offer positive content; not merely rule out errors. It rebukes Nestorianism strongly by arguing that there is one prosopon and one hypostasis. Riches thus commends us to take heed of the official Magisterial document released for the 1500th anniversary of Chalcedon, Pius XII's *Sempiternus Rex*. This condemns those who 'make an erroneous use of the authority of the definition of Chalcedon ... [in order to] emphasize the state and condition of Christ's human nature to such an extent as to make it seem something existing in its own right (*sui juris*), and not as subsisting in the Word itself (*quasi in ipsius Verbi persona non subsistet*)'.[31]

Before moving on to Thomas Joseph White O.P and then Bonhoeffer himself, let me conclude by pointing to why *Ecce Homo* evinces a 'metaphysical turn'. As

---

27. Ibid., 72n52.

28. Ibid., 72n56.

29. See note 22 above; Riches analysis ultimately depends on the question of whether Rahner's exploration of the 'rational soul' Chalcedon names as pertaining to the human nature of Jesus is unwittingly pushed to a level that requires there to be a human prosopon, but this is not under discussion here.

30. Riches, *Ecce Homo*, 73.

31. Pius XII, *Sempiternus Rex* §31 (https://www.vatican.va/content/pius-xii/en/encyclicals/documents/hf_p-xii_enc_08091951_sempiternus-rex-christus.html, accessed 22 August 2022), see Riches, *Ecce Homo*, 1.

mentioned above, Riches' book is unabashedly postliberal. The domain of 'secular reason' as allowing for the autonomous and self-sealed understanding of a neutral reality matches exactly the issues with Christ's humanity as something *sui juris*, not an instantiation of human nature which exists only and exclusively as rooted or subsisting in the divine Logos. He therefore recommends a turning back to premodern metaphysics. This holds that the Enlightenment neglect or forsaking of classical metaphysics was not only deeply problematic, but even makes genuine orthodoxy to Christian tradition impossible. However, Riches' own terminology does not present the post-Enlightenment scene as 'post-metaphysical', but rather as evincing a particular set of metaphysical assumptions, which he describes in ways which seem to imply Kant is to blame. The Nestorian logic of modernity is thus described in terms of a 'singular metaphysical a priori', namely to proceed from 'a *separatio* of divinity and humanity in Christ'.[32] Hence his claim about a 'basic parallelism' between Christ's divinity and humanity.[33] I'm not sure Riches uses the right words here for his own stated ends, and I think the subtle nod to Kant (with the words 'metaphysical a priori') is more instructive than it seems. That is, it is not so much that the alleged resurgence of Nestorian Christologies, nor even modernity itself, has a particular metaphysics of humanity on the one hand and divinity on the other, so much so that one is *sui juris* over against the other. Surely Riches' issue is that metaphysics itself went the same way as 'classical metaphysics', and that the *sui juris* humanity of Christ is emphasised precisely because it does not require a priori acceptance of a metaphysical scheme to be deemed credible.

The alleged resurgence of Nestorianism in the twentieth century is not just the flowering of an ever-present instinct to make the paradoxical truth of Jesus more palatable to the human intellect. It happens because metaphysical conceptualities like physis and hypostasis have ceased to be the normative means for understanding truth and reality in the twentieth century. The alternative norms of historical–critical study, or existentialism, or phenomenology, or psychology, have become dominant instead. This is why the human nature of Jesus seems the most appropriate starting point for Rahner, and many others. The issue is that, by taking disciplines of empirical scholarship as primary for the discovery of truth and reality, twentieth-century Christology is left wide open to the criticism that the humanity of Jesus is approached as something *sui juris*. Christ's humanity is studied using the empirically discernible means which are then applied by analogy to Jesus on the basis that he is fully human. This requires a sort of suspension of belief in the divine Logos just like Nestorius' questioning of the term *Theotokos*. Metaphysics itself has been left to one side, the defining and interrelating of conceptualities like nature and hypostasis have ceased to have the importance they once did, so much so that Christ's human nature can be explored in such a way that it must require a prosopon, an 'observable character' which Chalcedon forbids.

---

32. Ibid., 8.
33. Ibid., 12, see also 11–12.

Rahner approaches Chalcedon as merely the residual scaffolding of the *depositum fidei*. It is dogmatically unquestionable, yet when shorn of a commitment to premodern metaphysics it has no positive content as such. Its authority is then taken in terms of rules. What the metaphysical conceptualities *signify* are regulative components, rather than the things-in-themselves. This is deeply Kantian, for Kant calls his noumena 'empty', something Paul Guyer glosses by describing them as 'entirely negative'.[34] If, however, the elements of Chalcedon are taken as more than limits on metaphysics but as the things-in-themselves, the implication is that the errors attending twentieth-century Christology would be less acute. For this reason, I would suggest Riches are actually commending a turn *to* metaphysics or metaphysical realism, rather than commending one set of metaphysics (premodern) over against another (modern). Riches is tackling a post-metaphysical tendency in modernity, and this tendency is behind both Rahner's neglect of Chalcedon's one prosopon *and* the 'end or beginning' approach to the definition.

My question for part four's discussion of Bonhoeffer is now specific. Bonhoeffer discusses Chalcedon as an example of 'negative Christology', and something there only 'to set limits' on Christology.[35] The question to be posed to Bonhoeffer surrounds whether or not his reading of Chalcedon must go the same way as Riches claims Rahner's does. That is, does Bonhoeffer similarly surrender too much to modernity, does Bonhoeffer's orthodoxy or his alignment to the formal definitions constitute a mere background set of commitments which fail to protect him from Christological problems on a par with Rahner's lapsing into Nestorianism?

III. Thomas Joseph White O.P. *The Incarnate Lord*

Turning now to Thomas Joseph White, I can work towards formulating a similarly precise question from his work. White's book is subtitled *A Thomistic Study in Christology*, and it is certainly that, although not in a simply retrograde sense. White does not straightforwardly demand a return to the thirteenth century, and he certainly does not perform what is commonly taken to be the great misstep of the neo-scholastics; pulling the drawbridge up on the modern age with deductively grounded assertions from the *Summa* intended to keep the world at bay. White's approach is rather to enter deeply into canonically modern Christologies, and engage in a critical reading of them with the primary interlocuter being Aquinas himself. It is not saying 'all this is wrong, and Thomas is right' so much as saying

---

34. Immanuel Kant, *Critique of Pure Reason*, trans. and ed. Paul Guyer and Allen W. Wood (Cambridge: Cambridge University Press, 1999), 356; Paul Guyer, *Kant* (London: Taylor & Francis, 2014), 136. (When Kant claims to be conducting a 'metaphysics of metaphysics', he means an enquiry into the possibility of an enquiry into the nature of reality as such), see Paul Janz, *God the Mind's Desire* (Cambridge: Cambridge University Press, 2004), 125–6.

35. DBWE 12:331–2 (DBW 12:315–6).

'this leads into specific problems, and Thomas has distinctions and definitions which will allow us to see how those problems arose and how best we might surmount them'. There is therefore an attentiveness to modernity at work in White, which means his book is valuable for people from many different perspectives and commitments, because he covers various interlocutors from a wide range of different perspectives.

A 'metaphysical turn' is explicit in *The Incarnate Lord*. The main errors he sees at work in modern Christologies stem from the modern stance towards classical metaphysics, in a way similar to Riches' condemnation of Rahner, but much more extensively discussed in detail. White takes the words 'ontology' and 'metaphysics' as almost synonymous, meaning 'the study of what exists or of what has being'.[36] He considers Christology to be 'intrinsically' ontological/metaphysical, 'because it is concerned with the being and person of Christ, and with his divine and human natures and actions'.[37] He goes even further, however, insofar as he claims, 'it can be said unequivocally that without the ontological study of the person, being and natures of Christ, Christology ceases to be an integral science'.[38] Christology, as an-logy or *Wissenschaft* necessitates, by definition, systematic inquiry into the metaphysics of Jesus. On one level, this is a matter of Catholic orthodoxy. White does not agree with those who hold that you can adhere to the teaching of the councils without subscribing to the classical metaphysics therein. To do so, he says, invariably conceals the truths they contain: '[w]ithout a robustly metaphysical form of thinking about Jesus, the truth of [the] councils becomes obscured'.[39]

The first modern interlocutor with whom he takes issue is perhaps paradigmatic for separating out the teaching of the councils from what can be discerned about Jesus via other means: Adolf von Harnack. Von Harnack of course wished to disambiguate 'a biblical, ethical Christology' from a 'philosophical, ontological Christology', because the findings of historical scholarship, and the centrality of practical reason, were so credible in the late-nineteenth-century German intellectual scene, unlike discussions about physei and hypostasei from the first five centuries after Christ.[40] White's first task, then, is to show how the New Testament actually *requires* the conciliar conclusions about the metaphysics of Jesus in order to make sense, a task he calls 'biblical ontology'. The divine nature is the only way to make sense of the Scriptural trope of Christ's pre-existence, his Lordship similarly for his hypostasis and hypostatic union, the narrative of his life for the human nature, and the singular subject as relayed by the evangelists for the *communicatio idiomatum*.[41] White does not make this comparison, but one is reminded of the move towards more doctrinal readings of Scripture, or

---

36. White, *The Incarnate Lord*, 5–6.
37. Ibid., 4.
38. Ibid., 5.
39. Ibid.
40. Ibid., 7.
41. Ibid., 11–12.

a 'theological interpretation of Scripture' one finds in, say, David S. Yeago, who concludes that 'the judgment about Jesus and God made in the Nicene Creed – the judgment that they are "of one substance [nature]" ... is indeed "the same" in a basically ordinary and unmysterious way, as that ... in a New Testament text such as Philippians 2'.[42]

Whites' book is a 'Thomistic study' because he uses Thomas as an antidote to the problems presented by modern Christologies. But there is a more subsidiary reason which will prove important in turning to Bonhoeffer shortly, and it pertains more to theological epistemology than 'content'. Thomism is of course associated in the popular mind not just with the forensic study of Aquinas, but with a set of philosophical and theological commitments, even if there remain certain variances among different Thomists. The commitments I have in mind are those with which many Protestant commentators are most concerned about Catholic theology, particularly in Bonhoeffer's time. They are centred on the high regard for natural reason, for the relative integrity of human nature after the Fall, and for the fundamental compatibility between truths discerned by natural reason and those revealed by God and accepted in faith. The most well-known caricature of the alleged differentiation between Thomas and the Reformers is to offset Calvin's 'total depravity' with Thomas' 'nature is perfected by grace'.[43] In and of itself this does not get us very far, but the distinction, as applied to Christology, means most basically that any Thomistic Christology must be fundamentally comprehensible or intelligible, that truths of faith do not contradict those of reason, but must fundamentally complement them.

Karl Barth and Dietrich Bonhoeffer will be spinning in their graves already, but perhaps this position can be softened by investigating how the Thomism of the *nouvelle theologié* accommodated itself to at least some broadly Barthian points of orientation. A primary exponent of such Thomism is Henri de Lubac, who in the nature and grace debates of the mid-twentieth century argued that 'pure nature' (*natura pura*) – and by implication natural reason, too – were never in Thomas held to be autonomous or fully separable from the life of grace, or 'supernatural' reason. It is rather that, accepting the basis or ground of faith, reason can operate better in discerning the truth. But without that faith-filled basis, reason is not entirely abominable (it does not become like Luther's 'Frau Hulda'). Rather, there is a difference of degree between reason as a handmaid purified by grace or just a handmaid operating as well as she can in her natural state. This rooting of reason as operating fully within faith, thus presents Aquinas' Five Ways at the opening of the *Summa* not as foundational arguments for God's existence *on the basis of which* people can have faith, but rather as examples of the fundamental integrity of reason

---

42. David S. Yeago, 'The New Testament and the Nicene Dogma: A Contribution to the Recovery of Theological Exegesis', in *Pro Ecclesia* 3 (1994): 152–64, 160.

43. See John Calvin *Inst.* 1.4 and *STh* I, q. 1, a. 8, ad 2 (Thomas Aquinas, *Summa Theologiae*, ed. and trans. Thomas Gilby O.P. [Cambridge: Eyre and Spottiswoode, 1964], 31, translation altered).

to draw correct conclusions even in its natural state, even if those conclusions are as nothing compared to the revelation of the Trinity and the Incarnation.

From White's book, however, it seems de Lubacian Thomism goes too far in downplaying the integrity of natural reason. White takes great care to hold to the basic position of de Lubac and company, that truths of faith are never grounded on or proved by natural reason, before giving more attention than his precursors do to the ways by which natural reason still proves itself not only compatible with faith, but necessary even for faith to function properly. This can be seen in the way White critiques both Schleiermacher and Barth in ways that suggest they are each guilty of approaching Nestorianism. The truths discerned by natural reason in these two cases are those of historical–critical scholarship, and classical metaphysics of nature and person respectively. White says Schleiermacher is guilty of a 'confusion or blending' of reason and revelation which 'obscures the supernatural mystery of Christ and confines his meaning to the reductionist speculations of historical-critical scholars and their conjectures'. Barth is the precise opposite, for he 'expurgates (or at least severely curtails) the possibility of such conjectures being used meaningfully', and does the same with classical metaphysics as well.[44] In Schleiermacher's case, the threat of Nestorianism is relatively self-evident. By placing undue authority on natural reason the unity of Christ's divine and human natures is located 'within' the humanity, in the *schlechthinniges Abhängkeitsgefühl*, not in the hypostasis of the Logos. With Barth, White holds that he 'seeks to place the "site" of the hypostatic union in an odd location: the transcendent identity of God is revealed in a voluntary act of the human Christ (the free and willing submission of Christ to God)'.[45] The implication here seems to be that Barth was too cautious about applying philosophical conceptualities to identify Christ. His reading of Scripture lacks a corresponding ontology, so he 'ends-up (ironically)' applying 'human categories after all'.[46]

Whites' Thomist antidote to this involves distinguishing the 'formal' and 'material' objects of the 'epistemological act of faith'. The material object is 'God himself … in Christ', and the formal object is 'the medium through which or by which we have access to God and to Christ': namely, 'the convergence of divine truth in Scripture, tradition, and the ecclesial Magisterium'.[47] But White points out that Aquinas uses this distinction 'to explain how it is that we might know God both through the formal medium of revelation *and* through the distinct formal medium of philosophical speculation simultaneously'.[48] His discussion of this is highly instructive as to the style of White's Thomism. He says the truths of the different formal media 'in no way conflict with one another', they 'do not remain alien to one another'.[49] But, importantly, there is no danger of reductionism here,

---

44. White, *The Incarnate Lord*, 61.
45. Ibid., 49.
46. Ibid., 50.
47. Ibid., 53.
48. Ibid., 53n40.
49. Ibid., 53–4.

there is no rational foundationalism: the divinity of Christ 'utterly transcends the domain of natural reason as such', for this is one of those truths that 'can only be received supernaturally by grace'.[50] But truths of reason '*might contribute* to a better understanding of the material object' as long as they remain '*illustrative*' and not '*demonstrative*'.[51] From this, we have a first question to be posed to Bonhoeffer from White. This question surrounds the place of White's 'formal objects'; ultimately revelation and reason. His 'metaphysical turn' includes a renewed attentiveness to natural reason, something Bonhoeffer often treats polemically. However, might Whites' cautious discussion, in which revelation remains entirely primary and the truths of reason remain '*illustrative*' and not '*demonstrative*', mean that Bonhoeffer's purely negative interpretation of Chalcedon can be rethought?[52]

There is another key element to this discussion which needs to be given attention before finally getting to Bonhoeffer. This is White's interpretation of Kant. He does not give much direct attention to Kant, but certainly considers him to be the root from which the errors of modern Christology grow. He asks, 'in light of Immanuel Kant's critique of classical metaphysics … what is the importance of the longstanding metaphysical tradition that was employed classically to articulate the mystery of the Incarnation in theological terms'? He goes on to ask, can 'these expressions retain the full weight of their classical expression in a post-metaphysical age, and if so, how can this be?'.[53] When he turns to Kant directly, he states, 'the transcendence of God incarnate as it is understood to be revealed in Christ is in fact something the mind simply does not have the capacity to entertain intellectually'.[54] Therefore, we 'can only conceive of the presence of the divine *in the world* univocally, in terms of the natural forms of our world'.[55]

These are curious statements. On one level, yes of course the Incarnation itself cannot be aligned with a religion ascribed within the bounds of reason alone, although I suspect even Kant would say it can be 'entertained intellectually', just never rendered verifiable or true philosophically. But there seems to be a slight contradiction in White with the second quote. He says 'we can only conceive of the presence of the divine in the world univocally, in terms of the natural forms of our world'. But conceiving, in Kant, is the apprehension of concepts, and these belong to the *Verstand*, not 'in the world' as such. Moreover, it goes to the heart of White's argument that our conceptual understandings of reality do genuinely point to God himself, and do indeed apply to him as indeed they apply to the world. What is left unanswered in White, is the question of to what degree our conceptual understanding manages to capture and give a full grasp of the divine reality, what he calls the 'material object'. When White says the divinity of Christ

---

50. Ibid., 56.
51. Ibid., 57.
52. Ibid., 57.
53. Ibid., 33–4.
54. Original has various italics removed for clarity.
55. White, *The Incarnate Lord*, 45.

'utterly transcends the domain of natural reason as such', there would still seem to some limits even on the classical definitions. That is, the Chalcedonian Definition is not Jesus, and a Thomist as much as a Kantian must therefore say the Definition is not the thing-in-itself. This presents the third and final question to pose to Bonhoeffer, centred on what White calls the 'material object', meaning God himself. Could Bonhoeffer's approach to Chalcedon as essentially about 'limits' be approached in a way which is less Kantian ('entirely empty') than Rahner's; might his understanding of 'limits' be a more generic understanding about concepts themselves, thus permitting Christ himself to overstep them?

IV. Dietrich Bonhoeffer's Christology lectures

We now have three questions to pose to Bonhoeffer. In the first place, does Bonhoeffer's approach to Chalcedon fail to protect him from Christological problems Riches detects in Rahner's lapse into Nestorianism? Secondly, might Whites' cautious epistemological approach mean that Bonhoeffer's construing of the metaphysics of Chalcedon purely negatively can be rethought? Thirdly, there is the question of whether or not Bonhoeffer's approach to Chalcedon as a set of 'limits' necessitates what White calls Kantian 'univocity'.

To answer each of these questions I need first briefly to describe the passage on Chalcedon from the Christology lectures. In Part II of these lectures, the discussion of Chalcedon occurs in a section titled 'Critical Christology or Negative Christology'. Bonhoeffer describes this as 'the part of Christology that seeks to make the incomprehensibility of the person of Jesus Christ comprehensible'.[56] However, it is not this simple, insofar as he maintains that rather than 'turn' the incomprehensible 'into' something comprehensible, 'that which can be comprehended should serve to let stand that which we cannot comprehend'.[57] He applies this approach to Chalcedon itself, arguing that it is a self-defeating edifice, that it 'cancels itself out'.[58] As he puts it, 'all options for thinking of all this together and in juxtaposition are represented as impossible and forbidden options'.[59] This seems to mean that a union of two natures in one hypostasis remains complete and utter mystery. It is no simple resolution to say the divine nature and hypostasis take flesh in Christ, it is not straightforwardly comprehensible, the scandal of the Incarnation does not cease to be a stumbling block, the paradox is not resolved. Rather, Chalcedon intensifies the paradox, or ensures its endurance, by setting out dogmatic terms which mean the paradox cannot be lessened or in any way rendered more palatable to the intellect.

---

56. DBWE 12:331 (DBW 12:315).
57. DBWE 12:331 (DBW 12:315).
58. DBWE 12:343 (DBW 12:328).
59. DBEW 12:342 (DBW 12:327).

Bonhoeffer claims this proceeds by a 'breaking' or destroying of the concepts themselves. He says the formula 'reveals the limitations of its own concepts', and 'brings the concept of substance [nature] that underlies this thinking to its high point and immediately goes beyond it, by saying that from now assertions about the substance of Jesus Christ will no longer be permitted'.[60] The rationale here seems to be one person in two natures is utterly paradoxical, and the making of the language of natures authoritative in this way means the term in question can no longer be used, that is, what he calls 'relationships between natures' has led to a self-defeating paradox. This is why Chalcedon is presented as a work of 'negative Christology': because it provides a paradigmatic attempt to make the incomprehensible comprehensible, and therefore shows, authoritatively, how every attempt to understand Christ is tested by this limitation. This is post-metaphysical: the classical metaphysics of Jesus are pushed to their summation, and this summation is their undoing.

Now the ground is clear to tackle the first question, from Riches. Recall that, for Riches, the merely negative reading of Chalcedon he finds in Rahner is a consequence of treating the definition as a 'compromise statement' between Nestorianism and Cyrillian monophysitism. At first glance, it does not look too good for Bonhoeffer, as he falls in with those who do exactly this: he writes that 'these are the two boundaries between which the real assertion about the mystery of Christ takes place',[61] viz. Nestorianism and Monophysitism. The first, he says, 'had to be rejected because it allowed the humanity and divinity to be so torn apart that the unity of Christ's person could no longer be conceived'.[62] The second 'had to be rejected ... because it allowed the human nature of Christ to be swallowed up in the divine nature'.[63] Moreover, Bonhoeffer connects monophysitism with the term Riches says is wrongly associated with this doctrine in Cyril, *mia physis*. In seeking to avoid each of these he says ('[i]n opposition to both these fronts') the 'classical formulation of the doctrine of Christ as the God-man was established in the Chalcedonian formula'.[64] He then launches into the 'negative' approach described above.

At first glance, it thus seems that Bonhoeffer's approach to Chalcedon is deeply symptomatic of the problems of twentieth-century Christology highlighted by Riches. For Riches, Rahner approaches the definition as a 'compromise settlement' between Cyril and Nestorius, and therefore understands it merely negatively, as a beginning and not an end. Riches considers the definition rather to be a victory for Cyril, for whom the term *mia physis* entailed one prosopon and one hypostasis corresponding to the divine nature, it did not preclude human nature. Moreover,

---

60. DBWE 12:343 (DBW 12:328).
61. DBWE 12:341 (DBW 12:326).
62. DBWE 12:342 (DBW 12:327).
63. DBWE 12:341 (DBW 12:326).
64. DBWE 12:342 (DBW 12:327).

taking Chalcedon merely as a set of boundaries, Rahner was left to explore what descriptive content of Christ's personhood might be most fitting for today's world, with his existential explorations of Christ's human consciousness. This last move inevitably presents Christ's humanity as *sui juris*.[65]

Notwithstanding this prima facie problem, nonetheless, the fact remains that Bonhoeffer's Christology lectures do not in any way present Jesus 'from below', as having a *sui juris* humanity, nor has implying there is a prosopon corresponding to that humanity. That is, Bonhoeffer's strongly negative reading of Chalcedon simply does not lead into the Nestorian cul-de-sac. The examples of this are manifold, but just the term he uses for Christ is demonstration enough: 'the God-human'.[66] He says 'it is impossible to ask how the human Jesus can be simultaneously with each of us – as if this Jesus could exist in isolation!' as well as saying 'it is just as impossible to how God can enter into time – as if such an isolated God could exist!'.[67] The paradox is left standing, this is why he says all Christology must begin 'in silence'.[68] For Riches, a proper understanding of Chalcedon is also paradoxical. He speaks of 'the paradox of the christlogical *unio*' which is 'brought to the ultimate breaking point … but does not break'. This refers to the crucifixion, the most troublesome moment for an avowed Nestorian, in which God himself suffers death. This means, then, that Chalcedon is, for Riches, an 'agonising perplexity'.[69]

There is thus more room for a rapprochement between Riches and Bonhoeffer than it first appears. Indeed, although Bonhoeffer offers a negative approach to Chalcedon which seems similar to Rahner's, it is actually different. For Bonhoeffer, Chalcedon *is* actually an 'end', and not a beginning. It is not an end in terms of a final resolution or last word. It is the end of a certain way of trying to answer the question of who Jesus is with these concepts. However, it could still be countered that Bonhoeffer's offsetting of the divine and human against each other as equally 'impossible' remains somewhat Nestorian, for the key issue is the union of each in the one divine subject or hypostasis. But here again Bonhoeffer provides resources to defend him against this charge – for the proper question to voice in encountering Christ is given as the singular 'Who?': there is very clearly one subjectivity at play in Christ, and he describes it by saying '[h]e *is* the Logos' (original emphasis).[70]

The second question to answer comes from White's *The Incarnate Lord*, and surrounds the use of reason in the Christology lectures. Again, it is quite clear

---

65. Mention should be made of the 'positive Christology' Bonhoeffer himself utilises to complement the negative Christology of Chalcedon. This is relevant because it also evades the problems with Nestorianism Riches finds in Rahner's existentialism, that is, in his use of *Gestalt* as a non-amalgamative category. See Jacob Phillips, *Human Subjectivity in Christ. Integrating Simplicity and Wisdom* (London et al.: Bloomsbury, 2019).

66. DBWE 12:313, 342 (DBW 12:294, 327).

67. DBWE 12:312–3 (DBW 12:294).

68. DBWE 12:300 (DBW 12:280).

69. Riches, *Ecce Homo*, 6.

70. DBWE 12:302 (DBW 12:281).

of course that there are very marked differences between the two Christologies. White holds firm that the conceptualities of classical metaphysics are uniquely able to express the mystery of Christ, and that human reason's thinking about ontology and metaphysics should be held in very high regard. He says 'theological knowledge of the mysteries of faith is much closer to the form of natural knowledge that is properly metaphysical, or ontological, than it is to mathematics or to the observational sciences'.[71] For Bonhoeffer, as we know, reason is much more problematic. Perhaps we are inevitably back to the old Catholic-Protestant debates. But let us recall how White differentiates his thinking from certain others by emphasizing his basic commitment to a non-foundational use of reason in service of faith. For Bonhoeffer, asking 'who?' prohibits any foundational use of reason. The forbidden question is to ask whether 'the answer that is given [meaning Jesus is God] is the right answer',[72] for the '"that" in "that God was revealed in Christ" cannot be theologically questioned'.[73] For this reason, he says the 'fact the Logos became flesh' is 'a prerequisite … never the proof'.[74] In other words, for both Bonhoeffer and White, the foundation is revelation.

There are without doubt significant differences between White and Bonhoeffer surrounding the inherent value of the 'formal object' of reason, and therefore the metaphysical conceptualities that go with it. For Bonhoeffer there is the danger of reason 'turned in on itself', the *cor curvum in se*.[75] This is reason that has not been exposed to its ultimate limits by faith, and not had its limits transcended by God's self-revelation. Yet, Bonhoeffer is at times more open to the proper use of reason than many of his contemporaries and co-religionists, such as in the famous passage in *Ethics* about the 'proper use of *ratio*'.[76] All this would require lengthy discussion to do it justice, but there is a key point to make before moving on. This is that Bonhoeffer's approach takes reason is much less discrete way than 'classical' theology like that of Aquinas. The approach to reason in Thomism would question an inherent or intrinsic detriment to reason, while not necessarily denying that reason cannot operate properly and fully when separated from the life of faith: from devotion, prayer and obedience. But this is presupposed by the monastic tenor of the theology, not as something telling us much about reason in and of itself. Reason does not intrinsically tend towards the *cor curvum in se*, for Thomas, although it may well often end up there in how it takes shape in people's lives.

To return to the question at stake, whether Bonhoeffer's reading of Chalcedon can bear Whites' demand for the necessity of metaphysics for understanding Christ,

71. White, *The Incarnate Lord*, 55.
72. DBWE 12:304 (DBW 12:284).
73. DBWE 12:304 (DBW 12:284).
74. DBWE 12:301 (DBW 12:281).
75. See DBEW 12:303 (DBW 12:283).
76. DBWE 6:115-6 (DBW 6:105-7).

the answer is again not as clear cut as it seems. Whites' issue with denigrating metaphysics as a work of natural reason is that it leads to a concentration on Jesus' humanity as the site of the union between humanity and divinity within him (hence, Nestorianism). But insofar as he takes metaphysics and ontology as almost synonymous, and bearing in mind how Bonhoeffer presents one divine subject throughout his lectures, this criticism does not apply to Bonhoeffer's Christology lectures. In fact, Bonhoeffer discusses ontology directly, precisely as a necessary and intrinsic concern of asking 'Who?'. He writes, 'the question of *who*' is 'the question of *being*', for 'the christological question is in its essence an ontological question'.[77] The main differences from White surround firstly how that ontology is inquired into, that is, the standing of different formal objects. That is, Bonhoeffer opts for more contemporary philosophical means than classical metaphysics. Secondly, there is the fact that, in Bonhoeffer, the material object actually grounds the ontology. For Bonhoeffer, to ask 'who' means one's own being is exposed as limited, and the being of that beyond oneself reveals himself: 'the question of "who" is the question about transcendence'.[78]

This leaves the third question: whether or not Bonhoeffer's approach to Chalcedon as a set of 'limits' necessitates what White calls Kantian 'univocity'? Again, there are fundamental differences, of course. Bonhoeffer is no metaphysical realist, and his attentiveness to the limits of concepts is certainly more Kantian than Thomist, of course. But the fact remains that Bonhoeffer does not understand Chalcedon merely negatively, despite the statements he makes. Chalcedon is uniquely important for Bonhoeffer, because the concepts are pushed to the point where they must lead into some apprehension of Christ himself, to the material object of Christology. Chalcedon's self-defeating character renders it a 'living assertion about Christ that goes beyond all conceptual forms'. It is unique because '[e]verything is encompassed in its very clear yet paradoxical agility [*Lebendigkeiten*]'.[79] Now, this is not too far from saying that reflection on metaphysics and ontology is uniquely capable for expressing theological knowledge. It is just much closer to John Henry Newman than it is White or Aquinas. Newman writes, 'theology both uses logic and baffles it'. It is necessary, to 'trim the balance of truth [as] at Antioch or Nicaea', but the process by which this balancing act takes place 'is circuitous and elaborate; and is conducted by means of minute subtleties which will give the appearance of a game of skill in matters too grave and practical to deserve a mere scholastic treatment'.[80]

---

77. DBWE 12:304 (DBW 12:284).
78. DBWE 12:302 (DBW 12:282).
79. DBWE 12:343 (DBW 12:328).
80. John Henry Newman, *Mary: The Virgin Mary in the Writings of John Henry Newman*, ed. Philip Boyce (Leominster: Gracewing, 2001), 276.

V. Conclusion

The foregoing discussion makes clear that the 'metaphysical turn' in contemporary Catholic Christology will probably place Bonhoeffer further to the periphery of Christological reflection than he is already. At first glance he offers a merely 'negative' reading of Chalcedon, he accepts the 'compromise formula' understanding he inherited, and seems pejorative towards natural reason and therefore metaphysics. However, a closer examination reveals three important points. He does not slip into Nestorianism, nor threaten to at any point. Nor is his non-foundational use of reason in theology entirely opposite to Whites', although it is different. Moreover, although Bonhoeffer is of course very sensitive to the limits of metaphysical concepts, Chalcedon itself is still considered uniquely capable of pointing to the mystery it seeks to articulate. This is an at least de facto acceptance of the authority of classical metaphysics, even if it is framed more in terms of what it cannot do rather than what it can. Indeed, ontology is even taken further than being a 'formal object' in Bonhoeffer, for Christ himself grounds the ontology of his Christology.

For these reasons, Bonhoeffer's Christology should not, I suggest, be covered as a mere precursor to Liberation Theology. The points mentioned above place him on a very different footing to Jon Sobrino, and might even suggest his Christology gestures towards today's concerns. While he would agree with Sobrino that we must 'dispel any illusion that the mere repetition of some dogma gives us access to the reality of Christ', he does more than simply hold the concepts of Chalcedon, like Sobrino, as mere 'limit-concepts not directly accessible to human intuition'. That is, in the unique combination of concepts that Chalcedon provides, it presents a 'living assertion about Christ that goes beyond all conceptual forms' and therefore presents us with Jesus himself.[81]

---

81. DBWE 12:343 (DBW 12:328).

Chapter 5

'TO CARRY ON IN THIS CHALCEDONIAN SENSE': CHRISTOLOGY IN *LETTERS AND PAPERS FROM PRISON*

Philip G. Ziegler

I. Introduction

Provoked by their fascinating history, relevant themes and arresting idiom, much of the engagement with Bonhoeffer during the twenty years following the publication of *Letters and Papers from Prison* in 1951 was dominated by debates concerning their proper interpretation and significance for post-war Christianity in the West.[1] From the first, commentators were alert to the potentially incendiary implications for Christology of the 'new theology' that came to 'fragmentary, yet systematic' expression in what had been preserved of the smuggled correspondence between Bonhoeffer – then imprisoned in Tegel Prison, Berlin – and Eberhard Bethge – conscripted into the *Wehrmacht* – over the course of 1943–4.[2]

Writing already in 1956 Ronald Gregor Smith, for example, observes that it was 'not easy to see' how on the basis of the striking Christological reflections of 1944 Bonhoeffer could ever have gone on and 'constructed an orthodox doctrine of the relation of Christ to the Father'.[3] And John A. Phillips' extended study of

---

1. DBWE 8 (DBW 8).

2. Eberhard Bethge, 'The Challenge of Dietrich Bonhoeffer's Life and Theology', in *World Come of Age: A Symposium on Dietrich Bonhoeffer*, ed. R. Gregor Smith (London: Collins, 1967), 75. The term 'New Theology' comes from Bethge, who uses it to designate the theology of the prison correspondence in his biography, *Dietrich Bonhoeffer: Theologe – Christ – Zeitgenosse* (München: Chr. Kaiser Verlag, 1967), rendered fully into English as *Dietrich Bonhoeffer: A Biography*, rev. and ed. Victoria Barnett (Minneapolis: Fortress Press, 2000). See in the latter, 'The New Theology', 853–91.

3. Ronald Gregor Smith, *The New Man: Christianity and Man's Coming of Age* (London: SCM, 1956), 103. On Smith see the study by Bonhoeffer scholar, Keith W. Clements, *The Theology of Ronald Gregor Smith* (Leiden: Brill, 1986).

the development of Bonhoeffer's Christology across the whole of his corpus, espied deep and unresolved tensions in these same late texts which rendered the coherence and viability of Bonhoeffer's account 'vulnerable'. One is forced to question, he concluded, just how and whether Bonhoeffer could, in fact, have ever constructed a 'complete Christology on this basis'.[4] For Phillips as for Smith, the fragmentary novelty of Bonhoeffer's final Christological reflections primarily leaves us with open questions which, while invaluable to ask, are difficult to answer unambiguously. Continuing in this same mode, the brief chapter on Christology in John Robinson's (in)famous tract *Honest to God* takes its title – 'The Man for Others' – from Bonhoeffer's 1955 'Outline for a Book', and looks positively to 'some such Christology' of the sort 'towards which Bonhoeffer was working and of which he left such tantalizing intimations behind' as an intellectually respectable and authentic way beyond the antique strictures of 'supernaturalism'.[5] Robinson was perhaps more sanguine than others about the doctrinal fruitfulness of the Christological uncertainties bequeathed to us by the prison correspondence.

Other readers drew even more confident conclusions from the letters. Hanfried Müller's 1956 Berlin dissertation published four years later as *Von der Kirche zur Welt* argued that it was Bonhoeffer's late emphasis on the worldly humiliation and 'messianic suffering' of Jesus Christ which provided the theological ground for an embrace of a non-nihilistic secularism analogous to that 'positive, productive, and progressive' atheism of Marxism. As he put it, 'in this way, through this change in his theology, Bonhoeffer becomes free to alter his view of history' in a direction Müller was convinced bent towards alignment with key features of the Marxist worldview.[6] Of course, by its nature, Müller's analysis has limited interest in questions of Christology proper as he keenly traces the dissolution of the Church into the world – and of Christology into anthropology – which he considered to be the 'intention and the tendency' of the final stages of Bonhoeffer's theological thinking.[7]

---

4. John A. Phillips, *The Form of Christ in the World: A Study of Bonhoeffer's Christology* (London: Collins, 1967), 197–8. For his discussion of 'Christ, the Worldly Man', see 185–98.

5. John T. Robinson, *Honest to God* (London: SCM, 1963), 64–83., especially 75–7.

6. Hanfried Müller, 'The Problem of the Reception and Interpretation of Dietrich Bonhoeffer', in *World Come of Age: A Symposium on Dietrich Bonhoeffer*, ed. Ronald Gregor Smith (London: Collins, 1967), 205. This essay offers a concise English-language account of key elements of the argument advanced in the book itself, *Von der Kirche zur Welt* (Leipzig: Koehler & Amelang, 1960).

7. Müller, 'The Problem of the Reception and Interpretation of Dietrich Bonhoeffer', 183. Bethge admitted that statements in the prison letters might be thought to suggest that his ecclesiology was 'once again being called into question by Christology', but on his view the upshot was not a churchless Christianity, but rather a vision of the Church conformed to the *theologia crucis* – see Bethge, *Dietrich Bonhoeffer: A Biography*, 887–8.

William Hamilton was a leading figure in the 'death of God' debates in English-language theology in the 1960s. Of all the 'radical theologians', as they were styled, he and his work were most closely associated with Bonhoeffer.[8] While acknowledging that his overall reading of the trajectory of the prison writings kept close company with Müller's, Hamilton sustained a more direct interest in their Christological teaching as such.[9] He too came to champion Bonhoeffer as a prophet of an unanxious and positive theological embrace of secularity. Crucial for him, was Bonhoeffer's repudiation of therapeutic, 'God of the gaps' religion and with it any vision of 'Christianity as problem-solving and need-fulfilling'.[10] Confronted with the challenges of life, modern secular humanity no longer expects the advent of the *deus ex machina*, nor should it lament his loss. The 'death of God' names the situation in which the dialectic between the presence and absence of God has collapsed into absence alone: there is no transcendent depth-dimension to the world as we traverse it. Whatever the continuing significance of Jesus Christ in such a world, it cannot be secured by appeals to the 'revelation of God'. What emerges instead is a 'quest for the post-Christian Jesus' and a 'godless Christology' to which there corresponds a free – Hamilton was content to call it 'arbitrary' – and obedient binding to Jesus, the man for others, being 'obedient to him and obedient as he was obedient'.[11] On such accounts as these from Hamilton and Müller, the Christology of *Letters and Papers from Prison* is a Christology for *taking leave* of Christology: Christology has no long-term future in the 'world come of age', and even now the radical development of its content contributes to its own dissolution. Read in this way, the late Christological reflections show us a doctrine imploding

---

8. See G. Michael Zbaraschuk, 'William Hamilton (American, 1924–2012)', in *The Palgrave Handbook of Radical Theology*, ed. Christopher D. Rodkey and Jordan E. Miller (Cham: Palgrave Macmillan, 2018), 241–7, as well as by the same author, 'God Is Still Dead: Retrieving the Lost Legacy of William Hamilton', in *Resurrecting the Death of God: The Origins, Influence, and Return of Radical Theology*, ed. Daniel J. Peterson and G. Michael Zharaschuk (Albany: SUNY Press, 2014), 71–82. Also see the very recent personal essay by his son, Don Hamilton, 'When My Dad Killed God', *The Christian Century*, 15 July 2022, https://www.christiancentury.org/article/first-person/when-my-dad-killed-god, accessed July 2022.

9. See William Hamilton, 'The Death of God Theologies Today', in *Radical Theology and the Death of God*, ed. Thomas J. J. Altizer and William Hamilton (Indianapolis: Bobbs-Merrill, 1966), 42n9 for his appreciation and acknowledgement of Müller's position. See also in the same volume his short essay, 'Dietrich Bonhoeffer', 113–18.

10. William Hamilton, 'The Shape of Radical Theology', in *The Christian Century* 82 (6 October 1965): 1219–22, 1219.

11. William Hamilton, *On Taking God Out of the Dictionary* (New York: McGraw-Hill, 1974), 18, 56 and 'The Shape of Radical Theology', 1221. In the former, Hamilton suggests that this Christology was only just beginning to be worked out, and pointed to John A. Phillips, 'Radical Christology: Jesus and the Death of God', in *CrossCurrents* 19, no. 3 (1969): 273–96, as an 'admirable start'.

in upon itself, as it were, a doctrine whose trajectory points towards the eventual evacuation of any specifically *theological* content from the discourse about Jesus in celebration of our 'coming of age'.[12]

Keen interest in the theological salience of the motifs of 'religiousness Christianity' and the 'world come of age' was not always pursued as reductively as this. As one of the most able and responsible readers of Bonhoeffer from this period, Ronald Gregor Smith, understood from the first that Bonhoeffer remained primarily concerned in this last period with the 'positive meaning of Christ and Christianity'. For this reason, Smith argued, the significance of his critique of religion, his new thinking about divine transcendence, and his assertion of the responsible secularity of the world lay 'not in an undialectical maturity of man, but once again in the question of God'.[13] Indeed, in his earliest writing William Hamilton too had actually shared this line of argument with his *Doktorvater*, emphasizing with him that Bonhoeffer's prison Christology was precisely a polemic about divinity itself, contending that 'in Jesus the Lord we see for the first time what Christian "divinity" must be taken to be'; in the spirit of the Christology of the young Luther, Bonhoeffer saw in the crucified Christ a radical 'correction and a transformation' of other unbaptized concepts of deity.[14] Indeed, it seems clear from the texts themselves – not least from the extensive role played by discussion of 'God's suffering' and the programmatic theme of Jesus' 'lordship' throughout the decisive letters of 1944 – that such atheistic reductions of the Christological discourse of the prison writings are out of place. As Wolf Krötke rightly observes, Bonhoeffer's late Christological reflection manifestly 'proceeds from the assumption that the man Jesus is true God' such that it is and could only be a misinterpretation – creative or otherwise – to reduce the idea of Jesus' 'being for others' merely to an 'anthropological maxim'.[15] On this score, the Christology of the prison letters remains tethered to divine revelation and serves to secure a more thoroughly evangelized concept of both God *and* humanity.[16]

---

12. See the sympathetic but critical discussion of such 'atheistic interpretations' by André Dumas, *Dietrich Bonhoeffer: Theologian of Reality*, trans. Robert McAfee Brown (London: Collier-Macmillan, 1971), 254–69.

13. Both these cited claims are drawn from Ronald Gregor Smith, *Secular Christianity* (London: Collins, 1966), 178.

14. William Hamilton, *The New Essence of Christianity* (London: Darton, Longman & Todd, 1961), 86, or again: 'Christianity's real contribution is this: when asked what it means by God, it points to the cross', 82, and see 87–94.

15. Wolf Krötke, '"Sharing in God's Suffering": Dietrich Bonhoeffer's Understanding of a "Religionless Christianity"', in *Karl Barth and Dietrich Bonhoeffer: Theologians for a Post-Christian World*, trans. John P. Burgess (Grand Rapids, MI: Baker Academic, 2019), 154.

16. I have suggested something along these lines is true of Bonhoeffer's theological programme more generally, see Philip G. Ziegler, 'God', in *The Oxford Handbook of Dietrich Bonhoeffer*, ed. Michael Mawson and Philip G. Ziegler (Oxford: Oxford University Press, 2019), 137–49, especially 147–9.

During the years before and after the publication of his monumental biography of Bonhoeffer in 1967, Eberhard Bethge himself was regularly drawn into debates concerning the contested interpretation of the theological substance of the prison writings. In these engagements he was insistent that throughout the various phases of their correspondence, 'the pivot of Bonhoeffer's liberating analyses was Christology'.[17] He also contended that there is an 'intimate connection' between Christology and the non-religious expression of Christian faith and witness. For Bonhoeffer, writing from Tegel,

> Christology not qualified by something like non-religious interpretation became an unrelated entity and suffered a fatal loss of reality; non-religious Christianity without Christocentricism became a Sisyphean endeavor of modern man to adjust to a newly discovered self and world.[18]

The concern then is twofold: one the one hand, for Christologically fielded defence of the graciousness of the God of the Gospel and the value of that Gospel for contemporary human beings and, on the other, an assertion of the crucial importance of the concreteness of Christological doctrine achieved by forging a connection with the actuality of the world 'come of age' which acknowledges the historical contingency of 'religion'.

The importance of these two *foci* is concisely communicated in Bonhoeffer's formulation of the question which controls the whole theological correspondence of the summer of 1944. The question as set out in the letter of 30 April 1944 runs: 'Who is Christ actually for us today?'.[19] The bare question of Christology – namely 'who is Christ?' – is here modified by 'actually for us today' so as to insist upon its being asked and answered only in concrete connection with our age of responsible secularity. Bethge thought this 'expansion' and 'enlargement' of the 'Who?' question – which Bonhoeffer had of course made central to his earlier Berlin lectures on Christology in 1933 – to be an important marker of just what was 'new' in this late 'new theology'.[20]

We can agree, in line with Bethge's long-standing suggestion, that the Christological reflections found in Bonhoeffer's final fragmentary work win their

---

17. The phrase comes from Martin E. Marty, *Dietrich Bonhoeffer's Letters and Papers from Prison: A Biography* (Princeton: Princeton University Press, 2011), 49. This little volume offers a valuable account of something of the long career of *Letters and Papers from Prison* since its publication in the 1950s.

18. Eberhard Bethge, 'Bonhoeffer's Christology and His "Religionless Christianity"', in *Union Seminary Quarterly Review* 23, no. 1 (1967): 61–77, 61. This essay is also reprinted in *Bonhoeffer in a World Come of Age*, ed. Peter Vorkink II (Philadelphia: Fortress Press, 1968), 46–72.

19. DBWE 8:362 (DBW 8:402).

20. See DBWE 12:303 (DBW 12:283). Bethge, 'Bonhoeffer's Christology and His "Religionless Christianity"', 65.

systematic quality precisely from the material connection between Christology and Bonhoeffer's experimental thinking concerning the 'world come of age', the 'religionless interpretation of biblical concepts', and 'religionless Christianity'. Bonhoeffer himself makes this clear when he writes on 30 June 1944 of 'the issue that concerns me: the claim of Jesus Christ on the world that has come of age'.[21] Bonhoeffer's overriding concern in Christology, here as previously, remains concreteness, now conceived with primary reference, first, to the evangelical specificity of divine transcendence met in its dynamic self-humbling for others, and, second, to the responsible secularity of the modern world.[22] Throughout the striking theological exchange inaugurated by the letter of 30 April 1944, Bonhoeffer's Christological thinking orbits unsteadily but relentlessly around these twin *foci* as he ventures several new formulae to clarify them and their relation. These efforts culminate – or perhaps simply break off – with the 'Outline for a Book' from August 1944 in the Christological formula: Jesus '*der Mensch für andere*'.[23] In this 'apparently simple and yet so meaningful and new title for Christ',[24] Bonhoeffer rivets his attention to the reality of the self-humbling God become human for us without reserve – a salutary enactment of *true* deity – which gives rise *in that very act* to true humanity, i.e., a human being for others without reserve, the man Jesus.

Bonhoeffer's contention throughout the prison writings is that the language of 'God' and of 'transcendence' have been rendered profoundly ambiguous under the historically contingent conditions he designates with 'religion' as an especial term of art. The struggle for a 'religionless Christianity' is therefore in no small part a struggle to disambiguate the contemporary theological meaning of these terms from their religious *Doppelgängers* and entangling logics. Only part of this crisis derives from what Robinson once called – perhaps knowingly echoing Johannes Weiss from decades before – the 'currency crisis' which besets 'doctrinal formulations, moral codes, liturgical forms and the rest' under the conditions of secularizing modernity and which he took to be the heart of Bonhoeffer's late thinking about the

---

21. DBWE 8:451 (DBW 8:504).

22. Christiane Tietz emphasizes that Bonhoeffer wins through to a 'new understanding of transcendence' in this late Christology, see her essay 'Christology', in *The Oxford Handbook of Dietrich Bonhoeffer*, ed. Michael Mawson and Philip G. Ziegler (Oxford: Oxford University Press, 2019), 166. Paul L. Lehmann identified 'concreteness' as the abiding concern of Bonhoeffer's theological work – 'The Concreteness of Theology: Reflections on the Conversation Between Barth and Bonhoeffer', in *Footnotes to a Theology: The Karl Barth Colloquium of 1972*, ed., H. Martin Rumscheidt (Halifax, NS: Corporation for the Publication of Academic Studies in Religion in Canada, 1972), 53–76.

23. DBW 8:559 (DBWE 8:501).

24. Bethge, *Bonhoeffer: Exile and Martyr*, 149. See also Bethge, 'Bonhoeffer's Christology and His "Religionless Christianity"', 75.

world's coming of age.[25] But the other and more fundamental aspect of this crisis in fact comes from the Gospel itself when these terms are rendered evangelically concrete precisely in Christological terms. On this score, the thesis advanced by both Ebeling (already in 1955) and also Bethge – namely that the 'religionless interpretation of biblical concepts' just *is* 'christological interpretation' because it arises in fundamentally out of 'an insight into the nature of the Gospel' itself – can only be affirmed.[26] At play is the 'unity and paradox of the *theologia crucis* and the world come of age' and the relentlessly dialectical thinking Bonhoeffer pursues in expressing it.[27] In their dialectical interplay, these two *foci* conspire to eliminate 'a false notion of God' so as to allow 'us to see the God of the Bible, who gains ground and power in the world by being powerless'.[28] Ernst Feil was not mistaken to claim that on the basis of 'Jesus Christ the "one for others" Bonhoeffer developed a new view of transcendence and an understanding of the world in which the two elements were inseparable'.[29] For it is precisely and only when acknowledged and attested as God for us in human form and thereby as the one who lives for the sake of others, that Jesus Christ can 'become Lord of the religionless'.[30]

II. *The Christology of* Letters and Papers from Prison

Building upon these insights, the Christology of the prison writings can, I submit, be well-understood when seen in the light of Bonhoeffer's expressed judgements of the Chalcedonian Definition set out in his earlier Christology lectures of 1933.

---

25. John T. Robinson, 'The Debate Continues', in *The Honest to God Debate*, ed. David L. Edwards (London: SCM Press, 1963), 242, see 243–8 where the metaphor is spun out. Weiss, for his part writing in 1892 – in *Jesus Proclamation of the Kingdom of God*, ed. and trans. Richard H. Hiers and David L. Holland (London: SCM Press, 1971) – spoke of the need for the old apocalyptic 'coinage' to be re-issued at a new 'rate of exchange' in the present. For insightful discussion see Christopher Morse, '"If Johannes Weiss is Right ..." – A Brief Retrospective on Apocalyptic Theology', in *Apocalyptic and The Future of Theology: With and Beyond J. Louis Martyn*, ed. Joshua B. Davis and Douglas Harink (Eugene, OR: Cascade, 2012), 139–55.

26. Gerhard Ebeling, 'The "Non-Religious Interpretation of Biblical Concepts"', in *Word and Faith*, trans. James W. Leitch (London: SCM Press, 1963), 127–8, and Bethge, 'Bonhoeffer's Christology and His "Religionless Christianity"', 62.

27. So Bethge, *Dietrich Bonhoeffer: A Biography*, 868. Ebeling also argued that Bonhoeffer's commitment to the *theologia crucis* must be recognized 'as the keynote of Bonhoeffer's thinking', 'The "Non-Religious Interpretation of Biblical Concepts"', 158.

28. DBWE 8:479–80 (DBW 8:533–6).

29. Ernst Feil, *The Theology of Dietrich Bonhoeffer*, trans. Hans Martin Rumscheidt (Minneapolis: Fortress, 1985), 95.

30. DBWE 8:363 (DBW 8:403).

There he pointed towards what would be involved in 'continuing' that tradition in which, as he understands it, the doctrine of the two natures has itself been 'surmounted' by the very definition itself with its 'very clear yet paradoxical agility'.[31] The Christological reflections of 1944 can be seen to constitute attempts – tentative and bold by turn – to answer the question Chalcedon bequeathed to Christian faith and dogmatics: namely 'who is this human being who is said to be God?'.[32] To ask and answer Bonhoeffer's 'new' question – 'who is Christ actually for us today?' – is simultaneously to ask and answer this 'old' question as well, and so to 'carry on in this Chalcedonian sense'.[33] And new answer Bonhoeffer gives can and must be understood in relation to that 'old' question as well. In 1933 the answer had been that 'Jesus Christ is the one who *is for me*', an answer which emphasized the ontological quality of the promeity of the Son as an originary ingredient of his identity.[34] In 1944 the answer is that 'Jesus is the man for others'. The definitive role played by *promeity* in the Christology of the Berlin lectures is, I suggest, both reprised and modified here in the prison correspondence.

Perhaps *the* decisive Christological passage is that found in the previously mentioned 'Outline for a Book' of August 1944. The second chapter of that imagined work is conceived under the heading 'What is Christian Faith, Really?' and the plan includes a paragraph-length answer to the question 'Who is God?'. In my view, the answer Bonhoeffer sketches quite naturally divides into three short sections, each of which notably climaxes in an invocation of Jesus's being-for-others. While certainly cautious about over-interpreting these fragmentary materials, we ought not to allow Bonhoeffer's apology to Bethge that all this is 'put very roughly and only outlined'[35] to dissuade us from close reading and careful consideration of the substance of these important remarks.

31. DBWE 12:350, 343 (DBW 12:336, 328).

32. DBWE 12:350 (DBW 12:336).

33. DBWE 12:350 (DBW 12:336). The only reference to Chalcedon in *Letters and Papers from Prison* is an oblique one where it is invoked in relation to the concept of the 'the polyphony of life'. Bonhoeffer writes 'Where the cantus firmus is clear and distinct, a counterpoint can develop as mightily as it wants. The two are "undivided and yet distinct", as the Definition of Chalcedonian says, like the divine and human natures in Christ. Is that perhaps why we are so at home with polyphony in music, why it is important to us, because it is the musical image of this christological fact and thus also of our *vita christiana*?', DBWE 8:394 (DBW 8:440). The description of the two natures in their differentiated unity as a 'christological *fact*' is not uninteresting here.

34. I have ventured to exposit this theme elsewhere, see Philip G. Ziegler, 'Christ for Us Today: Promeity in the Christologies of Bonhoeffer and Kierkegaard', in *International Journal of Systematic Theology* 15, no. 1 (2013): 25–41.

35. DBWE 8:589 (DBW 8:653).

The first part sets out the encounter with Jesus as the form and substance of our encounter with God:

> Who is God? Not primarily a general belief in God's omnipotence, and so on. That is not a genuine experience of God but just a prolongation of a piece of the world. Encounter with Jesus Christ. Experience that here there is a reversal of all human existence, in the very fact that Jesus only 'is there for others'. Jesus's being-for-others is the experience of transcendence! Only through this liberation from self, through this 'being-for-others' unto death, do omnipotence, omniscience, and omnipresence come into being. Faith is participating in this being of Jesus. (Becoming human [*Menschwerdung*], cross, resurrection.)[36]

The discussion begins, notably, with the question of God and of the divine identity. To this question a lengthy and decidedly Christological answer is given. At issue is nothing less than the difference between God and world. All the talk of 'transcendence' that follows is involved in trying to draw out *this* difference aright. Bonhoeffer's terse suggestion is that the 'way of eminence' – e.g., perfecting our experience of power in affirmation of unlimited divine power – confuses, rather than clarifies the divine identity. The necessary clarification comes not from conceptual or discursive manoeuvres of this kind but from the actual advent and encounter with Christ. A quite specific negation forms the core of this encounter, namely, the overturning of 'all human existence' which follows from acknowledgement that Jesus being is exclusively and exhaustively – unto death! – *for others*.[37] This specific negation is also expressed as the emancipation of the self from itself in a movement strictly antithetical to the being of the *homo incurvatus in se*. The event of this divine transcendence is thus the making of this *true* human life, and it is in this true humanity that Christians participate by faith. If the distinguishing marker of deity is concrete existence *for others* then, Bonhoeffer quickly suggests, other possible designations of divine transcendence – Bonhoeffer lists three classical incommunicable attributes here – are in fact simply qualifying predicates of *this* quality of being which *just is* transcendence, i.e., they offer further qualification of the positive freedom to be for others which God actually enacts in the life, death and resurrection of Jesus.

---

36. DBWE 8:501 (DBW 8:558).
37. Bonhoeffer amended his MS with '*only*' for emphasis: '... *daß Jesus nur "für andere da ist"*' – DBW 8:558n10 (DBWE 8:501n10). The English might more naturally read 'that Jesus is *only* there for others' or 'Jesus only exists concretely for others', taking the *nur* adverbially. In his 'Editor's Afterword to the German Edition', Christian Gremmels observes that Bonhoeffer's thinking here builds up a series of 'reversals' founded upon the fundamental reversal of religious expectations vis-à-vis God – see DBWE 8:589 (DBW 8:653).

The question at the heart of the second section is the specific quality of our *relationship* to God:

> Our relationship to God is no 'religious' relationship to some highest, most powerful, and best being imaginable – that is no genuine transcendence. Instead, our relationship to God is a new life in 'being there for others' through participation in this being of Jesus. The transcendent is not the infinite, unattainable task, but the neighbour within reach in any given situation.[38]

To speak Christianly of God is to speak of God in those encounters and relations to which the concrete movements of his love and grace give rise, and not otherwise: Bonhoeffer admits no talk of God abstracted from God's salutary relation with us. It is because God is known in act, and specifically, in the act of Jesus' being-there-for-others, that the entire discussion to this point has already in fact concerned the *relationship* of God and humanity. Indeed, properly understood all theological discourse is always already implicated in this relationship. As Rainer Mayer rightly observes, 'the nonspeculative way of understanding transcendence, therefore, is only possible in the act of obedient faith – that is to say, in discipleship'.[39]

Now, if we ask, 'what is the specific quality of the relation to which this act of God gives rise?' the answer is *faith*. Bonhoeffer explicitly contrasts faith in the God come low to save in Jesus Christ with a religious relation to an abstract god of eminent power. This faith, as he comments elsewhere in the prison letters, is 'something whole and involves one's whole life' because 'Jesus calls not to a new religion, but to life'[40] – or as he says here in our passage, to 'a new life'. This new life of faith is quotidian, this-worldly, and ventured 'in ordinary', as it were: enabled and directed to be for others by virtue of its participation in Jesus' own being, faith disposes us towards our neighbours in any and all circumstances. Faith, as Bonhoeffer famously explained to Bethge in July 1944, is therefore a 'living in the midst of life's tasks, questions, successes and failures, experiences, and perplexities' in which 'one takes seriously no longer one's own suffering but rather the suffering of God in the world' and thereby 'becomes a human being, a Christian'.[41] To the total claim of Christ corresponds faith's embrace of the whole of life in a way that repudiates and overruns the instrumentality and partiality of religion.

Jesus 'being-for-others' *is* God's suffering in the world; it is the determining reality with which the new life of faith reckons. The reality of Jesus' being-for-others

---

38. DBWE 8:501 (DBW 8:558), translation altered. Bonhoeffer writes of '*das Teilnehmen an diesem Sein Jesu*' but the DBWE renders this as 'participation in the being of Jesus'. The specification *this* seems an important emphasis.

39. Mayer, 'Christology: The Genuine Form of Transcendence', 189.

40. DBWE 8:482 (DBW 8:537).

41. DBWE 8:486 (DBW 8:541). Bonhoeffer concludes this passage: 'And I think this is faith; this is μετάνοια'.

is set forth here as the enabling environment, as it were, of Christian faith, life and action. This claim reprises the essence of Bonhoeffer's much more elaborate discussion of 'The Structure of Responsible Life' in *Ethics* where God's reality-making act of 'taking on human being in bodily form and thus reconciling humanity's world with God' funds the axiom that action 'in accord with reality' is 'action in accordance with Christ'.[42] Here, as there, Bonhoeffer envisages a moral ontology decisively determined by the reality of God's assumption of humanity in Jesus Christ and which comes to genuine expression in forms of human life which derive from it, depend upon it and comport with it.

Appropriately, the third and final section turns to address the *incarnation* directly:

> God in human form! Not as in oriental religions in animal forms as the monstrous, the chaotic, the remote, the terrifying, but also not in the conceptual forms of the absolute, the metaphysical, the infinite, and so on, either, nor again the Greek god – human form of the 'God-human form [*Gott-Menschgestalt*] of the human being in itself'. But rather, 'the human being for others'! therefore the Crucified One. The human being living out of the transcendent.[43]

This is as precise a discussion of the nature of the incarnation as Bonhoeffer offers in the context of the prison correspondence. The final paired sentences put two descriptions of the reality of the incarnation in apposition. In the first, God's assumption of humanity in Jesus Christ issues in 'the human being for others' whose life finds its property epitome and term in the cross. The emphasis here falls upon the totality and unrestrained realization of Christ's ontological promeity in the selfless humiliation of the Son in the flesh without reserve. In the second, the incarnate one is described as '*der aus dem Transzendenten lebende Mensch*', a phrase which defines the meaning the confession of Jesus as *vere homo*. The true humanity of Jesus has its ground and origin in the positive freedom of God himself to be for others, i.e., in divine transcendence as Bonhoeffer understands it. We might understand this as an idiomatic expression of the sinlessness of Christ, the reality and truth of whose humanity is a function of its undisrupted relation with the reality of God. That which constitutes the identity of Jesus *qua* human being – his being-for-others – has its sole and exhaustive basis in the dynamic of the self-humbling person and deity of the Son. In other words, just because it is that creaturely existence which is the locus and form of this singular and salutary divine humiliation, the being of Jesus Christ is a *truly human* being. For clarification, Bonhoeffer sets the *true* humanity arising in and from incarnation over against two other notions of divine descent and appearing: one in the advent of the god in *non*-human flesh and form; the other, the advent of the god in the

---

42. DBWE 6:261, 263 (DBW 6:260, 262).
43. DBWE 8:501 (DBW 8:558).

projected idea of a god-like human form. The latter is a clear echo of Bonhoeffer's characterization of the embrace of the false serpentine promise of the *sicut deus* as the basis of the forfeiture of true humanity in his gloss on Genesis 3 in *Creation and Fall*.[44]

This pattern and sequencing of Bonhoeffer's thinking here, which sees Christ's true human being to be a consequence of the gracious movements of the true deity of the Son – Bonhoeffer's 'the transcendent' – represents a kind of Chalcendonianism, reiterating in a nontechnical idiom something like the an-/enhypostatic logic of the early Christian teaching. Yet, this is also a Chalcendonianism inhabited and 'repaired'. It is repaired first by its relentless emphasis on the self-humbling of the Son as the concrete personal form of deity, of 'transcendence'. This tethers 'divinity' firmly and finally to the cross, and so identifies the creative and salutary power of God incarnate with *kenosis*, weakness, humility, suffering and vicarious responsible action – in short, with being-for-others even unto death. The first repair glosses Chalcedon by way a theology of the cross. Such a Christology is crucially concerned with the 'question of God', committed to identifying the crucial discrimen which differentiates between God and not-God, between God and the gods. That discrimen is the reality of divine 'being-for-others' epitomized in God's assumption of humanity in Jesus Christ, the dynamics of which render *this* human existence uniquely 'real' and 'true' as a human 'being-for-others'.[45] Bonhoeffer, it seems, understood this to be fundamental to a more fully evangelized discourse about God with deep roots in – as well as consequences for – Christology.

It is repaired, second, by an exhaustive interest in the figure of the man Jesus as the one Christological reality whose mystery is properly opaque to further analysis in terms of divine and human natures as such. Bonhoeffer's late Christology faithfully honours the imperative conclusion of the 1933 lectures: namely that Christological thinking must 'not begin with the two natures in isolation, but rather with the fact that Jesus Christ is God. The *is* may not be interpreted any further. It has been established by God …'.[46] Bonhoeffer largely maintains his disciplined disinterest in the question of the two natures, concentrating instead upon the single identity of Jesus as God for us. Yet, the late Christological sketch does, as we have seen, speak of the true humanity of Jesus – his being-for-others – as arising out of God's own being-for-others which is the hallmark of genuine divine freedom, and so of true deity. While not a retreat into two-natures speculation, to be sure, this does suggest a judgement on Bonhoeffer's part that doing justice to the 'Who?' question in Christology admits – even requires – some account of the divine source of the

---

44. DBWE 3:111–4 (DBW 3:102–6).

45. This direction had already been intimated in the 1933 lectures when Bonhoeffer remarks that 'If we speak of the human being Jesus Christ as we speak of God we should not speak of him as representing an idea of God, that is, in his attributes as all-knowing and all-powerful but rather speak of his weakness', DBWE 12:254 (DBW 12:226).

46. DBWE 12:350 (DBW 12:336).

Saviour's true humanity. Certain claims about the priority, agency, graciousness and self-humbling of God are analytic, so to speak, in the identity description of Jesus Christ – the man for others and so *vere homo* – as the one in whom God takes up human being. The reason to elaborate these claims, even if only minimally, is precisely to honour the 'fact that Jesus Christ is God' and its entailments. In this, Bonhoeffer contributes to a tradition of Lutheran Christological doctrine committed 'to interpret the reality of God by what happens with Jesus: by his "flesh", the historical actuality of one man. Christology in the Lutheran movement works to put God "deep" in that flesh: to assert without qualification that as God meets us in the human Jesus, so God *is*'.[47] With its intense witness to the lordship of Jesus the man-for-others and the Crucified One – a 'lordship which strangely disqualifies all other lordships' as Bethge emphasizes[48] – Bonhoeffer's late Christology shares in this work, for it too looks to 'put God "deep" in that flesh' of the man Jesus in the actuality of his being-for-others.

Much of the essence of these two lines of argument is artfully expressed in the poem, 'Christians and Heathens' which accompanied Bonhoeffer's letter of 8 July 1944.[49] In its second stanza God is described boldly as 'in need', 'poor, reviled, without shelter or bread', 'devoured by sin, weakness, and death' and afflicted by 'pain'.[50] Each of these theological predicates and all of them taken together are obviously derived from the enacted pro-existence of Jesus Christ attested in the New Testament. In this way the poem performs a *theologia crucis* in miniature, looking as it does exclusively to 'comprehend the visible and manifest things of God seen through suffering and the cross'.[51] It describes the concrete form of divine self-humbling by means of which God 'goes to all people in their need' to feed 'body and soul with God's own bread' and to 'forgive' as the third stanza puts it. The divine identity and the form of divine movement attested here are utterly Christological in their conception. Bonhoeffer gives terse poetic expression to the second distinctive claim we have identified: namely that it is precisely *in* and *as* the human pro-existence of Jesus Christ that the divine pro-existence is encountered, known and owned. The single Christological fact that 'Jesus Christ is

---

47. Eric W. Gritsch and Robert W. Jenson, *Lutheranism: The Theological Movement and Its Confessional Writings* (Philadelphia: Fortress, 1976), 106.

48. Bethge, *Bonhoeffer: Exile and Martyr*, 150.

49. All citations from the poem that follow are from DBWE 8:460-1 (DBW 8:515-16). For discussion see Jürgen Henkys, *Dietrich Bonhoeffers Gefängnisgedichte. Beiträge zu ihrer Interpretation* (Berlin: Evangelische Verlagsanstalt Berlin, 1986), 57-65, and Bernd Wannenwetsch, '"Christians and Pagans": Toward a Trans-Religious Second Naïveté or How to Be a Christological Creature', in *Who Am I? Bonhoeffer's Theology through His Poetry*, ed. B. Wannenwetsch (London: T&T Clark, 2009), 175-96.

50. DBWE 8:461 (DBW 8:515).

51. Thesis 20 of Martin Luther, 'The Heidelberg Disputation', in *The Selected Writings of Martin Luther, 1517-1520*, ed. Theodore G. Tappert (Minneapolis: Fortress, 2007), 66, 78.

God' dominates Bonhoeffer's interest, precisely *because* of this acknowledgement of its internal architecture. All this is 'owned' in faith, that total life act in which, as Bonhoeffer strikingly writes, 'Christians stand by God in God's own pain', a clear reiteration of the definition of faith as 'sharing in the sufferings of God at the hands of godless world', offered elsewhere in the letters. For Bonhoeffer, this seemingly extraordinary human act hopes to 'honour God as manifested in his works' and is itself made possible only because 'Jesus's being-for-others *is* the experience of transcendence'.[52]

III. Conclusion

Writing in his *Ethics* Bonhoeffer remarks: 'What is decisive here is only *that there is a genuine worldliness only and precisely because of the proclamation of the cross of Jesus Christ*'.[53] We have seen that precisely this constructive connection between Jesus Christ, the Crucified One, and the question of genuine worldliness lies close to the heart of the Christological reflections to be found in *Letters and Papers from Prison*. The 'new' question of this late Christology – 'Who is Jesus Christ actually for us today?' – is formulated precisely at the point where acknowledgement of the responsible secularity of a 'world come of age' and pursuit of a better evangelization of the received concept of God intersect. This intersection is also the place from which Bonhoeffer's critique of religion emerges. This critique is motivated firmly from frank recognition of the historical contingency of religion as an exigent 'way of being in the world' rather than an anthropological given (*homo religiosis*). But its even deeper and more decisive mainspring lies in the contradiction of human religiosity by the uninvited and unsettling self-humbling movement of God come low in Jesus Christ in the concretion of divine transcendence *in* and *as* the pro-existence of this man. This movement is the 'messianic suffering of God in Jesus Christ'[54] into which the Christian is drawn in faith. Of course, this messianic movement into suffering – which for Bonhoeffer just is the transcendence of the God of the Gospel – meets with not only religious but also irreligious resistance: God bears the repudiation of a world replete with gods, to be sure, but as Bonhoeffer poignantly records here, God also 'suffers at the hands of a godless world'.[55] This is the cost of divine pro-existence as this becomes concrete in the pro-existence of the man Jesus. Christology is the school wherein Christians contemplate the humanity and humility of their God.

Indeed, the Christology of *Letters and Papers from Prison* is itself an experiment in the 'non-religious interpretation of biblical concepts'. For here, Bonhoeffer thinks and speaks of God become human in Christ, as 'the opposite of

---

52. Luther, 'The Heidelberg Disputation', 78.
53. DBWE 6:401 (DBW 6:405). Emphasis original.
54. DBWE 8:481 (DBW 8:536).
55. DBWE 8:480 (DBW 8:535). See Krötke, '"Sharing in God's Suffering": Dietrich Bonhoeffer's Understanding of a "Religionless Christianity"', 158–60.

everything a religious person expects from God'.[56] Lifted out of religious strictures, Christ no longer appears as a miraculous solution – a *deus ex machina* – to the insoluble puzzles and intractable problems which encircle life at its margins. Rather, decoupled from the demands of human religiosity, Christ confronts responsible secular women and men in the midst of their lives just as the Gospels tell of him: as Jesus of Nazareth, the man for others and just so as the man of sorrows, the *stellvertretende* servant of all, whose pro-existence without remainder takes him to the cross. In this Jesus stands as that which is 'manifest and visible' of God, a truly human one whose true humanity has as its own source and guarantee true transcendence, i.e., true divine freedom to be *pro alium*.[57]

Sharing in this humanity means sharing in the positive freedom and so also in the suffering of God; in this lies the great vocation of the worldly faith of the future Bonhoeffer espies from his prison cell. Acknowledgement of the actual humanity of Christ as the very enactment and so revelation of God's own being for us [*das Fürsein Gottes*] is the key. There could be no dissolving of Christology into anthropology: Bonhoeffer maintains to the end that 'the experience of transcendence is to be sought not simply in being-for-others but in *Jesus'* being-for-others'.[58] Bonhoeffer's emphasis on the concretely enacted, personal, and so relational identity of Jesus distilled into the formula, 'being there for others', may represent a distinct – and distinctly important – contribution to modern Christology. As Christoph Schwöbel observes, Jesus' humanity is 'underdetermined when it just interpreted as factual humanity or as individual archetypal humanity. Dietrich Bonhoeffer's view of the pro-existence of Jesus … seems to point in the right direction when it sees the humanity of Jesus as the way in which true humanity is communicated to those who encounter him'.[59]

We have suggested that in all this, the 'new' Christology of Bonhoeffer's prison writings is also and in virtue of just these features an effort 'to carry on' in a 'Chalcedonian sense'. He sustains a disciplined interest in the man Jesus Christ as the irreducible 'christological fact', i.e., as the single subject of Christological discourse whose identity admits no further conceptual dissolution into a two-natures discourse. If the paradoxes of the Chalcedonian Definition itself, rightly barred *this* path, they did at the same time, in Bonhoeffer's judgement, authorize and inaugurate another kind of Christological reflection which sets out precisely

---

56. DBWE 8:480 (DBW 8:535).

57. 'If one considers the popularity of Dietrich Bonhoeffer's phrase that God suffers with us, one is tempted to speak of a new dogma of divine passibility in the twentieth century', Christoph Schwöbel, 'The Generosity of the Triune God and the Humility of the Son', in *Kenosis: The Self-Emptying of Christ in Scripture and Theology*, ed. Paul T. Nimmo and Keith L. Johnson (Grand Rapids: Eerdmans, 2022), 270.

58. Rainer Mayer, 'Christology: The Genuine Form of Transcendence', in *A Bonhoeffer Legacy: Essays in Understanding*, ed. A. J. Klassen (Grand Rapids: Eerdmans, 1981), 189.

59. Christoph Schwöbel, 'The Generosity of the Triune God and the Humility of the Son', 283.

from the irreducible fact and mystery of Christ. Bonhoeffer's denomination of Jesus as 'the man for others' and his associated thinking concerning divine and human pro-existence, humility, and suffering are precisely an exercise in this kind of reflection.

As we have noted, in all this Christology remains for Bonhoeffer a discourse at the heart of which is the question of God. One crucial upshot of his late Christology is an evangelical specification of the nature of deity as self-humbling pro-existence – an insight won from Christological reflection but then, reflexively, also one seen to be fundamental to acknowledging and bespeaking the origin and depth and consequences of Jesus's true humanity. The witness to divine love as the indelible positive form of divine freedom first announced in *Act and Being* is reiterated and culminates in the 'new Christological formula' at the heart of the correspondence of the summer of 1944, namely 'Jesus, the man for others'. For Bonhoeffer, invocation of divine self-humbling and suffering is not a conceptual device by means of which to resolve the metaphysical puzzle of Christ's two natures. It is rather a concise republication of the dynamic form of Christ's being as a being for us without reserve as attested in scripture. It names the fundamental shape and manner of his lordship as *humilitas*, lifting it up as the defining quality of the One who, in faith, 'we must hear, trust, and obey in life and in death' (Barmen I).

Part II

JESUS CHRIST: VERE HOMO, VERE DEUS

Chapter 6

BEING HUMAN IN LIGHT OF CHALCEDON: THE NECESSARY POSSIBILITY OF BEING ONE

Nadine Hamilton

I. Demigod Nor Divinely Mutated Human – on the 'Unity' of the 'Natures'

The dogma of Chalcedon with its elaboration of the doctrine of two natures is the founding document of dogmatic Christology and can therefore be understood as its constitutive moment. Even today this pointed emphasis on God's will to salvation in his incarnation in Jesus Christ is used as a reference for the dogmatic elaboration of Christology. Although there are voices in Germany who seek to distance themselves from the Chalcedonian doctrine of two natures,[1] it remains the undisputed foundation of Christology – for their opponents, of course, only in the fact that it serves as a counter-foil for their new perspective on Christology from a supposedly more intellectually respectable basis. Such theologians have often criticized (amongst other things) the Chalcedonian concepts of 'physis' and 'hypostasis' as particularly unintelligible to modern thought, and perhaps even theologically counterproductive in their own time.

One of these sceptics is Christian Danz, the chair of Protestant Systematic Theology at the University of Vienna.[2] His argument presents the elaboration of Christology, from its origin in the doctrine of two natures, as an infiltration of the biblical linguistic world by the metaphysics of Greek philosophy, mostly of middle Platonism.[3] Danz identifies this transformation particularly in the concept of 'nature' and its consequent theory of the 'person' of Jesus Christ as God-human.[4]

---

1. For example, Friedrich Schleiermacher and Adolf von Harnack leading to Christian Danz. Christoph Schwöbel speaks of the 'crisis in Christology', which he, amongst others, identifies in the two-natures doctrine. See Schwöbel, 'Christology and Trinitarian Thought', in *Trinitarian Theology Today: Essays on Divine Being and Act*, ed. Christoph Schwöbel (Edinburgh: T&T Clark, 1995), 113–46, 116.
2. See Christian Danz, *Grundprobleme der Christologie* (Tübingen: Mohr Siebeck, 2013), 106.
3. See ibid., 55.
4. See ibid., 190.

His criticism, therefore, questions the emphasis on the unity of two 'natures', as such 'unity' is logically impossible due to the incompatible components on which it is based – God and human. As a consequence, the doctrine has never been consistent, he argues, neither then nor now.[5] Accordingly, Danz understands the presentation of the history of Christology as a tracing of the wrong paths taken by patristic and medieval theology, which not only have 'proven to require a revision under the conditions of knowledge of modernity'[6], but had already led to obvious aporias and dead-ends in the doctrine's earliest development.[7] In contrast, he presents his own understanding as a success story that began with the Enlightenment and which left behind the old dogmatic interpretation of Jesus Christ as a 'God-human'[8] to change the perspective from a Christology based on theories of the person and work of Christ to one based on a 'self-representation of understanding the human being in relationship with itself'.[9]

Even if Danz's approach itself appears problematic because he does not present any developed constructive Christology but instead a departure from the content of Christology itself,[10] he rightly points to a problem faced by everyone engaged in contemporary Christology: namely the postulation of the unity of two components that by their very definitions are incompatible (at least traditionally understood): God and human nature. But how then can we speak, with Chalcedon, of a unity of these two natures? Is it not therefore necessary to agree with Danz that a Christology that bases all of its insights on the unity of two incompatible components has always been obsolete, and that this is especially apparent after the advent of modernity? Must not today's Christology turn away from its old foundation and look for new paths, as Danz does?

I should say in advance that take issue with the wording of the wording of these questions. Danz's fundamental criticism of Christology and the Chalcedonian doctrine of two natures should be taken seriously. However, his objections seem to point out something other than what Danz is getting at, for they do not so much question the unity itself, but rather the terms with which this 'unity' – whatever it may be – is construed. What I want to point out with Danz's argument is, therefore, our frequently unreflective use of the terms 'nature' and 'person', and in this context probably also the term 'unity' itself. What do we mean when we talk about the 'nature' of God and the 'nature' of humanity? Is it about properties or is it about

---

5. See ibid., 1.
6. Ibid., 193.
7. See ibid., 79.
8. Ibid., 193.
9. Ibid., 240; find similar quotes at 203, 204, 205, 208, 217, 210, 220, 221, 231, 237, 239, 240. Danz repeats the formulation of 'understanding oneself' in almost identical form, without actually exploring and clarifying it in detail in his elaboration.

10. Danz programmatically asks the question whether 'a Christology without Jesus [is] possible' (ibid., 205–6. Danz cites Christian Wenz, *Christus: Jesus und die Anfänge der Christologie*, [Göttingen: Vandenhoeck & Ruprecht, 2011], 74).

physical characteristics? Is it a (materialistic substance-ontological[11]) distillation of the genera 'god' and 'human', which are then mixed, glued or juxtaposed in the 'unity' of the 'person'? If so, how should such a distillation be understood? I do not want to linger here on these questions as they are presently phrased, as it should be clear that such questioning will soon come to a dead end. For we cannot speak of an abstract 'nature' of God or humanity. Rather, it turns out that any definition of the 'nature' of God and the 'nature' of humanity goes astray and that, as accounts show, this was already the case at the time of the doctrine's emergence. At the same time, it should not be forgotten that the semantic content of the term 'nature' or 'physis' has changed since the doctrine was first developed.[12] Thus, in my opinion, contrary to Danz's assessment, the difficulty lies initially less in the 'unity' of the 'natures' than it does in the two underlying components of this 'unity'.

In this context, the possible overemphasis of one component over against the other, namely the divine and human natures, in this 'unity' must then be regarded as a consequence of the fact that they are unclearly defined rather than of the 'unity' itself. Only in a second step does it come into view. Then, of course, it is absolutely necessary to avoid claiming that Jesus Christ mutates into a demigod, or that a divine being mutates into a human, in this 'unity'.[13] Both 'natures' are to be preserved in their integrity; this is what Chalcedon emphasizes, and only in this way the events of salvation can be understood according to Scripture. Jesus Christ is God, but he does not resemble a God in his 'nature'; he is a human being, but he does not resemble an abstract 'nature' of humanity. If one follows Danz's criticism, however, it is inherent in the Christological doctrinal form itself, as a 'birth defect'[14] as he calls it, that the 'construction of the unity of a person from a divine and a human nature … is possible only in such a way that one of the

---

11. Substance is understood here in the sense of an almost material-factual occurrence. Of course, it can be questioned whether such a materialistic concept is not anachronistic. See, for example, Aristotle's understanding of substance. The concept of substance could in this understanding be helpful to understand the patristic use of terms as 'nature' and 'unity' in a deeper sense, as it is not a third person observation.

12. Coakley states that the precise meaning of the terms 'physis' and 'person' always has been unclear in the document of Chalcedon even though these terms 'had a pre-history' that 'was an ambiguous one and the "Definition" does not clear up the ambiguity.' (Sarah Coakley, 'What Does Chalcedon Solve and What Does It Not? Some Reflections on the Status and Meaning of the Chalcedonian "Definition"', in *The Incarnation: An Interdisciplinary Symposium on the Incarnation of the Son of God*, ed. Stephen T. Davis, Daniel Kendall SJ and Gerald O'Collins [Oxford: Oxford University Press, 2018], 143–63, 148.)

13. Danz bases his account of the early development of the dogma and beyond on Harnack's *Lehrbuch der Dogmengeschichte* and his *Grundriß der Dogmengeschichte* and largely agrees with Harnack's judgements on the development of the dogma. See Danz, Grundprobleme, 55; see especially 61–85.

14. Ibid., 106.

two natures is eliminated'.[15] Accordingly, for the history of theology, he sees 'the humanity within the framework of the doctrine of two natures' evaporating and not getting beyond a 'mere assertion of the humanity of Christ'.[16] If this assessment is correct, however, then the question that remains concerning Danz is how God's incarnation should be meaningfully spoken of. How is this 'unity' to be grasped without abstracting and/or weakening or evaporating the components? How can we speak of Jesus Christ as *true* God and a *true* human being? Should Jesus' humanity[17] not be understood differently than ours, if his 'person' is a unity of God and human?[18]

My initial answer to the last question is 'no', although I will go on to qualify this. It is the basic claim of the doctrine of two natures that God becomes *fully* human in Jesus Christ and that his humanity is fully our humanity. Jesus Christ is *truly* human, therefore he alone can save us humans and the whole creation. At the same time, however, the foremost question of the Church Fathers was how to avoid worshipping a human being for salvation. It is therefore also important to keep in mind that Chalcedon was not concerned with a formulation of an abstract theory, but with a directive for worship. Accordingly, it was up for discussion on how to speak of this man in a way that was not idolatry. It must be stated, on the other hand, that Jesus' humanity differs from our humanity because he is *truly* human and we are not (at least anymore). When we speak of the two 'natures' united in Jesus Christ, it is mainly the *divine* 'nature' that seems to cause us problems – and indeed it does – but we pretend to know what the *human* 'nature' means too quickly. However, as has already been shown, it is not at all easy to get to the heart of what constitutes our human 'nature'. What does it mean to be human, and what does it particularly mean in the God-human Jesus Christ? This question, obviously, cannot stand on its own but has strong ethical implications. Only when humanity is rightfully understood can we understand what community is and what its constitution is. If Chalcedon originated in the domain of worship, then its 'definition' has a political impact, because it establishes a conception of the communion of God and human beings. I would now like to take a closer look at this.

It should first be noted that in the case of Danz, the basic problem of Chalcedonian Christology (then and now) can be characterized on the one hand, in terms of content – in the 'unity' of two diametrically different 'natures' – and

---

15. Ibid., 106–7. Danz refers to Friedrich Daniel Ernst Schleiermacher, *Der christliche Glaube 1821–1822*, vol. 2, (Berlin/New York: De Gruyter, 1984), §117.1, 35 and Friedrich Daniel Ernst Schleiermacher, *Der christliche Glaube nach den Grundzügen der Evangelischen Kirche im Zusammenhange dargestellt* (1830/31), vol. 2, (Berlin/New York: De Gruyter, 1999), §96.1, 53–4; as well as to Wolfhart Pannenberg, *Grundzüge der Christologie*, 2nd ed., (Gütersloh: Gütersloher Verlagshaus, 1966), 295.

16. Danz, *Grundprobleme*, 109.

17. In German, the difference between abstraction and concretion can be depicted well by the terms 'Menschheit' and 'Menschsein'.

18. The same applies, of course, to his being God. However, this is a separate discussion.

on the other, formally – in the concepts of 'nature' and the 'unity' of the 'person'. Both facets of the Chalcedonian dogma require a deep examination of the classical locus *De personae Christi*. I would like to pursue this, especially concerning Jesus' human 'nature'. For this purpose, a first step must consider what Chalcedon solves and what it does not. Sarah Coakley, in her essay of the same title, has presented a very striking elaboration on how Chalcedon is to be understood as the beginning of a conversation and framework[19] for discussion about the nature of the God-man of Jesus Christ, which still has to be the basic principle of Christian theology today. To do this, however, it is necessary to look more closely at the formation of the doctrines of an- and enhypostasia that follow Chalcedon, because they lead deeper into the traditional understanding of the person of Jesus Christ. I would like to examine whether, based on this, it is also possible for contemporary Christology to describe the true humanity of Jesus Christ. It will become clear that a meaningful further reflection on the question of human 'nature' must necessarily begin with these conceptions, but must not stop there. In turning away from the 'how' to the 'who' question of the person of Jesus Christ with the doctrines of an- and enhypostasia, Bonhoeffer re-describes the problem of the doctrines by rejecting all attempts to construct and abstract a God-human.[20] From there he works out an understanding of the humanity of Jesus Christ that grasps Jesus Christ's humanity as *our* true humanity solely in the foundation of our being in the triune God.

II. The concept of 'nature' and its 'definition'

In her essay, Sarah Coakley explores the 'apparently innocent and simple question',[21] as she calls it, of 'what sort of statement this statement about Christ is'.[22] She sees this question as 'a question of some subtlety and importance which is nonetheless often overlooked in contemporary Anglo-American' and we can add German 'philosophical debates about the Chalcedonian "definition" of 451'.[23] Accordingly, she identifies the fundamental 'error' of different theological trajectories in their treatment of Chalcedon in the fact that they established the doctrine of the two natures as a 'definition' and thus introduced a propositional character into

---

19. See similar to Coakley's approach: Christoph Schwöbel, 'Die Trinitätslehre als Rahmentheorie', in *Gott in Beziehung: Studien zur Dogmatik*, ed. Christoph Schwöbel (Tübingen: Mohr Siebeck, 2002), 25–51.
20. See DBWE 12:302–4 (DBW 12:281–5). Bonhoeffer even seems to reject the concept of the *enhypostasia* as it implies, as Rowan Williams points out, 'that something is lacking in Jesus' humanity', in Rowan Williams, *Christ the Heart of Creation* (London: Bloomsbury, 2018), 193n57.
21. Coakley, 'Chalcedon', 144.
22. Ibid., 143–4.
23. Ibid., 143.

Chalcedon's claims so that the terms 'nature' and 'person' would be understood correspondingly as something static and substance-ontological.[24] She, on the other hand, elaborates 'a properly *apophatic* reading of the "definition" that understands Chalcedon as the "horizon" (*horos*) of defining what can, and cannot, be said'.[25] In doing so, the term 'horizon', with its original semantic field of 'boundary', 'horizon' and 'demarcation', as well as its later development to mean 'standard', 'pattern' and (monastic) 'rule',[26] provides itself the horizon for her answer to the question of what *kind of theology* Chalcedon wants to accomplish and what kind it does not.

With this semantic background, Coakley is not only able to explain the bishops' refusal of the emperor's demand for more precision,[27] but also to point out that in this text a complete systematic exposition of Christology was intended even less than a complete and precise metaphysics of the figure of Christ. Rather, she sees the text as drawing a 'line' between what could and could not be said. Accordingly, she recognizes in this admittedly *vague* definition a nevertheless *distinct* demarcation against divergent interpretations of Christ,[28] a *clear* speech regulation to distinguish duality (*physis*) and unity (*hypostasis*) in Christ, and a *deepened* (if more undefined) understanding of reality through the 'paradox' of the negatives. Accordingly, Coakley can conclude that the intention of the Chalcedonian Creed, and with it the two-nature 'doctrine', was precisely not a doctrine in the sense of a fixed dogma but instead an 'apophatic' document that did not seek to explain or grasp the reality to which it referred.[29] Following Chalcedon, she thus understands the two 'natures' of Christ in one 'hypostasis', not as a specifying 'definition' but as a shimmering (though still normative) 'horizon' to which one must constantly return, but which equally demands constant further thinking in all directions. Coakley is also able to identify clearly the problem at hand for this argument: in contrast to the East, which always understood Chalcedon as a moment (albeit a decisive one) in the Christological clarification process that continued in the following centuries, she sees the West as tending from the beginning to stop at Chalcedon and to expect from it something metaphysically and substantially more precise than was ultimately given. In her view, the West makes demands on the document which the document itself, however, never intended to fulfil: it does not seek to establish what human and divine physis consist of, nor does it seek to specify what hypostasis means when applied to Christ. Moreover, it does not seek to explain how hypostasis and physis, or how the physeis, are related to each other.[30]

---

24. A similar understanding of Chalcedon can also be found at Williams, Christ, 88. Williams therefore points out: 'Like most or many formulae of settlement, Chalcedon defines an agenda rather than a solution to the problems that have generated it.'

25. Coakley, 'Chalcedon', 144.

26. Coakly refers to Lampe's *Patristic Lexicon*.

27. Coakley, 'Chalcedon', 158.

28. Such as Apollinarianism, Eutychianism and extreme Nestorianism.

29. See ibid., 161. See also, ibid., 162.

30. Ibid., 162.

What is thus apparent with Coakley's interpretation is, first, that Chalcedon and its development of the two 'natures' of Christ in one 'person' should not be expected to provide a specific and precise answer to pressing Christological questions. Rather, the intention of the text, which is often pejoratively (mis-) understood as a compromise must be taken seriously precisely because it is not a narrow definition, but rather a realm of conversation that has been opened up. Chalcedon and its so-called 'two-nature doctrine' must be understood with Coakley as an invitation to reflect on God's presence in Jesus Christ in the world. In doing so, Chalcedon, in its apophatic manner, makes clear at the same time that there cannot be one 'correct' interpretation, but that different approaches should and can be brought into conversation with one another. If understood in this way, Chalcedon is in fact a boundary and an expanded horizon at the same time. The constructive approach presented in the following elaboration is understood as just that: a broadening of the realm given by Chalcedon with the doctrine of two natures; as a reflection on the given possibilities of speaking of the 'natures' and their 'unity' in the 'person' of Jesus Christ; and as a proposal for how, with Chalcedon as the horizon of understanding, the language of Jesus Christ's humanity can be appropriate and relevant today.

III. The true *humanity of Jesus Christ*

According to Coakley's argument, the difficulty of the Chalcedonian doctrine of two natures lies in the fact that we (always) demand an unambiguous answer and thus a fixed definition of the nature of the God-man Jesus Christ from this document. However, we thereby ask something of the text that it itself does not offer. Chalcedon, in its doctrine of two natures, does not intend to define the 'nature' of the God-man Jesus Christ; it does not intend to *define how* God can be human and how this particular humanity is then to be elaborated. Rather, as Coakley makes wonderfully clear in her treatment of Chalcedon's propositional intent, the doctrine intends to open a discourse whose realm is delineated, in the sense of a 'horizon', by the text itself. The exploration of this realm, however, is left to the believers themselves. The history of theology that follows Chalcedon seems to be such a discourse, but it also seems to me that there is always a need to define this realm in terms of its inventory.

The doctrines of an- and enhypostasia that followed Chalcedon seem to do just that.[31] To make the unity of both natures conceivable, the doctrine of the Logos as the person-forming hypostasis of both natures was added to the doctrine along with the elaboration of the concept of hypostasis. The negatively accentuated view of the doctrine was thus to be positively balanced in the formulation of the union of the two natures. It was understood to be the 'chief way in which to conceive the

---

31. See Ingolf Dalferth, *Der auferweckte Gekreuzigte: Zur Grammatik der Christologie* (Tübingen: Mohr Siebeck, 1994), 144.

unique yet real humanity of Christ',[32] as British theologian Colin Gunton points out, whose approach to Christology itself relies on an engagement with these two doctrines.[33] In the context of the interpretation of the doctrine of two natures, the doctrine of an- and enhypostasia occupies a central place in that it expresses the initiative and prerogative of God. It is emphasized that the person-forming moment of the human being Jesus of Nazareth is the Logos, the second person of the Trinitarian God, who takes the anhypostatic, i.e. non-personal human nature of Mary into himself and thus in the enhypostasia into the divine community in the Logos.

Today, these doctrines seem difficult to understand, and their significance for contemporary Christology appears questionable. Not infrequently, therefore, these doctrinal formations are passed over or considered superfluous, as Danz's argument presented at the beginning shows. However, these doctrines should not be jettisoned too hastily, as I believe that with them a clear perspective is offered on what we need for a constructive interpretation of Christology today. I would therefore like to look again at what these doctrines have to offer and what they do not. If taken biblically, the concepts of an- and enhypostasia seek to express the unique yet real humanity of Jesus Christ.[34] Both terms thereby point to how the one hypostasis of Jesus Christ can be understood in relation to history and creation on the one hand and God on the other.[35] This doctrine attempts to grasp the duality of the unity in the fact that the basis of the person of Jesus Christ is found not only in the finite processes of the world: by ascribing the initiative to God the Son, this doctrine also resists any deification of the human being Jesus. Enhypostasia, on the other hand, complements the negative aspect of anhypostasia – that Jesus' humanity does not have the same basis as that of human beings per se – positively: the person of Jesus Christ, his unique historical being, has its basis in the Son and the new act of the humanity of the eternal Son. Jesus is the eternal Son made flesh.[36]

Accordingly, what an- and enhypostasia want to convey is the gospel's message that in Jesus Christ we encounter God in God's redemptive presence in the Word made flesh. However, as interpretations in the tradition and the present show, caution is also required in order that these categories do not lead to a denial of the humanity of Jesus, even as they were originally established to avoid precisely this. For my question about the humanity of Jesus Christ, they retain their significance at least in that they point to the core soteriological problem of Christian theology by asking to what extent the redemption of all people can happen through this

---

32. Colin Gunton, *Christ and Creation* (Grand Rapids, MI: Eerdmans, 1992), 47.

33. See ibid., §2, 35–68.

34. See Thomas Torrance, *Incarnation: The Person and Life of Christ* (Downers Grove, IL: IVP Academic, 2008), 84.

35. See Gunton, *Christ and Creation*, 47. See also Bruce McCormack, 'The Person of Christ', in *Mapping Modern Theology: A Thematic and Historical Introduction*, ed. Kelly M. Kapic and Bruce McCormack (Grand Rapids, MI: Baker Academic, 2012), 149–73, 152.

36. See Gunton, *Christ and Creation*, 47–8.

one human being. The problem as well as the answer that these terms describe, therefore, lie within the question of how Jesus' humanity differs from the humanity of all other human beings so that in this humanity the work of reconciliation can be accomplished.

The doctrines of an- and enhypostasia can also serve to help to answer the question of Jesus Christ's humanity. I have already highlighted that the question concerning the human 'nature' of Jesus Christ and to what extent this 'nature' is also our 'nature' is not an easy one to answer. Frequently this distinction has been located in Jesus Christ's sinlessness. Often it is said that 'he is of one substance with ourselves, sin apart'.[37] However, this assumes that the *true* human 'nature' is a 'nature' without sin and thus without any possibility of sinning at all,[38] which this distorts our picture of human 'nature'. The New Testament temptation stories would not describe true *temptations* if Jesus Christ's human 'nature' could not actually fall prey to such temptations.[39] Accordingly, the difference between Jesus Christ's humanity from our humanity cannot be captured in his sinlessness.

Rather, it appears to be necessary to see this humanity in its particularity in the fact that this human being does not receive his humanity from himself but for God, and this is what the doctrines of an- and enhypostasia intend to emphasize. Consequently, these teachings can only speak of *true* humanity because this humanity *receives* its true form through its unity with the divine 'nature'. Thus, it is not a matter of understanding true humanity as our humanity minus sin; true humanity, on the contrary, is humanity distinguished by an extraordinary relationship with God.[40]

But how is this *extraordinary relationship* with God to be understood? Recent Christologies, such as Gunton's, attempt to circumvent this problem by expressing the distinctiveness of the humanity of Jesus Christ in the unique directedness of his life through the Holy Spirit.[41] The difference that Gunton rightly perceives in the directionality of the life of Jesus Christ in relation to all other human beings is hence not expressed negatively as sinlessness, but positively as faithfulness to God: as a human being in true relationship with God. This, he argues, is where the

---

37. Ibid., 41.

38. As Bonhoeffer writes in DBWE 3:119n9 (DBW 3:111n8): "'To be able to sin" and "not to be able to sin." The differentiation between *posse peccare* or *posse non peccare* (as applying before the fall), *non posse non peccare* (after the fall), and *non posse peccare* (the eschatological prospect) was developed by Augustine in his dispute with Pelagius.' See Adolf von Harnack, *History of Dogma*, on Augustine, vol. 4 (New York: Russell & Russel, 1958), 175–80; see also DBWE 2:145–6 (DBW 2:143–4.).

39. See Gunton, *Christ and Creation*, 53–5.

40. This says something about our understanding of being human in general. True humanity does not mean, as we traditionally formulate it clearly in this area in particular, human nature *minus* sin, but fallen humanity means human nature *plus* sin. I think this small but subtle difference has far-reaching consequences for anthropology as well.

41. See ibid., 50–9.

answer to the question posed by the doctrines of an- and enhypostasia must begin, and as a result, '[t]he weaknesses of the enhypostasia teaching are alleviated, if not removed'.[42] If Gunton understands the Holy Spirit as the perfecter of creation, he sees the Spirit also perfecting the human 'nature' of Jesus Christ: 'Just as the enhypostasia reminds us of the origin of our salvation in the eternal love and action of God, so attention to the Holy Spirit reminds us of how the saving action of Jesus is accomplished humanly in time. Too much stress on either can lose essential dimensions of the gospel.'[43]

As appropriate and important as I find the emphasis on the activity of the Holy Spirit at this point, however, two things should be kept in mind:[44] although the emphasis on God, the Spirit, is eminently important for the differentiation of the doctrine of the two natures, not all emphasis should be placed on the initiative of the Father in the Spirit alone.[45] For in doing so, one would risk substituting the Logos as the basis of the humanity of Jesus Christ, as classically expressed by enhypostasia, for the Spirit. Moreover, in such an interpretation lies the problem of understanding the Incarnation apart from the Logos[46] – a reading that causes difficulties especially Trinitarianly,[47] when according to Trinitarian understandings the works of the triune God are economically not to be assigned to a single hypostasis alone, but rather the one triune God is always involved in all works.[48] Likewise, for a Trinitarian interpretation of the 'unity' of the two 'natures', the Spirit cannot be ignored.

Nevertheless, one problem remains with the doctrines of an- and enhypostasia which cannot be avoided. If both doctrines try to express that Jesus Christ cannot have two hypostases, but rather only one, the only conclusion remains that the

---

42. Ibid., 50.

43. Ibid., 50. Gunton illustrates this balance of divine grounding and, at the same time, guidance by the Spirit in four examples from the life of Jesus: Virgin birth, baptismal account, temptation stories, and resurrection (50–9).

44. See therefore my forthcoming book: *Eine Ontologie des Namens Gottes: Zur Wiedergewinnung christologischer Grundgedanken*.

45. However, that seems to me to be the case in the Spirit Christologies that are relatively popular today. See Marco Hofheinz inquiry: Marco Hofheinz, 'Der geistgesalbte Christus: Trinitätstheologische Erwägungen zur umstrittenen Geistchristologie', in *Evangelische Theologie* 72 (2012): 337–56.

46. This is particularly evident in Gunton's summary quote on the virgin birth and the cross. See Gunton, *Christ and Creation*, 59.

47. See Schwöbel's argument, with which I agree, that the 'crisis in modern Christology is due to the neglect of the trinitarian logic of the Christian understanding of God and its implications for the Christian understanding of what it means to be human'. See Schwöbel, *Christology*, 120.

48. See Ernstpeter Maurer's wonderful elaboration of the reciprocal co-originality of the three Trinitarian hypostases in: Ernstpeter Maurer, *Der lebendige Gott: Texte zur Trinitätslehre* (Gütersloh: Gütersloher Verlagshaus, 1999), 48–50.

human 'nature' has its hypostasis in the divine one. Yet is this not exactly an example of what has already been presented above as one of the basic problems resulting from the doctrine of two natures, namely, of two entities made into one? In this understanding of an- and enhypostasia, are not human and divine 'nature' understood as two entities standing side by side, which are to be united into one? With this, however, the question arises as to whether an answer can be found to the problem posed by the doctrines of an- and enhypostasia, or whether they necessarily lead to substance-ontological thinking, which understands both 'natures' as two entities, in the modern understanding: subjects,[49] from which it is somehow necessary to make one?

The underlying difficulty of the doctrinal formation of an- and enhypostasia lies, in my opinion, in understanding both 'natures' as equivalent, i.e. as concretions of the underlying abstractions 'humanity' and 'divinity', which are differentiated from one another as parallel categories.[50] Ultimately, this is the problem faced by Gunton's approach to enhypostasia in the Spirit. In any case, an equal weighting of the two natures in the traditional interpretation is not only at the expense of Jesus Christ's humanity but also at the expense of his concrete *being human*. To do justice to the problem and the question of the doctrines of an- and enhypostasia, however, it, therefore, seems necessary to leave both behind, because it cannot be a matter of understanding Jesus Christ as the addition of two abstracts into a concretion. Consequently, the hypostasis philosophy cannot do justice to the matter in the logic peculiar to it. The following sketch is therefore to be understood as an attempt to formulate an answer to the problem posed by the an- and enhypostasis and in this sense can only be understood tentatively. The question of the humanity of Jesus Christ in contrast to that of all other human beings remains the starting point of the following considerations.

IV. Bonhoeffer and the Chalcedonian God-Human

As already indicated, the dispute concerning the humanity of Jesus Christ in relation to our humanity can only begin with the question of understanding true humanity. In their traditional formulation, the doctrines of an- and enhypostasia approach this question with fallen humanity, which they understand as something to be overcome for its corruption and fallenness. However, if it is to be said with

---

49. See Georg Essen, 'Geschichte – Metaphysik – Anthropologie: Diskurskonstellationen der Christologie in der Moderne: Eine katholisch-theologische Vergewisserung', in *Dogmatische Christologie in der Moderne: Problemkonstellationen gegenwärtiger Forschung*, ed. Christian Danz and Georg Essen (Regensburg: Pustet, 2019), 9–18, 11–2.

50. Hypostasis is understood in this sense as a concretion of what constitutes the individual. In this respect, Essen's analysis of the problem (see the previous footnote) hits the mark when it becomes clear there that the concept of hypostasis is understood in the sense of the modern concept of person and subject.

Paul that in Jesus Christ alone is it clear what being human is (see his Adam-Christ typology in Rom. 5:12-21; see also Eph. 4:24), what it means, and how it is manifested, then this approach seems to reveal another fundamental problem with the traditional interpretation. Corresponding to this are the two creation accounts in Genesis. I would like to apply these according to Bonhoeffer's interpretation in his lecture on *Creation and Fall*. According to Bonhoeffer's understanding, Adam and Eve's original humanity is distinguished in the fact that it illustrates creatureliness in free obedience.[51] However, Bonhoeffer does not understand this freedom, which is paradoxically also something that is binding, according to an abstract concept of humanity, but from the one, true human being altogether: Jesus Christ.[52] The epistemological path is thus laid out in exactly the opposite way as is traditionally the case; it is not from an abstract understanding of humanity that the humanity or rather the human being of Jesus Christ is derived. Instead, Jesus Christ's humanness, which shows itself precisely in his life as concretely being human, stands as the starting point of all knowledge of the humanity of all human beings. Correspondingly, the epistemological-hermeneutical starting point cannot be the beginning of God's history with his people, but the end. Only from the end can we know about the beginning, as Bonhoeffer rightly emphasizes.[53] Only from the incarnation, the cross and the resurrection can the humanity of all people be recognized, namely not as true but as fallen humanity. Accordingly, the sinfulness of fallen humanity is not to be subtracted from the humanity of Jesus Christ, but this sinfulness is 'added' to humanity, so to speak. If sin, following the understanding of the Reformation, should be understood not as moral failure, but as an expression of a broken relationship between God and human being and, as a result, between human beings, then this must be thought of as the result of a preceding event, not as something added in the sense of a substance.[54] In contrast, true humanity, which shows itself in Jesus Christ, is sinless life, because it lives out of the perfect relationship with God the Father. To understand the problem correctly raised by an- and enhypostasia, we need to ask how this humanity of

---

51. See DBWE 3:62 (DBW 3:58–9).

52. Bonhoeffer continues in DBWE 3:63 (DBW 3:59): 'We can ask how we know this and whether it is not once again just speculation about the beginning that is part of the fall-out of being in the middle. The answer is that it is the message of the gospel itself that God's freedom has bound itself to us, that God's free grace becomes real with us alone, that God wills not to be free for God's self but for humankind. Because God in Christ is free for humankind, because God does not keep God's freedom to God's self, we can think of freedom only as a 'being free for. …' For us in the middle who exist through Christ and who know what it means to be human through Christ's resurrection, the fact that God is free means nothing else than that we are free for God.'

53. Bonhoeffer already points this out in his preface to his lecture on *Creation and Fall* in DBWE 3:21–2 (DBW 3:21–2).

54. See also Bonhoeffer's understanding of sin in *Creation and Fall*. Instead of the term sin, Bonhoeffer speaks of 'being dead in the semblance of life'. (DBWE 3:117 [DBW 3:108]).

Jesus differs from our fallen humanity, or more precisely, how this relationship to the Father differs from our relationship to the Father.

The emphasis on the sole activity of God towards humanity in the doctrines of an- and enhypostasia has its origin here, because this relational event, which takes place in Jesus Christ, must also for the human 'nature' of Jesus Christ always start from the divine 'nature'. The human 'nature' is not capable of establishing a relationship with God. That happens alone through the active agency of the divine 'nature'. Here lies Gunton's abiding insight, which he describes primarily through the activity of the Spirit. The relationship with God can happen solely through God's free outreach, God's grace. Bonhoeffer, therefore, elaborates likeness as *analogia relationis*, as a 'relation which God has established, and it is analogous only in this relation which God has established'.[55] Accordingly, the question of an- and enhypostasia is not to be answered in the way a philosophy of hypostasis does, but instead with a re-description of the question of that philosophy: firstly with the question of in what way the relationship of Jesus Christ to God the Father differs from that of Adam, and secondly, in what way this relationship is different from that of the original Adam to God.[56]

This leads to nothing less than the question of the structure of all created being. Dogmatically it is to be emphasized, based on the biblical account that the whole creation is created by the Logos, in him, through him, and towards him (Col. 1:15-16). In the statements on the pre-existence and on the mediatorship of Christ in creation, the 'powerful presence of God's sphere of life'[57] is shown in God's creation, as Thomas Söding emphasizes. If we combine this with Gunton's notion[58] that the Bible understands the action of the triune God to be completed in the action of the Holy Spirit, who is understood as a life-creating power (Gen. 2:7), a multidimensional event emerges in which creation, incarnation, and consummation must be interpreted reciprocally. This grounding of Christology in creation and equally in consummation, which is not only significant in the Christological hymns but basically spearheads the entire New Testament's understanding of Jesus Christ,[59] must therefore be applied to a constructive Christology. If it is testified in

---

55. DBWE 3:65-6 (DBW 3:61).

56. Schwöbel's and my argument seem to be quite similar in many ways, but he seems to evaluate the doctrines of an- and enhypostasia in their meaning for a valuable Christology for today differently. See Schwöbel, *Christology*, 142-3.

57. Thomas Söding, 'Gottes Sohn von Anfang an: Zur Präexistenzchristologie bei Paulus und den Deuteropaulinen', in *Gottes ewiger Sohn: Die Präexistenz Christi*, ed. Rudolf Laufen (Paderborn/München et al.: Schöningh, 1997), 57-93, 90.

58. See Gunton, *Christ and Creation*, 92.

59. See, for example, the gospels, which in the emphasis on the sonship of Jesus Christ assume a power for Jesus Christ on which creation is based. See the stilling of the storm (Mk 4:41 asks, 'Who then is this, that even wind and sea obey him?' and Mt. 8:27 varies it, 'What sort of man is this, that even winds and sea obey him?'). See Gunton, *Christ and Creation*, 16-21. See more on this in my forthcoming Habilitation.

the New Testament that all creation has its beginning, its (life) foundation and its destiny in the Logos through the Spirit, it must be asked what this means for the understanding of (true) humanity.

If all creation is preserved in, through and towards the Logos, then theologically this means that creatures partake in creation in a particular way. The question, therefore, is in *what way* creatures partake of the Logos, that is, in what way this foundation of life constitutes being human. In my understanding, this is the core not only of the human 'nature' of Christ but also of anthropology itself. As already indicated, it cannot be a matter of constructing an abstract humanity from which the human component of both 'natures' of Jesus Christ can be reconstructed. Rather, this genuine constitution of humanity must be understood based on concrete human beings. Admittedly, only two human beings come into consideration as they signify the entire history of God with humans: Christ and Adam. In my understanding, the answer to the enduring question of the doctrines of an- and enhypostasia lies in these two figures and their difference from each other. Again: in their (life) stories, not in any abstraction of them.

When Genesis recounts Adam and Eve, the focus of this narrative – if one follows Bonhoeffer's interpretation – is their relationship with their Creator. Bonhoeffer emphasizes the difference between this relationship before and after the so-called 'Fall'. Bonhoeffer sees this relationship as changed not only with the transgression of the life-giving commandment[60] (Gen. 2:16–17), but already in the self-responsible answer to the suggestive question of the serpent ('Did God really say, You shall not eat from every kind of trees in the garden?',[61] see Gen. 3:1–3). What constituted the relationship before this transgression against God, the Creator – free, loving, devoted obedience – has now turned into anger and hatred

---

60. With Bonhoeffer's interpretation, a distinction can be made between the life-giving commandment and the life-ending prohibition, both of which denote the same thing, but each of which has different effects depending on whether humanity is in an original or fallen relationship with its Creator. What Adam and Eve still understand as God's love for them before the 'fall', they must see as God's hatred after the fall. Bonhoeffer indicates this difference in the peculiarly obscure image of the boundary in the middle. The editors of *Creation and Fall* write: 'In *Creation and Fall* the "middle" or "center" ["Mitte"] is a metaphor with a double meaning. *After* the fall humankind finds itself in a middle point that is, as it were, one point amidst others in a circle thought of as an empty ring lacking a center. As Bonhoeffer stated in *Act and Being*, the human spirit curving in upon itself constitutes a ring like that. Humankind at this 'middle point' knows no center outside itself. The reality, however, is that in the center of the fallen world there stands the cross of the "mediator" ["Mittler"], Jesus Christ, the source of life' (DBWE 3:165 [DBW 3:155]).

61. DBWE 3:106 (DBW 3:98).

against the Creator as well as the fellow-creature.⁶² The original relationship of the creature to its creator has changed into a lack of relationship. Yet, while Bonhoeffer characterizes the humanity of Adam and Eve in precisely this obedience, he also emphasizes the genuine constitution of humanity in its orientation to the Creator. The serpent, in the first 'sermon' ever given, one might say, shows that Adam and Eve need this orientation of their life to the Creator constitutively for their whole being. They themselves lack self-orientation; they need their creator to give them orientation for their lives. In listening to the serpent's 'sermon' they try to find orientation not from the serpent, as Bonhoeffer points out, as the serpent only suggests understanding God even better,⁶³ but from themselves. The possibility of sinning (which means, following a direction that is not the creator) is therefore a possibility of that human 'nature' that is not oriented by its creator anymore and therefore lacks orientation and as a result needs to be orientated anew. In the sense of Bonhoeffer, who presents this difference as *imago-dei* human versus *sicut-Deus* human,⁶⁴ one could probably say that human nature has fundamentally changed with this transgression of the commandment. What previously constituted the essence of humanity was its unclouded bond with the Creator,⁶⁵ which turns into its opposite in the transgression. Humanity finds itself torn loose from this bond apart from itself, alone for itself and against the other.⁶⁶ In a sense, in this interpretation, one must go so far as to say that *Adam's humanity turns into its opposite: Adam is no longer human, he is no longer God's creature. Instead, he is dehumanized because he has made himself his own God.*⁶⁷ Within this interpretation, what has been postulated above is concretized: sin is not something to be added to

---

62. Bonhoeffer describes Gen. 3:8–13 as Adam and Eve's flight from God. Both can no longer stand before each other, they have covered themselves in Gen. 3:7, before God they hide. Adam and Eve can only recognize God's call 'Where are you?' from Gen. 3:9 and thus God's renewed establishment and possibility of relationship as God's hatred and wrath, not as his gracious attention. See Bonhoeffer, DBWE 3:127–30 (DBW 3:119–22).

63. See DBWE 3:103–4 (DBW 3:96–7).

64. See DBWE 3:113–14 (DBW 3:104–5).

65. Following the Reformation tradition, Bonhoeffer interprets freedom as a bond with the Creator, from which a freedom for the other human being and a freedom from the powers of the world result. See DBWE 3:62–67 (DBW 3:58–63).

66. Bonhoeffer describes this separation from the bond with the Creator in reference to Luther's 'cor corvum in se ipsum' as disoriented humanity. See DBWE 2:137 (DBW 2:136) and DBWE 3:123 (DBW 3:116).

67. See DBWE 12:304–5 (DBW 12:285–6). See therefore Williams' summary on Bonhoeffer's Christology in *Christ*, 191: '[W]hat must die in the encounter with Christ is precisely *not* finitude or createdness but the delusion that we can live in denial of our finitude, our dependence on infinite agency.'

human 'nature', but something that deprives human 'nature' of its humanity, which has been constituted in its orientation through God all along. And so Adam's fallen humanity cannot be the basis for an understanding of human 'nature' in Christ, but Christ's human 'nature' precedes Adam's, constitutes it and makes it possible in the first place.

A different approach must therefore be taken. What becomes clear in Gen. 3, in Bonhoeffer's interpretation, is that being human, i.e., the human 'nature' consists in the relationship to the Creator.[68] This is exactly what constitutes the humanity of Jesus Christ – it is completely oriented towards God the Father. Yet, how is this to be understood? Bonhoeffer interprets this conception of being human, which is oriented towards its Creator, from Jesus Christ. In this sense, he takes seriously what Col. 1:16ff. and other passages highlight, that only in the context of Christ can the whole creation be understood in its being and orientation. This means that Adam and Eve receive their humanity not from themselves but from their creation in, through and towards the Logos. Only in this relation are they truly human, because only in this do they stand in a relationship to God, the Creator. True humanity is thus characterized by its being grounded in God Father through God Son – and on this point Bonhoeffer's theology must be supplemented[69] – in God Spirit.[70] Adam and Eve are creatures of God – human beings, if you will – because in the Creator's devotion to them in the Logos, through the Spirit, human beings receive the reality of being in a relationship with God. This relationship does not exist in itself in the sense of a substantially conceived property. It is solely God's gracious gift in God's free, loving devotion to the creature, God's human being. The essence of humanity, human 'nature', thus consists in the enabling of this relationship in the second through the third Trinitarian hypostasis. With the transgression of the commandment, however, this relational reality, its openness to God the Father in God the Son through God the Spirit and therein the humanity itself is lost, Adam and Eve cannot address their creatureliness, they each stand alone for themselves, they are without relationship.

The transgression of the commandment thus clearly shows that human 'nature' fundamentally changes. This does not mean a substance-ontological change that is to be understood as a materialistic change, but instead as a relational-ontological change. It is not to say that the essence of a human being in a substance-ontological understanding would have 'possessed' the Logos, only to lose it with the transgression. That is to say, however, that humanity lacks something after the transgression, namely its potential, which according to Bonhoeffer constitutes its whole reality, to recognize itself as a creature and thus in being in relation to the

---

68. Bonhoeffer understands the terms 'creature' and 'image' as being synonymous; this includes the term freedom, which he interprets, like the other two terms, as relational. See DBWE 3:62–6 (DBW 3:58–62).

69. In his theology Bonhoeffer himself speaks too rarely of the relationship of the Spirit for Christology, yet this must be avoided.

70. See Schwöbel, *Christology*, 139.

Creator.⁷¹ It seems obvious to say that humanity has lost its fundamental openness in the transition.⁷² However, this lost openness becomes recognizable solely in the infinite directedness of Jesus Christ to the Father.

Jesus Christ's humanity, his human 'nature', must therefore be understood as wholly in, through, and towards the Logos by the Spirit. The Bible expresses this difference not only by saying that the Logos became flesh, as is prominently seen in John's prologue, but also through its multifaceted stories of Jesus' life and death. I will therefore refer again to the temptations. Unlike Adam and Eve, Jesus Christ resists the temptations placed upon him and does not question God and God's commandment but points to God alone as the Lord (Mt. 4:1-11). Jesus' orientation in the Logos through the Spirit must therefore be understood as different from that of Adam and Eve. He is the sinless one in this sense because he is in a boundless relationship with the Father – but this is not something that needs to be subtracted from his human 'nature'. Rather, this is what constitutes his human 'nature' as true human 'nature', and his whole self-orientation derives from this relation to the father. It too is exposed to temptation – and in an exponential way if its temptations are messianic ones, as Gunton points out⁷³ – but unlike Adam and Eve it resists these temptations. The temptations of Jesus are thus to be read not only in the light of the temptation of the first human couple but also vice versa. From the standpoint of the resisted temptations of Jesus, the temptation of Adam and Eve can be seen as an open breach of the relationship. Yet these messianic temptations culminate in the last temptation on the cross, which does not stem from the devil but from another human being who was also condemned to death on the cross: '... help yourself, if you are the Son of God, and come down from the cross!' (Mt. 27:40). However, what follows is not Jesus' turning away from the Father, but the deepest cry for closeness in the abandonment experienced on the cross: 'My God, my God, why have you forsaken me?' (Mt. 27:46), an expression of the boundless relationship with God. Accordingly, in the Logos through the Spirit, his entire life, right up to the point of death, is oriented to the Father, in which Jesus Christ's true humanity proves itself.

Jesus' death on the cross, means that he dies out of, through and in this bond with the Father. Unlike in Adam, in Jesus Christ, the human logos is oriented towards the divine Logos. Because Adam and Eve set their own human logos as absolute,

---

71. In this context, in his *Ethics* Bonhoeffer speaks of the reality of God, the reality of the world, and the reality of Christ. See DBWE 6: 47–75 (DBW 6:31–61).

72. Luther's interpretation of sin as 'cor incurvatus in se ipsum' beautifully traces this lost orientation, when humanity in its sinfulness circles around itself, unable to lift its gaze to the other human being and to God. Plato draws a similar, at first paradoxical, image of the marionette, which alone is open to movement when it is erected by a single one of its features, the golden thread. Only then the rigid moves do not tug in opposite directions, but are free for movement. See Plato, *Nomoi*, 1.644–645.

73. See Gunton, *Christ and Creation*, 55.

detaching it from the connectedness with the Father and from the orientation to the Father, the divine Logos – Bonhoeffer can call it 'counter Logos'[74] – has to die. He dies because the human logos kills him in his self-assertion. The counter-Logos risen from death, however, cannot be killed by humans. But this divine Logos, as Bonhoeffer emphasizes, points the human being back to its humanity. It shows the human logos its limits not in its infinitude but in its self-referentiality (that is what Bonhoeffer calls 'death' with Paul[75]). It does this with his question of 'Who are you?',[76] a question that refers the human being back to its connection with the Creator, its free obedience to the Creator. Being human can thus be understood with Bonhoeffer solely in the connectedness of the human logos through the counter-Logos with the Father (and the Spirit, as Bonhoeffer's thesis has to be complemented on this point). In this, Jesus Christ is the only true human being, because in him the human logos and the divine Logos are consummately connected. Only in him do we see what a creature truly is, a creation in community and solidarity not just with the creator, but with all creation.

V. On the reciprocity of the two 'natures' in the 'unity' of the 'person'

Bonhoeffer begins this approach to Christology, which he identifies in his *Lectures* as being based on the Chalcedonian two-nature doctrine,[77] with the question of *who* Jesus Christ is – a fundamental decision that rejects all 'how' questions as inadequate.[78] Consequently, he does not begin his interpretation of the person of Jesus Christ and thus of God's will to save God's creation with the doctrine of two natures (and a correspondingly understood 'definition' of this event), but with the biblical account of God's relationship with creation. This means, on the one hand, that he recognizes a fundamental problem of the Christological discussion in the history of theology in the fact that the interpretation of the doctrine of two natures is not tied back to the biblical account of the incarnate God in Jesus Christ. Instead he shows that it is solely based on the apparent 'conceptual definition' of the doctrine of the two natures, in which both 'natures' are abstractly defined in their divinity and humanity. On the other hand, he himself does not want to deal with the speculative How questions ('How is this possible?', 'How is this to be understood?').

Therefore, a productive approach to a constructive Christology can be sought precisely in that *who* – 'Who are you?' – emphasized by Bonhoeffer, which demands a personal interpretation of the doctrine of two natures.[79] The question

---

74. See DBWE 12:302–6 (DBW 12:282–6).
75. DBWE 3:135 (DBW 3:127).
76. See DBWE 12:305 (DBW 3:286).
77. See DBWE 12:342–3 (DBW 12:327–9).
78. See DBWE 12:302–3 (DBW 12:282–3).
79. Here I differ from McCormack, 'Person', 149–50.

of the 'Who' immediately rejects all attempts to construct and abstract a God-man.[80] All 'thing-like' thinking that constructs, contrasts, or connects the two 'natures' in terms of entities is rejected. There can be no reflection on how divinity and humanity differ and relate to each other. Moreover, an ascertainable positive statement about Jesus Christ is also rejected, as if it were possible to speak about him in an undifferentiated way.[81] Rather, as Bonhoeffer shows, this who-question leads us to speak of God the Incarnate always given and based on the biblical *stories* within the framework and horizon of the doctrine of two natures.[82] Accordingly, the doctrine of the two natures, which is connected with the who-question, leads us into the biblical stories of Jesus Christ, which allow us to get to know his person and his actions without wanting to grasp them abstractly, i.e., without wanting to define them. The who-question invites us to understand the two 'natures' not detached from their background, but instead tied back to their origin and unfolded from there. In this way, Bonhoeffer understands the question of the person as an ontological one: 'it alone poses the question of existence as an ontological question about the being of Jesus Christ; insofar as the ontological question asked here is the question about the being of the person Jesus Christ; insofar as the ontological question asked here is the question of the being of Christ's person as clearly being the revealed Logos of God.'[83]

The questions Danz poses in his challenging of the Chalcedonian doctrine of the two natures thus culminate in a narrative-ontological understanding of the two natures. What 'nature' means in each case can thus only be grasped through the biblical narratives. – This applies not only to the divine but in the same way also to the human 'nature'. Neither 'natures' refer to abstract entities – they do not refer to an ominous deity or humanity, but to the God of Israel and the man Jesus of Nazareth. The human 'nature' of Jesus Christ must therefore indeed also be seen in its uniqueness and distinctiveness, in its person, in its actions and relationships with other creatures; the divine 'nature' must be understood trinitarian, this being the living triune God who makes Godself known to us in the biblical stories.[84] An

---

80. See DBWE 12:342 (DBW 12:327).

81. See Christian Welker, *Gottes Offenbarung. Christologie* (Neukirchen-Vluyn: Neukirchner, 2012), 254.

82. Welker understands Bonhoeffer's handling of the doctrine of two natures as an auxiliary construction, which Bonhoeffer used again and again, but at the same time left behind. The question arises to what extent Welker wants to see Bonhoeffer recur to the doctrine of two natures in order to recognize it as the basis of his theology. It seems to me, with Coakley, rather the case that Bonhoeffer builds his whole theology, especially his conception of the 'Christ-reality' entirely on the two-figure doctrine, admittedly not literally, but as a framework and horizon of thought for an understanding of reality. See ibid., 254.

83. DBWE 12:304 (DBW 12:285).

84. See Karl Barth, *Church Dogmatics IV/2: Doctrine of Reconciliation* (Edinburgh, Scotland: T&T Clark, 1958), 46–7.

elaboration of such a constructive Christology, which is not based on (materialistic) substance-metaphysical conditions, but which nevertheless does not omit to be, must be based on such a fundamental decision: Through the divine 'nature' alone, Jesus Christ's humanity is true humanity. However, from the comprehension of true humanity, it is possible to deduce the divine nature at least to the extent that it can be said that the divine 'nature' comes to its true divinity in this creative enabling of being human.[85]

---

85. Williams (Williams, *Christ*, 170) points out that the unifying theme in Bonhoeffer's Christology 'is one that has its roots in the Reformation principle that the essential thing to say about Jesus Christ is that his person and work must be understood as radically and entirely "for us". There is nothing to say about God that is not ultimately grounded in this understanding [...].' This theme has to be applied on understanding (his) divinity in my opinion, too.

Chapter 7

BONHOEFFER'S ECCE HOMO!: CHRISTOLOGY FROM THE CENTRE AND THE FULLNESS OF LIFE

Christian Schlenker

'Teaching about Christ begins in silence.'[1] However, it does not remain speechless. In *Ethics*, Bonhoeffer brings to speech a radical account of the significance of the humanity of Jesus Christ. '[T]here is no longer any reality, any world, that is not reconciled with God and at peace. God has done this in the beloved son, Jesus Christ. Ecce homo!'[2]

An important reason why Bonhoeffer emphasizes the humanity of Christ is found in his engagement with the contemporary theological landscape. Bonhoeffer studied under some of the most influential theologians of his time. His theological formation under Adolf von Harnack, Reinhold Seeberg and Karl Holl left little room for the traditional doctrine of the two natures. In post-Enlightenment theology, the metaphysical foundations that supported the Chalcedonian doctrine had crumbled, and to support it had become unreasonable. His teachers stressed that Jesus Christ was indeed but only a (remarkable) human being. While Bonhoeffer was not satisfied with their solutions to this problem he nevertheless took their critique seriously. Other than his teachers he did not abandon what he believed to be the undismissable theological claim of the Chalcedonian creed. In his Christmas meditation from 1939 Bonhoeffer summarizes the importance that he sees in the Chalcedonian doctrine: 'In fact, if Jesus Christ is not true God, how could he *help* us? If Christ is not true human, how could he help *us*?'[3]

This paper examines how Bonhoeffer understood the humanity of Christ with special attention to *Ethics*. As Ernst Feil notes in *Ethics* Bonhoeffer's Christology is intensified and culminates in a radical account of what God's embrace of the world in Christ amounts to.[4] In a first step, I will show one central aspect of how

---

1. Dietrich Bonhoeffer, *Christology*, trans. John Bowden (London: Collins, 1966), 27. The translation by J. Bowden follows E. Bethge's edition of the text. DBW(E) chooses another manuscript that does not include this line. See below, *note 102*.

2. DBWE 6:83 (DBW 6:70).

3. DBWE 15:531 (DBW 15:541).

4. See Ernst Feil, *Die Theologie Dietrich Bonhoeffers: Hermeneutik, Christologie, Weltverständnis* (München: Kaiser, 1979), 192.

Bonhoeffer's account differs from his teachers Harnack, Seeberg, and Holl, as well as from Emanuel Hirsch who, like Bonhoeffer, was a student of Holl. The thesis of this section is that for Bonhoeffer *Jesus Christ was not an exemplary and perfect human being but was perfectly humane*. In a second step, I will analyse how Bonhoeffer understands the revelation of Christ in the perfectly humane and finite human existence in dialogue with Karl Barth and Søren Kierkegaard. Here, my thesis is that Bonhoeffer argues *that the divinity of Christ is only understood in his Incarnation in the centre and fullness of life.*

I. The Teachers

Bonhoeffer studied under Adolf von Harnack, Karl Holl and Reinhold Seeberg in Berlin, three teachers that have been central figures of the German academic theology of that time. In this section I will in addition refer to Emanuel Hirsch as a fellow student of Holl. Of course, this is not a representative sample of the theological discussion of that time in its entirety but it is rather supposed to highlight a then widespread line of thought. All four theologians share a critical stance towards the Chalcedonian doctrine, stating that it relies on metaphysical assumptions that have become obsolete in a modern, post-Enlightenment world. Their intention is not to dismantle tradition but to safeguard the essence of Christianity. Integral to this is, that Christ can be understood as a concrete and historical human being because otherwise, he would be an abstract and speculative idea: What is essential about Christ's humanity cannot be expressed through the metaphysical language of natures. I argue that Bonhoeffer takes this critique seriously while trying to find new ways to articulate what Chalcedon pointed towards by using the metaphysical language of natures.

1. Condemning the Metaphysical Language of the Two Natures

Although in different forms all of Bonhoeffer's teachers – but most famously Harnack's 'Hellenization thesis' – mention and criticize the shortcomings of the ancient metaphysical framework of the Chalcedonian creed. As Christoph Markschies points out this neither is a thesis proper to Harnack but rather a widely accepted assumption at that time nor does Harnack rigorously condemn all Hellenistic elements as some of his critics suggest.[5] Bonhoeffer in his *Lectures on the History of Systematic Theology in the 20th Century* follows schematic lines in his portrait of the Hellenization thesis.[6] I will demonstrate briefly that it can be traced through the works of Harnack, Holl, Seeberg and Hirsch that they considered the Chalcedonian language to be problematic because it obscured the true humanity of Christ, and that there are strong tendencies within these

---

5. See Christoph Johannes Markschies, *Hellenisierung des Christentums: Sinn und Unsinn einer historischen Deutungskategorie* (Leipzig: Evangelische Verlags-Anstalt, 2021), 53–6.

6. DBWE 11:202 (DBW 11:167).

approaches to understand Christ primarily if not exclusively as teacher and moral exemplar. In the next subsection, this will serve as the background against which Bonhoeffer articulates his Christology.

According to Harnack, the original and biblically attested Christianity was mixed with the world views of the ancient Mediterranean region, which were dominated by Greek philosophical patterns of thought.[7] For Harnack, this is best seen in the identification of Christ with the Logos.[8] The identification which tried to integrate the new religion and the Hellenistic world culminates in clouding the human personality of Christ. Christ is seen primarily as the Logos of God and no longer as the man from Nazareth. This personality, Harnack argues, eventually became replaced by the abstract language of nature.

> When the Logos Christology obtained a complete victory, the traditional view of the Supreme deity as one person, and, along with this, every thought of the real and complete human personality of the Redeemer was in fact condemned as being intolerable in the Church. Its place was taken by 'the nature', which without 'the person' is simply a cipher.[9]

Harnack searches for the 'Essence of Christianity' – the more literal translation of his work *What Is Christianity* – as the historical core of the proclaimed Gospel free of all subsequent Hellenistic (or Hegelian)[10] systematizations of doctrine. Especially two Hellenistic elements are problematic for Harnack. First, as has been shown above, that Jesus was artificially identified with the Logos and, second, that the human personality was replaced by the two natures, which obscured the true relation between the Son and God.[11] The historical Jesus had an extraordinary

---

7. See esp. Adolf von Harnack, *What Is Christianity?* (New York and Evanston: Harper & Row, 1971), 200.

8. See ibid., 202–3, 231.

9. Adolf von Harnack, *History of Dogma*, vol. 3 (New York: Russel; Russell, 1958), 10; see Adolf von Harnack, *Lehrbuch der Dogmengeschichte: Die Entstehung des kirchlichen Dogmas*, unveränderter reprografischer Nachdruck der 4., neu durcharbeiteten und vermehrten Auflage, Tübingen 1909, vol. 1 (Darmstadt: Wissenschaftliche Buchgesellschaft, 1980), 704–5.

10. See Karl-Heinz Menke, *Jesus ist Gott der Sohn: Denkformen und Brennpunkte der Christologie* (Regensburg: Verlag Friedrich Pustet, 2008), 312.

11. Interestingly, what Chalcedon did in Harnack's opinion was to retain a 'minimum of historical conception which the Church still possessed regarding the person of Christ, by cutting short the logical results for the doctrine of redemption which threatened completely to destroy the Christ of the Gospels' (Adolf von Harnack, *History of Dogma*, vol. 4 (New York: Russel; Russell, 1958), 223; see Adolf von Harnack, *Lehrbuch der Dogmengeschichte: Die Entwicklung des kirchlichen Dogmas I*, Unveränderter reprografischer Nachdruck der 4., neu durcharbeiteten und vermehrten Auflage, Tübingen 1909, vol. 2 (Darmstadt: Wissenschaftliche Buchgesellschaft, 1980), 397.

God-consciousness and proclaimed the work of the Father – but not himself as God.¹² 'The Gospel', Harnack summarizes his account, '*as Jesus proclaimed it, has to do with the Father only and not with the Son*'.¹³ Bonhoeffer quotes this sentence in his *Lecture on the History of Systematic Theology* and argues that Harnack reduced Jesus to an *exemplar* who lives and proclaims the ethical will of God: 'Intentionally, no mention of the person of Jesus Christ; [he is seen] only as an example.'¹⁴

Differently, a reduction of Christ to a moral exemplar as a result of the rejection of the metaphysical language of Chalcedon can also be observed in Holl's famous exegesis of Luther. He argues that Luther *almost* taught monophysitism, modalism and subordinationism because he found these tendencies enfolded in the Chalcedonian language rather than being a flaw in Luther's own piety or reasoning.¹⁵ The *metaphysical language* of 'nature', 'substance' and 'person' obscured the heart of the problem rather than clarifying it.

> The fault in all this lies with the ancient dogma, not with Luther. A piety centered upon the will and a community of will was bound to collide everywhere with concepts like 'substance' and 'nature' – derived from the ancient *natural* metaphysics, and regarded as abiding entities of purely ontological determinateness – and with the correspondingly shallow conception of the person.¹⁶

Holl sees the difficulty arising with the metaphysics and the ontology of nature. Luther's piety and his central experiences of Justification, his reformatory insight, instead was based on an ontology of will. If Luther, Holl argues, has any relevance for us today, we need to be able to have the same existential experiences of faith and Justification as him. Holl sees it as the fundamental insight of Luther that this experience takes place in conscience, where the human will is in conflict with the unconditional will of God. Christ for Holl is understood as a walking model of the union with the will of God:¹⁷ 'In Christology Luther regarded it as an essential point that the divinity of Christ is revealed in his very humanity. ... To learn the true will of God, one must keep to the humanity of Christ.'¹⁸ It follows, that the *inhabitatio christi* is a '*personal* will, a personal moral power, that acts upon him'.¹⁹ Christ,

---

12. See Menke, *Jesus ist Gott der Sohn*, 210.
13. Harnack, *What Is Christianity?* 210, emphasis in the original.
14. See DBWE 11:203 (DBW 11:168).
15. See Karl Holl, *What Did Luther Understand by Religion?* (Philadelphia: Fortress Press, 1977), 78.
16. Ibid.
17. See Risto Saarinen, *Gottes Wirken auf uns: Die Transzendentale Deutung des Gegenwart-Christi-Motivs in der Lutherforschung* (Stuttgart: Franz Steiner Verlag Wiesbaden GmbH, 1989), 91–112.
18. Holl, *What Did Luther Understand by Religion?* 79.
19. 'Ein persönlicher Wille, eine persönliche, sittliche Macht ist, die auf ihn wirkt.' (ibid., 121).

therefore, is understood to be divine in the sense that he transmits the moral power which puts the justified human being within the realm of God's justice. Christ is understood as the work of God in the world. He is thus demarcated from God's being as the *instrument* through which the work of God is realized. It is important to note that not only Christ is seen as instrument by Holl, but every human being through which God works.[20] This may be, for example, the emperor who wages war to punish others;[21] the preachers who proclaim God's word;[22] the church itself;[23] Luther[24] and other individual heroes.[25] Christ, therefore, is seen mainly as an *example* of the workings of the moral will of God.[26] Consequently, Christ is not necessary for Justification.[27] In Christ, it only has been shown to us how Justification is worked by God. Bonhoeffer comments: 'Then Christ, through what he has done for me, has made himself superfluous; this is why, for Holl, the doctrines of justification and Christology are no longer the main focus.'[28]

The same point can also be made for Hirsch, for whom the old doctrine and its language of Greek philosophy constructed a Christology which reduced the humanity of Christ to an abstract concept.[29] Hirsch summarizes that the metaphysical language of Chalcedon has led to a point where it is impossible for us to see the humanity of Jesus.

> Firstly, the dogma took away the own human person of Jesus. Hence, we are not used to see the true humanity of the Lord. Here, we have to learn anew from the Gospels which portray him as a real individual human being.[30]

20. See Karl Holl, 'Luther', in *Gesammelte Aufsätze zur Kirchengeschichte*, 6. neu durchges. Aufl., vol. 1 (Tübingen: Mohr, 1932), 46. 100. 107; see also Saarinen, *Gottes Wirken auf uns*, 92–5.
21. See Holl, 'Luther', 285.
22. See ibid., 293.
23. See ibid., 301.
24. See ibid., 396.
25. See ibid., 528.
26. See Tomi Karttunen, 'Die Luther-Lektüre Bonhoeffers', in *Bonhoeffer und Luther: Zentrale Themen ihrer Theologie*, ed. Klaus Grünwaldt (Hannover: Amt der VELKD, 2007), 19.
27. See Michael P. DeJonge, *Bonhoeffer's Reception of Luther* (Oxford: Oxford University Press, 2017), 30.
28. DBWE 11:239 (DBW 11:208).
29. See also Reinhold Seeberg, *Christliche Dogmatik* (Erlangen and Wien: A. Deichertsche Verlagsbuchhandlung Dr. Werner Scholl, 1924), 2:149.
30. Emanuel Hirsch, *Jesus Christus der Herr: Theologische Vorlesungen*, 2., fast unveränd. Aufl. (Göttingen: Vandenhoeck & Ruprecht, 1929), 73. (translation, C.S.): 'Einmal, das Dogma hat Jesus die eigene menschliche Person genommen. So sind wir nicht daran gewöhnt, die wahre Menschheit des Herrn zu sehen. Da müssen wir neu aus den Evangelien lernen, die ihn uns als einen wirklichen individuellen Menschen schildern.'

Seeberg and Hirsch conclude that the Incarnation is an unreasonable assumption by Greek metaphysics. A union at levels of the will aptly describe the relation of God and Jesus of Nazareth.[31] Son of God then, as with Holl, only denotes the complete submission and obedience under the will of God. The hypostatical union, therefore, is an *ethical union* grounded in an *ontology of the will*.[32] God cannot be recognized in any other way than that his will manifests itself as the unconditional 'ought to', which one experiences in conscience. The demand of God, the unconditional 'ought to' is revealed in Jesus Christ. Hirsch writes: 'He is "the exemplar", in which God's demand is expressed, has become a visible reality for us.'[33]

The solutions of the teachers shift the problem into the realm of ethos[34] or an ontology of will.[35] It is evident in *Sanctorum Communio, Act and Being* and also his *Barcelona Lectures* that Bonhoeffer himself started his theological thinking deeply rooted in this tradition.[36] Only later does Bonhoeffer sharply criticize the resulting consequences: 'Hirsch, Holl, Reibi replace Christ [through – C.S.] conscience [setzen an Stelle Christi – Gewissen]. Always theology without Christology.'[37]

Unlike his teachers and Hirsch, Bonhoeffer sees a double achievement of Chalcedon that must be preserved: On the one hand, the language of Chalcedon made it possible to express a concern in the language of a metaphysical framework. Nevertheless, the concern itself originates in Christology and not in the Greek worldview. On the other hand, trying to recover the origins of a true Christianity does not yield a greater certainty. It is the context of the Hellenization thesis that Bonhoeffer comments in the *Lectures on Christology*: 'nothing is further from being a product of Greek thinking than the Chalcedonian formula.'[38] This assertion shares an important assumption with the Hellenization thesis. Bonhoeffer does not claim that the metaphysical articulation of the Chalcedonian doctrine is true because it is a remnant of Greek philosophy, but that this articulation is important because it says something true about Christ. The question then becomes, what theological significance of the humanity of Jesus Christ is lost when it is reduced to a (moral) exemplar.

---

31. Seeberg, *Christliche Dogmatik*, 2:159–60.

32. See Saarinen, *Gottes Wirken auf uns*, 130–48; DeJonge, *Bonhoeffer's Reception of Luther*, 33.

33. Hirsch, *Jesus Christus der Herr*, 52 (translation C.S). 'Er ist ja "das Vorbild", in dem Gottes Forderung ausgedrückte, uns anschaubare Wirklichkeit geworden ist.'

34. Bonhoeffer criticizes this about Harnack's approach, see DBWE 12:306 (DBW 12:339).

35. See Holl, *What Did Luther Understand by Religion?* 84: 'The union attained is only a union of will; an "affective" union, as Luther put it, not a "substantial" union.'

36. See Martin Rumscheidt, 'The Significance of Adolf von Harnack and Reinhold Seeberg for Dietrich Bonhoeffer', in *Bonhoeffer's Intellectual Formation: Theology and Philosophy in His Thought*, ed. Peter Frick (Tübingen: Mohr Siebeck, 2008), 202; Wolfgang Huber, *Dietrich Bonhoeffer: Auf dem Weg zur Freiheit* (München: C. H. Beck, 2019), 71–5.

37. DBWE 14:380 (DBW 14:363).

38. DBWE 12:306 (DBW 12:339). See DBWE 15:531 (DBW 15:541).

2. Not a Perfect Human Being but Perfectly Humane

While Bonhoeffer certainly presents and refutes the positions of his teachers in a strongly schematized way, he never blindly rejects them without considering the seriousness of their concerns.[39] If one searches for a common denominator in the Christologies of Harnack, Holl, Seeberg or Hirsch, one finds their endeavour to preserve the humanity of Christ. According to them, the dogma of the early Church buried the fact that Jesus of Nazareth was a human being. It is important to keep in mind this inner tension that the four scholars faced: They felt that the humanity of Christ had to be preserved because if there was any connection of the Transcendent to humanity, it had to be found in humanity and not in untimely metaphysical speculation.[40]

Bonhoeffer repeatedly accentuates that the significance of Jesus Christ's human nature cannot be found in any idealized and/or abstract version of Christ. For Bonhoeffer, this can mean either two things: On the one hand, Christ cannot be understood exclusively as a teacher, be it by teachings or by example. On the other hand, he cannot be reduced to an ideal human being.

Christ as a human being cannot be confined to a teacher who proclaims a teaching and becomes the founder of a 'new ethical ideology' or an 'ethic of Jesus'.[41] Bonhoeffer stresses rigorously that Christ cannot be reduced to a fixed set of abstract principles because that would fail to account that he was a concrete historical person, who lived in situations that were different from what any teaching could be. This 'grave misunderstanding … gives rise to an eternal conflict between the necessities of historical action and the "ethics of Jesus"'.[42] When we consider the humanity of Christ, we can never lose sight of this concrete historical existence.

> God became human in Jesus Christ, that God entered history, so that he was born at the time of the emperor Augustus, when Quirinius was governor of Syria, that he was a man during the time of the emperor Tiberius, and was crucified under Pontius Pilate.[43]

In short, Jesus cannot be identified with a teaching because this would fundamentally neglect one aspect of what it means to be human: to live a life within history, to be a temporal being.

---

39. See Nadine Hamilton, *Dietrich Bonhoeffers Hermeneutik der Responsivität: Ein Kapitel Schriftlehre im Anschluss an 'Schöpfung und Fall'* (Göttingen: Vandenhoeck & Ruprecht, 2016), 146; Huber, *Dietrich Bonhoeffer*, 49–50.

40. See Rowan Williams, *Christ the Heart of Creation* (London: Bloomsbury Continuum, 2018), 157.

41. DBWE 6:229 (DBW 6:228).

42. Ibid.

43. DBWE 6:228 (DBW 6:227–8).

Holl throughout his interpretations of Luther makes it abundantly clear that what is essential about faith is not an unchangeable teaching but that it is grounded in an existential experience.[44] While Bonhoeffer understands faith in an existential manner too, he points out an important difference to his teacher.[45] Whereas Holl stressed that Luther unveiled a religious experience that can be repeated, Bonhoeffer argues that the truth of the experience can never be found in the repetition of Luther, Paul, or any other role model of faith, but always remains to be formed by Christ:

> From the beginning, the qualitatively ultimate word of God forbids us from looking at the way of Paul or the way of Luther as if we had to go that way again. There are ways that are condemned. Strictly speaking, we should not repeat Luther's way any more than the way of the woman caught in adultery, the thief on the cross, Peter's denial, or Paul's zealous persecution of Christ.[46]

Essentially, for Holl, the experience of Justification follows human categories, both in its formation and in its measurement. This also happens, whenever 'we strive "to become like Jesus"',[47] and try to repeat his actions. In this case, the action would, again, be reduced to something that is in principle repeatable. While Bonhoeffer, too, emphasizes that the existential experience of the encounter with Christ is essential, he argues that this encounter has no natural predisposition in human nature. One cannot align oneself with Christ according to one's own measure; instead, one must be aligned by Christ. Bonhoeffer stresses this point in *Ethics*:

> Christ remains the only one who forms. Christian people do not form the world with their ideas. Rather, Christ forms human beings to a form the same as Christ's own. However, just as the form of Christ is misperceived where he is understood essentially as the teacher of a pious and good life, so formation of human beings is also wrongly understood where one sees it only as guidance for a pious and good life.[48]

What Bonhoeffer carefully tries to avoid here, considering the Christological implications, is to judge Christ's human nature as if it was a perfected and abstract nature. What we see by looking at the historical human existence of Jesus of Nazareth, is a human being that is in no regard exempt from the toils and plights, but also the joys and pleasures of life. '[B]y entering as a human

---

44. See e.g., Holl, 'Luther', 120.
45. See Friederike Barth, *Die Wirklichkeit des Guten: Dietrich Bonhoeffers 'Ethik' und ihr philosophischer Hintergrund* (Tübingen: Mohr Siebeck, 2011), 106.
46. See DBWE 6:150 (DBW 6:140–1).
47. DBWE 6:93–4 (DBW 6:81).
48. Ibid.

being into human life, by taking on and bearing bodily the nature, essence, guilt, and suffering of human beings.'[49] Bonhoeffer continuously highlights that vulnerability and fragility are a part of what it means to be a living human being.[50] This includes and reaches its pinnacle in the 'godlessness and godforsakenness of the world'[51] that Jesus Christ took upon himself. At the cross, Bonhoeffer argues, 'human glory has come to its final end in the image of the beaten, bleeding, spat-upon face of the crucified'.[52] Looking at the human, temporal existence of Jesus Christ all ideals and abstract concepts of humanity fail. The world and what it means to be a human being does not abide by any principle or abstraction. *This entails that the Incarnation of Christ cannot be grasped by philosophical language in the eyes of Bonhoeffer for the same reason that all abstract concepts fail to grasp what it means to be a concrete human being.* In this respect, Bonhoeffer strikes a Lutheran tone. In *Verbum caro factum est*, Luther addresses the limits of philosophical language in a similar manner: 'It is false and an error in the area of measurement',[53] philosophical language is the wrong measure regarding the Incarnation – and for Bonhoeffer it is paramount that it is at least problematic to measure the human being by abstract and idealized measures, as he makes abundantly clear in *Ethics* regarding any kind of principal ethics.[54] Here we have a first glimpse at what Bonhoeffer meant when he stressed that the Chalcedonian Creed is not the product of Greek thinking.[55]

By restricting their Christologies to the exemplary character of Christ in the sense of a walking example of a morally perfect human, Bonhoeffer's teachers undercut all the imperfections and shortcomings that make human existence what it truly is. Bonhoeffer summarizes this account in his dismissal of any understanding of Jesus Christ that reduces him to a teacher.

> Christ was not essentially a teacher, a lawgiver, but a human being, a real human being like us. Accordingly, Christ does not want us to be first of all pupils, representatives and advocates of a particular doctrine, but human beings, real human being before God.[56]

---

49. DBWE 6:84 (DBW 6:71).

50. See Williams, *Christ the Heart of Creation*, 190.

51. DBWE 6:401 (DBW 6:405). See H. Gaylon Barker, *The Cross of Reality: Luther's Theologia Crucis and Bonhoeffer's Christology* (Minneapolis: Fortress Press, 2015), 366.

52. DBWE 6:168 (DBW 6:150).

53. Martin Luther, 'The Disputation Concerning the Passage "the Word Was Made Flesh" (John 1:14) [1539]', in *Luther's Works: Word and Sacrament IV*, trans. Martin E. Lehmann, vol. 38 (Philadelphia: Fortress Press, 1971), 241. = WA 39 II, 5, Th. 31: 'Falsum est et error in genere mensurum'.

54. See DBWE 6:279–80 (DBW 6:280).

55. See DBWE 12:306 (DBW 12:339).

56. DBWE 6:98 (DBW 6:86).

Holl, Harnack, Seeberg, and Hirsch are unable to recognize the human being in the midst of her everyday life and her imperfections as having a truly human existence. Repeatedly Bonhoeffer formulates that in Christ we cannot search for the perfection of humankind. 'Jesus does not want to be considered the only perfect one, to look down on a humanity perishing under its guilt.'[57] Therefore, Bonhoeffer takes seriously the problem that his teachers brought up, that the humanity of Jesus Christ has to be regained but his solution is more radical than theirs. Bonhoeffer reinterprets what the Chalcedonian Creed formulated as 'καὶ τέλειον τὸν αὐτὸν ἐν ἀνθρωπότητι', 'and equally *perfect* in humanity'.[58] While τέλειον, in general, designates something that has reached its potential, its τέλος and therefore is 'perfect', Bonhoeffer interprets it to always include the vulnerability of life.[59] To be τέλειον ἐν ἀνθρωπότητι and ἄνθρωπον ἀληθῶς, is not a perfect and the one true human but to be perfectly and truly human, not an exemplary embodiment of the flawless and abstract human nature but a concrete human being.

> God does not seek the most perfect human being with whom to be united, but takes on human nature as it is. Jesus Christ is not the transfiguration of noble humanity but the Yes of God to real human beings, not the dispassionate Yes of a judge but [the] merciful Yes of a compassionate sufferer.[60]

Bonhoeffer transfigures the meaning of the human nature, that Christ can redeem humankind because he takes on all human suffering qua genus of sufferings, to a description of human beings that focuses on life. Human existence, as Bonhoeffer articulates inspired by Dilthey's *Lebensphilosophie*[61] as well as Heidegger's existential analysis of human *Dasein*,[62] is the life that spans from birth until death.[63] Thereby Bonhoeffer discards the problematic ontological assumptions that his teachers scrutinized and maintains what is at stake in what the Chalcedonian tradition articulated as *nature*. Bonhoeffer summarizes this thesis at various points in *Ethics*:

> However, the strictest concentration of all thoughts and statements about love on the name of Jesus Christ now must not reduce this name to an abstract

---

57. DBWE 6:233 (DBW 6:232).
58. Cited after, *The Oecumenical Documents of the Faith*, ed. Th. Herbert Bindley (Westport: Greenwood Press, 1950), 193, line 111.
59. The word τέλειος can be understood in this way too, see, e.g., Herodotus, *Histories: Book 1*, ed. Carolyn Dewald and Rosaria Vignolo Munson (Cambridge: Cambridge University Press, 2022), Hdt. 1.183: τὰ τέλεα τῶν προβάτων, the full-grown cattle.
60. DBWE 6:85 (DBW 6:78).
61. See Barth, *Die Wirklichkeit des Guten*, 148–95.
62. E.g., DBWE 6:220 (DBW 6:219).
63. See Martin Heidegger, *Being and Time*, trans. Joan Stambaugh (Albany: State University of New York Press, 1996), 342.

concept. Instead, this name must always be understood in the concrete richness of the historical reality of a living human being.[64]

Bonhoeffer goes into great detail to describe how life describes human existence in a way formerly articulated through the concept of nature. When situating the ethical question Bonhoeffer argues, '[t]he question about the good always finds us already in an irreversible situation: we are living.'[65] This basic element of what it means to be human is further described as a deep relationality which makes human beings *essentially* who they are. When Bonhoeffer describes the function of the Church, for example, he states that its concern is not religion as a natural quality – a function that reminds of Seeberg's assumption of a *religious a priori*[66] – but that it is concerned 'with the human existence in the world of whole human beings in all their relationships.'[67]

If this life in its relationships to fellow human beings, the environment, and history, is what it *essentially* means to be human, and this is what Christ the Incarnate faces and takes upon himself in his earthly life, *then* Bonhoeffer must describe *what* and *how* we learn anything of God by looking at this human being. And it is this *human* being, that we must look at and point to him, as Kierkegaard puts it, and must be able to say: 'Look, there he stands – the god? Where? There.'[68] Bonhoeffer, in a dense section of *Ethics* formulates what the Incarnation, the Crucifixion and the Risen One tell us with repeated insistence: 'Ecce homo – behold the human being.'[69]

II. Barth, Bonhoeffer and an Infinite Controversy

The transfiguration of 'human nature' into an existential grammar of life yields the question of what the assumption of this human life and existence in the Incarnate means. Bonhoeffer is careful not to restrict the divinity of the Incarnate God by means of his Incarnation *as well as* not to undermine the humanity of the concrete human life of Jesus Christ. If the former were the case, Jesus Christ wouldn't be truly God, if the latter not truly human. Again, we can quote Bonhoeffer's Christmas meditation from 1939 to see what is at stake here: 'In fact, if Jesus Christ is not true God, how could he *help* us? If Christ is not true human, how could he help *us*?'[70] In this section, I will analyse how Bonhoeffer articulates the relation of the Incarnate to his human nature.

---

64. DBWE 6:335 (DBW 6:338).
65. DBWE 6:246 (DBW 6:245).
66. Seeberg, *Christliche Dogmatik*, 1:102.
67. DBWE 6:97 (DBW 6:84).
68. Søren Kierkegaard, *Philosophical Fragments*, ed. Howard V. Hong and Edna H. Hong, Kierkegaard's Writings, VII (Princeton: Princeton University Press, 1985), 32.
69. DBWE 6:91 (DBW 6:78).
70. DBWE 15:531 (DBW 15:541).

In the Protestant tradition, this was traditionally debated between the Lutherans and the Reformed considering the question of whether the *finite is capable of bearing the infinite (finitum capax infiniti)*. Further, the in/capax distinction has been controversially discussed in Bonhoeffer research as either a difference or the merging point between Barth and Bonhoeffer.[71] Therefore, in a first step, I will show how both Barth and Bonhoeffer articulate the problem.

1. The Origin of the In/Capax Problem

In short, the *capax/incapax* question is, whether the finite world can (*capax*) bear the infinity of God or not (*non capax*), *while preserving the humanity and the divinity of Jesus Christ*. Bonhoeffer notes precisely this for the Reformed tradition in particular: 'In Reformed Christology, the emphasis is on preserving clearly what belongs to God and what belongs to humanity.'[72]

Without going into too much detail, the question emerged debating the *enhypostasia*, whether the humanity of Christ only is real *in and as* the Word (which both the Lutherans and the Reformed theologians approved) *also* implied that the Word of God only is real *in and as* the humanity of Christ.[73] Luther affirms this question:

> Christ is God and man, and his humanity has become one person with God, and is thus wholly and completely drawn into God above all creatures, so that he remains perfectly united with him. How is it possible, then, for God to be somewhere where Christ as man is not?[74]

---

71. James H. Burtness, 'Als ob es Gott nicht gäbe: Bonhoeffer, Barth und das lutherische finitum capax infiniti', in *Bonhoeffer und Luther*, ed. Christian Gremmels (München: Chr. Kaiser, 1983), 167–83; Andreas Pangritz, 'Dietrich Bonhoeffer: Within, Not Outside, the Barthian Movement', in *Bonhoeffer's Intellectual Formation: Theology and Philosophy in His Thought*, ed. Peter Frick (Tübingen: Mohr Siebeck, 2008), 245–82; Andreas Pangritz, *Karl Barth in der Theologie Dietrich Bonhoeffers: Eine notwendige Klarstellung* (Westberlin: Alektor Verlag, 1989); Karttunen, 'Die Luther-Lektüre Bonhoeffers'; Tomi Karttunen, 'Die Bedeutung der Berliner Zeit für das Denkmodell Dietrich Bonhoeffers', in *Dietrich Bonhoeffer – Orte seiner Theologie* (Paderborn et al.: Ferdinand Schöningh, 2008), 45–59; DeJonge, *Bonhoeffer's Reception of Luther*; Karten Lehmkühler, 'Christologie', in *Bonhoeffer und Luther: Zentrale Themen ihrer Theologie*, ed. Klaus Grünwaldt (Hannover: Amt der VELKD, 2007), 55–78.

72. DBWE 12:346 (DBW 12:332). See Karl Barth, *Die Christliche Dogmatik im Entwurf: Die Lehre vom Worte Gottes. Prolegomena zur Christlichen Dogmatik*, ed. Gerhard Sauter and Karl Barth Gesamtausgabe (Zürich: Theologischer Verlag Zürich, 1982), § 16, 363.

73. See Barth, *Die Christliche Dogmatik im Entwurf*, 359. For *enhypostasia* in Bonhoeffer, see the contribution of Nadine Hamilton in this volume.

74. Martin Luther, 'Confession Concerning Christ's Supper (1528)', in *Luther's Works: Word and Sacrament III*, ed. and trans. Robert H. Fischer, vol. 37 (Philadelphia: Muhlenberg Press, 1961), 228–9. See WA 26, 340, 14–7.

Barth emphasizes in his discussion of the in/capax debate in his Göttingen dogmatics that Luther – as well as Calvin – does not want to compromise in any way that the full revelation of God happened in Jesus Christ.[75] The Reformed tradition assumes that this statement must include a distinction – not a separation – of a reality of the Word outside (*extra*) of the humanity of Jesus Christ. If there was no such reality, the attributes of majesty (omnipresence, omnipotence, omniscience, eternity, …) would only have their reality in the human reality of Jesus Christ. This, however, is a highly problematic conclusion since then the attributes of majesty would be compromised. Barth states in terms of the in/capax question:

> But this would be the case if one wanted to think him enclosed in the humanity of Christ, thus in a creature, thus in a finitum, a finite quantity, as it were, because 'finitum non capax infiniti'.[76]

Hence, for the Reformed tradition *finitum non capax infiniti* became central. The Lutherans while affirming the Reformed conclusion feared that with this Calvinist *extra* – thus named *Extra Calvinisticum* – not only a distinction was articulated but an actual separation of the divine Logos into incarnate Logos (λόγος ἔνσαρκος) and the unincarnated Logos (λόγος ἄσαρκος) was introduced. Nevertheless, if such a separation was to be attested, then the hypostatic union and the unmixed and unseparated unity of the natures could no longer be maintained.[77] In response, the Lutherans upheld that in the case of the Assumption in Christ all attributes of majesty are communicated to the humanity of Christ. One important element of this is the teaching of ubiquity. After the Ascension, also the human nature of Christ is to be thought of ubiquitous. If Christ after all *is* present in the Eucharist, but we can only know what we know of God *as and through* the human nature of Christ, then the human nature of Christ must also be capable of being present in the Eucharist. Again, the Reformed upheld that in this case, Jesus Christ would stop being human because it is not particularity human to be ubiquitous. In other words, an omnipresent body would no longer be the finite being which was supposed to bear the infinite. Barth summarizes this account:

> If the humanity of Christ is a finitum, which is capax infiniti, if it is eternal, omnipresent, omnipotent like the Word itself, then it is no finitum, no real humanity and therefore no organ of revelation.[78]

---

75. See Barth, *Die Christliche Dogmatik im Entwurf*, 359.

76. Ibid., sec. 16, p. 360 (translation CS): 'Das wäre aber der Fall, wenn man ihn in der Menschheit Christi, also in einer Kreatur, also in einem finitum, einer endlichen Größe gleichsam eingeschlossen denken wollte, denn "finitum non capax infiniti"'.

77. See *CD* I,2, §15, 170 (*KD* I,2, §15, 186).

78. Barth, *Die Christliche Dogmatik im Entwurf*, 361 (translation CS): 'Sei die Menschheit Christi ein finitum, welches capax infiniti, sei sie also ewig, allgegenwärtig, allmächtig wie das Wort selber, dann sei sie eben kein finitum, keine wirkliche Menschheit und also kein Organ der Offenbarung.'

In contrast, the Reformed response with the Extra-Calvinisticum seeks precisely to preserve the finitude of the humanity of Jesus Christ as finitude. After a period of enthusiastic affirmation, Barth becomes critical of the *Extra* until he reaches a qualified account of it in *CD IV,1*.[79] In a lecture from 1947, he even goes so far as to call it a 'theologischer Betriebsunfall', a theological accident.[80] In *CD I,2*, written around the same time, Barth comes close to the account of Bonhoeffer's *Lectures on Christology* which upholds the intentions while dismissing the solutions of both Lutherans and Reformed. For Barth, the Lutherans fail to show how without the *extra* God can be truly human and truly God, while the Reformed cannot show how the *extra* does not introduce a dangerous duality in the divine Logos.[81] Bonhoeffer's critique similarly raises two points: First, the discussion of Ubiquity and the Extra Calvinisticum ask the wrong questions because they conflate discussions of the Eucharist and the Divinity and humanity of Christ. Secondly and as a consequence of the former, they try to navigate the 'maze of problems'[82] by asking only the *how*-question and thereby are applying a human measure to issues that cannot be measured by it. Both the Reformed and the Lutheran traditions start investigating the question of how the divine Logos is present in Christ and how the glorified Christ is present in the Eucharist starting with an inadequate antithetical pair of finite/infinite.

Seeing how both Barth (the Barth of *CD I,2* at least) and Bonhoeffer position themselves critically against both traditional articulations and take seriously the intentions of both the Lutheran and the Reformed theologians, it becomes questionable to articulate the differences between Barth and Bonhoeffer according to confessional diversity. In recent discussions, Michael P. DeJonge argued against Andreas Pangritz eloquently and convincingly for the relevance of this confessional distinction.[83] While for *CD I,2* the positions of Barth and Bonhoeffer overlap, the

---

79. See *CD* IV,1, §59, 180–2 (*KD* IV,1, §59, 197–8). For the discussion how Barth positions himself in regard to the *Extra Calvinisticum*, see Bruce McCormack, 'Grace and Being: The Role of God's Gracious Election in Karl Barth's Theological Ontology', in *The Cambridge Companion to Karl Barth*, ed. John Webster (Cambridge: Cambridge University Press, 2000), 95–101; Darren O. Sumner, 'The Twofold Life of the Word: Karl Barth's Critical Reception of the *Extra Calvinisticum*', in *International Journal of Systematic Theology* 15, no. 1 (2013): 49–56; Matthias D. Wüthrich, 'Ein "theologischer Betriebsunfall"? Erwägungen zum sog. *Extra Calvinisticum* ausgehend vom Heidelberger Katechismus', in *Theologische Zeitschrift* 70, no. 2 (2014): 104–7; Christian Link, 'Die Entscheidung der Christologie Calvins und ihre theologische Bedeutung: Das sogenannte Extra-Calvinisticum', in *Evangelische Theologie* 47, no. 2 (1987): 102–3.

80. Karl Barth, *Die Christliche Lehre nach dem Heidelberger Katechismus* (München: Chr. Kaiser Verlag, 1949), 71.

81. See *CD* I,2, §15, 170 (*KD* I,2, §15, 186).

82. DBWE 12:320 (DBW 12:302).

83. See DeJonge, *Bonhoeffer's Reception of Luther*, 47.

same can't be said for *Christliche Dogmatik im Entwurf* which DeJonge uses for his comparison because it is the main reference text of Barth in Bonhoeffer's *Act and Being*. In *Christliche Dogmatik im Entwurf* the affirmation of the *Extra* is evident and positioned clearly against the Lutheran doctrines.[84] Yet, in the context of the *Lectures on Christology* Bonhoeffer is much closer to what Barth will later say in *CD* I,2 – where both take rather mediating positions between the confessions.[85] In this context, Pangritz has a strong point that DeJonge seems to have missed in his critique: In the context of the *Lectures on Christology* the confessional differences regarding the solutions are not in the foreground but the intentions of the respective questions.[86]

It is paramount to see that Bonhoeffer does not dismiss the claim of Christ's omnipresence as such but rather identifies it as a *how*-question. It tries to go beyond a mystery it cannot solve, because it tries to explain it by a human measure. Before looking deeper into Bonhoeffer's own account of the problem, I will elaborate in conversation with the Barth of the *Church Dogmatics* on how the problem articulates itself in the terms 'finite' and 'infinite'.

2. Articulations of the In/Capax in Barth, Kierkegaard and Bonhoeffer

In *CD* II,1 Barth revisits the capax problem and elaborates on the question of the human measure. His main critique is that if omnipresence is subsumed under infinity, God becomes a question modelled after a problem of human existence – not after what God has revealed of himself.[87]

Barth explains how the concept of infinity developed in the footsteps of the Greek term ἄπειρον which for him necessarily results from the determination *omnis mensurae aut termini expers*, free from the limits of any measure.[88] In being 'purely negative … [i]t speaks of the non-finiteness'[89] as the infinite. Hence, this ἄπειρον remains being measured by the measure of finitude.

> What pretends to be this ἄπειρον, even if only in pride and revolt against the finite, is eventually infinite, created spirit, with all the demonic self-will which is its characteristic in the world of sinful men. … We have therefore no reason to try to see the essence of God in this proud and rebellious ἄπειρον.[90]

---

84. See Barth, *Die Christliche Dogmatik im Entwurf*, 363–4; DeJonge, *Bonhoeffer's Reception of Luther*, 60.
85. See also for *CD* IV,1 McCormack, 'Grace and Being', 97; also, Wüthrich, 'Ein "theologischer Betriebsunfall"?' 105.
86. See Pangritz, *Karl Barth in Der Theologie Dietrich Bonhoeffers*, 56.
87. *CD* II,1, §31, 464 (*KD* II,1, §31, 522).
88. *CD* II,1, §31, 467 (*KD* II,1, §31, 523).
89. *CD* II,1, §31, 465 (*KD* II,1, §31, 523).
90. *CD* II,1, §31, 467 (*KD* II,1, §31, 526).

If the in/capax question is modelled accordingly, the finite would be capable of the infinite insofar as it defines what the infinite is. But since the finite is the created measure, the infinite would be fully measured by human terms and hence seize to be infinite. The infinite, therefore, cannot be considered as an abstract infinity.[91] The measure of God's infinity can only be God himself and what we can know of God's infinity can only be known through God's revelation.[92] This infinity is different from all abstract notions of infinity – even if it is the presupposition of logic itself, which is always ready for annulment and dissolution[93] – that ultimately always remains determined by human measure. Barth's intention is to address the ever-greatness of God, which shows itself in his in-finity (εἰσπέραμαι, to continue the play on words).

Both Barth and Bonhoeffer are indebted to the Kierkegaard of the *Philosophical Fragments* here.[94] What the questions considering the *Extra* and the *Ubiquity* point to, is how – if the Incarnate is truly human – God reveals himself in humanity without undermining what this humanity entails. In this context, Kierkegaard compares Socrates and Jesus as teachers. Socrates reminds his students of what they already know,[95] that is, all that can be known potentially through reason and logic. That implies that everything that can be thought, even if it is infinity, is in the realm of reason. Reason, when tackling the infinite tries to think what it cannot think.[96] Kierkegaard sees this attempt as the condition of reason that tries to posit itself as the absolute truth. The actual encounter with what reason cannot think is different from reason attempting to 'discover something that thought itself cannot think'.[97] It can neither be thought *via negativa*, nor *via eminentiae*, nor be dialectically deduced.[98] What Kierkegaard tries to express is that there is an infinite qualitative distance between defining something as absolutely different in relation to reason and encountering something that basically has not been – not even not been – before the encounter.[99] *Jesus as a teacher does not remind the student of what he already knows by potentiality but instead posits a new condition.*[100]

---

91. See *CD* II,1, §31, 468 (*KD* II,1, §31, 526–7).

92. See *CD* II/1, §31, 472 (*KD* II/1, §31, 531).

93. This argument against the Hegelian logic is famously brought forward by Søren Kierkegaard, *Concluding Unscientific Postscript to Philosophical Fragments*, ed. Howard V. Hong and Edna H. Hong, Kierkegaard's Writings, XII.1/2 (Princeton: Princeton University Press, 1992), 1:109–17.

94. See the contribution of Lea Weber in this volume. See also Tim Boniface, *Jesus, Transcendence, and Generosity: Christology and Transcendence in Hans Frei and Dietrich Bonhoeffer* (Lanham: Lexington Books / Fortress Academic, 2018), 134–41.

95. See Kierkegaard, *Philosophical Fragments*, 23–6.

96. See ibid., 37.

97. Ibid.

98. Ibid., 44.

99. Ibid., 51.

100. Ibid., 55–6.

At this point, it seems more important to emphasize with Kierkegaard that the measure of infinity should not be seen in the object of its measurement, but in what is conditioned by it beyond what could be a speculative insight.[101] Kierkegaard sees Hegel as the pinnacle of speculative reason. For the derivation of the Hegelian true infinity to be possible, the paradox of the presence of infinity in the finite is weakened and diluted in its radicality through an *antecedence* of logic. In contrast, for Kierkegaard, the offence of the paradox only *retrogradely* can be addressed negatively by logic and thought. Here, the problem reaches beyond the definition of any bad or true infinity. If God is supposed to be identified with any infinity, it must be due to the revelation of God as the infinite. God's infinity must then have been posited, not deducted from a logical problem. Thus, while Hegel's true infinity always is properly defined only through itself and includes the finitude inside itself, what Kierkegaard points to here is that God's infinity works differently by being absolutely different. As example of this *absolute paradox*, Kierkegaard points towards the Incarnation. In the Incarnation, the condition (of faith) is given. The infinite reveals itself in the finite, giving meaning both to infinity and to finitude. If the question of how the finite is capable of the infinite is resolved by the measure of logic, it remains measured by human measures and therefore cannot be a proper divine attribute.

Christology, therefore, must 'begin [...] in silence. "Be silent, for that is the absolute" (Kierkegaard)'.[102] The first word on Christology can only be the revealed Word.[103] In his *Lectures on Christology* Kierkegaard's paradox is reflected in the *how* and the *who* question, as Rowan Williams points out.[104] The how-question is defined as everything that can be qualified by human measure. This becomes most evident when Bonhoeffer argues that the who-question often shifts into asking *what are you?*[105] In comparison, the who-question is not initiated by the questioner. The question of who is in its essence a passive and pathic event: we encounter

---

101. See Williams, *Christ the Heart of Creation*, 187.
102. Bonhoeffer, *Christology*, 27. The Bethge-edition of Bonhoeffer's *Lectures on Christology* includes a reference to Kierkegaard. The transcripts of Bonhoeffer's lecture are particularly divergent in the beginning of the lecture. Of all transcripts available at the Staatsbibliothek zu Berlin only *Nachl. 299 B 7,2 (Hartmut Gadow)* (and the compiled typescript of Bethge *Nachl. 299, B 7,4*) mentions Kierkegaard at the beginning. Gadow's transcript is available only in a typewritten transcript from 1960. There, however, Kierkegaard's name is misspelled ('Kiergegard'), which can either be interpreted as an error in the preparation of the typewritten transcript or as an indication of whether Gadow, unaware of Kierkegaard's name, wrote it down incorrectly in the lecture. The quote refers to Søren Kierkegaard, *Practice in Christianity*, ed. Howard V. Hong and Edna H. Hong (Princeton: Princeton University Press, 1991), 62: 'Be quiet, it is the absolute.'
103. See Rachel Muers, *Keeping God's Silence: Towards a Theological Ethics of Communication* (Malden et al.: Blackwell Publishing, 2004), 116–18.
104. See Williams, *Christ the Heart of Creation*, 186–91.
105. See DBWE 12:303 (DBW 12:283).

the question from outside of ourselves: 'There is only one possibility for me to be truly searching for God – that I already know who God is.'[106] The question turns itself against us: 'Who are you, that you ask this question?'[107] This is why we only can – in Bonhoeffer's words – kill Jesus or die in the encounter with him. Either we remain in the position of trying to secure the question and the truth of the answer from within us, then we do not grasp whom we encounter and hence kill him; or we have to give up all that so far defined who we are and therefore must die.[108] What finitude is, what it means to be human, can in light of the condition posited from outside ourselves not be considered in denial of its dependence on infinite agency. With this, Bonhoeffer expresses the thought of that reason which tries to think beyond itself, and of the encounter which defies all speculation. To attempt this speculation, however, is the very characteristic of reason as the *cor curvum in se*: to exalt itself self-referentially, as Bonhoeffer famously elaborates in many of his writings.[109] However, it is in the *Lectures on Christology* that the Christological relevance is most clearly evident and the proximity to Kierkegaard is most visible.

To summarize, when Bonhoeffer dismisses both the Lutheran and the Reformed solution as examples of the how question, it is because they are attempting to condition the revelation of Christ by means of constructing 'metaphysical hypostatizations'.[110] If the intention of their discussion is valid – that Christ's humanity must remain human and that in this humanity God has revealed himself completely without compromising his divinity – all we can know, we can only know through the passive and pathic encounter with Christ. In *Ethics* Bonhoeffer stresses that passivity in this context is not to be understood psychologically, it is a *theological passivity*.[111] This passivity embraces and 'concerns the existence of human beings before God'.[112]

3. Christology from the Centre and Fullness of Life

As discussed in comparison to his teachers, Bonhoeffer stresses that in the Incarnation, God revealed himself in the perfectly humane depths of life. 'In Christ all human reality is taken on',[113] not only the non-existent ideal of humanity.

---

106. DBWE 12:303 (DBW 12:284).
107. DBWE 12:305 (DBW 12:286).
108. See DBWE 12:305–6 (DBW 12:285–6).
109. See *DBWE* 2, 137 (DBW 2, 136), see Michael P. DeJonge, *Bonhoeffer's Theological Formation: Berlin, Barth, & Protestant Theology* (Oxford: Oxford University Press, 2012), 124.
110. DBWE 6:312 (DBW 12:304).
111. See DBWE 6:337 (DBW 6:340).
112. DBWE 6:337 (DBW 6:340).
113. DBWE 6:224 (DBW 6:223).

If God is to be described in his infinity, it hence always is from the midst of the world into which he lowered himself. Yet this does not imply automatically that God's infinity is constructed from finitude as Barth had criticized. Bonhoeffer sees the Chalcedonian Christology, as Rowan Williams puts it, 'as a way of dismantling a false account of the finite/infinite distinction'.[114] Bonhoeffer, beginning with the *Lectures on Christology* far into *Ethics*, is looking for a Christological language that starts with the revelation. Because of the Incarnation, the Crucifixion and the Ascension we are given a new limit.

> The world that is passing away has been claimed by God. We must therefore continue to reckon with the world's worldliness but at the same time reckon with God's rule over it. What actually exists is given anew its legitimacy and its limits.[115]

Bonhoeffer's answer revolves around a different conceptualization of finitude and infinity that mirrors what we have seen in Kierkegaard above. It is paramount to see that Barth constructed the account of the 'rebellious infinity'[116] along the lines of the definition of ἄπειρον, that which has no boundary (πέρας). Bonhoeffer, with Kierkegaard in the background, rethinks the definition of boundary in his *Ethics*. Christ is in the middle of life and from the centre he gives meaning to finitude, and therefore it is infinity that makes finitude significant as finitude. Essentially, what this amounts to for Bonhoeffer is that any adequate Christological language can neither argue from above nor from below, but only from the midst, from the fullness of life.[117]

A Christology 'from above', that starts from God to explain what the Incarnate needs to be is inadequate because inevitably such speculation would condition what can be revealed in the Incarnate. A Christology 'from below' that would first look at the historical Jesus and then to the Glorified, would inevitably lose sight of the fact that in the historical person of Jesus the Work and the being of God is revealed. Rather in Christ, what is revealed is both what the infinite and the finite are.

> As the limit, Christ is at the center that I have regained. As boundary, the boundary can only be seen from its other side, outside the limit. Thus it is important that we human beings, in recognizing that our limit is in Christ, at the same time see that in this limit we have found our new center.[118]

---

114. Williams, *Christ the Heart of Creation*, 195.
115. DBWE 6:224 (DBW 6:223).
116. *CD* II,1, §31, 467 (*KD* II,1, §31, 526).
117. Already in the *Lectures on Christology* Bonhoeffer emphasizes that Christ is the centre of existence, history and nature. See DBWE 12:324 (DBW 12:307).
118. DBWE 12:324 (DBW 12:306–7).

Bonhoeffer's *Ethics*, then, underlines a line of Kierkegaardian thought that is already present in the *Lectures on Christology* as the *pro-me* structure, which here is interpreted in terms of responsibility. The re-envisioned world in the light of faith is a world that, most fundamentally, only has meaning because it is put into a relation of possibility *for us*. The *pro nobis* of Christ shines a new light upon the very limits of our finitude. The infinity of God that is revealed in Jesus Christ does not go beyond the finitude of human life, instead, it radiates from within it. As God revealed himself in the martyred finitude, he shows us our finitude under a different horizon. It is not an otherworldly paradise that is shown but that the worldliness of everyday life with everything that that implies is seen under the horizon given in Christ. In the *Lectures on Christology* Bonhoeffer highlights, what this amounts to:

> The earth wants us to take it seriously. It will not let us escape, not into the salvation of otherworldly piety nor into the utopia of this-worldly secularism. Instead, it comes right out and shows us how it is enslaved in finiteness [zeigt uns ihre geknechtete Endlichkeit].[119]

The horizon constitutes a different kind of limiting the finite than the ἄπειρον. In the history of philosophy, the Greek word ὅρος not only has the meaning of boundary but also designates the horizon as that limit on which we *orient* our world.[120] For instance, in Plotinus' *Enneads*, *number* is understood as the category which allows for things to be differentiated and hence is the condition of both the possibility of determination and definition (ὁριστός), and the indeterminate, undefined, and hence debatable (ἀόριστος). However, *horizon* does not touch the absolute transcendence of the One, because speaking about it in philosophical language would always already have established a determination or at least indeterminateness. However, as the One circumradiates (περίλαμψεῖν[121]) from the centre, it constitutes the condition for any horizon to be formed but cannot be deduced from it. While Bonhoeffer is *not* adopting a Neoplatonic framework, the language of horizon as limitation and demarcation of finitude that leaves the One untouched in silence articulates a possibility to understand of how Bonhoeffer's Christology approves of the capability of the finite to bear the infinite 'non per se, sed per infinitum'.[122] As such, the infinite gives meaning to finitude and infinite alike

---

119. DBWE 12:290 (DBW 12:269–70). See Barker, *The Cross of Reality*, 364–7.

120. For ὅρος in the context of Chalcedonian discussions, see Sarah Coakley, 'What Does Chalcedon Solve and What Does It Not? Some Reflections on the Status and Meaning of the Chalcedonian "Definition"', in *The Incarnation: An Interdisciplinary Symposium on the Incarnation of the Son of God*, ed. Stephen T. Davis et al. (Oxford: Oxford University Press, 2002), 160–1.

121. Plotin, *Enn.*, 5.1.6.28; see Paul North, *Bizarre-Privileged Items in the Universe: The Logic of Likeness* (New York: Zone Books, 2021), 109.

122. DBWE 12:346 (DBW 12:332). See Pangritz, *Karl Barth in der Theologie Dietrich Bonhoeffers*, 54; similarly, Kierkegaard, *Philosophical Fragments*, 44–5.

from the centre of life. In a letter from prison to Bethge, Bonhoeffer stresses exactly that 'God is the beyond in the midst of our lives'.[123] But this circumradiating centre must, for Bonhoeffer, be a person. Analogically, in all our personal encounters in the world, we are left with the who-question, which is neither determinate nor debatable.

> Since the Chalcedonian formula, we can no longer say, how shall we think about the difference of the two natures and the unity of the person? but rather: who is this human being who is said to be God?[124]

The Chalcedonian Creed is precisely not a formula to be explained by philosophical language, but on the contrary, as an expression of the absolute paradox, that highlights the limits of thinkability. Here Bonhoeffer stresses that Christ can neither be understood from below – because this would be a violation of his humanity as he would be glorified into a perfect human being – nor from above – because this would be a diminution of his divinity since it would subvert the unfathomable and encompassing generosity of His love and thus of His revealed nature.

Bonhoeffer develops the contemporary relevance of this thought through the distinction between the ultimate and the penultimate, which leads to the determination of Christ-reality. The ultimate is eschatological in the sense that it is always the ultimate (ἔσχατος) word (λόγος). When Bonhoeffer speaks in this sense about the qualitative and the temporal ultimacy of the word, the latter depends on the former. For Justification, which the ultimate word reveals, is qualitatively different from what any human measure could grasp. It is temporally ultimate in the sense that, because of its qualitative irrefutability, it is at every moment the permanently ultimate word from which the whole world appears under the light of a new horizon. This new light that falls onto the world does not first reveal it as what it always has been, but rather is a continuous new creation of all that is. 'In this saving light, people recognize God and their neighbours for the first time.'[125] This happens without anything being changed in the 'physical existence' of the world. Like a child for whom a stick is a fishing rod one moment and a magic wand the next, the world changes without the need for any change in the substance of the world. Thus, reality becomes the reality of the penultimate. The reality that has been signified by the ultimate. The Word breaks ground in the reality of human beings. As Word, Christ is thus always present for the world. This permanent and ubiquitous omnipresence emphasizes the 'temporal' character of the presence. It is

---

123. DBWE 8:367 (DBW 8:408).

124. DBWE 12:350 (DBW 12:336). See Williams, *Christ the Heart of Creation*, 193–4: 'Bonhoeffer is wary of attempts to "go beyond" Chalcedon, since he sees these refinements less as grammatical fine-tuning than as covert strategies for returning to the "how" question which Chalcedon, rightly understood, prohibits.'

125. DBWE 6:146 (DBW 6:137).

only ubiquitous because it is always present. Nevertheless, it is only present insofar as it remains the ultimate Word and thus remains permanently in the coming. Christ-reality is not an explanation of Chalcedon but an expression of how Christ is still with us today. What was revealed in Christ and still is present as the light of the ultimate shines on our finitude as his presence. Omnipresence in the classical sense in which Luther described it as ubiquity is defined by spatial language, for Bonhoeffer, it rather becomes a presence *pro nobis* that shows us the significance of the finitude in which we live.[126] What is present is not his human nature purely by means of its humanity but who is present is the human existence of Christ through, in and as the divine Word.

> Only because there is one place where God and the reality of the world are reconciled with each other, at which God and humanity have become one, is it possible there and there alone to fix one's eyes on God and the world together at the same time. This place does not lie somewhere beyond reality in the realm of ideas. It lies in the midst of history as a divine miracle.[127]

This insight is also ultimately guiding Bonhoeffer's assessment of the question of ubiquity. After the caution articulated in the *Lectures on Christology*, Bonhoeffer ultimately tends towards a Lutheran solution. When in 1940 Bonhoeffer meditates on the Ascension of Christ, he approves that the *humanity* of Christ is eternally present. 'He remains human forever. His human nature, assumed within time, is taken up into eternity.'[128] Bonhoeffer, in the end, is a Lutheran who transforms his tradition within the Barthian movement.[129] The specific Bonhoefferian solution emphasizes that the starting point cannot be speculation, but the action of a divine agency. With that, Bonhoeffer emphasizes that all we can say about the finite and the infinite we only can say because the infinite has posited and remains the condition to speak about this relation at all.

> The assumed humanity, the human being Jesus Christ, enters the eternity of the Father. In order, however, to protect against philosophical speculation

---

126. Bonhoeffer does not address the traditional question of how Christ is present in the Eucharist. See Williams, *Christ the Heart of Creation*, 213–14: 'Bonhoeffer's reticence in spelling out a Eucharistic theology – influenced no doubt by his impatience with the importance ascribed to confessional disputes on this subject between Lutheran and Reformed Protestants – might yet be filled out by an understanding of how Eucharistic practice could embody precisely the non-competitive, non-territorial territory of a visible sign of God's future.'
127. DBWE 6:82 (DBW 6:68).
128. *DBWE* 16, 476 (DBW 16, 475).
129. See Christiane Tietz, 'Barth und Bonhoeffer', in *Barth Handbuch*, ed. Michael Beintker (Tübingen: Mohr Siebeck, 2016), 115; Eberhard Bethge, *Dietrich Bonhoeffer: Eine Biographie*, 8. Auflage (Gütersloh: Kaiser, 1994), 219; Boniface, *Jesus, Transcendence, and Generosity*, 112.

that allows humanity and divinity to merge into each other, that is, in order to confront any mysticism of identification, the Lutheran fathers teach that, ... the assumed humanity (i.e. Jesus Christ's human nature) is not itself assumed into the Trinity but remains eternally subject to it.[130]

III. Ecce homo!

In the one true exclamation about Jesus Christ – 'Ecce homo – behold, what a human being!'[131] – the limit is signified but not demarcated as the horizon of finitude from the centre. It is not a fixed boundary constructing a supernatural reality, which could be expressed by a speculative idea or a logical calculus. It is a limit that only arises from the fact that it springs from within human finitude. Already in his *Lectures on Christology*, Bonhoeffer had emphasized that in the encounter with the Logos – with the Word in person – one experiences the limit of one's own understanding. The question of infinity can never go back beyond this limit, which gives meaning to finitude. The Who question itself appears rather as that which breaks open the world and as such makes it questionable in a way that makes it possible to experience the world as signified by the love of God.

With the Who question, Bonhoeffer moves towards a gesture of what could be an adequate language that preserves the inarticulateable core of Christology. The Chalcedonian Creed, then, is a gesture itself, pointing towards the unaddressable in the middle of life. It is important to keep in mind that Bonhoeffer never tries to 'solve' Chalcedon with a positive account,[132] but rather sees the articulation of the inarticulateable as expressed in the silence of the paradox, which is a testimony to the *new language*, namely the Word's presence among us, as Luther positioned his own account of the Incarnation against all metaphysical speculation:

> We would act more correctly if we left dialectic and philosophy in their own area and learned to speak in a new language in the realm of faith apart from every sphere.[133]

---

130. DBWE 16, 476–7 (DBW 16, 475–6).

131. DBWE 6:82 (DBW 6:69).

132. As Williams, *Christ the Heart of Creation*, 184. puts it for the *Lectures on Christology*: 'The lectures have been described as tantalizingly lacking in positive dogmatic proposals ... They are more than a ground-clearing exercise; the very fact of identifying – as Bonhoeffer does – a fresh starting point carries doctrinal implications, to be spelled out in his later writing.'

133. Luther, 'The Disputation Concerning the Passage "the Word Was Made Flesh" (John 1:14)', 242. = WA 39 II, 5, Th. 40: 'Rectius ergo fecerimus, si Dialectica seu Philosophica is sua sphaera relictis, dicamus loqui *novis linguis in regno fidei* (emphasis CS), extra omnem sphaeram.'

Pilate's exclamation – *Ecce homo!* – brings to light the different aspects of what it means to have the gaze *directed* to Jesus Christ. 'Faith means to be captivated by the gaze of Jesus Christ.'[134] This means that finitude appears under a different horizon as something that is entirely the same while being wholly other. *From the centre of life, the whole of life, history and humanity is interpreted by Christ* – contrary to an interpretation of Christ through life, history or humanity.[135] Pilate's words portray the entire unveiling of God in human form. For Pilate, these words signify precisely what their literal meaning is: This Son of Nazareth is not a God, he is only human. However, at the same time, this sentence describes how God revealed himself, and what he took upon himself to bring about justification. Bonhoeffer takes seriously that all we can say about the Incarnation, the Crucifixion and the Resurrection we can say only in light of the humanity of Christ.

> This love of God for the world does not withdraw from reality into noble souls detached from the world, but experiences and suffers the reality of the world at its worst. The world exhausts in rage on the body of Jesus Christ. But the martyred one forgives the world its sins. Thus reconciliation takes place. Ecce homo.[136]

Pilate's exclamation is transformed into a fundamental theological articulation of revelation. For Bonhoeffer, this corrects a problem of the Christologies of his teachers, as they focus on the humanity of Christ, trying to avoid any metaphysical speculation but are left with an all-too-human Christ, who misses what it means to be human.

> Ecce homo – behold God become human, the unfathomable mystery of the love of God for the world. … Not an ideal human, but human beings as they are; not an ideal world, but the real world.[137]

God takes on the real world and becomes a truly human being and therein not only reveals who He is, but also what it means to be a true and finite human being that is loved by God.

---

134. DBWE 6:147 (DBW 6:138).
135. See DBWE 6:226 (DBW 6:225), Matt Jenson, 'Real Presence: Contemporaneity in Bonhoeffer's Christology', in *Scottish Journal of Theology* 58, no. 2 (2005): 145.
136. DBWE 6:83 (DBW 6:79).
137. DBWE 6:84 (DBW 6:70).

Chapter 8

THE SUFFERING GOD: BONHOEFFER AND CHALCEDONIAN CHRISTOLOGY

Matthias Grebe

This is the decisive difference between Christianity and all religions. Man's religiosity makes him look in his distress to the power of God in the world; he uses God as a *deus ex machina*. The Bible, however, directs us to the powerlessness and suffering of God; only a suffering God can help. To this extent we may say that the process we have described by which the world came of age was an abandonment of the false conception of God, and a clearing of the decks for the God of the Bible, who conquers power and space in the world by his weakness.

— Dietrich Bonhoeffer, *Letters and Papers from Prison*

In some ways suffering ceases to be suffering at the moment it finds a meaning, such as the meaning of a sacrifice.

— Viktor E. Frankl, *Man's Search for Meaning*

From his prison cell in 1944, shortly before his execution, Dietrich Bonhoeffer penned the famous words to his friend Eberhard Bethge that 'only a suffering God can help'.[1] According to Jürgen Moltmann, Bonhoeffer was the first theologian in the nineteenth and twentieth centuries who dared to speak of a 'suffering God' within the context of German Protestantism.[2] Not only this, but Bonhoeffer's

---

Thanks is due to the Deutsche Forschungsgemeinschaft (DFG) for supporting Matthias' research fellowship on theodicy and the problem of evil.

1. DBWE 8:479 (DBW 8:534).
2. See Jürgen Moltmann, 'Theologie mit Dietrich Bonhoeffer: Die Gefängnisbriefe', in *Bonhoeffers Theologie heute: Ein Weg zwischen Fundamentalismus und Säkularismus? Bonhoeffer's Theology Today: A Way between Fundamentalism and Secularism?*, ed. John W. de Gruchy, Stephen Plant, and Christiane Tietz (Gütersloh: Gütersloher Verlagshaus, 2009), 17-31. Moltmann writes: 'Nach meiner Kenntnis ist es in der gesamten deutschen Theologie des 19. Und 20. Jahrhunderts [bis zu diesem Zeitpunkt] einzigartig, dass einer vom "leidenden Gott" zu sprechen wagt', 29.

writings from prison were said to have sparked a 'theology of God's suffering'[3] and a 'turnaround in the conception of God in the 20th century.'[4] The second half of the last century witnessed a significant change within Christian theology, especially in post-war Germany. Theologians including Jürgen Moltmann,[5] Dorothee Sölle, Johann Baptist Metz and Eberhard Jüngel critically revisited the doctrine of divine impassibility, embracing instead the doctrine of the suffering God.

As Richard Bauckham highlights, the idea of divine suffering 'has appeared in many other theological traditions',[6] expounded by scholars as diverse as the Japanese Lutheran theologian Kazoh Kitamori,[7] Thomas F. Torrance, Paul Fiddes, Richard Bauckham and James H. Cone,[8] and to the extent that it is justified to ask if *theopaschism*, the belief that a God can suffer, has become the 'new orthodoxy'.[9]

This chapter's interest, then, is the underlying question of whether it is theologically and/or biblically correct to speak of the suffering God. This raises further questions: *Did* God suffer? *Does* God suffer? Is God *able* to suffer relationally with us, and what difference does that make for us personally? And of course, what has brought about such a radical re-conceptualization of God?

This chapter does not attempt to provide a theodicy. Rather, it engages with the doctrine of divine impassibility (*apatheia*) and the suffering God in light of Chalcedon, and expounds the thesis *Gott leidet, weil er liebt* – God suffers, because he loves. This thesis could be concretised in light of the triune God who loves in freedom (Barth) as follows: God suffers, because he loves his creation, the world and humanity.

In order to address the thesis, this chapter engages with Bonhoeffer's Christology and outworking of Chalcedon, for which we will turn to his *Lectures on Christology*.[10] Here we are told that Bonhoeffer finds it necessary to engage

---

3. See Jan Rohls, 'Der leidende Gott in der Theologie des 20. Jahrhunderts', in *Der leidende Gott: Eine philosophische und theologische Kritik*, ed. Peter Koslowski und Friedrich Hermanni (München: Wilhelm Fink Verlag, 2001), 31–56.

4. Christiane Tietz, 'Der leidende Gott', in *Panorama* 23 (2011): 107–20, 107. See also Jan Bauke-Ruegg, *Die Allmacht Gottes: Systematisch-theologische Erwägungen zwischen Metaphysik, Postmoderne und Poesie* (Berlin: De Gruyter, 1998), 36.

5. See Jürgen Moltmann, *The Crucified God: The Cross of Christ as the Foundation and Criticism of Christian Theology*, trans. R. A. Wilson and John Bowden (London: SCM, 1974).

6. Richard Bauckham, '"Only the Suffering God Can Help": divine passibility in modern theology', in *Themelios* 9, no. 3 (April 1984): 6–12, 6.

7. See Kazoh Kitamori, *Theology of the Pain of God*, trans. Shinkyo Shuppansha (Richmond: John Knox Press, 1965).

8. See James H. Cone, *The Cross and The Lynching Tree* (New York: Orbis Books, 2011).

9. See Ronald Goetz, 'The Suffering God: The Rise of a New Orthodoxy', in *Christian Century* 103, no. 13 (16 April 1986): 385–9, 385.

10. DBWE 12:299–360 (DBW 12:279–348).

with heresy, as the 'concept of heresy is a necessary, nonnegotiable factor' because 'doctrine must always be set over against false doctrine; otherwise one does not know what doctrine means'.[11] Thus I shall follow Bonhoeffer's advice and in a first step contrast the doctrine of impassibility with passibility. Then secondly, I shall look at Luther's Christology, especially the *communicatio idiomatum*, before in a third step engaging with Bonhoeffer and Chalcedon. The fourth and final section will expand Bonhoeffer's understanding of the suffering and crucified God and the ramifications of this for 'religionless Christianity' in a 'world come of age'.

I. Divine Impassibility and the Greek Doctrine of Apatheia

From the Patristic Period of the early Greek Fathers onwards, Christian theology has held as axiomatic the doctrine of divine impassibility (*apatheia*), which asserts that God is not a subject of passions, pain and suffering. Early Christology was developed in dialogue with Greek philosophy, which is why many modern scholars stress that the idea of *apatheia* was a 'Greek philosophical inheritance in early Christian theology'.[12]

But what did *apatheia* mean for the Greeks; how exactly did they understand the term? When Greek philosophy asserts that God cannot suffer, what is meant is that God can neither be *passive* nor *affected* by something or someone else. Instead, God is the unmoved mover (Aristotle/Aquinas) who is independent, absolutely self-sufficient and self-determining.[13] Thomas Weinandy defines passibility in the following way:

> For God to be 'passible' then means that he is capable of being acted upon from without and that such actions bring about emotional changes of state within him. Moreover, for God to be passible means that he is capable of freely changing his inner emotional state in response to and interaction with the changing human condition and world order. Last, passibility implies that God's changing emotional states involve 'feelings' that are analogous to human feelings.[14]

---

11. DBWE 12:332 (DBW 12:316).

12. Bauckham, 'Only the Suffering God Can Help', 7. Bauckham writes that 'The great hellenistic Jewish theologian Philo had already prepared the way for this by making *apatheia* a prominent feature of his understanding of the God of Israel, and virtually all the Christian Fathers took it for granted, viewing with suspicion any theological tendency which might threaten the essential impassibility of the divine nature'. See also Bonhoeffer's bold claim in the lecture 'Jesus Christ and the Essence of Christianity' where he writes: 'wherever the Greek spirit is regnant, the Christian idea of God is not understood', DBWE 10:356 (DBW 10:318).

13. See Bauckham, 'Only the Suffering God Can Help', 7.

14. Thomas Weinandy, *Does God Suffer?* (London: T&T Clark, 2000), 39.

Furthermore, the notion of divine *pathos*, suffering, which includes both the idea of pain and passion (emotion – both pain and pleasure) is, in Greek philosophy, associated with *passivity* and closely linked with other features of the changing material world, such as time and matter. Since God is atemporal and incorporeal, he is also unchangeable, since 'any change (even change which he wills rather than change imposed on him from outside) could only be change for the worse'.[15] As Bauckham explains:

> Suffering is what comes upon one, against one's will. It is something of which one is a passive victim. Thus suffering is a mark of weakness and God is necessarily above suffering. But, for the Greeks, one is also passive when one is moved by the passions or emotions. To be moved by desire or fear or anger is to be affected by something outside the self, instead of being self-determining. Again this is weakness and so God must be devoid of emotion. To suffer or to feel is to be subject to pain or emotion and the things that cause them. God cannot be subject to anything.[16]

Therefore, if God is the ground of all being, from whom everything else derives existence, then it must follow that God is immutable and impassible.

In terms of the Church's response, it could hardly deny that the central teaching of Christ's passion and death on the cross and the notion of divine impassibility were not straightforwardly compatible with the biblical witness and Christian experience, if we think of martyrdom and discipleship [*Nachfolge*].[17] The biblical narrative and Greek philosophy on *apatheia* seem to stand somewhat at odds, as an apathetic god does not seem to match the picture of the biblical God. A look at Scripture, especially the Hebrew Bible, reveals a God intimately involved in the history of his people, a God sharing in Israel's suffering (Jer. 31:20 and 30; Isa. 63:9; Hos. 11:7-11). And both the Passion narrative in the Gospels and the letters portray Jesus as a sufferer (Lk. 22:62; Jn. 11:35; Heb. 2:18; 1 Pet. 3:18, 4:1).

In light of this, did the Church abandon the Greek idea of the divine impassibility and embrace the biblical concept of a suffering God? The Nicene Creed merely

---

15. Bauckham, 'Only the Suffering God Can Help', 8. See also Christiane Tietz, 'Der leidende Gott', in *Die Spiegelschrift Gottes ist schwer zu lesen: Beiträge zur Theologie Dietrich Bonhoeffers* (Gütersloh: Gütersloher Verlagshaus, 2021), 138–40, who writes: 'Platon und Aristoteles nehmen diese Impulse auf. Platon, der Gott als "in jeder Hinsicht das Beste" beschreibt, betont, Gott könne sich nicht wandeln, sondern bleibe sich selbst gleich; denn wenn er jetzt das Beste, d.h. vollkommene ist, dann könnte er sich nur wandeln zu etwas Unvollkommenerem hin', 131.

16. Bauckham, 'Only the Suffering God Can Help', 7.

17. See Harmut Rosenau, 'Vom Leid der Nachfolge und der Nachfolge im Leid – Bonhoeffer und die Theodizee-Frage', in *Interesse Am Anderen: Interdisziplinäre Beiträge zum Verhältnis von Religion und Rationalität*, ed. Gerhard Schreiber (Berlin: De Gruyter, 2019), 705–22., passim. Vortrag auf der Jahrestagung der Internationalen Bonhoeffer-Gesellschaft 2018.

states that Christ 'suffered and was buried' and does not actually explain the suffering per se. However, when the Church *did* address the issue, it affirmed that God cannot suffer in his *divine* nature. The classical statement of theism is found in Cyril of Alexandria's second letter to Nestorius, (written about 429 AD), a view which was confirmed both at the first Council of Ephesus (431) and at the Council of Chalcedon (451). Cyril writes:

> In a similar way we say that He [Christ] suffered and rose again, not that the Word of God suffered blows or piercing with nails or any other wounds in His own nature (for the divine, being without a body, is incapable of suffering), but because the body which became His own suffered these things, He is said to have suffered them for us. For He was without suffering [*apathes*], while His body suffered.[18]

In this passage we see that Cyril is operating within the classic Greek understanding of suffering, which applies the concept to the *body*. And since God does not have a physical body, it logically followed for them that God cannot suffer. But even though early Church Fathers such as Cyril maintained the impassibility of God, they did so in the context of a paradox: constrained by the 'Alexandrian Christology to attribute the sufferings of Jesus to the Logos',[19] they navigated the paradox of God suffering impassibly in the idea that the impassible God is passible as the incarnate Word. In this way, aware of the suffering of the human nature, the divine Logos was *unaffected* by suffering.

How do we explain the dominance of the axiom of divine apathy in the early Church? Were the Fathers 'captivated by the spirit of Greek metaphysics which in turn distorted their understanding of Scripture'?[20]

Scholars vehemently disagree on this point. Paul Gavrilyuk points out the flawed antithesis in that the patristic dilemma, in that it amounted to a choice between 'the unemotional and uninvolved God of the Hellenes and the emotional and suffering God of the Hebrews'[21] and opposes what he sees as a false dichotomy made by some scholars between patristic impassibilty and modern *theopassianism*. However, whereas Gavrilyuk argues against the 'Theory of Theology's Fall into Hellenistic philosophy',[22] Jürgen Moltmann argues that the Fathers made the error

---

18. Norman P. Tanner, *Decrees of the Ecumenical Councils: Volumes 1 and 2: From Nicaea I to Vatican II* (Washington, DC: Georgetown University Press, 1990), 42.

19. Bauckham, 'Only the Suffering God Can Help', 8.

20. Jeffrey G Silcock, 'The Truth of Divine Impassibility: A New Look at an Old Argument', in *LTJ* 45, no. 3 (December 2011): 198–207, 199.

21. Paul Gavrilyuk, *The Suffering of the Impassible God: The Dialectics of Patristic Thought* (Oxford: Oxford University Press, 2004), 46.

22. Ibid., 5.

of seeing only two alternatives: 'either essential incapacity for suffering, or a fateful subjection to suffering'.²³ He explains that 'there is a third form of suffering – the voluntary laying oneself open to another and allowing oneself to be intimately affected by him; that is to say, the suffering of passionate love'.²⁴ We will return to this thought later.

We still need to consider what is actually at stake in this debate. The passibilists argue that 'if God does not suffer with the world he created, he is and will be seen to be cold, detached, uncaring, and devoid of compassion … theology must be determined by the biblical narrative, and in particular the narrative of salvation. The transcendent God cannot be quarantined from the contingencies of time and history.'²⁵ The heart of the issue for impassibilists is at least twofold: first, they want to safeguard against any fluctuations of 'emotion' in God, over which God has no personal control, i.e. human pain should not be said to stir up *involuntary* sorrow within God. Secondly, they want to safeguard the transcendence and otherness of God. God's life is different to creaturely life. For theologians like Weinandy, who advocate impassibility, the 'ontological distinction between Creator and creature is … the fundamental positive reason why God does not suffer'.²⁶

It is important to mention at this stage that many advocates of divine passibility would not disagree outright with the sort of statements which argue in favour of impassibility, and many would want to recognize the importance and the elements of truth in them. Not only does God not have a body, but God's lordship and sovereignty over creation make it inconceivable that God could ever be subjected to an external force that is more powerful. In this way any heresies and gnostic dualistic tendencies are immediately ruled out.

To sum up this discussion: we saw that the classical doctrine of divine impassibility affirms that God is not (negatively) *affected* by anything which transpires in God's creation. Suffering was understood as physical and emotional pain in the body, inflicted by an external force, which is why God cannot suffer, because God is incorporeal and incapable of being acted upon by an external force. In the event of Christ's passion and death on the cross, then, impassibilists argue that it was only the *human nature* of the God-man which suffered and experienced pain and death. Ultimately, for the Greeks and some of the early Church Fathers, the understanding of God as impassible highlighted stability and constancy. Arguably, for the modern mind, this idea of god might appear rather static.

---

23. Jürgen Moltmann, *The Trinity and the Kingdom of God: The Doctrine of God*, trans. Margaret Kohl (Minneapolis: Fortress Press, 1983), 23.
24. Moltmann, *The Trinity and the Kingdom of God*, 23.
25. Silcock, 'The Truth of Divine Impassibility', 200.
26. Weinandy, *Does God Suffer?*, 154.

II. Martin Luther: Communicatio Idiomatum

Luther makes an important contribution to the debate on the suffering God[27] in his creative development of two of the early Church Christological motifs – the theopaschite formula and the concept of *communicatio idiomatum*.[28] Luther's stark protest against the doctrine of divine impassibility is seen in his *theologia crucis*, contained within the Heidelberg Disputation of 1518. Here he not only uses the phrase *deus crucifixus* ('crucified God') to speak of God's sharing in the sufferings of Christ on the cross, but also comments in thesis 21: 'God can be found only in suffering and the cross.'[29] In this way, Luther revises 'Chalcedonian metaphysics as he faithfully explicates the christological dogma of Chalcedon'.[30]

In Luther's 1539 'Disputation concerning the passage "The Word was made flesh"'[31] and his 1540 'Disputation on the divinity and humanity of Christ',[32] he expounds the logic of the *communicatio idiomatum* and develops a new language that differentiates between *abstract* statements and the *concrete*. For Luther, theology needs to begin with the *concrete* particularity of God in Christ rather than an *abstract* god of philosophy. He rejects any metaphysics that speaks of the humanity and divinity of Christ in abstract terms. Luther argues that theology should not speak of God in general terms, as separated from Jesus, but always about the God who became human in Jesus Christ, who lived, suffered and died in the flesh.[33] He starts from the 'identity of the person of Christ in its unity as depicted in the New Testament'.[34] However, for Luther, God's passibility is not 'established by the *communicatio idiomatum* but ... rather is a theological means to realize or articulate that God, in Christ, did suffer and die'.[35] Luther argues for a *real* exchange, a communication of attributes 'which teaches that Christ's human nature is suffused by the divine and receives the attributes of the divine nature'.[36]

---

27. For an analysis of Luther's doctrine of *communicatio idiomatum* topic see Dennis Ngien, *The Suffering of God According to Martin Luther's* Theologia Crucis (Vancouver: Regents College Publishing, 2005), 68–86.

28. 'The concept of the communication of attributes was not invented by Luther but had already been used by Cyril in his dispute with Nestorius, but Luther develops it further as he comes up with a new theological language (*nova lingua*), with its own new grammar (*nova grammatica*), which is distinct from the general language of philosophy and is grounded in the biblical narrative and particularly the story of Jesus Christ', Silcock, 'The Truth of Divine Impassibility', 201–2.

29. *Heidelberg Disputation*, LW 31:52–3. See also DBWE 8:479n41 (DBW 8:534n38).

30. Silcock, 'The Truth of Divine Impassibility', 201.

31. LW 38:235–77.

32. WA 39 II:92–121. Translated from the Latin text of WA 39/2 by Christopher B. Brown.

33. See J. Silcock, 'The Truth of Divine Impassibility', 202.

34. Ngien, *The Suffering of God*, 68.

35. Ibid.

36. DBWE 12:346 (DBW 12:332).

Thus, Luther explains, because of the unity of the two natures, the divine nature via the *communicatio idiomatum* suffers along with the human nature. This notion of divine suffering, which brings together Christology and soteriology, is made lucid in Article 8 of the Formula of Concord (1577):

> We Christians must know that if God is not also in the balance, and gives the weight, we sink to the bottom with our scale. By this I mean: If it were not to be said [if these things were not true], God has died for us, but only a man, we would be lost. But if 'God's death' and 'God died' lie in the scale of the balance, then He sinks down, and we rise up as a light, empty scale. But indeed He can also rise again or leap out of the scale; yet He could not sit in the scale unless He became a man like us, so that it could be said: 'God died,' 'God's passion,' 'God's blood,' 'God's death.' For in His nature God cannot die; but now that God and man are united in one person, it is correctly called God's death, when the man dies who is one thing or one person with God.

In light of this, if the doctrine of impassibility is maintained, we might argue that the work of Christ on the cross is 'merely a human work, and His death on the Cross is the death of a man not the death of the Son of God'. However, salvation is achieved by Jesus because on the cross, he is 'doing something that man should do, but which only God *can* do'.[37]

Space does not allow for a further elaboration on Luther's new language and grammar of the Spirit in relation to the communication of attributes, but what has become clear from this short excursus on Luther's theology on the *concrete* and the *abstract* is that it compels us to articulate in precise language the doctrine of the suffering God. As Silock points out:

> [M]uch of the contemporary discussion is misdirected and misinformed because it uses terms like God and suffering in an abstract, philosophical way and does not employ the necessary linguistic rigour that Luther brought to the debate with his new language and new grammar of theology which makes a careful distinction between the concrete and the abstract. Simply to argue that God suffers or can't suffer, is passible or impassible, misses the point because it lacks precision. Luther reminds us that God *per se* is an abstraction; the only God we know is God in the flesh. God is not passible in the abstract, but only in the flesh of Christ.[38]

Ultimately then, there is at one level consensus between the patristic theology and Luther's theology on the axiom of divine impassibility, but only when speaking about the divine nature in itself, in *abstract* terms (which Luther ordinarily seeks to avoid!). There is, however, also disagreement when speaking *concretely* about

---

37. T. E. Pollard, 'The Impassibility of God', in *SJT* 8, no. 4 (1955): 353–64, 363.
38. Silcock, 'The Truth of Divine Impassibility', 205.

the incarnate Logos, the *deus pro nobis* who has revealed himself in Jesus Christ on the cross. Here, in Luther's treatment of the union of the divine nature and human nature – at times he uses the traditional language in order not to lose the distinction of the natures – he does position it in terms of the God who suffered and died.

III. Bonhoeffer and Chalcedon

The question of divine suffering emerged in the neo-Chalcedonian theopaschite controversy, which erupted after the Council of Chalcedon (451). In Chalcedon, the Council agreed that in Jesus Christ, two natures are united in one person. However, the debate 'continued over whether there are two active subjects corresponding to the two natures of the God-man'.[39] In opposition to the Apollinarian confusion of natures and the Nestorian separation of subjects, Cyril's theology of the hypostatic union and the theopaschite formula – in which one of the Trinity was crucified and suffered in the flesh – prevailed and became the via media,[40] which 'allowed one to speak of the suffering of God in Christ without attributing the suffering to the divine "nature"'.[41]

In his *Lectures on Christology* Bonhoeffer discusses the classical formulation of the doctrine of Christ as God-human as it was established in the Chalcedonian Formula of 451. He contends that the decision of the Church councils 'expressed only the conclusions of critical Christology'[42] and challenges his reader to think creatively about the Chalcedonian Formula, arguing, in agreement with Luther, that we cannot think about the two natures in isolation: 'Since the Chalcedonian formula, we can no longer say, *how* shall we think about the difference of the two natures and the unity of the person? but rather: *who* is this human being who is

---

39. See ibid., 200.
40. See Aloys Grillmeier SJ in collaboration with Theresia Hainthaler, 'Chapter One: "One of the Trinity Was Crucified"', in *Christ in Christian Tradition: From the Council of Chalcedon (451) to Gregory the Great (590–604)*, Part Two: The Church of Constantinople in the sixth century, trans. John Cawte and Pauline Allen (Westminster: John Knox, 1975), 317–43, 336.
41. Oswald Bayer, 'Das Wort ward Fleisch', in *Creator Est Creatura: Luthers Christologie als Lehre von der Idiomenkommunikation*, ed. Oswald Bayer and Benjamin Gleede (Berlin: De Gruyter, 2007), 5–34. See also Silcock, who writes: 'This is a way then of distinguishing between an heretical (Apollinarian) and a Chalcedonian (orthodox) theopaschism. However, even though the theopaschite formula was eventually accepted by the Council of Constantinople, it was and will always be a "persistent stumbling block" for those who held to the patristic axiom of the apathetic, impassible God', in 'The Truth of Divine Impassibility', 201.
42. DBWE 12:332 (DBW 12:316).

said to be God?'⁴³ Bonhoeffer makes clear that 'Chalcedon, as important as it is for setting the parameters for christological reflection, does not limit, but rather sets the bare minimum necessary for defining Christology'.⁴⁴

In these lectures Bonhoeffer reveals his 'core conviction, which is one he shares with Luther. He insists that if one wants to speak of God, it is necessary to point to the man Jesus'.⁴⁵ Thus it is understandable that for Bonhoeffer the concern is always to safeguard 'the fully divine and the fully human nature', to be mindful of the fact there is only '*one* Christ',⁴⁶ who has two natures. He writes:

> What is being said with the Chalcedonian formula is this: *that all options for thinking of all this together and in juxtaposition are represented as impossible and forbidden options* … In him we are to think of all possibilities [about God and human being] at once … This means that from the Council of Chalcedon onward, it is no longer permissible to talk about the human and divine natures of Jesus Christ as about things or facts.⁴⁷

For Bonhoeffer, the notion of Luther's differentiation between the *abstract god* and the *concrete deus pro nobis* is expressed in the how-question, which risks various heresies,⁴⁸ and the who-question and the *pro-me* structure, respectively.⁴⁹ He writes that '[t]he very core of his person is *pro-me* … I can never think of Jesus Christ in his being-in-himself, but only in his relatedness to me.'⁵⁰ Thus, when

---

43. DBWE 12:350 (DBW 12:336). Bonhoeffer writes that 'The Chalcedonian formula is an answer to the "how" question, but it is an answer in which the "how" question has already been surmounted. In the Chalcedonian formulation, the doctrine of the two natures has itself been surmounted. We must carry on in this Chalcedonian sense. This can only happen when we have overcome our way of thinking about the divinity and humanity of Christ as objects that are before us, when our thinking does not begin with the two natures in isolation, but rather with the fact that Jesus Christ is God.'

44. H. Gaylon Barker, *The Cross of Reality: Luther's* Theologia Crucis *and Bonhoeffer's Christology* (Minneapolis: Fortress Press 2015), 240.

45. Barker, *The Cross of Reality*, 115. Bonhoeffer writes that 'If we speak of the human being Jesus Christ as we speak of God, we should not speak of him as representing an idea of God, that is, in his attributes as all-knowing and all-powerful, but rather speak of his weakness and manger', DBWE 12:354 (DBW 12:341). This emphasis on 'weakness' is something which will become important again in Bonhoeffer's prison writings.

46. DBWE 12:342 (DBW12:327).

47. Ibid.

48. See DBWE 12, 'Part 2. The Historical Christ', 328–36, *passim* (DBW 12:311–48).

49. On the Christological who-question, see Matthias Grebe, 'Suffering, Sin-bearing, and *Stellvertretung*: Revisiting the Theology of Dietrich Bonhoeffer', in *Polyphonie der Theologie: Verantwortung und Widerstand in Kirche und Politik*, ed. Matthias Grebe (Stuttgart: Kohlhammer, 2019), 178–9.

50. DBWE 12:314 (DBW 12:295–6). Bonhoeffer explains that 'what is decisive about the *pro-me* structure is that, with it, both the *being* and the *works* of Christ are maintained', DBWE 12:315 (DBW 12:296), some *italics* added.

discussing Chalcedonian Christology, Bonhoeffer highlights the importance of the who-question. Since 'the concept of God's becoming human is negatively determined in such a way that its theological interpretation must reject any diminishment of full humanness or full divinity',[51] the who-question should be our guiding principle for every theological move. Bonhoeffer goes even further and cautions against speaking of God '*becoming* human [*das Menschwerden*]' as opposed to 'the God who *became* human [*der Menschgewordene*], for the former is a "how" question'.[52]

Furthermore, in his *Lectures on Christology* Bonhoeffer is developing a 'humiliation Christology à la Luther'.[53] He follows Luther – though not wholly uncritically[54] – in emphasizing that what is crucial is that 'the union of the two natures develops a *communicatio idiomatum*, a sharing of the individual attributes of the two natures',[55] which is conceived in the following terms: (1) *the genus idiomaticum*; (2) *the genus apostelesmaticum*; and (3) *the genus majestaticum*, which was at the core of Lutheran theology.[56] According to Bonhoeffer, Luther spoke of the 'divinity and humanity of Jesus as if they were one nature … This is the origin of the doctrine of *genus majestaticum*, which teaches that Christ's human nature is suffused by the divine and receives the attributes of the divine nature'.[57]

The Lutheran Christology of condescension became the basis for Bonhoeffer's own Christology on the suffering God, with the central conviction *finitum capax infiniti non per se sed per infinitum*, that the fullness of the Godhead dwelt in bodily form (Col. 2:9) in this weak, limited and humiliated person Jesus, who took

---

51. DBWE 12:340 (DBW 12:325).

52. DBWE 12:354 (DBW 12:341), *italics* added.

53. Ronald A. Carson, 'The Motifs of "Kenosis" and "Imitatio" in the Work of Dietrich Bonhoeffer, with an Excursus on the "Communicatio Idiomatum"', in *Journal of the American Academy of Religion* 43, no. 3 (1975): 542–53, 548. See also Barker, *The Cross of Reality*, 33–76, who highlights that Bonhoeffer was influenced by the Luther renaissance represented by Karl Holl.

54. This essay focuses on the suffering God and in terms of this doctrine, we can find an affinity between Luther and Bonhoeffer. However, there is no suggestion of an affinity found throughout Bonhoeffer's work, and it would be a stretch to call Bonhoeffer a 'Lutheran'.

55. DBWE 12:344 (DBW 12:330).

56. See DBWE 12:345 (DBW 12:330). However, as Andreas Pangritz points out, 'the consciously Lutheran theologian Bonhoeffer admits that at this point Lutheran theology comes "into conflict with what the Bible states" and with the Chalcedonian Definition: "There is … danger of the return of monophysitism, because the humanity becomes deity"', in 'Who Is Jesus Christ, for Us, Today?', in *The Cambridge Companion to Dietrich Bonhoeffer*, ed. John W. de Gruchy (Cambridge: CUP, 1999), 134–53, 141. Bonhoeffer repeats the danger of the *genus majestaticum*: 'Because the danger was sensed here that one might find oneself talking of a deified human being, this doctrine of the *genus majestaticum* was complemented [by] the doctrine of the two states of Christ', DBWE 8:346-7 (DBW 8:332).

57. DBWE 12:346 (DBW 12:332).

the risk of utter human concreteness. Bonhoeffer makes the person of Jesus, 'the God-man for others, the driving force that gives structure and movement to his theology.'[58]

IV. The Crucified and Suffering God

The idea of a passible God who suffers in solidarity with those who suffer was first expressed by Anglican theologians within the context of the industrial Britain of the late nineteenth century.[59] In the second half of the nineteenth century and particularly after the Second World War and in light of the horrors of Auschwitz, the dogma that God is impassible became no longer tenable for many, and in the later decades of the twentieth century and early part of this one, it has been 'progressively abandoned'.[60] Human suffering became the stimulus for embracing the doctrine of divine suffering. In *The Crucified God*, Moltmann reflects on his own experience:

> Shattered and broken, the survivors of my generation were then returning from camps and hospitals to the lecture room. A theology which did not speak of God in the sight of the one who was abandoned and crucified would have had nothing to say to us then.[61]

Early-twentieth-century Jewish theology manifested a strong trend towards 'the emancipation of the biblical understanding of God from the categories imposed on it by the influence of Greek philosophical theism', and in particular the attribute of impassibility.[62] In his major work *The Prophets*,[63] Abraham Heschel developed a theology of divine *pathos*, in which he goes so far as to say that 'God is in need of man'.[64] Moltmann picks up this notion of divine *pathos* when he argues that 'the theology of the divine passion is founded on the biblical tenet, "God is love"'.[65] If God is love, and if God's love is somewhat analogous to human love, then God must suffer, as love is vulnerable to suffering. For Moltmann, God is able to suffer, otherwise God would be loveless. He writes:

> [A] God who cannot suffer is poorer than any man. For a God who is incapable of suffering is a being who cannot be involved. Suffering and injustice do not affect him. And because he is so completely insensitive, he cannot be affected

---

58. Barker, *The Cross of Reality*, 115.
59. See Tietz, 'Der leidende Gott', 138–40.
60. Bauckham, 'Only the Suffering God Can Help', 6.
61. Moltmann, *The Crucified God*, 1.
62. Bauckham, 'Only the Suffering God Can Help', 9.
63. See Abraham. J. Heschel, *The Prophets* (New York: Harper and Row, 1962).
64. Heschel, *The Prophets*, 235.
65. Moltmann, *The Trinity and the Kingdom of God*, 57.

or shaken by anything. He cannot weep, for he has no tears. But the one who cannot suffer cannot love either. So he is also a loveless being.[66]

During his time in prison Bonhoeffer reflects anew on the cross and the suffering of Christ, and develops a 'religionless Christianity'[67] for what he calls a 'world come of age'. He famously argued that 'only a suffering God can help ... who conquers power and space in the world by his weakness'.[68] But how are we supposed to make sense of the paradox of only a 'weak' God being able to help us?

On the basis of the notion of a suffering God, which reveals the very essence of God's promeity, Bonhoeffer 'develops a new understanding of transcendence'.[69] As Ziegler maintains, 'at the heart of this extraordinary remark is the distinction between God and "God", i.e. between the God of the gospel whose transcendent reality is essentially *pro me* in Christ and the "false notion of God"'.[70] As we have seen, one of Bonhoeffer's central concerns is to 'explicate the reality of divine promeity as the quintessence of the Christian Gospel: God *is* for us'.[71] Crucial here is his understanding of God's promeity, that it is *Godself* who suffers. As in the *Lectures on Christology*, where he emphasized 'the first statements in theology – that wherever God is, God is wholly there',[72] here in his letter to Eberhard Bethge, Bonhoeffer also stresses that it is *God* – and not just a human being – who hangs on the cross. For Bonhoeffer, the cross and the passion reveal to

---

66. Moltmann, *The Crucified God*, 222.

67. DBWE 8:363 (DBW 8:404). He writes: 'If religion is only the garb in which Christianity is clothed – and this garb has looked very different in different ages – what then is religionless Christianity?'.

68. DBWE 8:479 (DBW 8:534).

69. Christiane Tietz, 'Christology', in *The Oxford Handbook of Dietrich Bonhoeffer*, ed. Michael Mawson and Philip G. Ziegler (Oxford: Oxford University Press, 2019), 150–67, 166.

70. Philip G. Ziegler, 'God', in *The Oxford Handbook of Dietrich Bonhoeffer*, ed. Michael Mawson and Philip G.Ziegler (Oxford: Oxford University Press, 2019), 137–49, 146. See also DBWE 8:479 (DBW 8:535).

71. Ziegler, 'God', 137. See also Philip Ziegler, 'Christ for Us Today – Promeity in the Theologies of Bonhoeffer and Kierkegaard', in *International Journal of Systematic Theology* 15, no.1 (2013): 25–41.

72. DBWE 12:349 (DBW 12:335). According to Carson, in this statement we see Bonhoeffer's 'unequivocal opposition to the Extra-Calvinisticum', 'The Motifs of "Kenosis" and "Imitatio" in the Work of Dietrich Bonhoeffer', 548. The issue with Extra-Calvinisticum might not be as clear cut for Bonhoeffer as Carson says it is. As Pangritz points out, Bonhoeffer also 'applauds the emphasis laid down by Calvinist Christology, "upon preserving clearly what God is and what humanity is; salvation depends upon retaining the true humanity of Jesus". On the other hand, the tries to preserve the Lutheran concern by proposing a mediating formula: "The finite can hold the infinite, not by itself, but by the aid of the infinite!"', 'Who Is Jesus Christ, for Us, Today?', 141.

us *who* this God is who helps us,⁷³ because in Christ God reveals Godself – God's true essence.⁷⁴ Following Luther, he acknowledges that God is 'present throughout creation, albeit in hidden form: it is only through God's own revelation in Christ on the cross that we know God *pro nobis*'.⁷⁵ The cross is the place where we see the weak and powerless God as the *deus pro nobis,* who is 'pushed out of a world come of age, from the realm of our knowledge and life'.⁷⁶ Bonhoeffer writes that 'God is weak and powerless in the world and in precisely this way, and only so, is at our side and helps us … not by virtue of his omnipotence but rather by virtue of his weakness and suffering!'⁷⁷

The passion and crucifixion highlight the passivity of God, i.e. God *passively* allows something to happen to himself. He not only allows himself to be pushed out to the peripheries of society, but he also allows himself to be nailed onto the cross by the evil powers of this world. Therefore, if Christian theology takes the cross of Christ as the central revelation of God's solidarity, then the cross is the 'point at which every genuinely Christian theology has found itself obliged to speak in some way of the suffering of God',⁷⁸ as the suffering of Christ on the cross reveals divine possibility.

This means that 'if God himself experiences suffering … then human suffering … is qualified anew'.⁷⁹ From now on, suffering has a 'place in God and thus no longer separate human beings from God.'⁸⁰ The God who in Christ enters into suffering is the immanent God who has changed sides to be in the place of those who are suffering, alongside those who suffer.⁸¹ By undergoing suffering in Christ,

---

73. On the primacy of Christ in revelation, see Christiane Tietz, 'Christology', who writes: 'Christ is God's Word speaking about Godself (DBEW 12: 301). In Christ, God communicates himself in person to human beings', 150.

74. See Tietz, 'Der leidende Gott', 133. Tietz writes: 'Das Kreuz ist vielmehr der Ort, an dem Gott sein Wesen zeigt und von der her Gottes Gottsein zu verstehen ist.' See also Eberhard Jüngel, 'Vom Tod des lebendigen Gottes', in *ZThK* 65 (1968): 93–116, 108.

75. Barker, *The Cross of Reality*, 115. On this see also Pangritz, 'Who Is Jesus Christ, for Us, Today?', who writes: 'the centrality of Christology is realised in a "hidden" way only … The reason for this seclusion lies in the fact that the presence of Christ himself is concealed', 138.

76. DBWE 8:450 (DBW 8:503).

77. DBWE 8:479 (DBW 8:534).

78. Bauckham, 'Only the Suffering God Can Help', 11.

79. Tietz, 'Christology', 165.

80. Ibid.

81. See Rosenau, 'Vom Leid der Nachfolge und der Nachfolge im Leid': 'Der leidende Gott hilft, weil er uns in unserem Leid nicht allein lässt und von sich abhält, weil Leid Gott nicht fremd und etwas Unmögliches ist und daher von ihm trennt. Weil Gott uns so mit seiner Nähe Kraft gibt, in der Mitte unseres Lebens eigenverantwortlich und mündig selbst – nach Möglichkeit – Leid zu verhindern und zu überwinden, anstatt an den Rändern unseres Lebens einen „Deus ex machina" (vergeblich) zu erwarten', 719.

who is fully God and fully human, God alters the *conditio humana*[82] of suffering from *within* and in doing so gives suffering a new meaning.[83] This is not an answer to theodicy and nor does it objectively change the fact that humans still suffer in this world. What it does mean is that the God revealed in Jesus Christ on the cross is with those who suffer, lamenting with those who suffer, and asking *with* them and *on their behalf* the why-question that they are asking (Ps. 22:2; Mt. 27:46).

This new understanding of divine and human suffering, as revealed in Christ, also challenges the religious mindset. Having reached the limits of her actions and possibilities, the religious person seeks an all-powerful God to help in her need. However, the cross shows that it is not possible to 'appeal to an almighty God to intervene in our circumstances like a *deus ex machina* from the outside'.[84] Bonhoeffer writes:

> Religious people speak of God at a point where human knowledge is at an end (or sometimes when they're too lazy to think further), or when human strength fails. Actually, it's a *deus ex machina* that they're always bringing on the scene, either to appear to solve insoluble problems or to provide strength when human powers fail, thus always exploiting human weakness or human limitations. Inevitably that lasts only until human beings become powerful enough to push the boundaries a bit further and God is no longer needed as *deus ex machina*.[85]

An impassible god cannot really help humanity, as this god would be conceived of as distant and as a counter model [*Gegenmodell*] to the world.[86] Such a god, as Christiane Tietz points out, cannot be of any help as he would either *determine* humans to their weaknesses and limits, or else *mislead* them into yearning for a supernatural intervention from God every time they are in trouble, rather than taking independent action themselves.[87] Thus, the suffering God of the Bible represents a reversal of and judgement on all the metaphysical caricatures *of* and conceptual approaches *to* God in which God is depicted as omnipotent, and all the erroneous religious ideas about *how* God should act in the world.

---

82. See Rosenau, 'Vom Leid der Nachfolge und der Nachfolge im Leid', who writes: 'Mag sein, dass das Leid zur Bedingung unseres Menschseins (*conditio humana*) gehört, weil Menschsein letztlich passivisch konstituiert und damit „passio" als Existenzial immer mitgesetzt ist', 707.

83. See Viktor Frankl: 'In some ways suffering ceases to be suffering at the moment it finds a meaning, such as the meaning of a sacrifice', in *Man's Search for Meaning* (New York: Washington Square Press, 1984), 135.

84. Tietz, 'Christology', 165.

85. DBWE 8:366 (DBW 8:407), *italics* added.

86. See Tietz, 'Der leidende Gott', 134.

87. See ibid., 134f.

Finally, the suffering God also helps humanity in another way. God's weakness, powerlessness and helplessness force human beings to take initiative, and stand autonomously and self-reliantly. In a 'world come of age' Bonhoeffer suggests we have to live '*etsi deus non daretur,* "as if there were not God".[88] This means that instead of fleeing from the world, the individual is called to independent, responsible living before God, and with God, and yet simultaneously also without God.[89] This independence brings about growth and development as she must live as one who manages her life without God.[90] This does not mean that humans have to live completely without God, but rather that we need to learn to live without the god of metaphysics, without the 'working hypothesis of God'[91] who is omnipotent and always intervenes,[92] knowing that the God of the Bible is with us – Immanuel – and guides us by his divine love.

V. Conclusion

The thesis at the outset was that God suffers, because he loves.[93] Because God loves his creation and wants to redeem and be in relationship with it, he *allows* himself to be pushed away. Though it is important to emphasize God's empathy and solidarity with those who suffer, it is also important to stress the dissimilarities between human and divine suffering. Whereas much human suffering occurs against our will and we are often powerless to avoid it,[94] God's suffering must always

---

88. DBWE 8:476 (DBW 8:530). Ziegler explains: 'For the world's coming of age does not render the God of the gospel unnecessary. Rather, as Bonhoeffer himself says directly, the secularizing trend of the modern world serves to eliminate "a false notion of God" and so to liberate human beings "to see the God of the Bible" afresh and unencumbered by dramatic, metaphysical, and psychological necessities such that "our coming of age leads us to a truer recognition of our situation before God" (DBWE 8: 478–80)', in Ziegler, 'God', 147.

89. See DBWE 8:479 (DBW 8:534).

90. See ibid.

91. DBWE 8:479 (DBW 8:534).

92. See Tietz, 'Der leidende Gott', 136.

93. See also William C. Placher, *Narratives of a Vulnerable God: Christ, Theology, and Scripture* (Louisville, KY: Westminster John Knox Press, 1994), who writes: 'God suffers because God is vulnerable, and God is vulnerable because God loves – and it is love, not suffering or even vulnerability, that is finally the point', 18.

94. In this chapter space precludes a closer look at the distinction between suffering and evil, which are not identical. Not all suffering contradicts the will of God and not all suffering is evil – the oft-given example being the child's experience of touching a hot plate, and the centrality of pain in teaching that heat has the potential to cause injury. For a detailed study of the differentiation between suffering and dysteleological suffering or affliction (Simone Weil) see Kenneth Surin, 'The Impassibility of God and the Problem of Evil', in *SJT* 35 (1982): 97–115, especially 103.

be understood as voluntary.[95] Therefore, the doctrine of the suffering God is not concerned with presenting a paradigm of suffering per se [*Leidensparadigma*], but seeks to emphasize that God, as revealed in Christ, is *with* the suffering humanity.[96] We saw that for the ancient Greeks, 'suffering implied deficiency of being, weakness, subjection, instability'.[97] However, as Moltmann already highlighted, God cannot be subject to suffering against his will, although that is not to say that he may not voluntarily expose himself to suffering. What the cross reveals is a *deus pro nobis* who 'suffers out of the fullness of his being because he is love. He does not suffer against his will, but willingly undertakes to suffer with and for those he loves. His suffering does not deflect from his purpose, but accomplishes his purpose.'[98] Thus, the cross does not make God a helpless victim of evil, but is in fact the bedrock of his power (1 Cor. 1:25) and the triumph over evil (Col. 2:15).

Ultimately, this poses a challenge to all human conceptual approaches *to* God or preconceived ideas *of* God which deny the passibility of God, annulled by the living person of Christ himself, 'the counter Logos',[99] as witnessed in the Bible. To ask the rather *abstract* question 'Can God suffer?' and answer it in the non-affirmative means limiting God, because what we see in the *concrete* revelation of Jesus Christ on the cross is that the God of freedom has bound himself to a human being.[100] Therefore we can conclude that in Christ (who is free *for* the other), God not only suffered, but graciously and freely chose to suffer *for* the other. In this way, it is in his very *passivity* that God can be active[101] – only a suffering God can help.

---

95. See Rosenau, 'Vom Leid der Nachfolge und der Nachfolge im Leid', who expounds this idea further when he writes: 'Wenn Bonhoeffer von der Ohnmacht Gottes und dem leidenden Gott spricht, wird damit das klassische Gottesprädikat der Allmacht von ihm nicht aufgegeben. Zunächst einmal muss man festhalten, dass Ohnmacht und Leiden, Leiden und Ohnmacht begrifflich nicht zwingend notwendige Implikationen sind. Auch der leidende Gott kann allmächtig sein und umgekehrt, zumal wenn – wie bei Bonhoeffer – ein voluntaristisches statt intellektualistisches Gottesverständnis vorliegt. Ohnmächtig im intellektualistischen Sinn (und dann hätten Kritiker der Rede vom leidenden Gott Recht) wäre Gott nur dann, wenn er eigentlich handeln und helfen möchte, aber es (z. B. aus logischen Gründen) nicht kann. Doch eine gewollte Ohnmacht, ein sich am Kreuz aus der Welt herausdrängen „lassen", ist keine Ohnmacht, sondern ein Verzicht auf Macht kraft Allmacht', 719.

96. See Dominik Weyl, 'Die Verwundbarkeit des Menschen und Gottes. Überlegungen im Anschluss an Dietrich Bonhoeffer', in *Hermeneutische Blätter* 1 (2017): 62–74, 74.

97. Bauckham, 'Only the Suffering God Can Help', 12.

98. Ibid.

99. DBWE 12:302 (DBW 12:282). See also DBWE 2:131 (DBW 2:129).

100. See DBWE 2:112 (DBW 2:109).

101. See Weyl, 'Die Verwundbarkeit des Menschen und Gottes', 71.

Chapter 9

HOW GOD SUFFERS: BONHOEFFER, MOLTMANN AND THEOLOGICAL LANGUAGE

Michael Mawson

In the last fifty years many theologians have shifted away from traditional doctrinal emphases on the impassibility and immutability of God, instead seeking to understand and speak of God as suffering in and with creation. This is apparent across a range of theologians with diverse commitments and agendas: Protestant systematic theologians such as Eberhard Jüngel and Robert Jenson,[1] Catholics like Hans Urs von Balthasar and Jean Galot,[2] political theologians,[3] liberation and postcolonial theologians,[4] feminist theologians,[5] open theists,[6] process theologians[7] and many others. Describing this situation in 1988, Paul Fiddes noted

---

1. See Eberhard Jüngel, *God's Being Is in Becoming: The Trinitarian Being of God in the Theology of Karl Barth*, trans. John Webser (Edinburgh: T&T Clark: 2001), 98–103; Robert Jenson, *Systematic Theology Volume 1. The Triune God* (Oxford: Oxford University Press, 2012), 123–45.

2. Hans Urs von Balthasar, *Mysterium Paschale*, trans. O. P. Aiden Nichols (Grand Rapids: Eerdmans, 1996), 89–147; Jean Galot, *Dieu Souffre-t-il?* (Paris: P. Lethielleux, 1976). On Galot, see also Eric L. Mascall, *Whatever Happened to the Human Mind?* (London: SPCK, 1980), 87–93.

3. Dorothee Sölle, *Suffering*, trans. Everett Kalin (Minneapolis: Fortress Press, 1984), 121–50; Jürgen Moltmann, *The Crucified God: The Cross of Christ as the Foundation and Criticism of Christian Theology*, trans. R. A. Wilson and John Bowden (Minneapolis: Fortress Press, 1993), 200–90.

4. Kazoh Kitamori, *Theology and The Pain of God* (London: SCM Press, 1966).

5. Elizabeth Johnson, *She Who Is: The Mystery of God in Feminist Theological Discourse* (New York: The Crossroad Publishing Company, 1992), 246–71; and Catherine LaCugna, *God: For Us: The Trinity and the Christian Life* (New York: HaperCollins, 2000), 209–42.

6. John Sanders, *The God Who Risks: A Theology of Divine Providence* (Downers Grove: InverVarsity Press, 2009), 173–248. Clark Pinnock, *Most Moved Mover: A Theology of God's Openness* (Grand Rapids: Baker and Paternoster, 2000).

7. Alfred N. Whitehead and David Ray Griffin (eds), *Process and Reality: An Essay in Cosmology* (New York: The Free Press, 1978), 342–52.

that 'whatever the popular view outside of academic theological circles, inside ... the idea that God suffers hardly needs to be argued any longer'.[8]

One of the foremost proponents of this turn has of course been the German theologian Jürgen Moltmann. In the *Crucified God* (published in German in 1972) and *Trinity and the Kingdom* (1980), Moltmann presents a trinitarian theology of the cross, one which makes the cross constitutive for the very being and identity of God. Moreover, Moltmann insists that only an idea of God as suffering does justice to God's passionate love for and involvement with the world. For Moltmann, recognizing suffering as bound up with God's love facilitates greater openness to God's presence in the midst of human suffering and despair. On this basis, a theology of divine passibility provides the basis for Christian hope and action in the midst of worldly suffering and evil.

Contesting this turn to divine suffering, other theologians responded by defending traditional emphases on divine impassiblity and immutability. In *Does God Suffer?* (2000), for example, the Dominican Thomas Weinandy insists that God in Godself, in God's inner mystery and perfection, is necessarily incapable of suffering and change: 'To say that God suffers, even in a very restricted sense would, I fear, inevitably cause confusion and misunderstanding.'[9] While recognizing the pastoral concerns driving Moltmann's theology, Weinandy nonetheless insists that 'a passible God is actually less personal, loving, dynamic and active than an impassible God'.[10] Indeed, he suggests that maintaining a clear distinction between God's impassible divinity and Christ's human suffering is necessary for having a God who is ultimately able to overcome and redeem suffering in the world. As Gilles Emery makes this point, 'the immutability that is proper to God guarantees precisely the transcendence and the perfection of his free action'.[11]

In light of this turn and ensuing debate, my interest in this chapter is in how Dietrich Bonhoeffer uses language of divine suffering in his late theology. In ways that resonate with Moltmann, Bonhoeffer famously proclaims in a letter from prison that 'only the suffering God [*der leidende Gott*] can help'.[12] Indeed, Moltmann and other proponents of divine passibility have often drawn on and appealed to Bonhoeffer in support of their position.[13] Nevertheless, in what follows I draw attention to some of the subtle yet important differences between how Bonhoeffer and Moltmann understand God's suffering.

---

8. Paul Fiddes, *The Creative Suffering of God* (Oxford: Oxford University Press, 1988), 1.

9. Thomas Weinandy, *Does God Suffer?* (Edinburgh: T&T Clark, 2000), 170.

10. Weinandy, *Does God Suffer?*, 26.

11. Gilles Emery, 'The Immutability of the Love of God and the Problem of Language Concerning the "Suffering God"', in *Divine Impassibility and the Mystery of Human Suffering*, ed. James F. Keating and Joseph Thomas White (Grand Rapids: Eerdmans, 2009), 29.

12. DBWE 8:479 (DBW 8:534). Bonhoeffer continues: 'It is not a religious act that makes one Christian, but sharing in God's suffering in the worldly life', DBWE 8:480 (DBW 8:535).

13. Moltmann, *The Crucified God*, 47. Also see Jürgen Moltmann, *A Broad Place: An Autobiography*, trans. Margret Kohl (Minneapolis: Fortress Press, 2009), 196.

I. Bonhoeffer's Christology Lectures

Scholars have long recognized the deeply Christological nature of Bonhoeffer's prison theology, including his statements about the suffering God.[14] Christians are those 'pulled along into the – messianic – suffering of God in Jesus Christ', as Bonhoeffer at one point writes.[15] To understand Bonhoeffer's use of this kind of language in his late theology, it will therefore be useful to initially turn to his more thoroughgoing treatment of Christology in some lectures from 1933.

In these lectures on Christology, Bonhoeffer develops his approach as a reflection on the Chalcedonian formula: 'One and the same Christ, Son, Lord, Only-begotten, acknowledged to be unconfusedly, unalterably, undividedly, inseparably in two natures.'[16] On the one hand, Bonhoeffer reads this formula as condemning various attempts to understand or conceptualize Christ directly. For Bonhoeffer, Chalcedon rules out attempts to conceptualize Christ's divinity and humanity by means of fixed or static philosophical concepts, that is, 'nature', 'person', etc. The basic problem with heresies such as Nestorianism or Monophysitism, for example, is that they begin with a fixed concept or preconceived idea of what is divine. They hold a particular idea of the divine and then proceed to approach or interpret Christ's humanity in ways that comport with this concept.[17] By beginning with a fixed idea of the divine, however, such heresies try to explain *how* Christ can be both divine and human, but they do so in ways that invariably compromise his full humanity.

On the other hand, Bonhoeffer maintains that the Chalcedonian formula is not in itself an attempt to establish or provide correct language for speaking about or understanding Christ, at least not straightforwardly. While this formula clearly affirms that Christ *is* both fully human and fully divine, it does not try to provide an explanation of *how* this is the case. Rather, in Bonhoeffer's reading, it simply advances a series of contradictory claims about Christ, thereby confounding or going 'beyond [its own] conceptual forms'.[18] In this way, he suggests, Chalcedon 'reveals the limitations of its own concepts' and indicates that in themselves 'these

---

14. Ernst Feil, *The Theology of Dietrich Bonhoeffer*, trans. Martin Rumscheidt (Minneapolis: Fortress Press, 1985), 90–5.

15. DBWE 8:481 (DBW 8:536). Before asserting that 'only the suffering God can help', Bonhoeffer writes that '*Christ* helps us not by virtue of his omnipotence but rather virtue of weakness and suffering' (italics added), DBWE 8:479 (DBW 8:534).

16. See Richard A. Norris, Jr. (trans. and ed.), *The Christological Controversy: Sources of Early Christian Thought* (Philadelphia: Fortress Press, 1980), 159.

17. Bonhoeffer asserts that for the Monophysites, 'Christ is not an individual person; instead, he put on nature like a garment', DBWE 12:340–1 (DBW 12:324–7). The Nestorians, by contrast, emphasize the necessary distance between Christ's divine and human natures.

18. DBWE 12:343 (DBW 12:328).

concepts are inappropriate and heretical forms'.[19] With this formula, concepts such as 'nature' and 'person' are juxtaposed and used in ways that stretch the ordinary meanings of these concepts to their breaking point.

This means that after Chalcedon the meaning and stability of ideas about divine and human natures can no longer be taken for granted. What Chalcedon affirms is that '[n]othing can be known about [either] God or human being, until God has become a human being in Jesus Christ'.[20] In other words, we know who God is and what it means to be human only from Christ, and hence only by looking to Christ. Following Chalcedon, we can know and speak of the divine and human natures only in reference to their unity in Christ's person. Bonhoeffer's basic claim, therefore, is that if we attempt to speak of or know God or human nature directly, otherwise than by looking to Christ, then we move into abstraction and idealism.

It is on this basis that Bonhoeffer briefly criticizes attempts by Reformed theologians to understand the divine logos as existent outside of or alongside the incarnate Christ.[21] Such attempts try to go beyond or behind the Chalcedonian formula as it stands, that is, by referring to the divine nature apart from Christ's concrete personhood. According to Bonhoeffer, these are essentially attempts to hold back or protect a part of God from the concrete Christ. Against such attempts, he is adamant that 'the λόγος no longer exists otherwise than in the σάρξ. God is no longer other than the one who has become human'.[22] Similarly, he asserts that 'we should speak not of God becoming human [*das Menschwerden*] but of the God who became human [*der Menschgewordene*]'.[23] Whereas the former implies the possibility of knowledge of God prior to and apart from God's becoming this particular human being, the latter more clearly affirms that all knowledge of and speech about God begins and remains with Christ.

For our interests, this clearly distances Bonhoeffer from Weinandy and recent defenders of divine impassibility, namely those who would insist on a clear distinction between the human and the divine natures of Christ in order to ensure God's freedom from creation. According to Bonhoeffer's logic, the problem with this move is that it again involves the attempt to speak of the divine nature prior

---

19. In a later essay Bonhoeffer reflects upon Chalcedon: 'Seldom was reason so willing to humiliate itself and surrender itself before the miracle of God as happened in these words', DBWE 15:532 (DBW 15:542).

20. DBWE 12:352 (DBW 12:339).

21. In his 1932 essay, 'Concerning the Christian Idea of God', Bonhoeffer writes: 'Since God is accessible only in his self-revelation, man can find God only in Christ. That does not exclude God's being elsewhere too, but he cannot and should not be grasped and understood except in Christ. God entered history and no human attempt can grasp him beyond this history', DBWE 10:456-7 (DBW 10:428-9).

22. DBWE 12:344 (DBW 12:329).

23. DBWE 12:344 (DBW 12:341).

to and apart from the person of Christ.²⁴ Theology should instead simply attend to God's revelation in Christ; it should not seek to speculate or speak about God (or humanity) otherwise or more directly.²⁵

This leads to a further move that Bonhoeffer makes in his Christology lectures. In line with this reading of Chalcedon, he endorses Luther's reading of the *communicatio idiomatum*: that what we know of Christ as a human being pertains to his divinity, and vice versa. This is encapsulated in Article VIII of the Formula of Concord: 'Everything human .... can be ascribed to and believed about God and everything divine ... can be ascribed to and believed about the human Christ.'²⁶ In endorsing this position, Bonhoeffer makes direct appeal to Luther: 'Luther spoke of the divinity and humanity of Jesus as if they were one nature' and 'felt it was important to see Christ's humanity as divinity.'²⁷ If Chalcedon means that we can only understand and speak of the divine and human natures in terms of their unity in Christ, then this in turn means we can only understand and speak of Christ's divinity with continual reference to his concrete humanity.

Bonhoeffer draws out the profound implications of this for theological language: 'If we are to describe Jesus as God, we would not speak of his being all-powerful or all-knowing; we would speak of his birth in a manger and of his cross.'²⁸ Accordingly, any knowledge of and speech about God proceeds from and depends on the life and death of Christ as a human being, meaning that concepts

---

24. This sets Bonhoeffer apart from those who understand theology as properly beginning with the immanent Trinity. In his theology, Bonhoeffer consistently avoids speaking of trinitarian persons and relations. On this basis Christopher Holmes has suggested that Bonhoeffer's Christology is therefore in need of a 'trinitarian supplement', and that 'without such a supplement, Bonhoeffer's Christology is hamstrung', Holmes, 'Bonhoeffer and Reformed Christology: Towards a Trinitarian Supplement,' in *Theology Today*, 71, no. 1 (2014): 28–42, 29. My worry with such a proposal is that it downplays the extent to which Bonhoeffer actively avoids (and does not just neglect) appealing to the immanent Trinity. On this issue also see Michael DeJonge, *Bonhoeffer's Theological Formation: Berlin, Barth and Protestant Theology* (Oxford: Oxford University Press, 2012), 106–14.

25. Bonhoeffer writes: 'The point of critical theology is to indicate the limits of every assertion [as they are found] in the actual reality of Jesus Christ', DBWE 12:352 (DBW 12:338).

26. DBWE 12:345 (DBW 12:331). In his 1937 'Mediation of Christmas', Bonhoeffer again quotes Luther in relation to this formula: 'Wherever you can say, Here is God, there you must also say, then Christ the man is also there. And if you point out a place where God is and not the man, the person would already be divided ... No my friend, wherever you place God for me, there you must also place the humanity for me', DBWE 15:533 (DBW 15:542-3).

27. DBWE 12:346 (DBW 12:332).

28. DBWE 12:354 (DBW 12:341).

such as impassibility or immutability have limited value for theology. We know and speak of God in terms of Christ's concrete humanity, or, as Luther succinctly formulates this point: 'Christ alone, and no other God.'[29]

To be clear, Bonhoeffer maintains that the humanity of Christ does not provide a basis for knowing or speaking of God directly and unambiguously. This is because of the particular form of Christ's concrete existence as divine and human: 'this God-human [*Gott-Mensch*] is veiled in his existence as the Humiliated One.'[30] When we look to the person of Christ in the Gospels, what we see is a humiliated human being, even a 'sinner among sinners'.[31] In Christ, God is at once revealed and hidden in suffering and crucifixion. In the final part of his lectures, Bonhoeffer thus describes this form as the stumbling block that frustrates and prevents any direct recognition of Christ for who he is.[32]

At the same time, however, he insists that it is this hidden presence of God (and true humanity) under the form of Christ's suffering and humiliation that facilitates faith. By confounding our own attempts to directly recognize and understand Christ as the God-human, this form of suffering and humiliation allows for something deeper. As Bonhoeffer writes, 'Faith exists when I yield myself to God ... even and especially there where it goes against all visible appearances. Only when I give up having visible confirmation do I believe in God.'[33] Put differently, the form of Christ's suffering and humiliation helps us to relinquish our own preconceived notions of what God is or should be. This form means that we no longer have to rely upon our own concepts or ideas about God (i.e. concepts such as omnipotence, impassibility, etc.).[34] By attending to how God comes to us in Christ's humiliation and crucifixion, we allow God to begin to teach us who God actually is.

---

29. Martin Luther, 'On the Councils of the Church', in *Luther's Works 41: Church and Ministry 3*, ed. Eric W. Gritsch (Minneapolis: Fortress, 1966), 286. Along similar lines, in the *Heidelberg Disputation*, Luther writes: 'None of us can talk adequately or profitably about God's glory and majesty unless we see God also in the lowliness and humiliation of the cross', 'Heidelberg Disputation', in *Luther's Works 31: Career of a Reformer 1, 1517-20*, ed. Howard J. Grimm (Philadelphia: Fortress, 1957), 52.

30. DBWE 12:356 (DBW 12:343).

31. DBWE 12:356 (DBW 12:343). Bonhoeffer's assertion in his lectures that 'Christ took on all the mortifying aspects of being human; otherwise he could not help us in our σάρξ' (DBWE 12:356 [DBW 12:344]) anticipates the later claim in his prison letters that 'only the suffering God can help', DBWE 8:479 (DBW 8:534).

32. DBWE 12:355-60 (DBW 12:342-8).

33. DBWE 12:358 (DBW 12:346).

34. Moltmann attributes the emergence of these concepts within Christianity to the influence of Platonic and Greek philosophy, *The Crucified God*, 127-35.

II. Bonhoeffer's Prison Theology

The language of the suffering God is at the very heart of Bonhoeffer's prison theology. In a series of letters, poems and other fragments composed during his incarceration, Bonhoeffer famously proposes a form of 'religionless Christianity' that takes seriously the 'world come of age'.[35] Moreover, he begins to reflect upon the implications of such religionlessness and worldliness for theological language; for concepts such as 'repentance, faith, justification, and sanctification'.[36]

In this late theology, Bonhoeffer is once again critical of attempts to understand or approach God conceptually: 'How do we talk about God – without religion, that is, without the temporally conditioned presuppositions of metaphysics, the inner life, and so on?'[37] Accordingly, for Bonhoeffer a religionless Christianity is one that no longer depends upon metaphysics or inwardness as prerequisites for faith. A religionless Christianity neither presupposes a 'religious a priori' in human beings nor insists upon God as a 'working hypothesis' for 'morality, politics, and the natural sciences'.[38] This kind of Christianity moves beyond many of the ways in which human beings have traditionally constructed and called upon God.[39]

Bonhoeffer's discussion of 'the world come of age' is similarly directed against conceptual approaches to God. In his analysis, one result of the progressive secularization of thought and culture, of God having been 'pushed out of a world come of age',[40] is that modern Christianity has often problematically sought to retain a place for God in 'ultimate questions' and 'unsolved problems'.[41] Bonhoeffer suggests that this is again an attempt to determine God from the standpoint of our own needs and ideas. The resulting God is a *deus ex machina* who is to 'solve

---

35. DBWE 8:363 (DBW 8:404). Bonhoeffer writes: 'How can Christ become Lord of the religionless as well? Is there such a thing as a religionless Christian? If religion is only the garb in which Christianity is clothed – and this garb has looked very different in different ages – what then is religionless Christianity?', DBWE 8:363 (DBW 8:404).

36. DBWE 8:373 (DBW 8:416).

37. DBWE 8:364 (DBW 8:405).

38. DBWE 8:478 (DBW 8:532).

39. Bonhoeffer endorses Barth's critique of religion: Barth 'led the God of Jesus Christ forward to battle against religion'. However, Bonhoeffer then insists that Barth himself did not go far enough. Barth effectively mobilized Christ against religious metaphysics and inwardness, but gave 'no concrete guidance' for 'the nonreligious interpretation of theological concepts'. Consequently, according to Bonhoeffer, Barth lapses into a 'positivism of revelation' by positing a new theological system or edifice in the place of religion, DBWE 8:429 (DBW 8:481).

40. DBWE 8:479 (DBW 8:534).

41. DBWE 8:406–7 (DBW 8:455).

insoluble problems or provide strength when human powers fail'.[42] Bonhoeffer endorses the world come of age, therefore, as an opportunity for something richer and deeper: 'the world that has come of age is no longer an occasion for polemics and apologetics' but should itself be understood 'from the Gospel and Jesus Christ'.[43]

In his letters, Bonhoeffer's discussions of religionlessness and the world come of age lead to and culminate in the language of the suffering God: 'one may say that the previously described development toward the world's coming of age, which has cleared the way by eliminating a false notion of God, frees us to see the God of the Bible, who gains ground and power in the world by being powerless'.[44] In particular, these developments help to release us from our dependence upon our own ideas about God, that is, in terms of power or immutability. These developments help us instead to attend to a biblical God who comes to us in and as the suffering and crucified Christ.[45]

Bonhoeffer reiterates this need to relinquish our own concepts and needs as a basis for approaching God in his brief 'Outline for a Book'.[46] He writes: 'Who is God? Not primarily a general belief in omnipotence'.[47] Rather, he continues, we know God in 'the Crucified One'.[48] As with the earlier lectures on Christology, this means that '[w]e must immerse ourselves again and again ... in Jesus's life, his sayings, actions, suffering, and dying in order to recognize what God promises and fulfils'.[49] In Bonhoeffer's prison theology, knowing God in Christ entails attending to Christ as he comes to us in Scripture: 'The Bible directs people towards the powerless and suffering of God'.[50]

This shift from attempting to approach God on our own terms to recognizing the one who comes to us as Christ is at the centre of Bonhoeffer's short poem, 'Christian and Heathens'.[51] In the poem's first stanza, he writes: 'People go to God

---

42. DBWE 8:366 (DBW 8:407).

43. DBWE 8:431 (DBW 8:482).

44. DBWE 8:479-80 (DBW 8:534-5).

45. On the relationship between Christology and Scripture in Bonhoeffer's theology, see Mawson, 'Scripture', in *The Oxford Handbook of Dietrich Bonhoeffer*, ed. Michael Mawson and Philip Ziegler (Oxford: Oxford University Press, 2019), 123-36.

46. This outline was composed in August 1944 after the assassination attempt on Adolf Hitler had failed. Bonhoeffer provides brief notes and possible headings for three chapters.

47. DBWE 8:501 (DBW 8:558) As Bonhoeffer continues, 'That is not a genuine experience of God but just a prolongation of a piece of the world.'

48. DBWE 8:501 (DBW 8:559).

49. DBWE 8:515 (DBW 8:572-3).

50. DBWE 8:479 (DBW 8:534).

51. Bonhoeffer enclosed this poem with a letter to Bethge on 20 July 1944. For a rich discussion of this poem and its theology see Bernd Wannenwetsch, 'Christians and Pagans: Towards a Trans-Religious Second Naiveté or How to Be a Christological Creature', in *Who Am I? Bonhoeffer's Theology through His Poetry*, ed. Bernd Wannenwetsch (London: Bloomsbury T&T Clark, 2009), 175-96.

when they're in need, plead for help, pray for blessings and bread.' All people instinctively appeal to God on the basis of our own human needs and desires. In the second stanza, however, he disrupts and overturns this movement: 'People go to God when God's in need/ find God poor, reviled, without shelter or bread/ see God devoured by sin, weakness, and death/ Christians stand by God in God's own pain [*Leiden*].'[52] A deeper encounter with God involves relinquishing our own needs and concepts as a basis for approaching God. We now recognize and stand beside the God who comes to us in God's own pain and suffering. We stand beside the one who has been 'devoured by sin, weakness and death', embracing the one who suffers in and as the concrete Christ.[53]

Moreover, by disrupting and subverting our own concepts of divinity, for Bonhoeffer the suffering God frees us to properly be in the world. In light of God's suffering, 'our lives are *allowed* to be "worldly", that is, we are delivered from false religious obligations and inhibitions'.[54] That God is fully present in the world in Christ's suffering means that we too are freed to embrace the world and recognize its claims upon us. The suffering God releases us from our dependence on religion to secure meaning or redemption from beyond this world.[55] As Bonhoeffer makes this point in another letter, 'the Christian is not a *homo religiosus* but simply a human being, in the way Christ was a human being'.[56]

In the 'Outline for a Book', Bonhoeffer gives further clarity to what it means for God to release us into worldliness. If we know of God only in the suffering of Christ, then this means that 'our relationship to God is no "religious" relationship to some highest, most powerful and best being imaginable … transcendence. Instead, our relationship to God is bound up with a life of "being there for others" through participation in the being of Jesus'.[57] The God who suffers frees us to follow Christ by attending to the needs of those around us: 'the neighbour within reach in any given situation'.[58]

Following Bonhoeffer, this indicates what it means to be Christian. To be Christian involves relinquishing our ideas about God and instead attending to God in God's own suffering presence. Bonhoeffer is clear, however, that this is not something that we ourselves achieve or enact. In his prison theology, he emphasizes the responsive nature of our participation in God's suffering. We are

---

52. DBWE 8:461 (DBW 8:515).

53. DBWE 8:460 (DBW 8:515).

54. DBWE 8:480 (DBW 8:535). As Bonhoeffer immediately continues, 'it is not a religious act that makes one Christian, but rather sharing in God's suffering in the worldly life'.

55. Bonhoeffer writes: 'Unlike believers in the redemption myths, Christians do not have an ultimate escape route out of their earthly tasks and difficulties into eternity', DBWE 8:487–8 (DBW 8:500).

56. DBWE 8:485 (DBW 8:541). As Bonhoeffer continues, 'I think Luther lived in this kind of worldliness'.

57. DBWE 8:501 (DBW 8:558).

58. Ibid.

'pulled along into the suffering of God' and 'pulled into walking the path that Jesus walks'.[59] We learn who God is only by being drawn into the suffering of Christ; we learn what it means to follow this Christ only in following him.

Finally, this means there is no clear pattern or stable model for being Christian or living by faith.[60] In one letter Bonhoeffer briefly reviews a number of examples of discipleship found in Scripture, including those of Zacchaeus, the shepherds, the centurion at Capernaum, Cornelius (Acts) and others: 'The only thing they have in common', he reflects, 'is their sharing in the suffering of God in Christ. That is their "faith".'[61] We cannot learn what faith or sharing in God's own suffering means, therefore, in advance or in abstraction from following Christ's call.[62] As Bonhoeffer makes this same point in his earlier *Discipleship*: 'how should disciples know what their cross is? They will receive it when they begin to follow the suffering Lord. They will recognize their cross in communion with Jesus.'[63]

In summary, Bonhoeffer's language of 'religionlessness' and 'the world come of age' is intended to disclose what it means to properly live before God and in the world, that is, without the support of traditional ways of conceptualizing or depending upon the divine. Religionless Christianity involves a willingness to have our notions of who and what God is interrupted and reshaped; it involves allowing God to come to us on God's own terms. In particular, it involves standing by and attending to the one who comes to us and is present in the world in the human suffering of Christ. And this means that we are Christians only by holding in faith that this one who suffers and dies for us really is God. We hold in faith that the one who has come to us in weakness and sin is the one who has saved us.

III. Moltmann's Trinitarian Theologia Crucis

In order to bring further clarity to Bonhoeffer's language of God's suffering, it will be useful to draw some comparisons with Jürgen Moltmann's more recent and better-known account of divine passibility. Like Bonhoeffer, Moltmann makes

---

59. DBWE 8:480 (DBW 8:536).

60. Bonhoeffer is clear that suffering per se does not provide a principle or method for sharing in God's suffering. It is only being drawn into God's suffering that provides the basis for faith and worldliness. Indeed, Bonhoeffer writes: 'If one has completely renounced making something of oneself ... then one takes seriously no longer one's own suffering but rather the suffering of God in the world', DBWE 8:486 (DBW 8:542). God's presence and suffering in the world directs us away from ourselves and towards the suffering of God and others.

61. DBWE 8:482 (DBW 8:537).

62. Luther writes: 'The only reason they [Christians] must suffer is that they steadfastly adhere to Christ and God's word, enduring this for the sake of Christ', Luther, 'On the Councils and the Church', 165-7.

63. DBWE 4:89 (DBW 4:82).

Luther's *theologia crucis* the centre of his theology. In *The Crucified God*, he provides a rich and nuanced account of this *theologia crucis*, positioning it against both theistic and atheistic attempts to approach God or divinity apart from the cross.[64] Moltmann too insists that we can properly know and speak of God only in the human suffering and humiliation of Christ: 'We see God most clearly in Christ's death upon the cross. God is not greater than he is in this humiliation.'[65] Like Bonhoeffer, he again frames this in terms of Luther's radical reading of the *communicatio idiomatum*: 'The divine being must encompass the human being and vice versa.'[66]

Moltmann also recognizes that this *theologia crucis* firmly places the human being into worldliness. He follows Luther, who 'sees in the cross God's descent to the level of our sinful nature and our death, not so that man is divinized, but so that he is de-divinized and given new humanity in the community of the crucified Christ.'[67] Moltmann thus endorses Luther's emphasis on God embracing human beings and thereby freeing them to properly be in the world. Moltmann's own theology of the crucified God is intended to facilitate engagement with and action in the world.

Nonetheless, Moltmann departs from Luther (and Bonhoeffer) when he insists that this *theologia crucis* needs to be developed in a more explicitly trinitarian direction. Indeed, he criticizes Luther for failing to clearly distinguish between trinitarian persons and relations in his language of the suffering God: '[H]e left out of his account the relationships in which this suffering and dying person of the Son is involved with the persons of the Father and the Spirit … his Christology was formed in terms of incarnation and the theology of the cross, but not always in trinitarian terms.'[68] In other words, Luther failed to identify the specific roles of the Son and the Father with respect to the work of cross. And Moltmann attributes this failure to Luther's reliance upon a Chalcedonian Christology.[69] Luther's language of the divine and human natures in Christ leads to paradoxical and convoluted ways of speaking of the suffering God: 'God died the death of the godless on the cross and yet did not die. God is dead and yet not dead.'[70]

Moltmann insists that more explicitly trinitarian language can bring clarity to this situation: 'The theological concept for the perception of the crucified Christ is the doctrine of the Trinity.'[71] Or, as he elsewhere writes, 'it is advisable to abandon the

---

64. See Moltmann: *The Crucified God*, 207–27.
65. Ibid., 205.
66. Ibid.
67. Ibid., 213.
68. Ibid., 235. Consequently, Moltmann continues, Luther arrives 'at paradoxical distinctions between God and God: between the God who crucifies and the crucified God'.
69. Against Luther, Moltmann writes: 'We have not interpreted the death of Jesus as a divine-human event but as a trinitarian event between the Son and the Father', ibid., 245.
70. Ibid., 244.
71. Ibid., 240.

concept of God and to speak of the relationships of the Son and the Father and the Spirit at the point at which "God" might be expected to be mentioned'.[72] Rather than using the language of God in relation to the cross, it would be better to think and speak in terms of the specific persons and relations of Father, Son and Holy Spirit.

On this basis Moltmann describes and locates the cross as a 'trinitarian event' between the Father, Son and Spirit. He employs trinitarian language to identify the distinct ways in which particular persons of the Trinity each suffer in and through the cross: 'The Son suffers dying, the Father suffers in the death of the Son.'[73] The Father suffers by surrendering the Son to crucifixion, whereas the Son suffers by surrendering to the cross in obedience to the Father. The Father and Son are united in suffering and surrender, even while each suffering and surrendering to one another in their own distinct ways.[74]

Moltmann's claim, therefore, is that attending to these more particular roles of trinitarian persons allows us to better recognize that God's suffering on the cross is ultimately God's love. It allows us to recognize that the suffering of the Father and the Son is not simply 'unwilling suffering', but instead an 'accepted suffering' precisely as the 'suffering of love'.[75] That the Father and the Son surrender to one another means that they each willingly embrace their suffering for the sake of the other. By speaking of God as Trinity, we can better recognize that God's suffering is a 'freedom to suffer as a result of the otherness of the other'.[76] This loving surrender for the other precedes and defines the event of the cross, thereby redeeming this suffering and showing it to be meaningful.[77]

Moltmann gives somewhat less attention to pneumatology in his trinitarian *theologia crucis*, but the Holy Spirit too plays a crucial role. Specifically, the work of the Spirit is to open up and extend this event of God's suffering love to the world. The Spirit draws the world and all human history and suffering into the sacrificial love of the Father and the Son.[78] Through the Spirit, Moltmann writes, '[a]ll human history, however much it may be determined by guilt and death, is taken up into this "history of God", i.e. into the Trinity, and integrated into the future of the "history of God".'[79] Through the work of the Spirit, God's trinitarian

---

72. Ibid., 207.

73. Ibid., 243.

74. Moltmann writes: 'In the cross, Father and Son are most deeply separated in forsakenness and at the same time are most inwardly one in their surrender', ibid., 244.

75. Ibid., 230.

76. Ibid., 230.

77. Moltmann writes: 'God allows himself to be forced out. God suffers, God allows himself to be crucified and is crucified, and in this consummates his unconditional love that is so full of hope', ibid., 248.

78. Moltmann writes: 'What proceeds from this event between Father and Son is the Spirit which justifies the godless, fills the forsaken with love and even brings the dead alive', ibid., 244.

79. Ibid., 246.

love encompasses all human history and provides a standpoint from which to interpret it. In this way the Spirit gives the cross its eschatological significance: 'The Trinity ... presses towards eschatological consummation, so that the "Trinity may be all in all", or put more simply, so that "love may be all in all".'[80]

All of this means that Moltmann's trinitarian *theologia crucis* is in the final instance a theology of hope.[81] The recognition that God's loving surrender precedes and redeems all human history and suffering provides a foundation for hope in the depths of our own experiences of suffering. As Moltmann writes, it is 'the ground for a love which is stronger than death and can sustain death. It is the ground for living with the terror of history and the end of history, and nevertheless remaining in love and meeting what comes in openness for God's future.'[82] A trinitarian theology of the suffering God, therefore, allows for recognizing the depth of worldly suffering while still retaining hope in its midst. This in turn provides a basis for human freedom and action in the world: 'Freedom in the light of hope is the creative passion towards the possible.'[83] For Moltmann, a theology of the suffering God provides the possibility for properly recognizing and responding to a suffering world.

IV. Bonhoeffer, Moltmann and Theological Language

There are subtle yet important differences between Moltmann's explicitly trinitarian *theologia crucis* and Bonhoeffer's Chalcedonian Christology.[84] As we have seen, Moltmann positions his trinitarian *theologia crucis* as an attempt to bring clarity to Luther's convoluted and paradoxical ways of speaking of God's suffering. At this point Bonhoeffer stands much closer to Luther. Specifically, Bonhoeffer's insistence that Chalcedon places limits on attempts to understand or conceptualize God stands in contrast to Moltmann's pursuit of clarity. Bonhoeffer writes: 'God as human being and human being as God must be held together in our thinking at the risk of sacrificing the rationality of such an assertion.'[85] This insistence also underlies Bonhoeffer's reflections on Christ as a stumbling block

---

80. Ibid., 255.

81. See Jürgen Moltmann, *Theology of Hope: On the Ground and Implications of a Christian Eschatology*, trans. James W. Leitch (London: SCM, 1964). And see Moltmann's more recent *Ethics of Hope*, trans. Margret Kohl (Minneapolis: Fortress, 2012).

82. Moltmann, *The Crucified God*, 278.

83. Jürgen Moltmann, *The Trinity and the Kingdom: The Doctrine of God*, trans. Margret Kohl (San Francisco: Harper & Row Publishers, 1981), 217.

84. To be clear, Bonhoeffer is not anti-trinitarian or against trinitarian language. When he does use such language, however, it tends be about God as *creator, reconciler* and *redeemer*, not triune persons or relations more directly that this. And he maintains the centrality of Christ even in discussions of God as creator or redeemer.

85. DBWE 12:340 (DBW 12:325).

in the final section of the Christology lectures; Christ's suffering and crucifixion is an offense to human thinking, in a way that makes room for faith. For Bonhoeffer, the point is not to better interpret or conceptualize God's suffering in Christ, but rather (as quoted above) to 'yield to God … even and especially there where it goes against all visible appearances'.[86]

On this basis Bonhoeffer also gives more attention to the structure and form of Christ's person as *'pro-me'* or *'pro-nobis'*.[87] That Christ as the God-human is a paradox or stumbling block for human thinking means we have no independent vantage point with respect to Christ.[88] In his lectures, Bonhoeffer asserts that 'the being of Christ's person is essentially related to me … The very core of his person is *pro-me*'.[89] We know and encounter Christ only as he comes to us and is related to us, not otherwise or more directly: 'I can never think of Jesus Christ in his being-in-himself, but only in his relatedness to me.'[90]

This commitment is apparent in Bonhoeffer's understanding of theological language as such. As we have seen, he maintains that theology cannot be, in the first instance, an attempt to understand or speak about God or Christ in the abstract, but only a kind of thinking and speaking that proceeds from the particular way that God comes to us in and as Christ. As Bonhoeffer writes elsewhere, 'theological thinking is not a construction a priori, but a posteriori'.[91] His basic point, then, is that we can only know of or speak about God by attending to how we ourselves are being formed by Christ.[92]

By contrast, Moltmann's attempt to understand the person of Christ primarily in relation to the Father (and Spirit) less clearly maintains this *pro-me* or existential structure. Moltmann's trinitarianism subtly shifts an emphasis away from theology as language *before* God (*coram Deo*), in its a posteriori attentiveness to Christ's call, to language *about* divine persons and relations. For Moltmann, the point seems to be to better understand Christ's suffering as the Son's loving surrender to the Father. In this way Moltmann's theology operates as a third-person discourse. Theology is the attempt to rightly speak about and understand God as Trinity, although in a way that also necessarily leads to engagement with and action in the world.

---

86. DBWE 12:358 (DBW 12:346).

87. That is, 'for me' or 'for us'. For more on Bonhoeffer on promeity, see Philip Ziegler, 'Christ for Us Today – Promeity in the Theologies of Bonhoeffer and Kierkegaard', in *International Journal of Systematic Theology* 15, no. 1 (2013): 25–41.

88. In light of the encounter with Christ, 'the "who question" interrogates the very existence of the one asking it', DBWE 12:303 (DBW 12:283).

89. DBWE 12:314 (DBW 12:295).

90. DBWE 12:314 (DBW 12:295–6).

91. DBWE 10:454 (DBW 10:426).

92. On being formed by Christ, see Bonhoeffer's manuscript 'Ethics as Formation' in his unfinished *Ethics*, DBWE 6:92–102 (DBW 6:79–90).

Finally, this demonstrates a difference at the level of anthropology. Moltmann's trinitarian *theologia crucis* displays greater confidence that human beings are able to know and speak of God. It displays more confidence that human beings are in a position to grasp the nature of God's suffering, as the sacrificial love of both the Father and the Son, and to then draw from this knowledge as a basis for interpreting and responding to reality. By contrast, Bonhoeffer's Christological approach places less confidence in human agency and reason; it consistently keeps an emphasis upon God's activity and on human beings as responding to or being drawn into this activity. For Bonhoeffer, the language of the suffering God thus marks the limits of attempts to theologically grasp or understand God. As he writes in an earlier essay, 'The real study of *theologia sacra* begins when, in the midst of questioning and seeking, human beings encounter the cross; when they recognize the endpoint of all their own passions in the suffering of God at the hands of humankind, and realize that their entire vitality stands under judgment.'[93]

V. Conclusion

At the beginning of this chapter, I indicated that my interest is in how Bonhoeffer uses the language of the suffering God in his late theology. My claim is that Bonhoeffer uses this language in ways that subtly differ from Moltmann and other more recent advocates (and also opponents) of divine passiblity.[94]

These differences are already anticipated in the main title of this chapter, 'How God Suffers', which has at least two possible meanings. The first and more common of these meanings follows the interrogative sense of the word 'how', as in questions like 'how *does* God suffer?' or 'how *is* God suffering?' According to this meaning, the title 'how God suffers' signals an intention to take a position on the questions at the heart of the recent debates about divine passiblity. Is God capable of suffering? And what is at stake with this question for responding to suffering in the world?

As we have seen, these kinds of questions are central to Moltmann's trinitarian *theologia crucis*. For Moltmann, it is necessary for God to be *capable* of suffering. Indeed, he insists that 'a god who is incapable of suffering is a being who cannot

---

93. This is the essay 'What Should a Student of Theology Do Today', DBWE 12:433 (DBW 12:417). Bonhoeffer continues: 'It is about responsible study and listening, becoming attentive to the Word of God, which has been revealed right here in this world; it is toning down one's self in the face of what is far and away the most important matter.' On this essay see also Michael Mawson, 'Studying Theology in a Time of Crisis: A Manifesto', in *Letters to a Young Theologian*, ed. Henco van der Westhuizen (Minneapolis: Fortress, 2022), 234.

94. As indicated above, Thomas Weinandy's basic question (the title of his book) is 'does God suffer?', and his interest is in the problematic implications of an affirmative response to this question. Moltmann and Weinandy therefore pursue and explore the same basic question with respect to God, even while arriving at opposite answers.

be involved … He cannot weep for he has no tears. But the one who cannot suffer cannot love either.'[95] It is only a God who suffers who is able to love.

There is, however, a second, less obvious meaning of the main title of this chapter. This meaning is tied to the more emphatic sense of the word 'how', as found in exclamations such as 'how wonderful to see you' or 'how I wish things were different'. Following this reading, the word 'how' would not so much signal a question or explanation, but rather it intensifies what follows. In light of an encounter with the crucified Christ, we exclaim or cry out, 'how God suffers!'

This is what Bonhoeffer seems to be pursuing with the language of the suffering God in his late theology. In other words, he has little interest in speculation or debates about whether God is able to suffer, or even what suffering might mean for who God is. In his earlier Christology lectures, he rules out such questions explicitly. With 'how' language, he writes, 'the object [i.e. God] is defined, recognized and understood by means of its possibilities, by means of its "how".'[96] Such questions about God proceed from and remain tied to our own conceptions and ideas about what is possible for God. Instead, Bonhoeffer proposes that we stand with God and attend to the one who has come to us (and is for us) in Christ's suffering and humiliation. For Bonhoeffer, the language of the suffering God affirms the cross as the beginning and end of all theological language.

---

95. Moltmann, *The Crucified God*, 222. Moltmann makes this same point positively: 'The one who is capable of love is also capable of suffering, for he also opens himself to the suffering which is involved in love', *The Crucified God*, 230.

96. DBWE 12:303 (DBW 12:283). Bonhoeffer continues: 'That we are always asking the "how" question shows we are chained to our own authority. It is the *cor cuvumn in se*.'

Part III

THE WORLD AND THE CHURCH

Chapter 10

CHRISTOLOGY'S COUNTERPOINT: BONHOEFFER ON KNOWING THE CHRIST WHO CALLS

Koert Verhagen

Dietrich Bonhoeffer's 1933 Christology lectures are tantalizing for a variety of reasons. Not only is the transcribed text as we have it reconstructed from student notes, but the arc of the course itself is incomplete. Indeed, the 'positive Christology' that Bonhoeffer was building toward is all too brief, breaking off in the midst of an uncharacteristically apologetic discussion of the miracles of Jesus. However, their historical situatedness – at a point of major transition in his academic and personal life which was causally connected to the rapidly growing power of National Socialism in Germany – and their singular focus on the person of Jesus Christ mark them as a sort of fulcrum in Bonhoeffer's theological development. As such, the content of the lectures is frequently and justifiably understood to stand in expanding continuity with his earlier work, while also grounding and illuminating later texts.

Because the Christology lectures are just that – academic lectures given at the University of Berlin – their form, progression and dense content does, on the surface, sit more comfortably alongside of texts from Bonhoeffer's oeuvre like *Sanctorum Communio*, *Act and Being* and the *Ethics* manuscripts. However, Bonhoeffer is nothing if not a Christocentric thinker in all phases of his theology.[1] As such, much can be gleaned from thinking of the 1933 Christology lectures in relation to Bonhoeffer's 'pastoral epistles', *Discipleship* and *Life Together*, as well. This chapter will be of the latter sort and my central claim is that when the introduction to Bonhoeffer's Christology lectures is properly understood, it becomes clear that *Discipleship* can and should be read theologically as the necessary counterpoint to his lectures.[2] Or, put another way, it claims that following after the incarnate, crucified

---

1. Nowhere is this point driven home more clearly in recent Bonhoeffer scholarship than in Phil Ziegler's 'Christologically Concentrated Treatment of Bonhoeffer's Doctrine of God in "God"', in *The Oxford Handbook of Dietrich Bonhoeffer*, ed. Michael Mawson and Philip G. Ziegler (New York: Oxford University Press, 2019), 137–49.

2. Throughout this chapter, when I reference the introduction to the 1933 Christology lectures, I am referring specifically to the section designated 'The Development of the Christological Question' in DBWE 12:299–308 (DBW 12:279–89).

and risen Christ is integral for Christology disciplined to the who-question.³ In order to defend this claim, I will begin by considering an alternative reading of the introduction to the Christology lectures, one that seeks to highlight the mutuality of the who-question and the full personhood of both members in the encounter between the human logos and the Counter Logos. Next, I will demonstrate the high degree of overlap between what Bonhoeffer identifies as the starting point for Christology and his description of the call to discipleship. Finally, in order to draw out the implications of this common starting point for the relationship between Christology and discipleship, I will draw on some recent work in theological epistemology that distinguishes between different forms of personal knowledge.

The central claim of this chapter hangs on a certain way of reading the introduction to Bonhoeffer's 1933 Christology lectures, a way that is hardly dominant in secondary literature. As such, it is important to justify this move here at the outset. Typically, the introduction is understood as something of an exercise in epistemic ground-clearing. Under the umbrella of what Andreas Pangritz has referred to as 'Bonhoeffer's Christology of encounter', the import of this introduction is regularly thought of in terms of Bonhoeffer's emphasis on the person of Jesus Christ (over against the idea of Jesus Christ) and the way encounter with this person creates the epistemic conditions necessary to undertake the Christological task. In doing so, these interpretations tend to assume that the who-question is aimed at one, obvious sort of knowledge – namely knowledge of a person. This line of interpretation tends to focus on the person of Jesus Christ and what Bonhoeffer has to say about the epistemic mortification and revivification necessary to rightly pursue the task of Christology under the auspices of the who-question. What I do *not* want to suggest is that such a reading is misguided, since it fits not only with the content of the introduction but also with the broader arc of the lectures. Furthermore, it makes good pedagogical sense as a starting point, preparing students for the sui generis nature of their subject matter and the particularly acute danger of imported presuppositions formed according to the 'how-question'. However, I believe such interpretations paint only a partial picture, one that my alternative reading seeks to remedy.⁴

---

3. In a similar manner, Ernst Feil draws attention to the fundamental significance of *Discipleship* for Bonhoeffer's Christology (Ernst Feil, *The Theology of Dietrich Bonhoeffer*, trans. Martin Rumscheidt [Philadelphia: Fortress Press, 1985], 78). However, since his focus is an account of Bonhoeffer's theological development he is primarily concerned with how *Discipleship* fits within Bonhoeffer's Christology more broadly. While what I am arguing here has some relevance for a more historical theological line of inquiry like Feil's, I am trying to identify and draw constructive insights out from Bonhoeffer's Christology for the Christological task more generally.

4. It remains possible that Bonhoeffer's intent when introducing the Christology lectures in the manner he does is adequately summarized by the more common interpretation. However, as I hope to show below, even if the themes my alternative reading seeks to highlight are not central to Bonhoeffer's intent, they are by no means insignificant, pointing to a nascent element in his Christology that is affirmed and unfolded in *Discipleship*.

What, then, does this alternative reading make of the introduction to Bonhoeffer's Christology lectures? First, it seeks to rectify what I take to be an imbalanced account of the encounter that is so central to his opening discussion. While Bonhoeffer's aim is undeniably corrective (i.e. refuting the human tendency to reduce Christ to an idea), it is also clearly the case that, for Bonhoeffer, the human person must be conceived of theologically in a threefold manner, namely as creature, sinner, and reconciled in Christ alone.[5] In other words, the encounter, insofar as it takes place between two persons, must take seriously the full personhood of both parties. Bonhoeffer affirms this towards the end of the lectures as we have them when he writes that 'the relation between God and human being should be understood never as the relation between two things but [only as that] between two persons'.[6] Jesus Christ cannot be reduced to an idea, but neither can the merely human person be reduced to the status of sinner or knower. Reduction in the former direction ignores God's loving affirmation of humanity in creation and reconciliation. Reduction in the latter direction may make space for the possibility of reconciled knowing in the task of Christology, but of a rather anaemic sort because in failing to take seriously the embodied creatureliness of human persons it reduces knowing to a centrally, if not solely, cognitive process. All this is to say that it is necessary to press beyond the critical, death-dealing encounter between counter-logos and human logos in the interest of highlighting the mutuality of the who-question. When Jesus Christ turns the who-question back around on the human logos he addresses and claims whole persons, and as a result, whole persons are inducted into the act of knowing Christ. Christology traditionally conceived then, is a task whose orientation to the who-question is dependent on it being nested within and inextricably bound up with wholistic (con)formation.[7]

This, then, is the second key feature of the proposed alternative reading: namely that conformation to the person of Jesus Christ is a hidden second prong to Bonhoeffer's account of Christology, albeit one that is not unfolded with any depth in the lectures themselves. We can rightly call this second prong another form or mode in which we come to know Christ, recognizing that knowledge is acquired in a variety of ways and cannot be reduced to one's cognitive mechanisms; I will return to this below. The introduction to the Christology lectures, then, establishes the pre-requisite for knowing the person of Jesus Christ in a manner that not only

---

5. I argue in more detail for the basic salience of this simultaneity for Bonhoeffer's theological anthropology in Koert Verhagen, *Being and Action* Coram Deo: *Bonhoeffer and the Retrieval of Justification's Social Import* (London: T&T Clark, 2021).

6. DBWE 12:352 (DBW 12:339).

7. Here I am gesturing towards Bonhoeffer's later work in *Ethics,* particularly the manuscript 'Ethics as Formation', where identifies the basis for Christian ethics as conformation to the incarnate, crucified and risen Christ. See particularly DBWE 6:92–6 (DBW 6:79–84) for how his account of formation unfolds as a rebuttal of false dichotomies between practical and dogmatic Christianity.

opens the door to multiple avenues of pursuit but, I would suggest, requires that they go hand-in-hand – point and counterpoint. This assertion will assume greater definition as I turn now to the deep resonance between the introduction to the Christology lectures and Bonhoeffer's account of discipleship.

In an early English translation of *Discipleship*, we find one of Bonhoeffer's most memorable formulations: 'When Christ calls a man, he bids him come and die.'[8] However, this translation is actually an expanding paraphrase of the more terse German, which, when translated more literally, reads: 'Every call of Christ leads to death.'[9] For Bonhoeffer, the way indicated by the call to discipleship is a way that begins with death. One could say, then, that discipleship presupposes a critical component, a critique aimed at some state of affairs that has to be changed or fixed in order for the conditions for true discipleship to exist. However, the language of death signals the need for something more total than a partial fix. While he is not referring to physical death (at least in most situations), nor is Bonhoeffer speaking of death in a purely metaphorical manner. Keeping with his Lutheran heritage, the death brought about by encounter with Christ and signified in the waters of baptism really does have ontological purchase on the person who undergoes it, bringing about a new way of being in the world.

This death is not something that sinful human beings can will for themselves. Indeed, when encounter with Jesus is conceived of as a human possibility '[t]he disciple makes himself available, but retains the right to set his own conditions. [… Discipleship] becomes a human program, which I can organize according to my own judgment and can justify rationally and ethically.'[10] If discipleship is reduced to a program in this manner, it inevitably relegates Jesus Christ to the status of an object or idea that can be comprehended and mastered. Over against this Bonhoeffer asserts that 'Jesus Christ in his word has to be our death and our life.'[11] What he has in view here is nothing less than the prerequisite for following after Jesus: namely call, encounter and death. 'The first Christ-suffering that everyone has to experience is the call which summons us away from our attachments to this world. It is the death of the old self in the encounter with Jesus Christ. Those who enter into discipleship enter into Jesus' death.'[12] Here though, entering into Jesus' death is not only the end of the old self, but also a mode of being in the world in which the disciple's whole existence is shaped by her being bound to the suffering God-human.

According to Bonhoeffer, then, encounter, death, and being bound to the risen Christ are essential to discipleship. And in his 1933 Christology lectures, Bonhoeffer makes almost the exact claim about the starting point for the task

---

8. Dietrich Bonhoeffer, *The Cost of Discipleship*, trans. R. H. Fuller and Irmgard Booth (New York: Touchstone, 1995), 89.
9. DBW 4:81: 'Jeder Ruf Christi führt in den Tod' (See DBWE 4:87).
10. DBWE 4:61 (DBW 4:49).
11. DBWE 4:88 (DBW 4:81).
12. DBWE 4:87 (DBW 4:80–1).

of Christology: namely that study of the person of Christ begins with a critical moment, where personal encounter with the risen Christ puts to death all the pre-conceived notions and convenient ideas projected onto him and in turn establishes the relational conditions according to which the who-question can properly be asked. As is the case in *Discipleship,* Bonhoeffer is also concerned here with human programmatic ways of knowing and their impulse to pursue the how-question: 'how does this object X fit into the classification that I already have at hand?'[13] He is also sensitive to the lengths humans will go to subvert or soften the encounter with Christ through self-negation.[14] Just as Christ's initiating call is the indispensable starting point for discipleship, the who-question can only be asked of Christ after a revelatory encounter. And in this encounter Bonhoeffer asserts:

> [O]ur question has been turned around. The question we have put to the person of Christ, 'who are you?' comes back at us: who are you, that you ask this question? Do you *live* in the truth, so you can ask it? Who are you, you who can only ask about me because you have been justified and received grace through me? Only when this question has been heard has the Christological question been definitively formulated.[15]

It is important to pause here and note not only the mutuality of the who-question, but also the form that Bonhoeffer gives to Christ's address: 'Do you *live* in the truth …?' Given that Bonhoeffer follows this question with a question about justification and grace, it seems safe to assume that 'truth' here is a reference to Jesus.[16] To live in the truth, then, is to live in Christ, and, of course, for Bonhoeffer since Christ is a person, risen and alive, he is also at work, so to live in him is to follow after him and participate in that work. Participatory language like this also abounds in *Disicpleship* as Bonhoeffer describes Christ's fundamental significance for determining the texture and pattern of a life spent following after him.[17] So, to live in the truth of Christ needs to be understood here not merely as a state of being, but also as an active way of life. Furthermore, it is also worth flagging that Bonhoeffer spends the first chapter of *Discipleship* attacking justification as a principle and the cheap grace that this understanding of Christ's work makes possible. Costly grace, on the other hand, 'costs people their lives' and 'justifies the sinner' – it is the means by which one is bound to Christ in discipleship.[18] And likewise, justification and grace are necessary for formulating the who-question aright.

---

13. DBWE 12:301 (DBW 12:281).
14. DBWE 12:302 (DBW 12:282).
15. DBWE 12:305 (DBW 12:286-5), emphasis KV.
16. See Jn 14:6.
17. See e.g. DBWE 4:49, 89, 120, 127, 285 (DBW 4:36, 83, 121, 129, 301).
18. DBWE 4:45 (DBW 4:31).

While Bonhoeffer's language of encounter, death, justification and participation is fairly intuitive and uncontroversial when it comes to describing the starting point for discipleship, it is much less so when it comes to describing the task of systematic theology, and more specifically Christology. There are preconceived notions of what sort of task Christology is or should be and they fit better with what follows from the introduction to Bonhoeffer's lectures than they do with the introduction itself. But this, in fact, seems to be part of the motivation behind the introduction: namely the destabilizing of these preconceived notions, and not merely as a matter of prolegomena that can be left behind, but rather in a way that has serious and fundamental significance for how Bonhoeffer's lectures were to be heard and received. That is to say, the introduction helps attune the reader to the fact that there is something deeply ironic and dissonant about a lecture series that is meant to emphasize the irreducible personhood of Christ and the importance of the who-question because the verbal/textual medium of a lecture itself already signals reduction. Bonhoeffer seems to be nodding to this paradox when he writes: 'As long as the christological question is one asked by our logos, it always remains within the ambiguity of the "how question." But as soon as it stands within the act of faith, it becomes a form of knowledge, which has the possibility of posing the "who question."'[19] In this one word, 'faith', Bonhoeffer sums up that which is created in and through justifying encounter with the counter Logos. Importantly, for Bonhoeffer, faith is not primarily a psychological reality or reducible to a set of beliefs. Rather, it is being in Christ and reflective articulation of that state of being which Christ creates prior to explicit, propositional belief.[20] Being able to pose the who-question, then, is all about having one's entire existence in and through the ongoing act of faith in Christ. 'Only *in faith* is there seeing.'[21]

It would seem that faith, insofar as it entails being in Christ, enables one to ask the who-question because it is the means by which Christ graciously makes himself available as a person. Thus, Christology is faith-enabled knowledge of a person. But what does that mean? While the how- and the who-questions structure Bonhoeffer's distinction between merely human knowing and human knowing in faith, there is still a fair amount of ambiguity involved when it comes to what sort of knowledge each question yields. Bonhoeffer is emphatic that the how-question reduces Christ to an idea and the who-question acknowledges the personhood of Christ, but there is certainly more than one way to know a person. Knowing facts about a person constitutes knowledge of that person. Yet, when asked if we know so-and-so, merely knowing things about that person without having ever encountered her rarely seems sufficient to warrant an affirmative

---

19. DBWE 12:307 (DBW 12:288).

20. On this see DBWE 2:116–23 (DBW 2:113–21). While it is beyond the scope of this chapter, a robust account of Bonhoeffer's understanding of faith would also need to consider the fact that individual faith cannot be thought of as existing independently of the community of faith.

21. DBWE 12:359 (DBW 12:347).

answer. This signals a general sense that interpersonal encounter is an important element of personal knowledge.[22]

However, at the same time, interpersonal encounter without self-revelation and self-interpretation also yields a thin sort of personal knowledge because the person is reduced to who they are in encounter. When this happens, the complex set of realities that constitute a person's identity – their past experiences, their self-understanding, their other relationships, etc. – is rendered opaque. In other words, it seems like both interpersonal encounter and the reception of self-revelation are important ingredients of deep personal knowledge.

Of course, if the hermeneutical turn has taught us nothing else, it is that the knower is ever the interpreter. As such, the self-revelation of the other in the form of self-description and interpersonal encounter is not known as such, but rather as it is interpreted by the knower. So, when asked if I know so-and-so, I might answer in the negative even though I frequently engage with her interpersonally and have learned quite a bit about her. This is because I have recently felt betrayed by this person and as a result, I am in the midst of questioning everything I previously thought I knew about her. More positively this form of knowing also relates to knowing what something is like. In terms of personal knowledge, this would be knowing what it is like to spend time with a person, what it is like to be hugged, loved or disappointed by that person.

To help us get a clearer sense of what is at stake here for knowing Christ, it is worth considering Joshua Cockayne's evaluation of these three forms of personal knowledge in his book, *Contemporary with Christ*. There he employs the useful and clarifying grammatical taxonomy of first-, second- and third-personal forms of knowledge. First-personal knowledge refers to what I have just described in terms of the hermeneutical turn and knowing what something is like.

> To describe the world from a 'first-personal' perspective is to talk only of an individual's experience of the world – the way it seems to them. Thus, to talk of first-personal knowledge is to talk of knowing the taste of a perfectly made cup of coffee or knowing the pangs of emotion felt in watching one's favorite film.[23]

While this way of knowing is an inevitable feature of our epistemic life, it certainly appears to be insufficient when it comes to grounding knowledge of Christ because this way of knowing is ultimately self-mediated. By itself, it fails

---

22. There are interesting sub-questions that emerge here with respect to letters, email, social media and video chats, and the degree to which these different mediums can facilitate interpersonal encounter. It seems to me that they can, but only in a limited sense. Furthermore, there are good theological, philosophical and sociological reasons for thinking that embodied interaction is an important ingredient that aids in the transition from interpersonal encounter to personal knowledge.

23. Joshua Cockayne, *Contemporary with Christ: Kierkegaard and Second-Personal Spirituality* (Waco: Baylor University Press, 2020), 12.

to recognize the 'otherness of the other', to riff on Bonhoeffer's description of the who-question.[24] Ultimately, when it comes to knowing persons, it is incumbent upon the knower to reckon with the reality of their independent, external existence rather than reducing them to self-constructed mental simulacra. This is especially true when it comes to knowing God in the person of Christ. Thus, Cockayne writes: 'God [is not] merely a feature of human consciousness, known only from the first-personal perspective. As such, growing in knowledge of God cannot be confused with growing in knowledge of oneself and one's own experiences.'[25]

Third-personal knowledge, in contrast, approaches the object of knowledge as a mind-independent reality. 'To have third personal knowledge of something is to know something about how the world is, independently of facts about one's personal experience.'[26] Awareness of historical events that happen and persons that lived before one's lifetime are characteristic examples of this form of knowledge. For instance, I might know that Karl Barth smoked a pipe, but my knowledge of this fact is not a product of my having shared said pipe with him on occasion. Rather, it is passed down to me via the testimony of others. When it comes to knowing Christ this form of knowledge clearly must play a role since no one alive today experienced Jesus first-hand in all of his particularity as a Jewish carpenter living in first-century Palestine. Without the testimony concerning Jesus' ministry and teaching that we encounter in Scripture and tradition, it seems quite clear that our knowledge of him would be greatly impoverished. However, the danger that lurks behind third-personal forms of knowing is the tendency to equate knowing *about* a person with knowing that person in a deep, personal manner. The very nature of God and persons more generally defies this sort of propositional objectification. So, again, but from a different angle, third-personal knowledge fails to do justice to the otherness of the other because it renders them two-dimensional, ironing out the complexity that dwells in the interstitial space between propositions. For Cockayne, '[t]his is not to diminish the importance of propositional knowledge for the life of faith. Indeed, as with any other person, to know God well will require knowing a great deal *about* God. But such thinking about God is entirely futile on its own if one is wanting to know God as subject.'[27]

What then of second-personal knowledge? According to Cockayne, this is the only form of the three that is 'unique to the experience and knowledge of other persons'.[28] The legitimacy of this form of knowledge becomes quickly apparent – even if it resists tidy definition – by performing a thought experiment in which a person creates a comprehensive account of everything they know about their spouse. If this account was read by someone on the other side of the world 200 years later, we could, in one sense, justifiably say that the reader knows just as

---

24. DBWE 12:303 (DBW 12:283–4).
25. Cockayne, *Contemporary with Christ*, 13–4.
26. Ibid., 13.
27. Ibid., 26.
28. Ibid., 13.

much *about* the writer's spouse as the writer. And yet, few would contend that the reader *knows* the writer's spouse anywhere near as well as the writer herself. This is because the writer possesses second-personal knowledge of her spouse and the reader only possesses third-personal knowledge. With this in mind, 'the second-personal perspective is unique to those experiences in which some *other* is the focus of one's experience, and it is appropriate to address this other as a "you".[29] When it comes to knowing Christ, the importance of this form of knowledge is immediately apparent, especially if one accepts Bonhoeffer's accounts of discipleship and Christology discussed above. Asking the 'who-question', knowing the person of Jesus Christ, and following after him seem to require second-personal knowledge. Yet, even here the danger of violating the otherness of the other presents itself when second-personal knowledge is prioritized in such a way that the knower refuses to countenance valid witness and testimony about the one who is known because it does not fit with the knower's experience up to that point.

In the course of expositing Cockayne's threefold account of personal knowledge, I have hinted at this framework's relevance for thinking through the point counterpoint relationship between Christology and discipleship, but now I want to make it explicit. First, two comments on the first-personal perspective, although it is less directly pertinent to the concerns of this essay. Although, at one level, the first-personal perspective is no more inherently problematic than human finitude and creaturely status, the tendency of sinful humanity to elevate this perspective to an authoritative level is undoubtedly one of the fundamental missteps that enable programmatic discipleship and reduction of Christ to an idea via self-negation. And yet, in acknowledging the goodness of God's creation, it is important to also recognize that Bonhoeffer's Christology of encounter allows space for affirming the importance of knowing what it is like to be known and loved by God, and what it is like to know God with us and for us.

More centrally, the second- and third-personal perspectives provide a clarifying angle from which to approach the tension identified above between the introduction to Bonhoeffer's Christology lectures and what follows. In the introduction, Bonhoeffer is asserting that the necessary starting point for the task of Christology is personal encounter with the person of Jesus Christ. And by emphasizing the way Christ's personhood requires that Christological enquiry is disciplined to the who-question, he is making it clear that the sort of knowledge aimed at is irreducibly second personal. However, and this is where the tension arises, the majority of the lectures assume a third-personal perspective. They aim to describe Christ as mediator, as the humiliated and exalted one, etc. Even in his reading of Chalcedon as negative Christology, Bonhoeffer is making propositional claims about what *cannot* be said about Christ. It might seem, then, that the lectures are not terribly well-suited to the task laid out in the introduction.

However, there are at least two other ways to understand the introduction's content and positioning vis-à-vis the lectures as a whole. One way is to take it

---

29. Ibid., 13.

as a sort of warning meant to alert his students to the limitations of Christology done in a descriptive and prescriptive key. In other words, it is Bonhoeffer's own peculiar way of saying:

> As you listen to and engage in these lectures, do not fool yourself into believing that Christology is reducible to what we are doing here. Instead, keep in mind that if it is a person whom we are seeking to know, then the sort of knowledge we are aiming at here must be woven together with another, more relational form of knowledge.

This is a possibility, but I think it is a bit of a stretch since reading the introduction as a sort of coded warning sounds too conspiratorial.

More likely is that Bonhoeffer intends the who-question to get at both second- and third-personal forms of knowledge but recognizes that the purview of the lectures limits his discussion to an orientation in the latter direction. Indeed, understood in this way, various elements of the Christology lectures can be understood in terms of Bonhoeffer's clear-sighted understanding that second-personal knowledge of Christ is indispensable to the task of Christology. His treatment of Chalcedon as an exercise in negative Christology fits the bill here. This is perhaps most evident when, in summarizing the value of 'critical theology', he asserts that its result 'is the recognition that this "how" of relationship is impossible to think through'.[30] In other words, without denying the value of third-personal knowledge about Christ, Bonhoeffer knows that when taken as the primary mode of Christology it attempts to do the impossible – namely make sense of a relationship between two persons – and in so doing it collapses all Christology into the how-question.

The concluding section on positive Christology is where Bonhoeffer is most evidently attempting to pursue the who-question in a mode that holds together second- and third-personal knowledge. This is typified when, in the course of discussing Christ's sinlessness, he rejects any reduction of the claim to merely third-personal knowledge: 'The statement about Jesus being without sin in his actions is not a judgment within a moral system but rather a recognition, through the eyes of faith, of the One who does these things, the One who is without sin for all eternity.'[31] To claim Christ's sinlessness, then, cannot and should not amount to the implicit compilation of a comprehensive list of the things he did and refrained from doing. Rather, it comes through faith-enabled, second-personal awareness of and engagement with the present person of Jesus Christ. Awareness of Christ's sinlessness clearly involves third-personal knowledge acquired through the witness of Scripture and tradition. But, unless this knowledge coheres in and is coordinated with the person who is known in and through personal encounter, it can always be re-interpreted or rationalized away.

30. DBWE 12:353 (DBW 12:340).
31. DBWE 12:357 (DBW 12:345).

10. Christology's Counterpoint

For Bonhoeffer, '[m]ystagogical silence is prattle', so the third-personal line of Christological enquiry cannot be thrown out the window in favour of second-personal knowledge, as is evidenced by the very existence of the Christology lectures.[32] Jesus Christ is indeed *pro nobis*, but the particular way in which *he is* for us is in the particularity of his first-century Jewish flesh and in his being 'very God from very God'. Of necessity, this means that his person is not reducible to what we can know through merely second-personal engagement with him. Instead, fully engaging with the person of Christ means knowing him in his particularity, and this requires third-personal knowledge about him that can only be acquired via witness and testimony. One possible objection to this claim echoes Barth's theology of revelation, asserting that, insofar as God is always subject and never object in the event of revelation, all knowledge of revelation is second-personal. Without contesting this, I think it is still important to keep in mind that because God reveals himself to real human beings it remains deeply helpful to distinguish the distinct ways in which we experience coming to know. Making such distinctions helps to stave off undesirable reductions, especially given the persistent effects of sin on our epistemic faculties. Without these distinctions, it becomes easier to slip into a mode of thinking where faith is seen to entail an automatic hypostasizing of knowledge about Jesus or, on the other end of the spectrum, he is reduced to our first-personal experience of him.[33]

Bonhoeffer's sensitivity to both the need for and the challenge of holding second- and third-personal knowledge together in Christology is nicely captured in his emphasis on the mystery of Christ in a circular letter he wrote to Confessing Church pastors in Pomerania in 1939.[34] In this letter, Bonhoeffer offers a theological meditation on Christmas that echoes many of the themes from the Christology lectures, right down to its discussion of natures, the personhood of Christ, and the *genus majestaticum*. However, of particular interest for our purposes here is the

---

32. It is worth noting that Bonhoeffer's not so veiled critique of patristic mysticism here is not entirely charitable, signalling a loose and, at times, condescending engagement with early church history, which is certainly one of the weaknesses of the Christology lectures. For a solid summary and assessment of this, see Stephen Plant, '"We Believe in One Lord, Jesus Christ": A Pro-Nicene Revision of Bonhoeffer's 1933 Christology Lectures', in *Christ, Church and World: New Studies in Bonhoeffer's Theology and Ethics*, ed. Michael Mawson and Philip G. Ziegler (London: T&T Clark, 2016), 45–60.

33. Some dangerous practical implications of ignoring the historical particularity of Christ's incarnate identity, which are known via witness and testimony, are highlighted in J. Kameron Carter, *Race: A Theological Account* (Oxford/New York: Oxford University Press, 2008). There, Carter persuasively makes the case that unless we coordinate our second-personal knowledge of Christ to the historical particularity of his covenantal, Jewish flesh we will reduce him to our experience and ideas of him. He argues that in the West this has historically yielded a white Christ.

34. On mystery as a *leitmotif* in Bonhoeffer's theology more broadly, see Feil, *The Theology of Dietrich Bonhoeffer*, 5–6.

way he sets the mystery of the person of Christ between the epistemic prioritization of experience on the one hand and reason on the other:

> The early church pondered the Christ question over several centuries. In so doing, it made reason captive to obedience to Jesus Christ and vividly testified, in stern and contradictory statements, to the mystery of the person of Jesus Christ. It did not yield to the modern illusion that this mystery could only be felt and experienced, because it knew about the corruption and egocentricity of all human feeling and experience. The church did not mean, of course, that this mystery could be logically conceived, but in that it did not shy away from uttering the ultimate conceptual paradoxes, it declared and glorified the mystery as mystery for all natural thinking.[35]

In the Incarnation, as the locus of divine mystery, God reveals himself in a way that is not reducible to human experience and far exceeds a compilation of facts and rational summations. It is the task of the theologian to engage this mystery without erasing it. Bonhoeffer knew that this entails venturing third-personal articulations, but was adamant that the coherence of such theological formulations could only be known in the mystery of second-personal engagement. And in a formulation that is as relevant for Christian theology today as it was then, he identifies the Scylla and Charybdis that lurk on either side of this tension:

> What foolishness, as if it were the task of theology to decode God's mystery, pulling it down to the commonplace, miracle-less words of wisdom based on human experience and reason! Whereas this alone is its charge – to keep the miracle of God a miracle, to comprehend, defend, and exalt the mystery of God, precisely as mystery. The early church meant the very same thing when it concerned itself with the mystery of the Trinity and the person of Jesus Christ with tireless fervor. What superficiality and thoughtlessness, particularly among theologians, when theology is disparaged, when they boast about not being and not wanting to be theologians, ridicule their own office and ordination, and nonetheless at the end of it all, they have and advocate a bad theology instead of a correct theology![36]

In the Christology lectures, Bonhoeffer seeks to navigate this tension by repeatedly drawing the reader back to the second-personal and acknowledging the limits of the third-personal. Yet, as has already been noted, the third-personal dominates. Turning our sights back to *Discipleship*, then, I want to suggest that it takes the road the lectures did not travel, providing a counterpoint to them by placing second-personal engagement at the centre of its subject matter. The

---

35. DBWE 15:529 (DBW 15:539).
36. DBWE 15:529 (DBW 15:538).

first question that must be addressed is whether it is even possible for a written work to focus on second-personal knowledge since the very existence of a text seems to signal reduction to a third-personal perspective. Cockayne's work is again helpful here. He acknowledges that theological descriptions of second-personal engagement are by no means a substitute for the engagement itself, and as such, there is always something less real or inevitably removed about them. The difference, he suggests, is like the difference between a map of the Atlantic Ocean and the ocean itself. 'If all one wants is to admire the beauty of the ocean, then they will get by fine without a map; indeed, a map might distract from this activity. Yet, if one wants to plot a course across the ocean in order to reach some destination, then a map is essential.'[37] Adopting this metaphor, we might say that *Discipleship* attempts to map knowing Christ from a second-personal perspective along with the formative, affective, and, ultimately, ethical implications of this way of knowing. In this, its basic presupposition is that second-personal knowledge is formative knowledge. Whereas third-personal knowledge can be held at arm's length, second-personal knowledge shapes us. From his earliest work on, Bonhoeffer was convinced that persons are relationally constituted. If this is the case, then there is no such thing as relational or second-personal knowledge as such, but only ever a knowing that constitutes in a manner peculiar to the relationship in question. Knowing Christ as a 'you' and being known by Christ means being called, bound and formed. This is the mode of knowing that takes centre stage in *Discipleship*, even as it is significantly informed by third-person witness and testimony about Christ.

In mapping second-personal knowledge of Christ, *Discipleship* should not be understood merely as consonant with or supplementing the subject matter of the Christology lectures. Rather, as indicated by their common starting point, they aim at knowledge of Christ in interconnected and complementary ways. More specifically they guide and are corrective in relation to each other. Without the second-personal knowledge which comprises the central focus of *Discipleship*, Christology will devolve into objectification and dead orthodoxy. Likewise, without the third-personal knowledge unfolded in the Christology lectures, discipleship will inevitably degenerate into following after an idea of Christ conformed to individual experience and preference. In both cases, the who-question devolves into the how-question.

In conclusion, by disambiguating what sort of knowledge the who-question aims at, we have seen that human knowledge of Christ's person is crucially second-personal, but also importantly draws on the third-personal perspective as well. This distinction enables a better understanding of the tightrope Bonhoeffer is attempting to walk in the Christology lectures, but it also explains the slightly disorienting disjunct between the introduction and the rest of the lectures. Furthermore, it opens the door to reading *Discipleship* as a necessary counterpoint

---

37. Cockayne, *Contemporary with Christ*, 12.

to the lectures, which, as I have argued here, helps to illuminate the full import and scope of the who-question in a manner that the lectures only gesture toward. Finally, although this would require more unpacking than I have space for here, one important implication of all this is that the road from the Christology lectures to Bonhoeffer's *Ethics* can and should lead through *Discipleship*.[38]

---

38. The stronger claim would be that much is lost if *Discipleship* is glossed over in these discussions. For an example of this sort of gloss, see Rowan Williams' otherwise excellent and compelling treatment of Bonhoeffer's Christology in Rowan Williams, *Christ the Heart of Creation* (London: Bloomsbury Continuum, 2018), 182–217. On the qualified continuity between *Discipleship* and *Ethics* see Florian Schmitz, '*Nachfolge*': *Zur Theologie Dietrich Bonhoeffers* (Göttingen: Vandenhoeck & Ruprecht, 2013), 407–10; Verhagen, *Being and Action* Coram Deo, 120–1.

Chapter 11

'PREPARING THE WAY' FOR GOD'S WORD: A CENTRAL MOTIF OF BONHOEFFER'S ETHICS AND ITS IMPLICATIONS FOR PUBLIC THEOLOGY

Hannah Bleher

I. Introduction – 'Preparing the Way' as a Leitmotif for Bonhoeffer's Ethics

In public theological discourses, Bonhoeffer's ethics and theology is a popular point of reference; in fact, he is called a public theologian par excellence.[1] Bonhoeffer's distinction between the penultimate and ultimate things is, in particular, prominent in this regard. In light of the Lutheran Two Kingdoms Doctrine and Barth's outline of Christian community and civil community, he describes with this distinction Christian life and being in the world from a unique temporal perspective. One dazzling motif in this context, however, tends to be overlooked and has so far received little attention in public theological discourses, although it has potential for the public theological discourse: the motif of 'preparing the way'.

---

1. See Christine Schliesser, 'Dietrich Bonhoeffer – Ein "Öffentlicher Theologe"?', in *Evangelische Theologie* 78, no. 3 (2018): 180–92; Heinrich Bedford-Strohm, 'Dietrich Bonhoeffer Als Öffentlicher Theologe', in *Evangelische Theologie* 69, no. 5 (2009): 329–41; although there is also criticism to this interpretation (see Johannes Fischer, 'Gefahr Der Unduldsamkeit: Die "Öffentliche Theologie" der EKD ist problematisch', in *Zeitzeichen* 17, no. 5 (2016): 43–5), there are nonetheless good arguments to relate Bonhoeffer's life and work to the paradigm of public theology (see Pascal Bataringaya, Traugott Jähnichen, Oliver Munyansanga, and Clemens Wustmans [eds], *Dietrich Bonhoeffer: Life and Legacy* [Zürich: LIT Verlag, 2019]; Dirk J. Smit, 'The Paradigm of Public Theology: Origins and Developments', in *Contextuality and Intercontextuality in Public Theology: Proceedings from the Bamberg Conference 23.-25.06.2011*, ed. Florian Höhne, Heinrich Bedford-Strohm, and Tobias Reitmeier [Zürich, Berlin: LIT Verlag, 2013]). The term and discourse of public theology emerged in the 1960/70s through Martin E. Marty in the United States as well as through Wolfgang Huber and especially through Wolfgang Vögele later in the 1990s in Germany, see Florian Höhne, *Öffentliche Theologie: Begriffsgeschichte und Grundfragen* (Leipzig: Evangelische Verlagsanstalt, 2015).

The motif can certainly be assigned an important role, for Bonhoeffer himself considered giving his ethics work the title 'Preparing the Way and Entering In'.[2] This suggests that the motif of 'preparing the way' reflects a *leitmotif* of his ethics. Within the *Ethics* fragments in the chapter 'Ultimate and Penultimate Things', Bonhoeffer describes 'preparing the way' very vividly: 'Preparing the way' means to give bread to the hungry, but it is not a social reform programme, but rather an inward and spiritual process of preparing the way for the divine word.[3] However, there is also a political-ethical potential associated with 'preparing the way'. What this means and how the motif can be understood in the overall conception of Bonhoeffer's ethics and, thus, contributes to public theological discourses, aims to be hermeneutically explored in this chapter.

For this purpose, this chapter conducts a close reading of the section 'Ultimate and Penultimate Things' in terms of 'preparing the way'. Conducting a close reading means that the nuances of meanings of the motif will be traced in the text. The article is based on a tripartite reconstruction in which textual boundaries, textual descriptions of the motif, and its textual coherence are traced. The aim is to grasp Bonhoeffer's understanding of the motif in terms of the *intentio operis* that oscillates between the *intentio auctoris* and *intentio lectoris*, as Umberto Eco states.[4]

Based on this hermeneutic reconstruction, the article argues that the motif vividly and succinctly relates Bonhoeffer's Christologically grounded understanding of being human as the point of departure for his socially and publicly oriented ethics and theology to his Christ-centred understanding of responsible life. In this regard, this contribution aims to analyse thoughtfully and detailed the term 'preparing the way' as a *leitmotif* of Bonhoeffer's ethics as well as to raise its political-ethical potential for public theology discourses. For this reason, first, a close reading of 'preparing the way' within Bonhoeffer's ethics is conducted. Second, the motif is discussed in terms of public theology. Three aspects of the motif are proposed as relatable to the public theology paradigm, namely sensitivity to ambiguity, the empowerment focus and action orientation.

---

2. As the editors of Dietrich Bonhoeffer's *Ethics* fragments note in a footnote with reference to a letter from 1940; see DBWE 6:161n64 (DBW 6:153n55).

3. See DBWE 6:146–70 (DBW 6:137–62).

4. See Umberto Eco, *Die Grenzen der Interpretation* (München: Carl Hanser Verlag, 1992). The criterion of interpretation within this hermeneutic approach to interpretation is the text itself. Each interpretation of the text should therefore be reflected in terms of its coherence to the overall textual context of the work in order to avoid over-interpretation. Given the fragmentary character of Bonhoeffer's ethics work, this hermeneutics seems particularly appropriate, as neither the trains of thought completed nor the original intention of the author or the text could ever be fully grasped or explained in further works. Against this background, the reader's interpretation should be particularly sensitive and stick to the textual boundaries to grasp the intention of the work, but not over-interpret it.

II. How Can 'Preparing the Way' Be Understood?

1. Exploring the Context: Bonhoeffer's Distinction of Ultimate and Penultimate Things

Close reading requires, as a first step, a contextual analysis of 'preparing the way', located in Bonhoeffer's interpretation of the doctrine of justification, which he examines in his manuscript of the 'Ultimate and Penultimate Things'. Bonhoeffer presents the event of justification as the origin and essence of the Christian life.[5] With this interpretation he sheds light on his anthropological assumptions that are deeply founded in his Christology. In concrete terms, the context of the motif of 'preparing the way' follows the following lines:

In his manuscript 'Ultimate and Penultimate Things', Bonhoeffer describes the event of justification as the event of an ultimate, more precisely: as the event of the bursting in of God's last word to the sinner.[6] In doing so, people recognize themselves and their neighbours for the first time in the light of God.[7] Or in other words, the word creates new being.[8] Following this thought, means, on the one hand, that the sinner addressed by God's word is justified, and on the other hand, that the life-world context of the human being now appears in a new light through the word of God. The word of God of mercy and justification is thereby the last word in two respects, namely qualitatively and temporally: Qualitatively, that is according to its content, it is the last word since no word of God goes beyond his word of grace; this means '[t]here is nothing greater than a life that is justified before God.'[9] Temporally, Bonhoeffer states, the word of God is the ultimate word, for the ultimate is always preceded by the penultimate. This means, there is 'some action, suffering, movement, intention, defeat, recovery, pleading, hoping – in short, quite literally a span of time at whose end it [the last word of God, HB]

---

5. See DBWE 6:146 (DBW 6:137).
6. See DBWE 6:146 (DBW 6:137).
7. See DBWE 6:146 (DBW 6:137).
8. See DBWE 6:96: 'In Christ the form of humanity was created anew.' (DBW 6:83). See for further interpretation Peter Dabrock, 'Wirklichkeit verantworten: Der responsive Ansatz theologischer Ethik bei Dietrich Bonhoeffer', in *Verantwortungsethik als Theologie des Wirklichen*, ed. Wolfgang Nethöfel, Peter Dabrock, and Siegfried Keil (Göttingen: Vandenhoeck & Ruprecht, 2009), 117–58. Peter Dabrock describes this as the mystery of Bonhoeffer's understanding of reality: 'Wort schafft Sein. Neues Wort lässt Sein neu sehen.' (Dabrock, *Wirklichkeit verantworten*, 136); see also Peter Dabrock, 'Responding to "Wirklichkeit": Reclaiming Bonhoeffer's Approach to Theological Ethics between Mystery and the Formation of the World', in *Mysteries in the Theology of Dietrich Bonhoeffer. A Copenhagen Bonhoeffer Symposium*, ed. Kirsten Busch Nielsen, Ulrik Nissen, and Christiane Tietz (Göttingen: Vandenhoeck & Ruprecht, 2007), 59–80, 60. Rowan Williams, too, interprets it in light of the solidarity of Creator and creation, see Rowan Williams, *Christ the Heart of Creation* (London: Bloomsbury, 2018), 202–5.
9. DBWE 6:149 (DBW 6:149).

stands.'[10] This implies, that only those who have become guilty of an accusation in a temporal sense can be justified.[11] The justifying word of God's grace remains the ultimate, therefore the path 'from the penultimate to the ultimate cannot be abandoned.'[12] The penultimate, in contrast, is everything that precedes the ultimate. However, it is not a state, but rather a judgement of the ultimate about what has gone before and what is past.[13] This means the ultimate conditions the penultimate – not vice versa. From the justification of the sinner by grace – the ultimate – the penultimate is determined as being human and being good.[14] Again, these determinations of the penultimate are not preconditions of justification but are determined by the ultimate. Being human, therefore, precedes being justified, but being human is conditioned by being justified – in other words: only the one justified becomes a human being.[15]

What being human means cannot be separated from Bonhoeffer's Christology.[16] To understand his justification-theological description of being human, his Christology[17] must be taken into account. Following Nadine Hamilton's interpretation, Bonhoeffer's Christological explanation of Jesus Christ's human nature enables an understanding of being human in general. In this sense, Bonhoeffer, echoing the Chalcedonian doctrine,[18] points out that Jesus Christ defines what it means to be truly human.[19] Following Bonhoeffer's Christological reflections, the true humanity of Jesus Christ is characterized by the extraordinary relationship with God, which is based on the fact that human nature has its origin in the divine nature of Jesus Christ, thus, no sin disturbs the relational event and there is an intact relationship happening.[20] Such a relational understanding of the

---

10. DBWE 6:150–1 (DBW 6:141).
11. See DBWE 6:151 (DBW 6:142).
12. DBWE 6:151 (DBW 6:142).
13. See DBWE 6:159 (DBW 6:151).
14. See DBWE 6:159 (DBW 6:151).
15. See DBWE 6:160 (DBW 6:152).
16. See Clifford J. Green, 'Ethical Theology and Contextual Ethics: New Perspectives on Bonhoeffer's Ethics', in *Religion im Erbe: Dietrich Bonhoeffer und die Zukunftsfähigkeit des Christentums*, ed. Christian Gremmels and Wolfgang Huber (Gütersloh: Chr. Kaiser/Gütersloher Verlagshaus, 2022), 255–86, 257.
17. See Christiane Tietz, 'Christology', in *The Oxford Handbook of Dietrich Bonhoeffer*, ed. Michael Mawson and Philip G. Ziegler (Oxford: Oxford University Press, 2019), 150–67; Ernst Feil, *Die Theologie Dietrich Bonhoeffers: Hermeneutik – Christologie – Weltverständnis*, 5th ed. (Münster: LIT Verlag, 2005), 135–220.
18. See Nadine Hamilton, *Dietrich Bonhoeffers Hermeneutik der Responsivität: Ein Kapitel Schriftlehre im Anschluss an 'Schöpfung und Fall'* (Göttingen: Vandenhoeck & Ruprecht, 2016), 260–78; see Williams, *Heart of Creation*, 185–99.
19. See Hamilton, *Being Human in Light of Chalcedon. The Necessary Possibility of Being One* article in this volume, 96; see also Clifford J. Green, 'Editor's Introduction to the English Edition', in DBWE 6:6–7.
20. See Hamilton, *Being Human* article in this volume, 101.

true humanity of Jesus Christ sheds light on what it means to be human at all: If Jesus Christ's humanity is truly human, being human means to be in relation with God.[21]

Jens Zimmermann exceeds this relational concept when he describes the unified self – unified through participation in Christ's life in which God and the world are reconciled.[22] Against this background, he speaks of a participatory mode of the being of selfhood.[23] The Christian subject participates in the humanity of Christ, his incarnation, by living, dying and rising in Christ's image.[24] Participation in the Incarnation of God in Jesus Christ is thus structured threefold by God's human life, cross and resurrection.[25] According to Bonhoeffer's ethics, furthermore, the Incarnation of God in Jesus Christ as a human being should not be considered without the perspective of the Crucifixion and Resurrection. Otherwise, in his opinion, Christian ethics either tips over into radicalism and enthusiasm or embraces compromise.[26] The awareness of not only the humanity, but also of the cross and resurrection of Jesus Christ should in this sense prevent a one-sided ethical orientation to the world or, conversely, to the hereafter. The triad of Incarnation, Crucifixion and Resurrection is, therefore, an important basis for Bonhoeffer's ethics of responsibility. Bonhoeffer unites Incarnation, Cross and Resurrection in his understanding of a Christian life. Along these lines, 'Christian life means being human [Menschsein] in the power of Christ's becoming human, being judged and pardoned in the power of the cross, living a new life in the power of the resurrection.'[27]

The penultimate must therefore be preserved for the sake of life and humanity.[28] This means for Bonhoeffer that human life should not be deprived of the conditions that belong to being human, as will be shown in more detail below, otherwise justification would be seriously hindered.[29] Deprivation of the necessities and conditions of life, in fact, prevents the word of God from being heard. Consequently, those who proclaim the word of God should care about the penultimate, otherwise, it does not meet the requirements of the word 'for free passage, for a smooth road.'[30] To take care of the penultimate and to ensure

---

21. Underlying this interpretation of humanity is an ontology of responsivity based on the communicative self-revelation of God in Jesus Christ. This means that human being is to be understood as a response to the being of Christ; see Hamilton, *Dietrich Bonhoeffers Hermeneutik der Responsivität*, 400–2; see also Dabrock, *Responding to 'Wirklichkeit'*, 56–68.

22. See Zimmermann, *Christian Humanism*, 134–42.

23. See ibid., 139–42.

24. See ibid., 139.

25. See ibid., 139–42.

26. See DBWE 6:157–63 (DBW 6:148–55).

27. DBWE 6:159 (DBW 6:150).

28. See DBWE 6:160 (DBW 6:152).

29. See DBWE 6:160 (DBW 6:152).

30. DBWE 6:160 (DBW 6:152).

that the ultimate may not be prevented or destroyed, that is, that justification may be heard, means: 'The way for the word must be prepared. The word itself demands it.'[31]

2. Describing 'Preparing the Way'

The text-based description of 'preparing the way' in light of the beforementioned context-analysis is the second step of this close reading: How does Bonhoeffer describe the motif? Bonhoeffer argues, by explaining the penultimate in his outline, that being in the penultimate is all about preparing the way for the word of justification, the ultimate. '[T]his preparation is not only an inward process, but a visible, creative activity on the greatest scale.'[32] Although Christ paves his own way, Bonhoeffer explains that people can oppose the coming of grace or rather act oppositely to facilitate the receiving of grace and the ability to believe.[33] Even if grace ultimately comes as it wills, there are conditions of the heart that make receiving grace difficult, and therefore, according to Bonhoeffer, human beings are not excused from preparing the way for grace, because '[t]he condition in which grace meets us is not irrelevant'.[34] Conditions that make the coming of grace difficult are in Bonhoeffer's perspective, for example, disgrace, desolation, poverty, helplessness, living in disorder, satiety, powerlessness, humiliation or disappointment.[35] Although God comes down precisely to these 'very depths of the human fall, of guilt, and of need',[36] these conditions are the task of 'preparing the way'. In other words, 'preparing the way' is about shaping the way of being human in light of the one human being, Jesus Christ.[37] This commission of 'immeasurable responsibility [is] given to all who know about the coming of Jesus

---

31. DBWE 6:160 (DBW 6:152–3).
32. DBWE 6:161 (DBW 6:153).
33. See DBWE 6:162 (DBW 6:154).
34. DBWE 6:162 (DBW 6:154).
35. See DBWE 6:162–3 (DBW 6:155).
36. DBWE 6:163 (DBW 6:155).
37. This means that one's own humanity is already suspended and reconciled in the light of Christ's humanity. The tension between the penultimate and the ultimate is resolved as Jens Zimmermann describes by referring to Bonhoeffer: 'The Christian experiences this ultimate-penultimate tension in a unified way because both aspects are held together by the collective person Jesus Christ. Only in Christ, writes Bonhoeffer, "is the ultimate-penultimate relation solved." (DBWE 6:149)' (Zimmermann, *Christian Humanism*, 141). Rowan Williams describes this state of human being in terms of agency: 'Bonhoeffer outlines a Christological ethic not primarily in terms of an "external" imitation of Christ but as the outworking of a transformation of human agency into the kind of life that is uninterruptedly embodied in Jesus – the consistent refusal of a place to defend and the allied readiness to stand in the other's place for their good or their rescue' (Williams, *Heart of Creation*, 215–16).

Christ'.³⁸ 'Preparing the way' refers, in this sense, to the task of meeting human needs, or as Bonhoeffer puts it: 'To bring bread to the hungry is preparing the way for the coming of grace'.³⁹

'Preparing the way' for Christ would be misunderstood if it were only a matter of fixing the world or creating conditions that are expedient or desirable, for then it would be more a matter of implementing a social reform programme according to Bonhoeffer's argument.⁴⁰ Of course, the concrete interventions in the world matter, but Bonhoeffer emphasizes that 'preparing the way' is, above all, also about the spiritual reality of an action, since the coming of Jesus Christ is at stake. 'This means that visible deeds, which must be done to make people ready to receive Jesus Christ, must be deeds of humility before the coming Lord, which means deeds of repentance'.⁴¹ In its spiritual dimension, Bonhoeffer describes 'preparing the way' as repentance. Following this line of argument, preserving the penultimate requires doing repentance as a concrete change in one's own behaviour.

Against this background of 'preparing the way' in deeds, as well as in repentance, within the context of justification light is shed on being human and being good as Bonhoeffer describes. Both can be recognized only from the coming of grace and both find fulfilment in it. In this context it is important that Jesus Christ comes to the fallen world and with this event the world becomes understandable as a 'world preserved and maintained by God'.⁴² In this perspective, 'preparing the way is to respect the penultimate and to enforce it, because of the ultimate that is approaching'.⁴³ 'Preparing the way', furthermore is to ensure that the word can be proclaimed and heard, for only through the preached word the call can be heard, followed, and faith be given.⁴⁴ In Bonhoeffer's view it is, therefore, necessary to enable people to hear God's word. Should the possibility to hear the word be disturbed by either physical inability, a hindrance in the way of life, or regarding the freedom of thought, the most important task must be to make it possible to hear God's Word.⁴⁵ 'That may mean', as Bonhoeffer states, 'that people must become human again'⁴⁶ before they are able to hear and respond.

---

38. DBWE 6:163 (DBW 6:155).
39. DBWE 6:163 (DBW 6:155).
40. See DBWE 6:164 (DBW 6:156-7).
41. DBWE 6:164 (DBW 6:157).
42. DBWE 6:165 (DBW 6:158). In the event of justification, it could be concluded with Peter Dabrock, the origin and essence of all Christian life is consummated, see Dabrock, *Wirklichkeit verantworten*, 146.
43. DBWE 6:166 (DBW 6:158).
44. See DBWE 6:166 (DBW 6:158-9).
45. See DBWE 6:166 (DBW 6:158-9).
46. DBWE 6:166 (DBW 6:159). Bonhoeffer's Christological founded understanding of being human is, as mentioned above, a cornerstone for understanding what Bonhoeffer implies here. On the Christological concept and the meaning of being human, see Hamilton, *Being Human*, article in this volume, 93-112.

Bonhoeffer describes 'preparing the way' as founded in the coming of Christ and the realization that He can only prepare the way for Himself: 'We are made preparers of Christ's way because, and really only because, Christ comes of Christ's own will, strength, and love; [...].'[47] The expectation of and the faith in the coming of Jesus Christ constitutes Bonhoeffer's motif of 'preparing the way', which he describes as possible solely in expectation of the ultimate and thus characterizes being human in the penultimate. However, this does not mean, following Bonhoeffer's description, that 'preparing the way', or Christian life in general, is directed exclusively towards the ultimate in order to overcome the penultimate, but 'Christian life is the dawn of the ultimate in me, the life of Jesus Christ in me. But it is also always life in the penultimate, waiting for the ultimate.'[48] The ultimate, therefore, has decisive consequences for being human in the penultimate, which in turn is destined to prepare the way.

3. Relating 'preparing the way' to Bonhoeffer's concept of life and responsibility

In light of this description and its contextual setting, 'preparing the way' presents itself as a pivotal point of Bonhoeffer's ethical reflections. To examine this observation and the coherence of the motif in the overall context of Bonhoeffer's *Ethics* fragments, the third step of the close reading elaborates the embedding of the motif in Bonhoeffer's overall conception of his responsibility ethics. What is of interest here is how the motif relates to Bonhoeffer's central thoughts and in particular to his understanding of life and responsibility, both deeply founded in his Christology.

Bonhoeffer's concepts of life and responsibility are significant for this in the following respects: 'preparing the way', as described, is closely linked to Bonhoeffer's understanding of being human. In order to further describe this basic situation or setting of ethics, Bonhoeffer resorts to the concept of life. The considerations on life or the situation: 'we are living',[49] occupy a prominent position in his manuscript 'History and Good' in its second version.[50] One could say, and this is also supported by this article, that Bonhoeffer's concept of life is a decisive prerequisite for his concept of responsibility.[51] Within the expression 'responsible life', furthermore, Bonhoeffer correlates the concept of life with his concept of responsibility. Thus, for the understanding of 'preparing the way', both concepts are essential. Both take on different functions. On the one hand, life can be interpreted as a setting of 'preparing the way' and, on the other hand, responsibility can be interpreted as its substantive determination.

---

47. DBWE 6:167 (DBW 6:159).
48. DBWE 6:168 (DBW 6:160).
49. DBWE 6:246 (DBW 6:245).
50. Compared to the first version, it can be assumed that this was probably consciously reconceptualized by Bonhoeffer as a starting point.
51. See Friederike Barth, *Die Wirklichkeit des Guten: Dietrich Bonhoeffers 'Ethik' und ihr philosophischer Hintergrund* (Tübingen: Mohr Siebeck, 2011), 146.

3.1. Bonhoeffer's concept of life In the manuscript 'History and Good', Bonhoeffer defines his concept of life first in distinction to other ethical theories. These theoretical conceptions, according to Bonhoeffer, are dominated by an idealistic abstraction, namely the abstraction of the isolated individual human being, who has to distinguish between good and evil according to an absolute criterion.[52] Bonhoeffer explains: 'Indeed, the basic scheme of this abstraction, in each of its elements, misses precisely the specifically ethical problem.'[53] The abstraction, Bonhoeffer argues, consists in the fact that there is no isolated individual per se, as well as the absolute ethical criterion is not available and the good, as well as the evil, do not appear in pure form in history.[54] Whenever an absolute good is identified as a criterion, an ideal is declared to be a value, virtue or duty. Then, according to Bonhoeffer, the good becomes 'a dead law, a Moloch, to whom all life and freedom are sacrificed'.[55] Instead, life is reduced to 'a static basic formula'.[56] Bonhoeffer notes that the ethical decision 'in which the whole person, with both understanding and will, seeks and finds what is good only in the very risk of the action itself, within the ambiguity of a historical situation'[57] is neglected. Instead, applying principles is regarded as an ethical task.[58]

Bonhoeffer thus criticizes any ethics based on idealism or rationalism. These theories fail upon life,[59] as he states, because they interpret the reality of life utilizing a spirit-nature scheme: 'Life is reduced to a quantité négligeable that can be disregarded at will. Life is understood, at best, as that part of "nature" that owes its origin, as well as its redemption to the spirit, to the idea.'[60] The good, according to Bonhoeffer, within these theories is thus detached from life and is about 'a realization of certain ideals and values that are independent of life'.[61] Bonhoeffer shares the critique of idealism and rationalism with both existential philosophy and the philosophy of life, which developed as philosophical currents at the same time, and adopts their criticisms.[62]

The philosophy of life, which developed as an intellectual current in the late nineteenth and early twentieth centuries, in particular, is an important element in Bonhoeffer's work, even though he does not specifically mention it in his

---

52. See DBWE 6:247 (DBW 6:246).
53. DBWE 6:247 (DBW 6:246).
54. See DBWE 6:247 (DBW 6:246).
55. DBWE 6:247 (DBW 6:247).
56. DBWE 6:248 (DBW 6:246).
57. DBWE 6:248 (DBW 6:247).
58. See DBWE 6:248 (DBW 6:247).
59. See DBWE 6:248 (DBW 6:246-7).
60. DBWE 6:249 (DBW 6:248).
61. DBWE 6:253 (DBW 6:252).
62. See Barth, *Die Wirklichkeit des Guten*, 146.

Ethics fragments.[63] The critical turn of the philosophy of life against idealism and rationalism is characterized primarily by a new concept of life, which detaches itself from the dualistic spirit-nature scheme and a general principle of reason.[64] The philosophy of life rejects the exclusive importance of the mind or the intellect for the knowledge of the world and living; in contrast, it primarily includes the non-intellectual, that means the physical and psychological aspects, as well as the social and historical contexts of life in its anthropology.[65] Bonhoeffer's reflections on life are related to concerns of the philosophy of life, for example, the idea of the unity of reality and human life, as well as its individuality and relation to this worldliness, and also the rejection of an absolute metaphysical point of view.[66] Rather, Bonhoeffer replaces an absolute point of view with life in its historicity and, thus, introduces life as the reference point of all existence, as well as of thought and action.[67]

The particular focus on the historicity of life establishes the essential relation between the question of the good and life that Bonhoeffer states programmatically at the beginning of the manuscript 'History and Good' in its second version: 'The question about the good is itself part of our life, just as our life is part of the question about the good.'[68] This indicates further, according to Bonhoeffer, that the question of the good is posed in the context of the concrete conditions of life:

> The question about the good is asked and decided in the midst of a situation of our life that is both determined in a particular way and yet still incomplete, unique and yet already in transition; it happens in the midst of our living bonds to people, things, institutions, and powers, that is, in the midst of our historical existence.[69]

On the other hand, life in its historical determination is always already ethically challenged, as Bonhoeffer states, and therefore cannot exclude the question of the good, which situationally always poses itself anew.

---

63. Friederike Barth provides a detailed account of the references and influences of the philosophy of life in Bonhoeffer's manuscript 'History and Good'. Nevertheless, she clearly states that rather the Christological foundation of the concept of life was Bonhoeffer's decisive intention and finally Rudolf Bultmann's commentary on John gave the impulse for this. See Barth, *Die Wirklichkeit des Guten*, 158, 145–95.

64. See Barth, *Die Wirklichkeit des Guten*, 152–3.

65. See ibid., 154.

66. See ibid., 157, 163: 'Die Absage an einen archimedischen Punkt des Denkens, von dem aus das immer im Wandel begriffene Leben erst seinen Sinn und seinen Maßstab erhielte, ist begründet in der Absage an einen rationalistischen Wirklichkeitsbegriff.'

67. See Barth, *Die Wirklichkeit des Guten*, 163.

68. DBWE 6:247 (DBW 6:245).

69. DBWE 6:247 (DBW 6:245–6).

Furthermore, the historicity of life alludes in Bonhoeffer's outline to the essential binding of life to the penultimate. This kind of attachment to the penultimate has consequences for ethical action, which, thus, does not follow a general principle or virtue, but is decided in the historical situation. The ethical decision[70] gains specific significance in Bonhoeffer's conception of ethics. There is, however, no absolute certainty about the right action, since historical change, the unique historical situation and human motivations have always been in the process of becoming. Instead the situation demands a decision, that is, to choose 'something relatively better over something relatively worse'.[71] Thus the penultimate as reality is the ethical starting point of life, as well as of ethics. Bonhoeffer's conception of ethics proves in this sense to be a situation ethics.

Bonhoeffer's theological identification of reality as ultimate and penultimate underlines in its anthropological consequence precisely this binding of life and thus a situational approach of ethics – however, it also exceeds it. The human being, because it is addressed by the ultimate, lives in the penultimate, from which arises the mandate for the ultimate as 'preparing the way'. This implies a concrete ethical action towards Christ. But here, the situational ethics is exceeded: The justification-theological explanation, as well as the Christological foundation of the ethical situation, makes it clear that being human as well as the concept of the good and ethics is grounded in the life, cross and resurrection of Jesus Christ. Through the Christological foundation of life, Bonhoeffer makes it clear that his historical concept of life is bound to Christ's being. Life itself is even ethically qualified by this Christological justification:[72] 'Good is not a quality of life but "life" itself. Being good [Gutsein] means "to live".'[73]

Bonhoeffer gains this insight by associating life with the self-expression of Jesus in John: 'I am the life' (Jn 14:6). Bonhoeffer justifies this linkage with the question: 'While we are still living and are thus ignorant of the limit of our life, namely, death, how could we be able to say what life is in itself?'; and he concludes: 'We can only live life, but not define it.'[74] In accordance with his Christological-relational approach to being human,[75] Bonhoeffer states that life is not in a human being, but outside of it: 'My life is outside myself, beyond my disposal. My life is another, a stranger, Jesus Christ [...]. Rather, Jesus Christ is life itself.'[76] Bonhoeffer further

---

70. '[T]he genuine decision in which the whole person, with both understanding and will, seeks and finds what is good only in the very risk of the action itself, within the ambiguity of a historical situation.' (DBWE 6:248 [DBW 6:246]).

71. DBWE 6:261 (DBW 6:260).

72. See Barth, *Die Wirklichkeit des Guten*, 178.

73. DBWE 6:253 (DBW 6:252).

74. DBWE 6:249 (DBW 6:248).

75. See Hamilton, *Being Human*.

76. DBWE 6:250 (DBW 6:249).

expands this argument based on Rudolf Bultmann's Commentary on John[77] and calls Christ the life of all created things.[78]

In light of his insight that life lies outside the human being's self in Jesus Christ, Bonhoeffer describes this not as self-recognition, but as a claim encountered from outside, which can be believed or contradicted.[79] The word of Jesus – 'I am the life' – once it affects the human being personally, reveals two things: On the one hand, the No about the apostasy of life from the origin, and on the other hand, the Yes to the new life, 'to the flourishing of life's strength'.[80] Human beings live in the tension between Yes and No, but in Jesus Christ, the new life is unified, because 'in each Yes already the No is perceived, and in each No also the Yes'.[81] This unity of life in Christ is, in this sense, the reconciliation of God with humanity, of the worldly with the Christian, is Jesus Christ as life itself.

In the motif of 'preparing the way', both central aspects of Bonhoeffer's concept of life coincide: first, a life that becomes historical and takes shape situationally, and second, life as a response to Christ's claim 'I am the life', his Incarnation, Crucifixion and Resurrection. In this sense, it can be argued that 'preparing the way' is a process of coping with situations of life. As Bonhoeffer's description made clear, 'preparing the way' is dealing with the historical, situational conditions that life implies. Life in this sense presents itself as the setting of 'preparing the way', or in more colourful words: Life is the stage on which the 'preparing of the way' is performed. At the same time, 'preparing the way' also presents itself in terms of Bonhoeffer's outline as a mode of responding to the call to the life of Jesus Christ. Thus, 'preparing the way' could also be formally described as answering.[82] The fundamental insight regarding 'preparing the way' in terms of Bonhoeffer's concept of life, however, is that life is the foundation of all 'preparing the way', of all related actions, and deeds. Ethics cannot be detached from this: There is no ethics beyond life – in other words, the ambivalence of Christian life between the divine claim as well as binding and the already reconciled reality through Christ is the setting of Bonhoeffer's ethics.

---

77. Again, it should be pointed out that the decisive impetus for the elaboration of Bonhoeffer's concept of life was probably not so much philosophical concepts of life, but rather Rudolf Bultmann's commentary on John, which Bonhoeffer mentions in a letter in March 1942 during his work on the first ethics version. Furthermore, two of the very few references Bonhoeffer himself makes in his ethics refer to this same commentary on John (see DBWE 6:250n1 [DBW 6:249n1]); see Barth, *Die Wirklichkeit des Guten*, 158.

78. See DBWE 6:250 (DBW 6:249).

79. See DBWE 6:250 (DBW 6:249).

80. DBWE 6:251 (DBW 6:251).

81. DBWE 6:252 (DBW 6:251).

82. See DBWE 6:254 (DBW 6:253–4).

3.2. Responsibility Bonhoeffer's concept of life is closely tied to his description of responsibility. In this respect, 'preparing the way' relates to responsibility as well. Bonhoeffer describes responsibility as '[t]his life, lived in answer to the life of Jesus Christ (as the Yes and No to our life)'.[83] Responsibility as response means for Bonhoeffer the wholeness and unity of life that responds to the reality given by Christ: 'Responsibility thus means to risk one's life in its wholeness, aware that one's activity is a matter of life and death.'[84] All of life is subsequently a response to God's claim. Bonhoeffer, thus, gives the concept of responsibility, as he states, 'a fuller meaning than is the case in everyday usage'.[85] He expands the concept of responsibility in this sense through a Christological justification of the concept of responsibility.

Bonhoeffer regards responsible life as being twofold structured, on the one hand, by the binding of life to human beings and God, on the other hand, by the freedom of one's own life. Furthermore, he determines formal criteria of responsibility: He outlines that the bond shows itself in the form of vicarious representative action and accordance with reality; the freedom proves itself in the willingness to take on guilt and in the risk of the concrete decision as a venture.[86] Wolfgang Huber describes this interplay of bond and freedom as 'Selbsttranszendenz und Lebensvollzug'.[87] This means that only in self-transcendence, in stepping out of oneself, and in giving one's life to God and one's neighbour, being human is possible. Bonhoeffer's concept of responsibility, subsequently, depends on his concept of life, as Bonhoeffer's introductory definition of responsibility already clearly states: 'This life, lived in answer to the life of Jesus Christ (as the Yes and No to our life), we call *"responsibility"* [*"Verantwortung"*].'[88]

This interrelation of Bonhoeffer's concept of responsibility and life, or in short: responsible life, relates to the motif of 'preparing the way' in two ways. Firstly, in relation to the Christological justification of life. As claim from outside, namely as the claim of Christ: 'I am the life,'[89] the concept of life relates to 'preparing the

---

83. DBWE 6:254 (DBW 6:254).

84. DBWE 6:255 (DBW 6:254).

85. DBWE 6:255 (DBW 6:254).

86. Bonhoeffer describes the structure of the responsible life inconsistently. Thus, the concept of freedom is sometimes determined as one's own accountability of life and action as well as venture; see DBWE 6:257 (DBW 6:256). In other parts of the text, he mentions the willingness to accept guilt and freedom as aspects of the responsible life, see DBWE 6:174, 288 (DBW 6:166, 289). However, Bonhoeffer predominantly refers to the basic structure mentioned above.

87. Wolfgang Huber, *Ethik: Die Grundfragen unseres Lebens von der Geburt bis zum Tod* (München: C. H. Beck, 2013), 120: 'Self-transcendence and life's consummation' (translation HB).

88. DBWE 6:254 (DBW 6:254), italics in original.

89. See Jn 11:27; 14:6; see DBWE 6:250-1 (DBW 6:250).

way' with responsibility. This means life provides a common background for responsibility and being responsible in the mode of 'preparing the way'. Life is, as argued in this article, the setting of Bonhoeffer's ethical considerations. Secondly, it is not only life but the underlying Christologically founded anthropology that connects responsible living with the concept of 'preparing the way'. In a nutshell, being human is the response to Christ's claim, which is responsibility. Again, at a glance, the constitution of life through the address of Christ is, as shown, reflected in the theological explanations of justification concerning the ultimate and penultimate. Here, the ultimate is described as a word event, which reconstitutes the human condition, and as the precondition of Christian life. Bonhoeffer describes the concept of life developing in a communicative event. Thus, it can be argued that an essentialist ontology is preceded by a communicative or responsive ontology.[90] This communicative ontology lays the foundation for the human being as a responsible being, in the truest sense of the word: Responding, and thus literally being responsible, is being.[91] This responsive anthropology is in turn at the core of 'preparing the way': 'preparing the way' is to pave the way for the Word, so that being human in response to Jesus Christ's call – as a responsive human being – is possible. In other words: Responsibility is the very substance of 'preparing the way'.

4. Understanding 'Preparing the Way'

Following this close reading, a brief summary will be given of how the motif can be understood. What is of importance here is the context in which it is described, namely in Bonhoeffer's justification-theological distinction of the penultimate and ultimate things. This context is the key to understanding 'preparing the way'. The distinction between the penultimate and the ultimate goes hand in hand with the basic anthropological determination that the way must be prepared for the word of justification to enable being human.

Bonhoeffer understands 'preparing the way' in order to enable human being in two ways: On the one hand, as concrete deeds and interventions in the visible world. It means that the penultimate as such is recognized by upholding human rights and living conditions; on the other hand, he emphasizes the spiritual reality of 'preparing the way' as repentance.[92] Both imply that human beings become preparers of the way, through the dawning of the ultimate in them, which, henceforth, determines their being human and their deeds. In other words, 'preparing the way' is the answer to this dawning of the ultimate as demand of

---

90. See Dabrock, *Responding to 'Wirklichkeit'*, 60; and Dabrock, *Wirklichkeit verantworten*, 136; see Hamilton, *Dietrich Bonhoeffers Hermeneutik der Responsivität*, 400–2.
   91. See Hamilton, *Dietrich Bonhoeffers Hermeneutik der Responsivität*, 402.
   92. See DBWE 6:164 (DBW 6:157).

Jesus Christ. Bonhoeffer, furthermore, describes 'preparing the way' as a necessary consequence of the knowledge of Christ's grace: 'Because we await Christ, because we know that Christ will come, therefore and only therefore do we prepare the way.'[93] 'Preparing the way' is happening to human beings, it is rather an urpassive attitude in response to the godly demand, as Dabrock describes it.[94] In other words, 'preparing the way' becomes an essential trait of a new humanity in the penultimate.[95]

In terms of Bonhoeffer's central concepts of life and responsibility, 'preparing the way' presents itself, as this article argues, as a formal shaping of life with a substantial focus on responsibility. Life is, thus, the background or the setting in which preparing the way can be located and performed. Responsibility, on the other hand, provides the inner orientation or content, the very substance of 'preparing the way'. Taken together, it can be said on a formal level that 'preparing the way' is the mode of responsible life. Oriented to the conditions and contexts of life temporally and materially, 'preparing the way' is about acting or living responsibly. This means that human beings, first and foremost, must be enabled to be responsive and live responsible – this literally captures 'responsibility' in the truest sense of the word, as responsibility is made up from 'responsible' and 'ability'. For Bonhoeffer, this is essentially a Christological argument. Enabling human being, this means 'preparing the way', is all about paving the way for the true human being, Jesus Christ. His concept of life is also oriented towards the Christological interpretation of Jesus Christ's saying 'I am the life'.[96] Likewise, responsibility as a response to Jesus Christ's claim is interpreted substantively. Only against this Christological background can the central role of 'preparing the way' as a mode of responsible life be grasped in its full scope.

III. 'Preparing the Way' and Its Political-Ethical Potential

Against this background, the political-ethical potential of the 'preparing the way' motif is now to be highlighted. Based on the understanding of the motif as a mode of responsible life, it is assumed that the political side of 'preparing the way' offers insights for political Christian agency in the (pluralistic) world. Bonhoeffer's ethics, understood as social ethics,[97] which addresses not only the church public but a public in the broader sense, is fundamental for the following explanations.[98] This becomes clear, on the one hand, through his understanding

---

93. DBWE 6:167 (DBW 6:160).
94. See Dabrock, *Wirklichkeit verantworten*, 142.
95. See DBWE 6:168 (DBW 6:160–1).
96. See Jn 11:27; 14:6, and also DBWE 6:250–1 (DBW 6:249).
97. See Wolfgang Huber, *Konflikt und Konsens: Studien zur Ethik der Verantwortung* (München: Chr. Kaiser Verlag, 1990), 143.
98. See Schliesser, *Dietrich Bonhoeffer*.

of reality, which sees world-reality and God-reality united in Christ-reality. The reality of the world is always already carried and reconciled in the reality of God.[99] With this understanding of reality, Bonhoeffer vehemently opposes the perverted interpretation of the Two Kingdoms Doctrine with its strong focus on the autonomy (*Eigengesetzlichkeiten*) of the temporal dimensions of the world. Especially within the distinction between the ultimate and the penultimate, it becomes clear how Bonhoeffer reinterprets the Lutheran Two Kingdoms Doctrine.[100] In terms of justification-theology, with his distinction, he takes the whole life and not only the realms of state and church into account. He replaces the reference to a spiritual kingdom and a temporal kingdom with the ultimate and penultimate.[101] It is against this background that he situates the motif of 'preparing the way' as a mode of responsible life and ethical action.

For the political-ethical interpretation of 'preparing the way', Bonhoeffer's fundamental ethical considerations should be summarized, which are consistent with the motif of 'preparing the way': First, Bonhoeffer's distinction between the ultimate and the penultimate and his concept of life clearly show that his ethical approach transcends any situational ethics. Life in its current reality and historical becoming is understood as a unified life. Second, Bonhoeffer's ethics is to be understood in light of the conduct of life. This may not be confused with an ethics of lifestyle. Rather, the situation 'we are living'[102] establishes the responsible action and is its content. It is about the responsible conduct of life itself, instead of a principle-oriented ethical approach of responsibility. Responsibility, moreover, is an inherent element of life, determined by the responsiveness of human life. Third, Bonhoeffer's ethics presents itself as relational-responsive ethics, knowing itself bound to the claim of God, as well as towards each other. In this sense, Bonhoeffer resists an abstraction of the individual and provides a social ethics by its relational grounding.[103] On this horizon, the political potential of 'preparing the way' is to be considered.

As described, 'preparing the way' can be interpreted as a mode of responsible life. This becomes particularly clear in Bonhoeffer's explanations of his doctrine of mandates, in which the mandates are represented in their formal determinacy and their reciprocity, for, with, and against each other, as 'preparing the way'. This aspect of Bonhoeffer's doctrine of mandates cannot be elaborated on further. The following short summary, however, helps to elaborate the political aspects of 'preparing the way': In Bonhoeffer's explanations, the mandates can be interpreted as a place of responsible action. The mandates are to be interpreted

---

99. See DBWE 6:55 (DBW 6:40).

100. See Michael DeJonge, *Bonhoeffer's Reception of Luther* (Oxford: Oxford University Press, 2017).

101. See ibid., 137–42.

102. DBWE 6:246 (DBW 6:245).

103. See Huber, *Konflikt und Konsens*, 143.

in light of Christ-reality and not as orders of creation or maintenance.[104] This is accompanied by his description that the mandates are instituted by God but are shaped by people, or as Gunter Prüller-Jagenteufel puts it: the mandates are spaces of responsibility shaped by people.[105] They emerge, as Bonhoeffer describes, as structures of God's preservation action, but only in cooperation of their with-one-anotherness, for-one-anotherness, and being-over-against-one-anotherness of the mandates, which implies a process of negotiation.[106] Bonhoeffer, at one level, wants to prevent the absolutization of a single mandate through their interwovenness and cooperation.[107] On another level, the mandates acquire their meaning and their cooperative character in a 'deconstructionist running against each other'.[108] Even if the doctrine of mandates remained, as Frits de Lange says, 'a torso',[109] it can be stated that the running against each other of mandates describes a cooperative and processual relationality and, in this sense, challenges the motif of 'preparing the way'. The motif of 'preparing the way' is indicated by Bonhoeffer in the explanations of the individual mandates, for example, when for the mandate of work the preparation of the way is described as the goal and task[110] or for the mandate of authority the protection of the created is to be requested through law and sword and thus a form of preparation is described.[111] In all brevity, it can be concluded that the mandates as places of responsible life can be understood and are determined as 'preparing the way'. This positioning as such indicates political potential, but 'preparing the way' is not to be reduced to the formulation of mandates. Instead, this contribution asks for insights offered by the motif in a triad with the concept of life and responsibility, for a theory of Christian action in (a pluralistic) world reality. Three political-ethical accents of 'preparing the way', in particular, can be derived: Sensitivity to ambiguity, empowerment orientation and orientation to action.

104. See Gunter Prüller-Jagenteufel, *Befreit zur Verantwortung: Sünde und Versöhnung in der Ethik Dietrich Bonhoeffers* (Münster: LIT Verlag, 2004), 343: 'Weil der Begriff der Erhaltungsordnung zu leicht im Sinne einer Zwei-Reiche-Lehre mißverstanden werden konnte, [...] gab ihn Bonhoeffer schon 1933 wieder auf; den Denkansatz im Erhaltungshandeln Gottes behielt er jedoch bei und konkretisiert ihn in seinen Ethikmanuskripten, indem er ihn in die Lehre von den göttlichen Mandaten weiterführte.'
105. See ibid.
106. See DBWE 6:393 (DBW 6:397).
107. See DBWE 6:393 (DBW 6:397): 'None of these mandates exists self-sufficiently, nor an one of them claim to replace all the others.'
108. Dabrock, *Wirklichkeit verantworten,* 152 (translation HB).
109. Frits de Lange, '"Miteinander, Füreinander, Gegeneinander": Bonhoeffers Mandatenlehre in einer Pluralistischen Gesellschaft', in *Bonhoeffer Rundbrief: Mitteilungen der Internationalen Bonhoeffer-Gesellschaft, Sektion Bundesrepublik Deutschland* 54 (1997): 13–32, 15.
110. See DBWE 6:71 (DBW 6:58).
111. See DBWE 6:71–3 (DBW 6:58–60).

With the distinction of the ultimate and the penultimate, with 'preparing the way', Bonhoeffer theologically describes the basic anthropological situation of human beings in the world as *simul iustus et peccator*. It is in this everlasting ambivalence of humanity that 'preparing the way' is founded and anchored. For this reason, a certain tolerance of ambiguity is demanded to prepare the way. This basic situation is spiritually strongly emphasized by the need for repentance. But it is not only in these terms that the motif oscillates between tensions: The concept of life and its bondage to the historical situation in its becoming, on the one hand, and the reality of the world suspended in the reality of Christ, on the other, further provoke a certain sensitivity to ambiguity between what is possible and what is demanded. Responsible action, as it is then described as a structural element of responsibility, remains in this sense a venture. This idea of sensitivity to ambiguity is reinforced when the willingness to accept guilt is described as an element of responsibility, as well as the adequacy to reality as binding for a responsible life.

The empowerment orientation is reflected concretely in the political tone of the description of 'preparing the way' when it comes to helping those who lack basic needs. This may mean 'that people must become human again'[112] before they are addressable for God's word or capable to respond. Bonhoeffer is concerned with enabling people to hear and participate in God's word. He makes this even clearer in his reflections on human rights,[113] in which, the orientation to the neighbour is remarkable. In his *Letters and Papers from Prison*, Bonhoeffer calls this shaping of orientation towards another as 'being there for others'.[114] This motif also appears as a structural element of responsibility in light of the binding element of vicarious representation. As described by Bonhoeffer, vicarious representation is characterized by selflessness and complete devotion to the other.[115] Its objective, it can be summarized, is to help others to be free and to fulfil his or her demands through 'being there for others'.[116]

There is finally a strong emphasis on the orientation to action, which highlights the political potential of 'preparing the way'. The priority of life and action within Bonhoeffer's ethics, in which ethical principles first prove themselves through life, could perhaps be interpreted as a pragmatic line of argumentation, for example, similar to the ethical approach of his contemporary John Dewey, who places action and experience at the beginning of ethics with his method of the experimental

---

112. DBWE 6:166 (DBW 6:159).

113. See DBWE 6:171–218 (DBW 6:162–217); see also Christiane Schliesser, '"The First Theological-Ethical Doctrine of Basic Human Rights Developed by a Twentieth-Century German Protestant Theologian": Dietrich Bonhoeffer and Human Rights', in *A Spoke in the Wheel. Reconsidering the Political in the Theology of Dietrich Bonhoeffer*, ed. Kirsten Busch Nielsen, Ralf K. Wüstenberg, and Jens Zimmermann (Gütersloh: Gütersloher Verlagshaus, 2014), 369–84.

114. DBWE 8:501 (DBW 8:558).

115. See DBWE 6:258–9 (DBW 6:257–9).

116. DBWE 8:501 (DBW 8:558).

inquiry.[117] Following this, in exploring the options between demands and reality, ends and means, and seeking appropriate possibilities, action is at the heart of 'preparing the way'. Preparation of the way is not only 'an inward process, but a visible, creative activity on the greatest scale'.[118] Bonhoeffer also emphasizes the spiritual dimension of visible deeds within 'preparing the way': 'This means that visible deeds, which must be done to make people ready to receive Jesus Christ, must be deeds of humility before the coming Lord, which means deeds of repentance'.[119] With the concept of life, which is embraced in the preparation of the way, the concrete deed, the doing or the concrete life becomes central. The bond to the concept of life is in this context a guardrail of action. Not principles or forever fixed legalities, but life itself is the criterion of ethical action. This strong concept of life, in which ethical action, being human, and being good underline a pragmatic ethical interpretation.

Beyond that, 'preparing the way' is strengthened also from the concept of responsibility regarding its action orientation, in terms of the venture of the concrete decision, as well as the willingness to guilt. Responsibility emerges in light of the free responsible action that takes place in the freedom of the own self, like in a free-floating space. No person or principle can ultimately justify these actions. Acting responsibly means to act in one's own freedom by 'considering all existing circumstances related to people, general conditions, or principles'.[120] If nothing comes to their defence this is a 'proof of [...] freedom'.[121] This is precisely the risk of an ethical action, because in the end there is a decision that has to be made in a specific situation. The justification of an act by the analysed motives, circumstances and intentions, however, cannot serve as an absolvement or excuse, because then this very decision-making process would become the law and the person would no longer be free.[122] According to Bonhoeffer, however, the risk of concrete decision and acting freely and responsibly, is

> bound to God and neighbor as they encounter me in Jesus Christ, the only bond that is liberating, totally liberating. Responsible action takes place in the sphere of relativity, completely shrouded in the twilight that the historical situation casts upon good and evil. It takes place in the midst of the countless perspectives from which every phenomenon is seen. Responsible action must decide not simply between right and wrong, good and evil, but between right and right, wrong and wrong.[123]

117. See John Dewey, *Logic: The Theory of Inquiry* (New York: Henry Holt and Company, 1938); see John Dewey, *The Quest for Certainty: A Study of the Relation of Knowledge and Action* (London: George Allen & Unwin Ltd, 1930).
118. DBWE 6:161 (DBW 6:153).
119. DBWE 6:164 (DBW 6:157).
120. DBWE 6:283 (DBW 6:283-4).
121. DBWE 6:283 (DBW 6:284).
122. See DBWE 6:284-5 (DBW 6:285).
123. DBWE 6:284 (DBW 6:284).

In his *Letters and Papers from Prison*, Bonhoeffer refers to the orientation to action in this way: 'Hover not over the possible, but boldly reach for the real' and, in addition, 'in action alone is found freedom'.[124]

In order to summarize this sketch: 'Preparing the way' in its relation to the concept of life and responsibility reveals a political-ethical orientation, insofar as public action in Bonhoeffer's sense expects and copes with ambivalences, which is oriented towards the other and their capabilities, and aims towards the concrete deed. These three accents will now be discussed regarding the public theological discourse.

IV. What Does 'Preparing the Way' Imply for Public Theology?

Bonhoeffer's ethics has repeatedly found reception in the public theological tradition; Christine Schliesser, for example, proposes to describe Dietrich Bonhoeffer as a public theologian *avant la lettre*.[125] Bonhoeffer's understanding of the reality of Christ, his concept of responsibility, or the willingness to take up guilt are received quite often in the public theological discourses. The motif of 'preparing the way', however, has rarely been examined in this context, although it bears potential for public theological discourses.

'Public theology', in light of this contribution, refers to the paradigm of public theology,[126] which globally developed in the mid-twentieth century. There are two roots for the term; it emerged from the discourses on civic theology in the United. States, Martin Marty first used it in this context. Slightly earlier, however, Wolfgang Huber argued for a public-theological approach, in response to the political theology movement in Germany.[127] In great diversity of concepts and motivated by liberation theology, the paradigm of public theology has arrived in the theological discourse worldwide, as in Brazil, South Africa and other countries.[128] Especially in Germany, the emblem of public theology introduces a plurality-sensitive and democracy-friendly theology and church practice after the Second World War and the experiences of the National Socialist regime.[129] Besides historical, cultural

---

124. DBWE 8:513 (DBW 8:571).
125. See Schliesser, *Dietrich Bonhoeffer*.
126. See Smit, *The Paradigm of Public Theology*.
127. Se Höhne, *Öffentliche Theologie*.
128. See for an overview of the different approaches Florian Höhne and Frederike van Oorschot (eds), *Grundtexte der Öffentlichen Theologie* (Leipzig: Evangelisches Verlagsanstalt, 2015); for current discussions and approaches compare the *International Journal of Public Theology*.
129. See the convincing interpretation of the public theology paradigm as a modern interpretation of the Lutheran Two Kingdoms Doctrine by Julian Zeyher-Quattlender, *Du sollst nicht töten (lassen)? Eine Rekonstruktion der Friedensethik Dietrich Bonhoeffers aus der Perspektive Öffentlicher Theologie in aktueller Absicht* (Leipzig: Evangelische Verlagsanstalt, 2021), especially 203–15.

or contextual events, public theology is influenced by liberation-theological approaches, as well as political theology, methodologically and conceptually. Materially, the term embraces the liberation-theological commitment for the disadvantaged and marginalized, as well as any efforts for justice of theological and church institutions. Formally, it includes the reflection of all Christian content in the public sphere, as well as the political and public discourse in the mode of translating religious content as a contribution to public reasoning.[130]

There are, however, also criticisms to this paradigm. Practical efforts to concretize public theology in its institutions, the churches and their ministers, have been strongly criticized in the German-speaking context. The critiques impute a rather one-sided party-political admonishment for justice and public reasoning: Christians, therefore, have increasing difficulties to identify with the public-theological political engagement, the diversity of opinions seems to be undermined, and finally, the churches are not even fundamentally responsible for policy-making.[131] Public theology is not only criticized in German-speaking countries: it is criticized as well, for example, by the South African theologian Tinyiko Maluleke, who understands the concept of public theology as a perpetuation of colonial, decidedly Western theology, which represents a categorical appropriation of particular discourses and interests.[132] Instead, he claims for a particular African and Black theology. The critics, thus, either call for greater political diversity or a fully diversified politicization of public theology, on the one hand, and at the same time for a strong, critical demarcation of theology from the political, as well as economic systems, on the other hand. Criticism varies widely, but it shows that the paradigm of public theology is challenged by an increasingly functionally differentiated society, pluralization, individualization and secularization of all spheres of life.

In light of these discourses on public theology, Bonhoeffer's motif of 'preparing the way' in particular offers further potential for these debates on public theology. For example with regard to the sensitivity to ambiguity, if both diversity and politicization are demanded and at the same time the demarcation from political, colonialist or economic positions, a public theology in the mode of 'preparing the way' would be seeking out precisely these ambivalences and paving the way in between. Or in Bonhoeffer's words: 'In any action that is truly in accord with

---

130. See Jürgen Habermas, 'Religion in der Öffentlichkeit. Kognitive Voraussetzungen für den "öffentlichen Vernunftgebrauch" religiöser und säkularer Bürger', in Jürgen Habermas, *Zwischen Naturalismus und Religion. Philosophische Aufsätze* (Frankfurt am Main: Suhrkamp, 2009), 119–29, 135–8.

131. See Christian Albrecht and Rainer Anselm, *Öffentlicher Protestantismus zur aktuellen Debatte um gesellschaftliche Präsenz und politische Aufgaben des evangelischen Christentums* (Zürich: Theologischer Verlag Zürich, 2017).

132. See Tinyiko Sam Maluleke, 'Reflections and Resources: The Elusive Public of Public Theology: A Response to William Storrar', in *International Journal of Public Theology* 5, no. 1 (2011): 79–89.

reality, acknowledgement of the status quo and protest against the status quo are inextricably connected.'[133] Bedford-Strohm calls this kind of public theology a 'biblical informed realism'[134] and describes its concern as follows: 'Für die Ethik bedeutet das genau den Weg zwischen Anpassung an das Faktische auf der einen Seite und Fundamentalopposition auf der anderen Seite, den die öffentliche Theologie zu gehen versucht.'[135] In the spirit of Bonhoeffer's 'preparing the way', public theology mediates between God's claim and the reality of life.

Also, through the empowerment orientation, the motif of 'preparing the way' might be fruitful for public theology. Both the central focus on the option for the marginalized and the spiritual orientation of empowering to hear the word of God offer a simultaneity to public theology, which may be an answer to critical positions. Public theology, in the sense of 'preparing the way', would then be seeking both a spiritual way and a way of concrete political action, meaning both: a proclamation of the word of God and the civil, and political commitment to justice.

This is emphasized even more when the action orientation of 'preparing the way' is transferred to the approach of public theology. Not only reflections on Christian contents, but also concrete actions would then be the watchword of a public theology. This becomes particularly interesting when diaconal, religious-pedagogical, or church-practical elements are incorporated into the discourses on public theology, as is currently increasingly happening.[136] Detachment from the political and turning to the actual public in concrete action and doing can offer new possibilities and a readjustment of the understanding of public theology in light of 'doing public theology'. Public theology performed through and within life would probably be an appropriate emphasis in terms of 'preparing the way', at least in Bonhoeffer's sense.

---

133. DBWE 6:261 (DBW 6:222).

134. Bedford-Strohm, *Dietrich Bonhoeffer*, 338 (translation HB).

135. Ibid., 337: 'For ethics, it is precisely this way between adjustment to the factual on the one hand and fundamental opposition on the other, which public theology seeks to follow' (Translation HB).

136. See Thomas Schlag, *Grundtheorien einer praktisch-theologischen Kirchentheorie* (Zürich: Theologischer Verlag Zürich 2012); Thomas Schlag, 'Vom Kopf auf die Füße: Öffentliche Theologie ist nicht nur etwas für Bischöfe und Bischöfinnen', in *Zeitzeichen* 18, no. 3 (2017): 16–18; Ulrich H. J. Körtner, *Diakonie und öffentliche Theologie: Diakoniewissenschaftliche Studien* (Göttingen: Vandenhoeck & Ruprecht, 2017); Werner Haußmann, Andrea Roth, Susanne Schwarz, and Christa Tribula (eds), *EinFach Übersetzen: Theologie und Religionspädagogik in der Öffentlichkeit und für die Öffentlichkeit* (Stuttgart: Kohlhammer Verlag, 2019).

Chapter 12

'GOING AHEAD' AS REAL HUMAN BEINGS IN THE *GEMEINDE:* BONHOEFFER'S CHRISTOLOGICAL FORM AND FORMATION IN SUFFERING AND DYING

Samuel Efrain Murillo Torres

I thank you today for going ahead of us on this road between Easter and Ascension; this is the blessing ... left to us. I too want to travel this road with Maria, of being wholly ready for the last things, for eternity, and yet wholly present for the tasks, for the beauty and the troubles here on earth. Only by keeping to this path can we become completely happy and at peace with one another.[1]

I. Introduction

Dietrich Bonhoeffer's corpus has shown its relevance to several aspects of public life. After several years of his work being exposed theologically in different languages and cultures, Bonhoeffer's corpus shows to be relevant in affirming more comprehensive concrete ways of direct impact on communities and society. This supports addressing polarized and divided communities in a world that experiences faith in every day less institutionalized and increasingly diverse societies. For Bonhoeffer, the way to reconcile faith and human experience in the concrete is through the lenses of the Christological prism.[2] Within this

---

1. Letter written from prison to Ruth von Wedemeyer in 10 April 1944. The letter refers to the longing after the passing away of beloved ones, specifically on Maria's father and brother that passed away in 1942, DBWE 8:57n8 (DBW 8:45n7). '[The daily texts from Ps. 31.6 & Phil. 1.23] They direct our thoughts to those who are calling to us from the eternal realm, who are with us – Father and Max.' Full letter in DBWE 8:341-2 (DBW 8:379-80).

2. Bonhoeffer's Christology is '... interpreted through the Christological (Chalcedonian) prism, because reality is "in him" and all Christian ecclesial life is carried within this reality ... A theological view that splits the world into two separated realms risks reducing Christianity to an individualistic project of saving one's soul.' in Brendan Leahy, "Christ

contextual complexity, this theological construction seeks to unfold Bonhoeffer's Christological account to explore an Aesthetic Public Theology from the margins.

Throughout this chapter, a possible theological point of departure is bringing together form [*Gestalt*] and formation [*Gestaltung*] from the *Ethics* concerning his Christological lectures; this unfolds the centrality of Bonhoeffer's Christological form [*Gestalt*] and formation [*Gestaltung*]. The account of this theological construction aims to link Bonhoeffer's account to the public sphere, being a real-human-being in the world, in the light of his Christology. I describe the formation [*Gestaltung*] according to the form [*Gestalt*] as an ontological reality that has an always dynamic, open analogical, and never enclosed Christ's form [*Gestalt*] concerning all possible finite spatio-temporal dynamics in the world. All this I refer to, as the aesthetics of Bonhoeffer's Christology.

Firstly, the account of the form [*Gestalt*] and formation [*Gestaltung*] in relation to Christ's being in Bonhoeffer's corpus is described. Bonhoeffer's explanation of the form [*Gestalt*] of Christ *in which* his *aesthetic-ontological-dynamic* occurs concerning His *pronosity*: (1) *Christ's being as Word*, (2) *Christ's being as Sacrament* and (3) *Christ's being as Gemeinde*.[3] This nature of Christ is the *nature to which we are beings* in the *Imago Dei*. Therefore, the exploration concerns the concreteness

---

existing as Community": Dietrich Bonhoeffer's Notion of Church', in *Irish Theological Quarterly* 73, no. 1 (2008): 50–1. Also see Michael Mawson, *Christ Existing as Community: Bonhoeffer's Ecclesiology* (Oxford: Oxford University Press, 2019), 121–4, and Ulrik Nissen, *The Polity of Christ: Studies on Dietrich Bonhoeffer's Chalcedonian Christology and Ethics* (London: T&T Clark, 2020), 39–48.

3. Word, sacrament and *Gemeinde* is Bonhoeffer's aesthetic in the Christology as actuality. See DBWE 12:315–23 (DBW 12:296–306). This is the ontological-dynamic of the formation in the form in which we are *real-human-beings*. For Bonhoeffer's sacramental theology, see Chris Dodson, *The God Who Is Given: Dietrich Bonhoeffer's Sacramental Theology and Religionless Christianity* (Lanham: Lexington Books/Fortress Academic, 2021). 'Bonhoeffer's terms for the church, especially Gemeinde, have been most challenging. He uses two categories of terms – theological and sociological – to discuss the *sanctorum communio*. The main theological terms are *Kirche* and *Gemeinde*, as in the axiom "Die Kirche ist Christus als Gemeinde existierend ..." *Gemeinde* has a range of meanings and usages in Bonhoeffer's text and therefore presents the most complex translation problem. In Bonhoeffer's most distinctive and fundamental usage in this book, *Gemeinde* means Christ present as *sanctorum communio*. *Gemeinde* in Bonhoeffer's preferred term; its meaning provides the theological norm for "church". When Bonhoeffer says, "the church [*Kirche*] is Christ existing as *Gemeinde*." This does not mean that an institution calling itself church defines where Christ is communally present. On the contrary, it is not a church organization that defines Christ, but Christ who defines the church. In other words, it is precisely where, and only where, "Christ-exists-as-Gemeinde" that we find the "church" (Kirche).' Clifford J. Green, 'Editor's Introduction to the English Edition', in *Sanctorum Communio*, DBWE 1:14–15.

of being formed [*Gestaltung*] as: (4) *real-human-beings*, (5) *real-suffering-dying-human-beings* and (6) *a-new-risen-humanity*.[4] This being formed [*Gestaltung*] is the *mode in which we are beings* in the likeness of the form [*Gestalt*] of Christ's being. However, this formation is meaningful only as it is placed in the ultimate reality *for which* Christ's being is: (7) *being the centre of the whole of our existence*, (8) *being the centre of the whole of history*, and (9) *being the centre of the whole of the creation*.[5] In this *aesthetic-ontological-dynamic* constant movement, humanity exists and is called to be formed [*Gestaltung*] in the never static form [*Gestalt*] of Christ. This theological account is what Bonhoeffer calls the penultimate being concerned by the ultimate.[6]

Secondly, Bonhoeffer's account of an *unconscious-ontological* response, as a way of living as *real-human-beings* in the world in total simplicity, wisdom and naïveté is focused upon.[7] For Bonhoeffer, this is the only possible way to witness Christ's

---

4. 'Formation occurs only by being drawn into the form of Jesus Christ, by *being conformed to the unique form of the one who became human, was crucified, and is risen*' DBWE 6:93 (DBW 6:80–1), emphasis in the original, also see DBWE 6:93–7 (DBW 6:80–5). This is the *aesthetic-ontological-dynamic* of the formation [*Gestaltung*] by which the likeness [*real-judged-suffering-new-risen-humanity*] of the form [*Gestalt*] is in the *Gemeinde*. For Bonhoeffer's understanding of being and becoming human, see Christian Schlenker's contribution in this book, and see the collection of essays in *Being Human, Becoming Human: Dietrich Bonhoeffer and Social Thought*, ed. Jens Zimmermann and Brian Gregor (Eugene: Pickwick Publications, 2010).

5. Creation, history and existence is Bonhoeffer's aesthetic Christology as placed. See DBWE 12:324–7 (DBW 12:306–11). This is the ontological-dynamic of the formation [*Gestaltung*] in the form [*Gestalt*] for which we are real-human-beings. For Bonhoeffer's contemporary contribution of Christ as placed in the church and the world, see the collection of essays in Michael Mawson and Philip Ziegler (eds), *Christ, Church and World: New Studies in Bonhoeffer's Theology and Ethics* (London: T&T Clark, 2016).

6. 'Going ahead' for Bonhoeffer is based in the time between; easter and ascension, penultimate and ultimate, 'In this saving light, people recognize God and their neighbors for the first time. The labyrinth of their previous lives collapses. They become free for God and for one another' DBWE 6:146 (DBW 6:137).

7. This is Bonhoeffer's central elements in *Nachfolge, Akt und Sein, and Ethik*: What is the relation of the 'Who' question of Christ with obedience, commandment and human agency in the concrete. Bonhoeffer engages with the unconscious-reflective response of the disciple and unfolds it with the theological categories of simplicity, wisdom and naïveté. 'Only the person who combines simplicity with wisdom can endure. But what is simplicity? What is wisdom? How do the two become one? A person is simple who in the confusion, the distortion, and the inversion of all concepts keeps in sight only the single truth of God. This person has an undivided heart, and is not a double-psyche, a person of two souls (James 1[:8]). Because of knowing and having God, this person clings to the commandments, the judgment, and the mercy of God that proceed anew each day from the mouth of God. … the wise person will seek to obtain the best possible information about the course

reality in a polarized *religionless* context.[8] Bonhoeffer's Christological approach avoids abstracted theological frameworks, or any simple romantic response that re-victimizes human experience by sacralizing their pain from privileged positions. In line with Bonhoeffer's conclusion in his Christology lectures, Christ is always offensive to the temporal ways of the *Gemeinde*.[9] Therefore, the formation of *real-human-beings* [*Gestaltung*] in the *Gemeinde* is always in disruptive, transgressive and subversive dynamic ways in the form [*Gestalt*] of Christ.[10]

In seeking, as this research does, therefore, to be an *aesthetic-ontological-dynamic* process that assists to engage in the public sphere, there is wisdom in recognizing Raimundo Barreto's insight that Public Theology 'emerged in response to the privatization of religion in the public sphere proposed by the theories of

---

of events without becoming dependent on it. Wisdom is recognizing the significant within the factual. Wise people know the limited receptivity of reality for principles, because they know that reality is not built on principles, but rests on the living, creating God' (DBWE 6:81 [DBW 6:68]). Bonhoeffer expands to explain simplicity with the naïve concept: '"Naïveté" is more an aesthetic concept (in theology too) … "Simplicity" is an ethical concept. One can become "simple," but one can only be innocently naïve. "Simplicity" can be attained by education – and is even one of the chief aims of education – while "naïveté" is a gift … naïveté it implies wholeness …' (DBWE 8:294–5 [DBW 8:323]). For a full study on this see Jacob Phillips, *Human Subjectivity 'in Christ' in Dietrich Bonhoeffer's Theology: Integrating Simplicity and Wisdom* (London: T&T Clark, 2020).

8. Religionless Christianity is Bonhoeffer's category for the being of the *Gemeinde* in the world come to age: 'if one wants to speak of God "nonreligiously", then one must speak in such a way that the godlessness of the world is not covered up in any way, but rather precisely to uncover it and surprise the world by letting light shine on it. The world come of age is more god-less and perhaps just because of that closed to God than the world not yet come of age' (DBWE 8:482 [DBW 8:537]). Also, see Wolf Krötke, *Karl Barth and Dietrich Bonhoeffer: Theologians for a Post-Christian World*, trans. John P. Burgess (Grand Rapids: Baker Publishing Group, 2019), 135–65, see Tom Greggs, *Barth and Bonhoeffer as Contributors to a Post-liberal Ecclesiology: Essays of Hope for a Fallen and Complex World* (London: T&T Clark, 2022), 133–46, and Matthew D. Kirkpatrick, *Attacks on Christendom in a World Come of Age: Kierkegaard, Bonhoeffer, and the Question of 'Religionless Christianity'* (Eugene: Pickwick Publications, 2011).

9. 'He who bore the form of *the* human being can only take form in a small flock; this is Christ's church. … The church is the human being who has become human, has been judged, and has been awakened to new life in Christ. … The starting point of Christian ethics is the body of Christ, the form of Christ in the form of the church, the formation of the church according to the form of Christ' (DBWE 6:96–7 [DBW 6:84]).

10. This disruptive and transgressive is always an act of resistance from the *Gemeinde*, see Michael P. DeJonge, *Bonhoeffer on Resistance: The Word against the Wheel* (Oxford: Oxford University Press, 2018), 57–68. For a biographical approach on this sense see Christiane Tietz, *Theologian of Resistance: Life and Thought of Dietrich Bonhoeffer*, trans. Victoria Barnett (Minneapolis: Fortress Press, 2016).

secularization'.[11] As an alternative, challenge, according to Tom Greggs, in light of this (and in dialogue with Bonhoeffer) is to make an

> articulation of a theology which is suspicious of religion for theological reasons, as the best way in the contemporary age, that one can seek to identify the direction in which Bonhoeffer was pointing, and join him in the journey that seeks to answer the question of what Christianity is, and who Jesus Christ is, for us today.[12]

This different approach will help to shape communities not from dogma or institutionalized religion, nor from an idealised view of humanity,[13] but from an organic and concrete experience of faith, which makes visible the irruption of Christ's *Gemeinde* in the world.

The account of this theological process aims to study Bonhoeffer's aesthetics in his Christology, contributing to the concrete public sphere, which constantly reveals Christ's *Gemeinde* at the margins of existence. The *Gemeinde* embraces all humanity as one, where particularity and experience embrace all in a common belonging, with the only point of reference and relation to the human being revealed exclusively in Jesus Christ. This theological exploration reflects on the human agency concerning suffering and dying considering Bonhoeffer's Christology. The concrete questions to reflect on in this chapter are: Who is Jesus Christ, in the concrete experience of despair, suffering, mourning, and even unbelief as real-human-beings?[14] 'Who' is this Christ's *Gemeinde* for the whole creation? 'Who' is Christ's being in the concrete testimony of the *Gemeinde* in tension with the usual boundaries of the *Kirche*?[15]

---

11. Raimundo Barreto, 'The Church and Society Movement and the Roots of Public Theology in Brazilian Protestantism', in *International Journal of Public Theology* 6, no. 1 (2012): 70–98. See Ralf K. Wüstenberg, 'Religion and Secularity', in *The Oxford Handbook of Dietrich Bonhoeffer*, ed. Michael Mawson and Philip Ziegler (Oxford: Oxford University Press, 2019), 321–30.

12. Tom Greggs, *Theology against Religion: Constructive Dialogues with Bonhoeffer and Barth* (London: T&T Clark, 2011), 73.

13. See DBWE 6:80 (DBWE 6:66–7).

14. '[E]tsi deus non daretur' (DBWE 8:476, see n23 [DBW 8:530n21]).

15. This theologizing is enriched by Tom Greggs' exploration of a theology that is against religion by identifying and reflecting on the being of Christ beyond all established boundaries: 'By reminding the theologian of the need to be self-critical in her religious speech about God, secular critiques of religion may come to help the theologian to focus on the true subject of theological enquiry – God in all of God's otherness to creation – rather than to confuse God with an idol of human religious imagining. Secular critiques of religion may help, therefore, to identify religion and the religious nature of speech about God, and thereby to make theology alert to the danger of confusing so-called "god" with God. By reminding us of the propensity to engage in acts of idolatry and religion, secular critiques point theologians towards the very Godness of God, which cannot simply be capture in human language, ritual or conceptualization' (Greggs, *Theology against Religion*, 9).

II. The 'Who' Question in Bonhoeffer's Christological Form and Formation

For Bonhoeffer, Christ cannot be categorized, defined, understood or met by any static defined system. He is the centre of all, 'the center of our sphere knowledge',[16] as he transcends is always only 'the prerequisite for our thinking, not the proof. ... Christology is the center of the realm of scholarship itself ... the invisible, unrecognized, hidden center of scholarship'.[17] Hence, any distracting questions related to 'what' or 'how' as a point of departure or centre must be set aside to be able to reach the relevance of the relational Christology in Bonhoeffer's corpus: 'Who' is Christ? 'Who' is He for us? Furthermore, therefore, 'Who' are we in Him?

In Bonhoeffer's approach, the only severe possible approach to the 'Who' question is that Christ is the only One, the same One throughout time, space and any human experience; Christ is the One who does not change.[18] This provides Christ's form *[Gestalt] aesthetic-ontological-dynamic* guiding principle for the way in which to understand our humanity, in relation to time, place, experience and context. He is the alpha and omega not as an abstracted theological formula but in all places and times within spatio-temporal history. Every day, we explore this same question that Bonhoeffer did in his time, from a different concrete place, moment, context, experience and culture. However, the answer is the same – whether in relation to Berlin in the 1930s or any other experience of despair today. Who is, then, this God-human, Jesus Christ? For Bonhoeffer, Christ is the ultimate human being, Ecce Homo.[19] He is the One Who is human as we are, and therefore, our humanity (in its contingency and concreteness in all contexts) is held in His being for us and for all. Bonhoeffer's answer is our own:

> He is completely human. Nothing human is foreign to him. The human being that I am is what Jesus Christ was also. We say of this human being, Jesus Christ, that he is God. ... If we speak of the human being Jesus Christ as we speak of God, we should not speak of him as representing an idea of God, that is, in his attributes as all-knowing and all-powerful, but rather speak of his weakness and manger. ... Jesus became like us? This question remains open, because the

---

16. DBWE 12:301 (DBW 12:281).

17. Ibid.

18. 'The form of Christ is one and the same at all times and in all places' (DBWE 6:98 [DBW 6:85]).

19. See DBWE 6:82 (DBW 6:68–9), see n22 (n21). For more on the influence from Nietzsche's to Bonhoeffer, see Peter Frick, 'Friedrich Nietzsche's Aphorisms and Dietrich Bonhoeffer's Theology', in *Bonhoeffer's Intellectual Formation*, ed. Peter Frick (Tübingen: Mohr Siebeck, 2008), 175–99 and Frits de Lange, 'Aristocratic Christendom: On Bonhoeffer and Nietzsche', in *Bonhoeffer and Continental Thought: Cruciform Philosophy*, ed. Brian Gregor and Jens Zimmermann (Bloomington: Indiana University Press, 2009), 73–83.

Bible leaves it open. God who became human is the God of glory; God glorifies himself in the human. This is the ultimate mystery of the Trinity. ... God's self-glorification in the human is thus the glorification of the human, which shall have eternal life with God the Three in One.[20]

The answer to 'Who' Christ is, does not come as expected in history, and certainly not according to expectations today and its contingent contemporaneity. 'Who' are you? He reveals:

[I]n a wholly new form, so that it is no longer an idea or a word that is turned against the autonomy of the [human] logos, but rather the counter Logos appears, somewhere and at some time in history, as a human being, and as a human being sets itself up as judge over the human logos and says, 'I am the truth'.[21]

For Bonhoeffer, this is the form [Gestalt] of Christ as *real-human-being* in all its unity. In the always *aesthetic-ontological*-dynamic and changing Gestalt of the being of Christ 'every possibility of classification must fall short, because the existence of this Logos means the end of my logos. He *is* the Logos. He *is* the counter Word.'[22] As created beings, we must never forget that Christ not only answers all our questions (not in conformity to our theological principles or historical expectations), but He is never a stranger to any human experience, but just as 'Who' He is, the same Christ in eternity: the relational *real-human-being*, Who meets and challenges us deep in our own existence regardless of our differing human logos.

Once we open ourselves to the encounter that emerges in the *aesthetic-ontological-dynamic* of the form [Gestalt] of Who Christ is, He is revealed as the One who is experienced in constant tension, and interruption at the limits and centre of the whole of our *existence, history, and creation*, in His own way, time and terms of being:

The mystery of *who* remains hidden from us. The ultimate question for critical thinking is that it *must* ask *who* but it *can* not. That means that one can legitimately ask *who* only after the self-revelation of the other to whom one puts the question has already taken place, after the immanent logos has already been superseded. That is, the question of *who* can only be asked on condition that the answer has already been given. And this in turn means that the Christological question can only be asked, as a scholarly question, within the sphere of the

---

20. DBWE 12:353–5 (DBW 12:340–2).
21. DBWE 12:302 (DBW 12:282).
22. DBWE 12:302 (DBW 12:282). For a study on the counter Word in Bonhoeffer see David S. Robinson, *Christ and Revelatory Community in Bonhoeffer's Reception of Hegel* (Tübingen: Mohr Siebeck, 2018), 93–124.

church, and the prerequisite for it is the fact that Christ's claim to be the Word of God is a just claim. There is only one possibility for me to be truly searching for God – that I already know who God is.[23]

Thus, for Bonhoeffer, Christ's being reveals within the form [*Gestalt*] of this *aesthetic-ontological-dynamic* exchange in the daily experience of *real-human-beings* placed within *creation, history, and existence*.[24] This is His interrupting *ontological-revealing* the way of being as *Word, Sacrament and Gemeinde*.[25] This way of being is towards relationship and community, with us and with all humanity. This uninterrupted encounter unsettles our life forms [*Gestalt*] such that 'the question of "who" expresses the otherness of the other … [and] interrogates the very existence of the one asking it. With the "who question," the person asking is queried about the limits of their own being.'[26] We dislike being confronted with our identity and relationship with otherness. That is why, in our irrational forms [*Gestalt*] of living, we try to erase His voice among us, trying to disappear the 'Who' question. The pious religious fantasy that Christ died happily for us should be rejected. This dogmatic approach erroneously justifies violence and celebrates that Christ is killed, killed by us. Today, human beings still attempt to disappear by all possible means all that He means in His life and reality for all. This is seen clearly in our insistence on claiming mastery over our *existence, history and creation* without Christ:

> The Word become human must be hung on the cross by the human logos. Then the person who was causing the worry has been killed, and along with that person, the question. But what happens when this counter Word, though it has been killed, raises itself from the dead as the living, eternal, ultimate, conquering Word of God, when it rises up to meet its murderers and rushes at them again, appearing as the Resurrected One who has overcome death? Here the question, 'Who are you?' becomes most poignant. Here it stands, alive forever, over and around and within humankind. … Now our question has been turned around. The question we have to put to the person of Christ, 'Who are you?' comes back

---

23. DBWE 12:303 (DBW 12:283–4).
24. See DBWE 12:324–8 (DBW 12:306–23).
25. 'That Christ is the Word means that he is the truth. Truth is only in the Word and through the Word' (DBWE 12:315 [DBW 12:297]). 'Christ is wholly Word, and the sacrament is wholly Word … The sacrament is Word of God, for it proclaims the gospel, not as a wordless action, but as action that is made holy and given its meaning by the Word … The Word in the sacrament is the Word in bodily form.' (DBWE 12:318 [DBW 12:300]). 'As Word and sacrament, Christ is present as church-community. … Christ is the church-community by virtue of his being-*pro-me*' (DBWE 12:323 [DBW 12:305]). For a study on Christ as Sacrament, see Robinson, *Christ and Revelatory Community*, 144–8, see a full study on Bonhoeffer's sacramental theology in Dodson, *The God Who Is Given*, 31–66.
26. DBWE 12:303 (DBW 12:283).

at us: who are you, that you ask this question? Do you live in the truth, so you can ask it? Who are you, you who can only ask about me because you have been justified and received grace through me? Only when this question has been heard has the Christological question been definitively formulated.[27]

However, this is not simply an individualistic set of abstract questions or issues. It is deeply communal as it relates to the form [*Gestalt*] of Christ's being, which is known only in His body, in the *Gemeinde*. Bonhoeffer establishes that it is 'in the church, where Christ has revealed Himself as the Word of God'.[28] And yet the church in every context and culture experiences the concrete answer to the 'Who' question while it is being formed [*Gestaltung*] to receive the will and commandment of Christ 'every day anew'.[29] Bonhoeffer then concludes that the 'Who' question ends up for systematicians relating to the extent to which the work of Christ is the means by which the person is interpreted and the person is the means by which the works are of interest.[30] For Bonhoeffer, 'there is no point in the works of Jesus to which one can unambiguously refer and say that here Jesus can truly be recognized, unambiguously and without doubt, as the Son of God on the basis of his works'.[31] Therefore, the Christological 'Who' as *the* theological question is before any other soteriological or eschatological questions.[32] We must know 'Who' Christ is before knowing His deeds and promises for us: 'This is the issue, that the Son entered into the flesh, that he wants to do his work within the ambiguity of history, incognito.'[33] This is 'Who' Christ is, interrupting our life, even today in the differing human contexts in which we live. He is 'the Christ of history, the whole Christ, whom we ask and who answers,'[34] Who remains the changeless in the form [*Gestalt*] as One.

Bonhoeffer establishes that Christ's person is unknown by any miraculous performance as if He should prove 'Who' He is by performing extraordinary actions: it is in His incognito form [*Gestalt*] that Christ enters the world and demands that the world asks, *Who am I?* Thus, at the same time, Christ's personhood presumes that His works are the works of God Himself, 'his works that last eternally in a new world of life'.[35] It is Christ in Whom the *Gemeinde* has found mercy, forgiveness and life to be *all and whole* anew.[36] Therefore, Bonhoeffer goes on: 'Only where the

---

27. DBWE 12:305 (DBW 12:285–6).
28. DBWE 12:304 (DBW 12:284).
29. Ibid.
30. See DBWE 12:308 (DBW 12:288–90).
31. DBWE 12:309 (DBW 12:291).
32. See DBWE 12:310 (DBW 12:291–2).
33. This is what Bonhoeffer develops as theological categories named 'hidden principle' or 'likeness of flesh', more in DBWE 12:309 (DBW 12:290–1).
34. DBWE 12:310 (DBW 12:291).
35. DBWE 12:309 (DBW 12:290).
36. See DBWE 12:309 (DBW 12:290).

risen Christ is understood as the ground and the prerequisite for Christology is it possible to grasp his presence as a person. The person of Jesus Christ is, in fact, its own work.' Theologically, this concept is explained through the following account:

> To be present means to be in the same place at the same time (presence). We are talking about Christ's ability to be simultaneously present to us all. Even as the Risen One, Jesus remains the human Jesus. Only because he is human can he be present to us. But that he is eternally with us here, eternally with us in the now – that is his presence as God. Only because Jesus is God can he be present to us.[37]

It is from this structure that Bonhoeffer establishes the *ontological-dynamic* form [*Gestalt*] of Christ's being in which he is present, and the relational Christ in the *likeness of flesh* of what he develops as a *hidden principle* becoming a stumbling block for all who listen.[38] As Bonhoeffer says: 'The presence of Christ is a veiled presence ... The hidden form in which Christ is present is, for us, the church's proclamation ... in the scandalous form of its preaching.'[39] The hidden form [*Gestalt*] of Christ's being will prove relevant in the light of public life in a concrete place and time. Once this foundation is established, the concrete reality of 'Who' Christ is, reveals the person of Christ in specific form [*Gestalt*] and in diverse places throughout history. From here, Bonhoeffer develops the concept of the *nunc et hic* of Christ's being in time and space.[40] This here and now structure of being present for us in His ultimacy as the ultimate reality in the penultimacy of creaturely life is the structure through which to understand the constancy of Christ in relation to the spatio-temporal contingencies of creaturely life. Since all of humanity as a whole is in Him ultimately, in the penultimacy of creaturely contingent reality, we are free to exist in the now in an open, analogic, dynamic, welcoming and never static *Gemeinde* which is for the Christian, the *aesthetic-ontological-dynamic* relationship of believers, the church as community.[41]

---

37. DBWE 12:312 (DBW 12:294).
38. Bonhoeffer makes a distinction between 'humanity of Christ' and 'humiliation of Christ'. He is human as humiliated and exalted. The hidden principle or 'likeness of flesh' belongs to the humiliation and Jesus Christ is a 'stumbling block' only as the humiliated. See DBWE 12:314 (DBW 12:295).
39. DBWE 12:313 (DBW 12:294-5).
40. 'Now and here.'
41. The use of *Gemeinde* is in an ontological theological category to refer to the church-community formed [*Gestaltung*] by Christ's being and is not to be confused with the church as the institutional or denominational established religion or a sociological community to be described. This is an important distinction made by Bonhoeffer. 'In his reflections on primal sociality, we have seen that Bonhoeffer draws insights and concepts from existing sociological philosophy (e.g. Scheler and Hegel) and sociology (e.g. Tönnies). In particular, he takes up Tönnies' classic distinction between community (*Gemeinschaft*)

III. The Promeity and Pronosity in Bonhoeffer's Christological Form and Formation

So far, I have reflected on the *aesthetic-ontological-dynamic* form [*Gestalt*] of Christ's being, 'Who' is being as Word, Sacrament and *Gemeinde*, placed in the centre-limits of the whole of our *existence, history and creation* while being changeless as *real-human-being*, and the cosmological tension of being formed [Gestaltung] in the dynamics of the 'Who' question, as *real-suffering-dying-human-beings* and *new-risen-humanity* by God,[42] when asking: 'Who' is asking?

These cosmological tensions of the ultimate reality of Christ and its constancy concerning the reality of Christ in the contingencies of space-time lead to the even more foundational issue of Bonhoeffer's conceptualizing of Christ as ontologically (and not just ethically or relationally) *pro me* and *pro nos*. Once the question of Christ's identity is understood, Bonhoeffer develops specifically the concrete, constant and total presence of Christ as the centre of all – a presence which can only be understood in light of the form [*Gestalt*] full of grace in Christ's *aesthetic-ontological-dynamic* being for us.

This can be understood as the question: in which form [*Gestalt*] and which place of this form [*Gestalt*] is the One, God-human, Jesus Christ for us? It is through the *pro me* structure of Bonhoeffer's account of the person of Christ that this is answered. This structure implies three things in terms of the relation of Christ to the new humanity and the call to follow in the formation [*Gestaltung*] according to the form [*Gestalt*]. First, for Bonhoeffer, '[Christ] is ... the historical Jesus.'[43] Second, Christ 'stands for his brothers and sisters ... for his new humanity before God, he is the new humanity and the church–community.'[44] This does not mean that Christ is for the *Gemeinde* as some empirical and institutional religious body, but in His suffering, dying and cry 'why hast thou forsaken me' upon death on the cross, He is for the new humanity known and seen in the *community* of the church [*Gemeinde*]. The church [*Gemeinde*] is not the condition for a new

---

and society (*Gesellschaft*). This has led some scholars to suggest that Bonhoeffer is simply restating Tönnies' distinction. In light of this, we must reflect on the relationship between Bonhoeffer's "specifically Christian sociology" and Tönnies formal sociology. The first point to note is that Bonhoeffer is not only drawing upon Tönnies for his Christian sociology, he is also attempting to correct him at a fairly fundamental level. ... Bonhoeffer is not simply adopting insights from formal sociology uncritically in *Sanctorum Communio*. Rather, his aim is to context and correct what he deems to be problematic in such approaches, that is, the genetic and historicist elements that result from their underlying atomistic social philosophy' (Mawson, *Christ Existing as Community*, 92–3).

42. See DBWE 6:92 (DBW 6:79–80).
43. DBWE 12:315 (DBW 12:296), also see DBWE 6:325–7 (DBW 6:327–30) and DBWE 6:104–5 (DBW 6:94–6).
44. DBWE 12: 315 (DBW 12:296).

humanity, but new humanity is the reality within which the church [*Gemeinde*] comes into being and should live.⁴⁵ Third, in Christ, 'God both judges the new humanity and pardons it.'⁴⁶ In order to explore what this might mean in the experience of suffering and dying, and the formation [*Gestaltung*] of those going ahead in wisdom and simplicity according to the dynamic form [*Gestalt*] of Christ's being,⁴⁷ it is necessary to unpack this account of promeity and pronosity in Bonhoeffer.

For Bonhoeffer, for all of the centrality of his account of promeity, it is not possible to think of Christ in individualistic or private terms concerning human beings. Instead, Christ must be thought of in terms of His always dynamic and analogic relationship with humanity as a whole. His presence is 'in the threefold form [*Gestalt*] of Word, sacrament and church-community [*Gemeinde*].'⁴⁸

---

45. Bonhoeffer affirms that in the understanding of the Church, we should avoid delimiting the visibility of the church in space and time as if the Gemeinde should fight the world for space to be visible. This means that the 'space of the church does not, therefore, exist just for itself, but its existence is already always something that reaches far beyond it. This is because it is not the space of a cult that would have to fight for its own existence in the world. Rather, the space of the church is the place where witness is given to the foundation of all reality in Jesus Christ' (DBWE 6:63 [DBW 6:49]). For more on Reformation-Lutheran understanding of the church, Tom Greggs develops on the invisibility of the church-community [*Gemeinde*] that 'it is in faith in the Spirit's coming to the community, and in faith in the Spirit's establishing it by the act of the Spirit's intensive presence in the givenness of space-time as a locus for the anticipatory redeeming work of God, that one can speak of the invisibility of the Church. But that very invisibility is meaningful strictly in relation to the visible community which stands across the variance and contingencies of quotidian space-time and, by the Spirit's provenience, calls on the promises of God in the act of the Holy Spirit to bring the church into being. It is the visible community of the Spirit's coming that the Spirit (invisibly) seeks to create' (Tom Greggs, *Dogmatic Ecclesiology: The Priestly Catholicity of the Church, Volume 1* [Grand Rapids, Michigan: Baker Academic, 2019], 21) and on the existence of the church-community [*Gemeinde*] he writes that 'The church signifies imperfectly and provisionally that grace in which it already actively participates by an event of the act of the Holy Spirit – a grace which is already for all creation in God's self-determination in Christ to be the one who is eternally for us. In this way, the church's existence is for God and for the world: it exists as it simultaneously lives its life vertically for the God who is for the world, and horizontally for the world God is for' (ibid., 131).

46. DBWE 12:315 (DBW 12:297).

47. Many authors reflect Bonhoeffer's intentions in relation with the integration of simplicity and wisdom as coherent within consciousness and reflective agency in response, the problem is described in Phillips, *Human*, 1–5.

48. DBWE 12:314 (DBW 12:295).

Christ's being lies always as the limit, the boundary, and the new centre of everything and all:[49]

> That is Christ's nature and way of existing. Being in the center means a threefold being there: (1) being-there for humankind, (2) being-there for history, (3) being-there for nature. This is the Christ *pro-me* translated into the 'where structure' [within the 'who structure' of the Christ]. Christ status as mediator must be proven in that he can [be] seen as the centre of human existence, of history, and of nature.[50]

Centrality and marginality will be crucial for the following dialogue surrounding the *pro-nos* structure of Christ's being as the centre of human existence: 'Who' is this Christ being as the centre of human existence in despair, suffering, dying and unbelief?[51] 'Who' is this Christ being as the centre of history, considering the narrative and role of history that rolls over those suffering in unfair ways in our societies?[52]

Once he has established that Christ is for us as an ontological and constant – always in the *aesthetic-ontological-dynamic* and therefore, never static – way of being,

---

49. This boundary lies between our old and new being, old and new creation, all in our formation [*Gestaltung*] according to the *aesthetic-ontological-dynamic* form [*Gestalt*] of Christ.

50. DBWE 12:324 (DBW 12:307).

51. Bonhoeffer engages seriously with harm in the *Ethik* when speaking about the harm inflicted and the huge pain and trauma of this recognizing that not all wounds and suffering inflicted heals but still insists on the relevance of diminishing the harm of others as individuals and societies, see DBWE 6:143–5 (DBW 6:134–5). Esther Reed refers on the Ethical implications in the formation according to the form in developing '… a post-liberal ethic of responsibility that reckons with situations where the agent-act-consequence line of traceability fails. The key argument is that in Christ and because of Christ, the meaning of responsibility is reversed from an I-You-I to a You-I-You dynamic … With Bonhoeffer, the affirmation is that when the ethical problem becomes "How can I live responsibly" and "How can I take responsible decisions?" rather than "What is the meaning of responsibility learned in Christ, neighbour and land?" the focus is ourselves rather than God as first and last …' in Esther Reed, *The Limit of Responsibility: Dietrich Bonhoeffer's Ethics for a Globalizing Era* (London: T&T Clark, 2018), xv.

52. 'What matters is only whether the past guilt is in fact scarred over. If so, then at this point, within the historical conflicts of the nations, both domestic and foreign, something like forgiveness takes place, though it is only a weak shadow of the forgiveness that Jesus Christ gives to believers. Here the claim to full atonement by the guilty for past injustice is renounced; here it is recognized that what is past can never be restored by human power, that the wheel of history can no longer be rolled back. Not all wounds that were made can be healed; but it is critical that no further wounds be inflicted' (DBWE 6:144 [DBW 6:135]).

Bonhoeffer explains more about his concept of the stumbling block experienced in faith, towards relationship and belonging in community:

> Faith exists when I yield myself to God [to the extent that] I will wager my life on God's Word, even and especially there where it goes against all visible appearances. Only when I give up having visible confirmation do I believe in God. The only guarantee that faith can bear is the Word of God itself. *Christus pro nobis* is the Christ who reconciles me with God, and that is only possible through this stumbling block and through faith. … [O]ur faith is continually tested. But this teaches us to pay attention to the Word. Faith comes through temptation.[53]

History, theology and institutional religion have tried to build an image of Christ in their static closed narratives, which make faith unapproachable, based on an idealised humanity in order to try to avoid the experience of Christ being a *stumbling block*.[54] 'No preaching is protected from leading to superstition, and superstition is never more dangerous than when entrenched behind pious sentences and convictions. All Christian preaching necessarily awakens superstition when for whatever reason it neglects Jesus's cross.'[55] While trying to flee our own created and *aesthetic-ontological-dynamic* way of being in Christ as *real-human-beings*, Christ becomes a religious concept among religious people, and the accompanying risk is that, as such, these religious Christians build mainly *religious* communities.

This dynamic in religious communities proves to be nothing more than an empty and superficial abstract way of life, based on subjective morals imposed as the way to the form [*Gestalt*]. This religious form [*Gestalt*] and formation [*Gestaltung*] are the opposite of 'Who' Christ is,[56] expressed in the not real *human-being* trying to cling to earthly life as eternal, in imposition and ruling

---

53. DBWE 12:358 (DBW 12:346).

54. See DBWE 6:80 (DBW 6:66–7).

55. Ernst Käsemann, *Church Conflicts: The Cross, Apocalyptic, and Political Resistance*, ed. Ry O. Siggelkow, trans. Roy A. Harrisville (Grand Rapids: Baker Academic, 2021), 69.

56. Bonhoeffer establishes that '[a]ll things appear as in a distorted mirror if they are not seen and recognized in God. All that is – so to speak – given, all laws and norms, are abstractions, as long as God is not known in faith to be the ultimate reality. That God alone is the ultimate reality, is, however, not an idea meant to sublimate the actual world, nor is it the religious perfecting of a profane worldview. It is rather a faithful Yes to God's self-witness, God's revelation. If God is merely a religious concept, there is no reason why there should not be, behind this apparent "ultimate" reality, a still more ultimate reality' (DBWE 6:48 [DBW 6:32]). This is also seen when the church makes its aims to fight for space in the world by creating religious organizations or being defined by pious superficial moral standards. This leads to spiritualizing Christ in the space of a cult, see DBWE 6:62–4 (DBW 6:47–50).

over others, while in Christ's form 'His lordship remains that of the Crucified, even after Easter, it is continually opposed to our own desires and longings'.[57] For this reason, such religious communities are distant from the concrete experiences of people living at the limits of their existence in faith, from where *real-human-beings* are continuously excluded, put against each other and even exterminated from societies. By making their communities correspond to the centrality of what humans believe life is, rather than the marginality of the life of Christ, which is the ultimate centre of all creation and its eschatological end, these religious people deceive themselves and form religious communities, making the body of Christ delimited or exclusive. On this, Bonhoeffer makes clear:

> [He] enters of his own free will into the world of sin and death. ... He comes among us humans not in μορφὴ θεοῦ [Godly form] but rather incognito, as a beggar among beggars, an outcast among outcasts; he comes among sinners as the one without sin, but also as a sinner among sinners. This is the central problem for all Christology. The doctrine that Jesus was without sin ... is the central point that decides everything.[58]

The One 'Who' is present for all is 'the human God-Jesus',[59] and the form [*Gestalt*] in which He as the ultimate reality of all creation is in the form [*Gestalt*] of the marginal, the outcast, the sinner. Those who seem peripheral to the world and religion, but are the centre of Christ's ultimate reality. The powerful and religious ignore Christ's question: 'Who am I?' They pretend to be the ultimate logos of the world. They pretend to have the ultimate dominion over what happens to those fragile and vulnerable, defining who becomes successful and excluded and who lives and dies. They even perpetuate polarizing and abstract metanarratives that continue to divide humanity, which aim to keep society within the confines of the imagination of the powerful. Within this metanarrative, emancipation is perceived as impossible. Instead of *real-human-beings* living as embraced subjects in society, they become disposable subjects of the metanarratives of privilege and power.

Building on a description from Walter Benjamin's thesis on history, we can say, that Bonhoeffer had an seismographic understanding of his present, past and future – an understanding, which, in his time, only offered confusion. The problem was that the consciousness of time contemporary to Bonhoeffer generally offered short-sightedness in terms of history and theology,[60] which pretended to

---

57. Käsemann, *Church Conflicts*, 76.
58. DBWE 12:356 (DBW 12:343-4).
59. DBWE 12:313 (DBW 12:294).
60. This is from Walter Benjamin First Thesis on History. Reality is understood as driven by an automaton [*Automaten*] that pretends to establish the only possibility of human history by overcoming the world by itself. The consequences for theology are devastating, as it becomes constantly confused about its past, aims and intentions, not surprisingly failing to see Christ's *Gemeinde* in the very concrete reality. This reality pretends to depart from

rule over facts in history while ignoring reality's formation in *Christ-reality*. This contrast between the *Gemeinde* and the false account of the community based upon pretence is explained in Bonhoeffer's terms when he speaks of the villain and the saint in public life:[61] 'evil appears in the form of light, of beneficence, of faithfulness, or renewal, that it appears in the form of historical necessity, of social justice.'[62] This contrast is relevant for those being formed to the reconciler, Christ-form [*Gestalt*] – the real, judged and renewed human being.[63] Those being formed in Christ are being formed towards witnessing in the common belonging of guilt, justification and renewal.[64] Yet, those in the *Gemeinde* as much as those outside of it face the danger of falling away. This danger of falling away [*Abfall*][65] is tremendous: it is all too easy to fall prey to the *Filling-Station* in the *One-Way street*[66] where one encounters frustration, failure or even an anonymous death without reason

the myth of progress and idolatry of success to justify its annihilating present and actions of death toward the future. It forgets about real-human-beings, of all living and even those killed, rolling over them, harming and destroying. This way of life disintegrates societies, cultural heritage, and academic and theological thinking worldwide. It obscures faith (act) within institutional religion with the imposition of closed structures trying to objectivize God. In practice, it is proclaiming a gospel that ends up with annihilation and enmity of life, human beings, and the whole world. The thesis says: 'There was once, we know, an automaton constructed in such a way that it could respond to every move by a chess player with a countermove that would ensure the winning of the game. A puppet wearing Turkish attire and with a hookah in its mouth sat before a chessboard placed on a large table. A system of mirrors created the illusion that this table was transparent on all sides. Actually, a hunchbacked dwarf – a master at chess – sat inside and guided the puppet's hand by means of strings. One can imagine a philosophic counterpart to this apparatus. The puppet, called "historical materialism", is to win all the time. It can easily be a match for anyone if it enlists the services of theology, which today, as we know, is small and ugly and has to keep out of sight.' (Walter Benjamin, 'On the Concept of History', ed. Michael W. Jennings and Howard Eiland, *Selected Writings: Volume 4 1938-1940* [Cambridge, Mass.: Harvard University Press, 2006], 389).

61. See DBWE 6:76 (DBW 6:61–2).
62. DBWE 6:77 (DBW 6:63).
63. See DBWE 6:134 (DBW 6:124–5).
64. See DBWE 6:134–45 (DBW 6:124–35).
65. See DBWE 6:77 (DBW 6:62–3).
66. This is Walter Benjamin on those who fail in their convictions to nurture the *Gemeinde* which in this case is towards Christ-reality: 'The construction of life is at present in the power far more of facts than of convictions, and of such facts as have scarcely ever become the basis of convictions. Under these circumstances, true literary activity cannot aspire to take place within a literary framework; this is, rather, the habitual expression of its sterility. Significant literary effectiveness can come into being only in a strict alternation between action and writing; it must nurture the inconspicuous forms that fit its influence in active communities better than does the pretentious, universal gesture of the book – in leaflets, brochures, articles, and placards. Only this prompt language shows itself actively

in nothingness.⁶⁷ However, in this context, Christ asks in his *aesthetic-ontological-dynamic* being: 'Who am I?', leading *real-human-beings* back to His historical life, to the underway path of witness as *real-suffering-dying-human-beings*, and a *new-risen-humanity*, that He brings about in Himself, in which the marginal and oppressed are the central, and to the *aesthetic-ontological-dynamic* community of His body [*Gemeinde*] in which this form [*Gestalt*] takes place in his pronosity for all.

IV. Christ's Form and Pronosity as Ultimate Reality

The main aim of Bonhoeffer's *Ethics* is to establish the concreteness and true nature of the form and formation within reality. Bonhoeffer's *Ethics* are all about being aware and living consciously as *real-human-beings, real-suffering-beings, and new-risen-humanity* in the time between Christ's ascension and the *Parousia*. They concern Christ's wholeness in all as the total reality of creation and the eschaton known in Him, and how this ultimate reality is lived in the penultimacy of creaturely temporal existence. First, Bonhoeffer's *Ethics* begins with the question of what the good is.⁶⁸ This question directs one's attention to the task of discerning what the will of God as *Creator, Reconciler and Redeemer* is.⁶⁹ Second, Bonhoeffer addresses the nature of the ultimate reality constituted in the affirmation that Christ is the only source of all good,⁷⁰ and this is revealed in faith.⁷¹ And third, the *Ethics* then seeks to establish the fundamental task of witnessing to Christ in His self-announcing, self-witnessing, self-revealing of the reality that Christ is the God-man Who is present among all God's creatures and creation,⁷² which is 'the one realm of Christ-reality'.⁷³ For Bonhoeffer, these themes are the subject matter of Christian ethics and, further, the subject matter of the ultimate reality.⁷⁴

Ultimate reality or Christ-reality requires that one intentionally recognize that all the thesis-antithesis structure that forms other ethics, norms, ideals, laws, etc.,

---

equal to the moment. Opinions are to the vast apparatus of social existence what oil is to machines: one does not go up to a turbine and pour machine oil over it; one applies a little to hidden spindles and joints that one has to know' (Walter Benjamin, 'One-Way Street', ed. Michael W. Jennings and Howard Eiland, *Selected Writings: Volume 1 1913–1926* [Cambridge, MA: Harvard University Press, 2006], 444).

67. See DBWE 6:129 (DBW 6:120–1).
68. See DBWE 6:47 (DBW 6:31).
69. See DBWE 6:48 (DBW 6:31–3). This is Barth's ordering in *Church Dogmatics*, see ed. note 5.
70. See DBWE 6:49 (DBW 6:33–4).
71. See DBWE 6:75 (DBW 6:61).
72. See DBWE 6:49 (DBW 6:33–4).
73. DBWE 6:58 (DBW 6:43), italics in the original.
74. See DBWE 6:49 (DBW 6:33–4).

are based on the subjective approach of human judgement, culture or context.[75] These other forms, while grounded in human subjectivity, are at the same time trying to always apply themselves as an equivalent metanarrative applicable everywhere through unilateral morals and values. This metanarrative pales in comparison to Christ-reality. This Christ-reality is no longer about 'ought and is, idea and realization, motive and work',[76] but is now about faith in this Christ as the only source of good[77] in the concrete. These issues are addressed in terms of Christology and pneumatology:

> [In] the relation between reality and becoming real, between past and present, between history and event (faith) or, … the relation between Jesus Christ and the Holy Spirit. The question of the good becomes the question of participating in God's reality revealed in Christ. … Only by participating in reality do we also share in the good.[78]

When *real-human-beings* are participants in this reality, Bonhoeffer establishes that one's person and work are always united.[79] The good desires the whole[80]; '*human beings are indivisible wholes, not only as individuals in both their person and work, but also as members of the human and created community* to which they belong.'[81] This indivisible whole is called 'creation' in origin and the 'Kingdom of God'[82] in its goal. Here we can see fulfilled the *aesthetic-ontological-dynamic*

---

75. Bonhoeffer refers to these ethical agendas and programmes as having the aim of a 'noble humanity' (DBWE 6, 77–80 [DBW 6:62–7]), with the risk that it end up either by hating humanity or making a demigod of it as the only aim of life, this results against the form [*Gestalt*] and formation [*Gestaltung*] in Christ's being, which is only experienced and found through the aesthetic of faith in true simplicity and wisdom (see DBWE 6:81 [DBW 6:67]). These other forms against Christ mentioned by Bonhoeffer: all aim and wisdom of life based in success (see DBWE 6:88–91 [DBW 6:53–4]), divinizing death (see DBWE 6:91–2 [DBW 6:78–81]), cult of ratio, divinization of nature or faith solely in progress (see DBWE 6:115 [DBW 6:105–6]), resulting all in a way of life full of fear, having nothingness as god (see DBWE 6:127 [DBW 6:118–19]).

76. David Hume, Hegel and Kant ethical forms [*Gestalt*] and formation [*Gestaltung*] in DBWE 6:50 (DBW 6:33), see n13 (n12). For more studies on Hegel, Hume or Kant's influence or interaction in Bonhoeffer see Robinson, *Christ and Revelatory Community, passim*, also see Wayne Floyd, 'Encounter with an Other: Immanuel Kant and G. W. F. Hegel in the Theology of Dietrich Bonhoeffer', in *Bonhoeffer's Intellectual Formation*, ed. Peter Frick (Tübingen: Mohr Siebeck, 2008), 83–120.

77. DBWE 6:75 (DBW 6:61).

78. DBWE 6:50–1 (DBW 6:34–6).

79. See DBWE 6:51 (DBW 6:35–6).

80. See DBWE 6:53 (DBW 6:37–8).

81. DBWE 6:53 (DBW 6:38), emphasis in the original.

82. DBWE 6:53 (DBW 6:38).

exchange, *to which* we are in actuality *real-human-beings*, *by which* we are in potentiality formed [*Gestaltung*] as *real-suffering-dying-beings*, and *for which* we are a *new-risen-humanity* placed in God alone.[83] This is the formation to the form of Christ's being. Actualising the good centres on realising this indivisible whole in the ultimate reality of God in Christ. This is how Christianity transforms the question of the good.[84]

In Christ as ultimate reality, every static opposition or eternal conflict between the good and the bad, the religious and not religious, sacred and profane, godliness and worldliness are avoided.[85] Every sort of dualism either between ideas, conceptual norms, ethics, or division between God and the world is left behind.[86] This theme is highly relevant for this theological proposal since in some public and religious narratives there remains this propensity towards dualism: between perpetrators and victims, government and citizens, the academic and the professional, the religious and the secular. As will be seen, these dualisms bring conflict between one another without ever overcoming the world. But for Bonhoeffer, in the light

---

83. A partial parallel structure of Bonhoeffer's aesthetics of the form [*Gestalt*] and formation [*Gestaltung*] in Christ is found in Maximos the Confessor describing the motion and rest of created beings as 'portions of God': 'He is a "portion of God", then, insofar as he exists, for he owes his existence to the logos of being that is in God; and he is a "portion of God" insofar as he is good, for he owes his goodness to the logos of wellbeing that is in God; and he is a "portion of God" insofar as he is God, owing to the logos of his eternal being that is in God. In honoring these logoi and acting in accordance with them, he places himself wholly in God alone, forming and configuring God alone throughout his entire being, so that he himself by grace is and is called God, just as God by His condescension is and is called man for the sake of man, and also so that the power of this reciprocal disposition might be shown forth herein, a power that divinizes man through his love for God, and humanizes God through His love for man. And by this beautiful exchange, it renders God man by reason of the divinization of man, and man God by reason of the Incarnation of God' (Maximos the Confessor, 'Ambiguum 7', in *On the Difficulties in The Church Fathers: The Ambigua*, vol. 1, ed. and trans. Nicholas Constas [Cambridge Massachusetts: Harvard University Press, 2014], 105–7). The parallel is in being *real-human-beings* (nature-existence in actuality), *real-suffering-dying* (to move in goodness/likeness as mode in potentiality), and as a *new-risen-humanity* (to live in as eternal beings for reason and end).

84. See DBWE 6:53 (DBW 6:37–8).

85. Every heritage that ends up in dualisms or abstractions is proved false, see DBWE 6:56 n33. 34. 35. 36 (DBW 6:41–2 n32. 33. 34) 'Thinking in terms of two realms understands the paired concepts worldly-Christian, natural-supernatural, profane-sacred, rational-revelational, as ultimate static that designate certainly given mutually exclusive entities. This thinking fails to recognize the original unity of these opposites in the Christ–reality and, as an afterthought, replaces this with a forced unity provided by a sacred or profane system that overarches them. Thus, the static opposition is maintained' (DBWE 6:58–9 [DBW 6:44]).

86. See DBWE 6:59 (DBW 6:44–5).

of Christ as ultimate reality, we are challenged to see mutual, fruitful development as a cohesive whole through Christ. It is in Christ that we are all called to take part in this one God-world reality simultaneously,[87] recognizing that the whole reality of the world is 'already borne, accepted, and reconciled in the reality of God'.[88] Bonhoeffer puts this extremely powerfully: '*In Jesus Christ the reality of God has entered into the reality of this world.*'[89] When we partake in Christ we are always at the same time in the owned, inhabited, reconciled and embraced God-world reality which is the one and only realm of the Christ-reality.[90] This is the one and only ultimate reality, *in which, by which, to which, and for which*, we are continuously formed [*Gestaltung*] in Christ.

The unity of the God-world reality is established in Christ's being.[91] Instead of affirming static independence between or against each other, the God-world reality affirms a polemical relation between their common reality and the unity in Christ that is witnessed.[92] This polemical use of the worldly is for a better Christianity and for Christianity to discover a better worldliness.[93] Every way of life in terms of abstractions, dualisms or realms is overcome by faith in the revelation of ultimate reality in Jesus Christ.[94] This means that this world must confess together the God-world reality while confessing the ultimate reality in Christ.[95] In Christ, ultimate reality is, therefore, about belonging as a unified whole. In the terms of our theological aim, this is the *aesthetic-ontological-dynamic* account of life and reality, for individuals and communities, as they are formed [*Gestaltung*] into the *Gestalt* of the one Christ reality.

Against dualisms and abstractions, Bonhoeffer proposes a change in spatial analogies drawn from the New Testament.[96] This change avoids abstracting the space of the church as a spiritual entity where Christ ends up being spiritualized or monopolized.[97] Bonhoeffer makes this clear in the following way:

> When God in Jesus Christ claims space in the world – even space in a stable because 'there was no other space in the inn' – God embraces the whole reality of the world in this narrow space and reveals its ultimate foundation. ... The space of the church does not, therefore, exist just for itself, ... it is not the space of a cult that would have to fight for its own existence in the world ... is not there

---

87. See DBWE 6:55 (DBW 6:40–1).
88. DBWE 6:55 (DBW 6:40).
89. DBWE 6:54 (DBW 6:39), emphasis in the original.
90. DBWE 6:58 (DBW 6:43–4).
91. See DBWE 6:59 (DBW 6:44–5).
92. See DBWE 6:60 (DBW 6:45–6).
93. Ibid.
94. See DBWE 6:61 (DBW 6:46–7).
95. See DBWE 6:62 (DBW 6:47–8).
96. Ibid.
97. See DBWE 6:63 (DBW 6:48–9).

in order to fight with the world for a piece of its territory ... [i]t is not true that the church intends to or must spread its space out over the space of the world ... [T]he space of the church is the place where witness is given to the foundation of all reality in Jesus Christ ... where it is proclaimed and taken seriously that God has reconciled the world to himself in Christ ... It desires no more space than it needs to serve the world with its witness to Jesus Christ and to the world's reconciliation to God through Jesus Christ. [It] can only defend its own space by fighting, not for space, but for the salvation of the world.[98]

The *Gemeinde* experiences this when it realizes that its only task is to be a witness to the world that is the world, the world created, loved and reconciled by God in Christ. When there is silence regarding the consummate reality, this is a sign of either decay or corruption in the religious institution that has failed to be witness to Christ as *Gemeinde*.[99] Institutional religion and theology exemplify this in their corruption and decay over the centuries mainly in the modern West. Instead, the *Gemeinde* should understand its reality and be witness to this reality in Christ, equipped by the Holy Spirit. The space and place of the church is 'already been broken through, abolished, and overcome in every moment by the witness of the church to Jesus Christ'.[100] Therefore, the *Gemeinde* is never static but always dynamic, not closed or delimited by space or places but always open, free. This becomes and is shaped as an *aesthetical Gemeinde*.[101]

Christians often uncritically reproduce popular narratives and ideas of their age. This becomes problematic because the centre of their witnessing proclaims a kingdom of evil that is against the church and Christ. They speak of what they are against in their self-deceiving dualisms. Even today in the twenty-first century, institutional religion [*Kirche*] is haunted by witches and demons of its own invention that exclude, victimize and inflict vast amounts of suffering and trauma on *real-human-beings*. Bonhoeffer affirms from the God-world ultimate reality in Christ that:

[E]ven the devil, unwillingly, must serve Christ, and, willing evil, must ever again do good ... the kingdom of the devil is always only under the feet of Christ ... For it is just the 'evil world' that is reconciled in Christ to God and has

---

98. DBWE 6:63–4 (DBW 6:49).
99. See DBWE 6:64 (DBW 6:49–50).
100. DBWE 6:64 (DBW 6:50).
101. 'The body of Jesus Christ, especially as it is presented to us on the cross, makes visible to faith both the world in its sin and in its being loved by God, and the church-community as the company of those who recognize their sin and gratefully submit to the love of God. This belonging together of God and world that is grounded in Christ does not allow static spatial boundaries, nor does it remove the difference between church-community and world' (DBWE 6:68 [DBW 6:54]). Bonhoeffer makes clear the unity and dynamic boundaries of the *Gemeinde* in the World.

its ultimate ... reality ... in Christ. The world is not divided between Christ and the devil; it is completely the world of Christ, whether it recognizes this or not ... The dark, evil world may not be surrendered to the devil, but [must] be claimed for the one who won it by coming in the flesh, by the death and resurrection of Christ. Christ gives up nothing that has been won, but holds it fast in his hands ... [T]he lost and condemned world is being drawn ceaselessly into the event of Christ.[102]

Only once every possible static abstraction of the kingdom of evil is resolved, then it is possible to develop the practical and concrete experiences of life within this ultimate reality: the realization of Christ as ultimate reality among us, here and now, in our context and time, in our world. Central is the issue, in ethics, therefore of partaking in this reality, realizing as individuals and communities that we have been reconciled with God in Christ, which is something revealed, fulfilled and achieved in Christ. This will of God *pro-nos* embraces the whole. In this theological description, the experience of Christ's ultimate reality in the *Gemeinde* as it bears witness to all of creation in its reality offers insight into the embracing of every human experience, as this chapter aimed to describe; even in experiencing the highest levels of despair, suffering and unbelief, Christ is present among us as the ultimate reality in our penultimacy.

V. Bonhoeffer's 'Going Ahead' as Real-Human-Beings in Suffering and Dying

Having established that Christ's being is with and for all as individuals and communities and that He is not a stranger to any human circumstance, it is still important to explore Bonhoeffer's meaning of 'Going ahead' between Easter and Ascension. Bonhoeffer's 'Going ahead' is the existence of the *Gemeinde* 'not with the so-called religious functions of human beings, but with the existence in the world of whole human beings in all their relationships. The church's concern is not religion, but the form of Christ and its taking form among a band of people.'[103] For Bonhoeffer, the *Gemeinde* is fully present, fully aware of the past and present, and fully aware of Christ's reality in embracing and responding to the future. In Bonhoeffer's account:

> Where, however, it is recognized that the power of death has been broken, where the miracle of the resurrection and new life shines right into the world of death, there one demands no eternities from life. One takes from life what it offers, not all or nothing, but good things and bad, important things and unimportant,

---

102. DBWE 6:65–6 (DBW 6:51–2).
103. DBWE 6:97 (DBW 6:84–5).

joy and pain. One doesn't cling anxiously to life, but neither does one throw it lightly away. One is content with measured time and does not attribute eternity to earthly things. One leaves to death the limited right that it still has. But one expects the new human being and the new world only from beyond death, from the power that has conquered death.[104]

This is the constant movement in the being of Christ in the *aesthetic-ontological-dynamic*, as a way of being formed [*Gestaltung*] with a very tangible experience within time, place and space that exceeds all possible spatio-temporal limitations; it all begins and ends with and in Christ's form [*Gestalt*] in being fully honest in embracing life as *real-human-beings*.

For Bonhoeffer, 'Going ahead' means the constant underway as *real-human-beings* in the never-ending formation [*Gestaltung*] in a total embracement of the call *in which, by which, to which and for which* we are disciples, in tension with the never static, *aesthetic-ontological-dynamic*, indivisible form of Christ. 'Going ahead' in likeness to the form [*Gestalt*] is not something to be achieved as a linear spatio-temporal goal, not even to think of 'going ahead' as being physically over others as a status or way of life. This is the dualistic narrative of success.[105] Nevertheless, 'Going ahead' is the 'humanity [that] still lives, of course, in the old, but is already beyond the old. Humanity [that] still lives, of course, in a world of death, but is already beyond death. Humanity [that] still lives, of course, in a world of sin, but we are already beyond sin.'[106] Bonhoeffer adds to the road between Easter and Ascension, we are in Christ in the community, this is to be continuously underway and on the move.[107]

> [W]e must immerse ourselves again and again, for a long time and quite calmly, in Jesus's life, his sayings, actions, suffering, and dying in order to recognize what God promises and fulfills ... what is certain is that in suffering lies hidden the source of our joy, in dying the source of our life; what is certain is that in all this we stand within a community that carries us.[108]

---

104. DBWE 6:92 (DBW 6:79).

105. 'Actually it's a *deus ex machina* that they're always bringing on the scene, either to appear to solve insoluble problems or to provide strength when human powers fail, thus always exploiting human weakness or human limitations. Inevitably that lasts only until human beings become powerful enough to push the boundaries a bit further and God is no longer needed as deus ex machina' (DBWE 8:366 [DBW 8:407], see n25 [n24]).

106. DBWE 6:92 (DBW 6:79).

107. Being underway, '[i]t is he very mark and nature of the people of God, which otherwise does not exist. ... The prophets all proclaim a departure, an exile and a return, thus a continually being underway' (Käsemann, *Church Conflicts*, 77).

108. DBWE 8:515 (DBW 8:572–3).

'Going ahead' means resisting a false soteriological description or portrayal of the gospel road between Easter and Ascension.[109] It is to leave behind a simplistic idea of the Resurrection,[110] as if soteriology could be the central aim of the person of Christ.[111] It is not to reduce the Resurrection to a moral framework to achieve. Even the resurrection alone is irrelevant as an optimistic, easy way out in denial of our suffering and despair,[112] as 'His lordship remains that of the Crucified, even after Easter, it is continually opposed to our own desires and longings'.[113] As with the performing of miracles, the Resurrection alone is proof of nothing in our faith, but it is in the *aesthetic-ontological-dynamic* exchange in the likeness to the form [*Gestalt*] that we experience the being of Christ in the midst of all.

To be faithful to Christ's form [*Gestalt*] implies not to rush in confessing an antiseptic, totally clean, and white, resurrected Christ. But Christ, as the *real-human-being*, that is God, 'Who' was subject to trauma and violence in his body, 'Who' expressed not a cry for survival from the cross but that in him 'his death cry is the new creation call'.[114] The resurrected 'Who' after such failure and

---

109. 'It is a profound mistake to present the Christian gospel as if it were something that immediately showed itself, that authenticated itself without reflection it is of the manner of the coming of Jesus that he comes so close to the ordinary ways of men that they hardly notice him, that they treat him as one of themselves' (Donald Mackinnon, *Borderlands of Theology and other Essays* [Eugene: Wipf & Stock, 2011], 93).

110. 'It is a common place of traditional theology that in speech concerning God and the things of God "the negative way" must precede "the way of eminence". If men would give sense to what they say, they must be agnostic before they dare invoke the resources of anthropomorphic imagery; they are always properly more confident concerning what they must deny than concerning what they may affirm. ... In knowing what it is not, they know that it is not a descent from the cross postponed for thirty-six hours. It is not the sudden dramatic happy ending which the producer of a Hollywood spectacular might have conceived. In the stories as we have them, it is only to his own that the risen Christ shows himself with the marks of his passion still upon him; his commerce with them is elusive and restricted, as if to guard them against the mistake of supposing that they were witnesses of a reversal, and not of a vindication, of those things which had happened' (Mackinnon, *Borderlands of Theology*, 95–6).

111. 'God has made Jesus the eternally present Lord by raising him from the dead. This answer, however, is too facile if it obscures the cross with the message of the resurrection ... there is no presence of the Risen One other than in the call to and service of the cross' (Käsemann, *Church Conflicts*, 68–9).

112. 'Christianity takes the history of Jesus and urges the believer to find, in the endurance of the ultimate contradictions of human existence that belongs to its very substance, the assurance that in the worst that can befall his creatures, the creative Word keeps company with those whom he has called his own' (Mackinnon, *Borderlands of Theology*, 93).

113. Käsemann, *Church Conflicts*, 76.

114. Ibid., 74.

betrayal, and after three days of such desolation and pain; Could they still smell decomposed flesh from his body? Could they see His vulnerability in the atrocity of his wounds? Could they truly see? 'The Risen One will and must be recognized by his nail marks. Otherwise he does not remain Jesus.'[115] It is because of this path in simplicity, wisdom and naïveté that we realize once again that only in the formation [*Gestaltung*] to the form [*Gestalt*] we can truly see and live.

It is in this likeness to the form, 'Going ahead', that human beings realize Christ even in the most extreme desolation, pain and unbelief, as it is in the most uncomfortable religionless life that the being of Christ is revealed in the splendour of His changeless form [*Gestalt*]; revealing the reconciled *new-risen-humanity*.

'Going ahead' is to realize that our call as *real-human-beings* is to be aware and proclaim 'Who' Christ is for me, for us and for all. This means, in Christ's form [*Gestalt*], to always appear too profane for the *Kirche,* while at the same time, appear too religious to the logos of man. Religionless Christianity is to recognize ourselves in the always embracing form [*Gestalt*] of Christ, in the always *aesthetic-ontological-dynamic* formation [*Gestaltung*]. Hence, it is the *aesthetic-ontological-dynamic* by which the never-ending exchange, beyond the spatio-temporal, in which the formation [*Gestaltung*] to the form [*Gestalt*] of Christ's being emerges as an anomaly and interruption to our expectations of life. It is this *aesthetic-ontological-dynamic* in which, as part of the agency of *real-human-beings*, they come to belong in Christ's *Gemeinde*, and in his ever-flowing Word, arises the very nature and cosmic existence of *Christus als Gemeinde existierend*.[116]

Finally, the *aesthetic-ontological-dynamic* is for which the margins become the unexpected already embraced and borne centrality. In the deepest despair and unbelief, the human agency realizes the total pessimism of faith as the way to salvation for all.[117] Christ's form [*Gestalt*] is beyond any possible mastery, dominion, control or knowledge. Hence, we realize the *aesthetic-ontological-dynamic* is in 'Going ahead' in the *Gemeinde, in which, by which, to which and for which* all realize to be on the move, not in eternal human noble contradictions and dualisms, and not tired of each other in annihilation, but resonating in

---

115. Ibid., 75.

116. See Christiane Tietz, 'Christology', in *The Oxford Handbook of Dietrich Bonhoeffer*, ed. Michael Mawson and Philip Ziegler (Oxford: Oxford University Press, 2019), 150–67; Tom Greggs, 'Ecclesiology', in *The Oxford Handbook of Dietrich Bonhoeffer*, ed. Michael Mawson and Philip Ziegler (Oxford: Oxford University Press, 2019), 225–40; Mawson, *Christ Existing as Community*.

117. 'When we emphasize universal salvation as a result of Christian sinfulness, salvation is no longer ours to offer in a slightly superior way to the others, now the salvation of the other is the only hope of our own salvation: not "us then them," but "only us if them," or an "if even us then surely them … with Bonhoeffer, only if there is hope for them can there be hope for us – ultimately because there is no simple us and them with regard to sin and unbelief"' (Greggs, *Barth and Bonhoeffer*, 202, 205).

our mutual tiredness and vulnerability in shared unbelief,[118] not responding in useless human effort aiming for superficial religious conversion, but allowing to experience Christ's being in the midst of all, as a testimony in His form [*Gestalt*] to the contradictions of the world. This is Christ's being as *Gemeinde* holding the whole of the creation, history and existence. This is the Glory of God, and this is our eternal rest in God, in whom we find wholeness for peace with one another.[119] This is the Glory of 'Who' Christ is for all!

VI. Conclusion

Throughout this proposal developed by Bonhoeffer we have explored its relevance towards concreteness as an Aesthetic Public Theology in the *aesthetic-ontological-dynamic*. Bonhoeffer concludes:

> The human being, accepted, judged, and awakened to new life by God – this is Jesus Christ, this is the whole of humanity in Christ, this is us. The form of Jesus Christ alone victoriously encounters the world. From this form proceeds all the formation of a world reconciled with God.[120]

A world reconciled with God, even while in despair, pain and unbelief. This is the Word revealed in the *Gemeinde's* simplicity, which emerges in the silent interval-suspension (Zwischen) that conveys the painful mourning of the world.[121] It witnesses Christ's reality in a *religionless* time, despite the constant

---

118. In relation with work-time tension, the *Gemeinde* is not looking for any advantage over chronological time, therefore it is useless for the functional ways of the world, the *Gemeinde* is witnessing that it is all Christ's: 'The tiredness of exhaustion is the tiredness of positive potency. It makes one incapable of doing *something*. Tiredness that inspires is tiredness of negative potency, namely of not-to. The Sabbath, too – a word that originally meant stopping [*aufhören*] – is a day of not-to; speaking with Heidegger, it is a day free of all *in-order-to*, of all care. It is a matter of interval [*Zwischenzeit*]. After He created it, God declared the Seventh Day holy. That is, the day of in-order-to is not sacred, but rather the day of not-to, a day on which the use of the useless proves possible. It is a day of tiredness … The interval is a time without work, a time of, and for, play [*Spielzeit*] … The interval, in-between time, is a period of in-difference as friendliness … The "Pentecostal company" that inspires not-doing stands opposed to the society of activity … It is a society of those who are tired in a special way. If "Pentecostal company" offered a synonym for the society of the future, the society to come might also be called a society of tiredness' (Byung Chul-Han, *The Burnout Society* [California, Redwood City: Stanford University Press, 2015], 33–4).

119. DBWE 8:341–2 (DBW 8:379–80).

120. DBWE 6:92 (DBW 6:80).

121. 'The silence of the church is silence before the Word. In proclaiming Christ, the church falls on its knees in silence before the inexpressible, the ἄρρητον. To speak of Christ is to be silent, and to be silent about Christ is to speak' (DBWE 12:300 [DBW 12:280]).

unawareness of the *Kirche*, as institutional religion. Therefore, it is in the radical response to discipleship as individuals and communities, as part of Christ's being as *Gemeinde* as nothing else but honest, real, fragile and vulnerable *real-human-beings*.[122] The formation [*Gestaltung*] according to the being of the form [Gestalt] of Christ 'demands more of us than devotion and emotion – that is, it demands our preparedness for acting and suffering'.[123] In unbelief and total naïveté realizing that 'the night is not yet over, but day is already dawning'.[124] this beautiful aesthetic exchange of our beings in the being of Christ's form [*Gestalt*] takes place; in dying and suffering *real-human-beings*, all placed and reconciled in God alone.

122. A visible process of an Aesthetic Public Theology in Bonhoeffer's account is noticeable in the collectivity of Mexican families in the search for those harmed by enforced disappearances. The reconciled Gemeinde in a necropolitical context, with a voice of truth in simple acts, contrasts with the *Kirche* and other institutions in the public sphere. For more on necropolitics in the public sphere, see Silvana Mandolessi and Katia Olalde (eds), *Disappearances in Mexico: From the 'Dirty War' to the 'War on Drugs'* (London: Routledge, 2022), and Karina Ansolabehere, Barbara A. Frey, Leigh A. Payne (eds), *Disappearances in the Post-Transition Era in Latin America* (Oxford: OUP, 2021). For more on theology in the public sphere in Mexico and Latin America, see William A. Walker, *A Theology of the Drug War* (London: Lexington Books/Fortress Academic, 2020) and William Cavanaugh, *Torture and Eucharist* (Oxford: Blackwell Publishing, 1998).
123. Käsemann, *Church Conflicts*, 76.
124. DBWE 6:92 (DBW 6:79–80).

Chapter 13

JESUS CHRIST: THE CENTRE OF THE CHURCH

David Emerton

In his 1902 work, *L'Évangile et l'Église*, the Roman Catholic modernist Alfred Loisy wrote that 'Jesus announced the kingdom, and it was the church that came'.[1] Loisy's oft-quoted – but far from ironic or sardonic[2] – sentiment gives voice implicitly to the concern of this chapter: the relationship between Jesus and the Church, or, more formally, the relationship between Christology and ecclesiology, as this relationship is conceived in the theological thought of Dietrich Bonhoeffer. It is commonplace in extant Bonhoeffer scholarship to take as a central *leitmotif* of Bonhoeffer's ecclesial thinking what he writes in the context of his doctoral dissertation, *Sanctorum Communio*: '*Die personale Einheit der Kirche ist "Christus als Gemeinde existierend"*'.[3] That is, 'the church is "Christ existing as church-community"'.[4] What is far less commonplace in such scholarship, however, is any consideration of how the coinherence between the Church and Christ which Bonhoeffer suggests by this *leitmotif* actually exists as Bonhoeffer understands it. Such a consideration is thus the focus of this chapter. And to articulate its response to the question of *how* the Church is, for Bonhoeffer, 'Christ existing as church-community', the chapter turns, taking its cue from the trajectory of Bonhoeffer's own theological thinking, to Bonhoeffer's pneumatology – to his understanding of the person and work of the Holy Spirit, as the Holy Spirit relates to the church-community existing as Christ. In light of this pneumatological indexation of the coinherence between the Church and Christ which exists in Bonhoeffer's understanding of how the Church is 'Christ existing as church-community', the chapter considers the extent to which Christology really is the foundation of Bonhoeffer's ecclesiology as it is often considered to be in extant Bonhoeffer

---

1. Alfred Loisy, *The Gospel and the Church* (New York: Prometheus, 1988), 145.

2. See Paul Avis, *Jesus and the Church: The Foundation of the Church in the New Testament and Modern Theology* (Theological Foundations of the Christian Church, vol. 1, London: T&T Clark/Bloomsbury, 2021), 137–42.

3. DBW 1:133 (DBWE 1:199).

4. See, for example, DBWE 1:141. 190. 199. 280 (DBW 1:87. 127. 133. 191).

scholarship. As a corrective to this well-trodden path, the chapter suggests, instead, that whilst Christology is the *central* dogmatic *res* of Bonhoeffer's ecclesiology, its *foundational* dogmatic *res* is, in fact, pneumatology.

I. A Systematic Concern?

To speak in these terms – of Christology, ecclesiology and pneumatology – and to use such (Latin) language – of '*res*' (which admittedly is not readily associated with Bonhoeffer himself)[5] – is to situate the concern of this chapter squarely within the register of systematic theology. This itself, given the varied, diffuse and sometimes fragmentary nature of Bonhoeffer's body of work, but also the kaleidoscopic legacy of his theological thinking, might not be an obvious move. Indeed, in light of the question posed by André Dumas just over half a century ago as to whether Bonhoeffer can be said to 'really have a systematic point of view if his readers can organize his thought into so many contradictory systems',[6] Wayne Whitson Floyd drew attention to the need to dispel any illusion as to the systematic unity or '*coherence* of Bonhoeffer's theology'[7] as a whole. And in his provocative dissent thesis of 1975, the late David H. Hopper gave voice to what he saw as the inherent and paradoxical tension in successive Bonhoeffer interpreters who sought to identify a basic or systematic unity in Bonhoeffer's thought, but appealed to different hermeneutical keys to do so.[8] To situate Bonhoeffer's theological thought

---

5. The language of '*res*' is taken from John Webster and Tom Greggs, and is used alongside 'dogmatic' to refer to the object or subject matter of either theological thinking per se, or a specific Christian doctrine. See John Webster, '"In the Society of God": Some Principles of Ecclesiology', in *Perspectives on Ecclesiology and Ethnography*, ed. Pete Ward (Grand Rapids: Eerdmans, 2012), 200–22; and Tom Greggs, 'Bearing Sin in the Church: The Ecclesial Hamartiology of Bonhoeffer', in *Christ, Church and World: New Studies in Bonhoeffer's Theology and Ethics*, ed. Michael Mawson and Philip G. Ziegler (London: Bloomsbury T&T Clark, 2016), 77–99.

6. André Dumas, *Dietrich Bonhoeffer: Theologian of Reality*, trans. Robert McAfee Brown (London: SCM Press, 1971), 276.

7. Wayne Whitson Floyd, *Theology and the Dialectics of Otherness: On Reading Bonhoeffer and Adorno* (Lanham: University Press of America, 1988), 6.

8. See David H. Hopper, *A Dissent on Bonhoeffer* (Philadelphia: The Westminster Press, 1975). Within Bonhoeffer scholarship the number of different hermeneutical keys for reading Bonhoeffer is significant. For example, Christology has been accorded ultimacy by John A. Phillips, *Christ for Us in the Theology of Dietrich Bonhoeffer* (New York: Harper & Row, 1967) and Ernst Feil, *The Theology of Dietrich Bonhoeffer*, trans. Martin Rumscheidt (Minneapolis: Fortress Press, 1985), amongst others; 'reality' has been proposed (ironically perhaps) by Dumas, *Dietrich Bonhoeffer* and Heinrich Ott, *Reality and Faith: The Theological*

in a systematic register, therefore, might be contentious, as too might be the related identification of Bonhoeffer's 'pneumatology', 'ecclesiology' and 'Christology', given there is no regular systematic presentation of these doctrinal loci within the corpus of his writings. Nevertheless, they are suggestions that, I think, can be made, and, in fact, treat Bonhoeffer primarily as he himself understood himself – that is, as a *Dogmatiker* or systematic theologian.[9]

Throughout his life, Bonhoeffer works methodologically and intentionally with theological categories for the purpose of prosecuting the primary theological task of elucidating Christian doctrine as a function and in service of the Church.[10] Bonhoeffer does so, however, not in any regular dogmatic sense in terms of offering a systematic account of the whole of Christian doctrine ordered locus by locus. Instead, Bonhoeffer's writings form an irregular dogmatics,[11] or, to follow the more recent and helpful differentiation offered by Anna Williams, a 'relational' – as opposed to a 'conventional' – systematic theology.[12] In contrast to the concern of conventional systematics to offer a coherent and comprehensive account of Christian doctrine in toto, relational systematic theology is as Williams describes it, concerned primarily with tracing links between different Christian

---

Legacy of Dietrich Bonhoeffer, trans. Alex A. Morrison (Philadelphia: Fortress Press, 1972); 'sociality' has been offered as a key by Clifford J. Green, *Bonhoeffer: A Theology of Sociality*, rev. ed. (Grand Rapids: Eerdmans, 1999); 'life' by Ralf K. Wüstenberg, *A Theology of Life: Dietrich Bonhoeffer's Religionless Christianity*, trans. Doug Stott (Grand Rapids: Eerdmans 1998); 'freedom' by Ann L. Nickson, *Bonhoeffer on Freedom: Courageously Grasping Reality* (Aldershot: Ashgate, 2002); and the concept of 'person' by Michael P. DeJonge, *Bonhoeffer's Theological Formation: Berlin, Barth, and Protestant Theology* (Oxford: Oxford University Press, 2012).

9. See DBW 1:172 (DBWE 1:251) and DBWE 10:198–9 (DBW 10:161–3).

10. In a working note to *Ethics*, Bonhoeffer writes: 'Today we find "Christian ethics" freed from Christian doctrine, Christian behaviour that is not at all aware of its Christianness [*Christlichkeit*]. Only recently have people again come to ask after the foundation of their behaviour and thus come back to doctrine and to the church. The issue is this: the unification of the two, to lead-back to faith', Dietrich Bonhoeffer, *Zettelnotizen für eine 'Ethik'*, Ergänzungsband zu DBW 6, ed. Ilse Tödt (München: Chr. Kaiser Verlag, 1993), 32. On the suggestion for reading Bonhoeffer with a dogmatic hermeneutic, see also Eva Harasta, 'Bonhoeffer's Lutheran Ecclesiology and Inter-Religious Dialogue: A Dogmatic Reading of Bonhoeffer', in *Bonhoeffer and Interpretative Theory: Essays on Methods and Understanding*, ed. Peter Frick (Frankfurt am Main: Peter Lang, 2013), 239–40.

11. On 'regular' and 'irregular' dogmatics, see Karl Barth, *Church Dogmatics*, I/1, ed. and trans. G. W. Bromiley and T. F. Torrance (Edinburgh: T&T Clark, 1975), 275–87.

12. See A. N. Williams, *The Architecture of Theology: Structure, System, and Ratio* (Oxford: Oxford University Press, 2011), 1–22.

doctrines and indicating how any one doctrine – often as the single subject of theological discourse – is informed by or determines another, and thereby exhibits 'an impetus towards coherence and comprehensiveness'.[13] For Williams, this impetus thus likens theology that is in this sense systematic to a jigsaw:

> [E]ven if one does not have all the pieces, the shape of any one of them reflects its orientation towards others as parts of a larger pattern. When there are enough such pieces to hand, a complete picture forms, but even in the absence of a whole, unified image, a solitary piece displays by its very shape its trajectory towards linkage.[14]

To speak, then, of both the systematic nature of Bonhoeffer's theology and his 'Christology', 'ecclesiology' and 'pneumatology', is not only to be dependent, therefore, on the whole corpus of his writings and on moving freely between those writings in order to construct the material content of such doctrines, but to assume and to apply to those writings a definition of systematicity that trades not on conventionality but on relationality.

What is more, from this relational systematic vantage point, a major task for the systematic theologian comes (perhaps) more sharply into view. Systematic theology itself is concerned with the substance and arrangement – or ordering – of doctrine, and how the relationship between doctrines is subsequently understood, especially in relation to the proportionality of the doctrines represented and which doctrine (if any) is considered foundational.[15] The systematic theologian is alive, therefore, to the way in which any one doctrine is shaped and potentially misshaped by another, and to how the expansion or contraction – or indeed prioritizing – of one doctrine in relation to another doctrine can distort the coherence of Christian doctrine as a whole. A major task for the systematic theologian is thus to register and repair any such distortions or deformations.[16] The importance of this systematic theological task and the 'aliveness' that it requires of the systematic theologian cannot be overstated: it is the case that no one doctrine is treatable in isolation from other doctrines, and (as Williams' differentiation between conventional and relational systematicity underscores) any one doctrine must be treated always in reference to the way it interconnects coherently with Christian doctrine as a whole. However, it is also the case that the doctrine considered by the theologian to be foundational to that whole, or prioritized and attended to particularly within that whole, will tend to shape – and

---

13. Ibid., 1.
14. Ibid.
15. See John Webster, 'Introduction: Systematic Theology', in *The Oxford Handbook of Systematic Theology*, ed. John Webster, Kathryn Tanner, and Iain Torrance (New York: Oxford University Press, 2007), 1–15, 12–13.
16. See Webster, 'Introduction: Systematic Theology', 13.

potentially misshape – the doctrines which subsequently are related to it.[17] As Sarah Coakley writes, '*wherever one chooses to start* [one's systematic theology] *has implications for the whole, and the parts must fit together*'.[18] Put otherwise, 'dogmatic topography'[19] in theology matters. It matters, in other words, where (doctrinally speaking) the theologian chooses to start her speech about the Church from; and it matters because different doctrinal foundations to ecclesiological speech give rise to different theological accounts of the Church. And those accounts – because of those different doctrinal foundations – carry the potential to be misshaped (doctrinally speaking) and thus to one extent or another deficient theologically. This potential for theological deficiency in ecclesiological discourse, especially when it comes to articulating the relationship between Jesus and the Church, thus stands as the backdrop against which this chapter proceeds to consider the relationship between Christology and ecclesiology as Bonhoeffer understands it in connection to 'Christ existing as church-community'. Before turning to consider this relationship in Bonhoeffer's own theological thinking, however, and in order to draw out subsequently something of the constructive force of Bonhoeffer's articulation of how the Church is 'Christ existing as church-community', it will be helpful, first, to sketch something of the way in which the relationship between Christology and ecclesiology is often conceived in contemporary ecclesiological discourse.

II. Mislocating the Church Christologically?

Without doubt, the relationship between the doctrines of Christology and ecclesiology is something over which much theological ink has been spilt. This itself is perhaps not surprising. After all, it is the Apostle Paul who first describes the Church as 'the body of Christ' (1 Cor. 12:27) and it is this Christologically indexed ecclesiological image that continues to offer fertile ground for thinking theologically about the Church today.[20] Indeed, the impulse to coordinate

---

17. See John Webster, *God without Measure: Working Papers in Christian Theology, Volume I: God and the Works of God* (London: T&T Clark/Bloomsbury, 2016), 3–10; see also Tom Greggs, 'Proportion and Topography in Ecclesiology: A Working Paper on the Dogmatic Location of the Doctrine of the Church', in *Theological Theology: Essays in Honour of John B. Webster*, ed. R. David Nelson, Darren Sarisky, and Justin Stratis (London: T&T Clark/Bloomsbury, 2015), 89–106.

18. Sarah Coakley, *God, Sexuality, and the Self: An Essay 'On the Trinity'* (Cambridge: Cambridge University Press, 2013), 41.

19. Tom Greggs, *Dogmatic Ecclesiology Volume One: The Priestly Catholicity of the Church* (Grand Rapids: Baker Academic, 2019), xxx.

20. For a brief but helpful summary discussion of the image, see Arland J. Hultegren, 'The Church as the Body of Christ: Engaging an Image in the New Testament', in *Word & World* 22, no. 2 (2002): 124–32.

ecclesiology with Christology in contemporary accounts of the Church and to do so in virtue of Paul's image of the Church as Christ's body is frequent, and regardless of whether such accounts trade on more Protestant, Catholic or Orthodox theologies. This impulse itself may, in part, be symptomatic of the all-important ecclesiological point of the Reformers – of Luther, in particular – that the Church is *creatura verbi divini* ('the creature of the word').[21] Reflecting on this ecclesiological point and summarizing it helpfully, Edmund Schlink writes: 'The Church is, because Jesus Christ constantly is acting upon her. She was not before this action; and she is not for an instant without this action.'[22] Or, as Anders Nygren argues, also writing from a Protestant Lutheran perspective, 'what the Church is, in the deepest sense, emerges only as the Church is seen in its indissoluble relationship with Christ: it is the Church as the "Body of Christ"'.[23] And in this sense, 'the Church is nothing in itself'.[24] For Nygren, what the Church is is conditioned exclusively by Christ, and Christ – seemingly – is conditioned exclusively by the Church: 'The Church cannot exist without Christ; Christ cannot be present without his Church.'[25] And this coordination of Christ and the Church, further, is such that Christology and ecclesiology are understood by Nygren as mutually conditioning; if the former does not 'include' the latter it is 'false', and the latter, if it is not 'fixed' by the former, is said to go 'astray'.[26] In this sense, then, and in the words of Emil Brunner, 'Ecclesiology is Christology'.[27]

In a fashion similar to Nygren, the Roman Catholic theologian Henri de Lubac likewise conditions what the Church is Christologically. Whilst tracing the foundation of the Church to the divine processions of God's own internal life,[28] and thereby viewing the Church as 'a mysterious extension in time of the Trinity',[29] de Lubac writes: 'the church is a mystery because, coming from God and entirely

---

21. For Luther, of course, Word and Spirit can never be separated. For discussion of the Reformer's conception of the church as *creatura verbi divini*, see Christoph Schwöbel, 'The Creature of the Word: Recovering the Ecclesiology of the Reformers', in *On Being the Church: Essays on the Christian Community*, ed. Colin Gunton and Daniel W. Hardy (Edinburgh: T&T Clark, 1989), 110-55.

22. Edmund Schlink, *The Coming Christ and the Coming Church* (Edinburgh: Oliver & Boyd, 1967), 116.

23. Anders Nygren, *Christ and His Church*, trans. Alan Carlsten (Philadelphia: The Westminster Press, 1956), 14.

24. Ibid., 100.

25. Ibid., 31.

26. Ibid.

27. Emil Brunner, *The Christian Doctrine of the Church, Faith, and the Consummation: Dogmatics Vol. III*, trans. David Cairns (London: Lutterworth Press, 1962), 84.

28. See S. J. Henri de Lubac, *The Splendour of the Church*, trans. Michael Mason (London: Sheed and Ward, 1956), 71.

29. S. J. Henri de Lubac, *The Church: Paradox and Mystery*, trans. James R. Dunne (Shannon: Ecclesia Press, 1969), 24.

at the service of his plan, she is an organism of salvation, precisely because she relates wholly to Christ and *apart from him has no existence, value or efficacy*'.[30] At every step of the ecclesiological way, the ecclesiologist must therefore insist, in the words of Douglas Farrow, that 'it is only Christ who makes the church the church'.[31] Or from the perspective of Greek Orthodoxy, John Zizioulas argues that the Church comes to be the Church truly – that is, 'the Body of Christ' – only as (and each time) the Holy Spirit constitutes the Church thus in the eucharistic *synaxis*.[32] Zizioulas' pneumatologically indexed eucharistic determination of the Church's true being as Christ's body is echoed by the catholic Lutheran theologian Robert Jenson. For Jenson, whilst the being of the Church is grounded in the *in se* life of God and so linked ontologically as Christ's body to the second person of the Trinity, the Church is nevertheless a work of God *ad extra* in creation: 'The unmediated and wholly antecedent will that is the Father dictates that there be the church', and as Jenson continues, that the Church chosen in God's divine intention 'as something other than the world' 'be exactly the one that exists' in the world by the action of the Holy Spirit.[33] It is the Holy Spirit who creates (according to Jenson) the *communio* that the Church is by animating in the Church's life the perichoretic *communio* of God, and such that the Church becomes Christ's body in its being epicletically and anamnetically united to the Son's created body.[34] Ultimately, the work of the Holy Spirit in constituting the Church truly is thus indexed most properly, Jenson argues, eucharistically;[35] only in the Eucharist does the Church realize what the Church is truly, since in the Eucharist the Holy Spirit makes the Church Christ's body and thus at once *signa et res*: 'the event of the remembered Jesus as the presence of the coming one'.[36]

This, of course, is a crude over-simplification of the complexities of the ecclesiological work of these individual theologians, and indeed a severely truncated sketch of the way in which the relationship between Christology and ecclesiology is often conceived in contemporary ecclesiological discourse. Despite the limited nature of the sketch, however, it does serve to illustrate sufficiently, I think, what is a frequent impulse in contemporary accounts of the Church – the impulse, that is, to coordinate (either to a greater or lesser extent) ecclesiology with Christology. But more specifically, and if the ecclesial thinking of these individual theologians is probed further, what becomes apparent is not just a coordination of

---

30. Ibid., 15, emphasis DE.

31. Douglas Farrow, *Ascension & Ecclesia: On the Significance of the Doctrine of the Ascension for Ecclesiology and Christian Cosmology* (Edinburgh: T&T Clark, 1999), 3.

32. See John D. Zizioulas, *Being as Communion: Studies in Personhood and the Church* (London: Darton, Longman & Todd, 1985), 22 and 160–1.

33. See Robert W. Jenson, *Systematic Theology*, vol. 2 (New York: Oxford University Press, 1999), 167–83, 173.

34. See ibid., 211–27.

35. See ibid., 212–13.

36. Ibid., 259.

ecclesiology with Christology, but, in fact, a problematic coinherence of the two doctrines (problematic at least in light of the concerns of the systematic theologian noted above).

In Nygren's work, for example, the relationship between Christ and the Church as Christ's body is seemingly collapsed without remainder so as to elide intentionally any distinction between the Church and Christ, and such that as the body of Christ the Church *is* (according to Nygren) Christ himself.[37] As Nygren writes:

> To designate the Church as the body of Christ and Christ as the head of the Church is not to imply that one part is allocated to Christ and another to the Church; on the contrary, it emphasizes their indissoluble relationship and unity. Christ is not the head pure and simple, but he is the head of his Church. Similarly, the Church is not the body in itself, viewed apart from the head, but *it is just the body of Christ*.[38]

Thus, without due concern seemingly for Christ's ascension – and for what Farrow subsequently has described as 'the Christological enigma'[39] of the *Christus absens* and the *Christus praesens* which, ultimately, the doctrine of the ascension introduces into ecclesiological discourse – Nygren proffers his definition of the Church: 'The Church is Christ *as he is present among and meets us upon earth after his resurrection*.'[40]

Similarly, de Lubac too might be said to over-identify the Church's being with Christ himself: 'the Church is not just a body, but *the* body of Christ'.[41] For de Lubac, between Christ and the Church there is 'a certain relation of mystical identity', which in ecclesiological discourse must never be separated, and such that '[p]ractically speaking, for each one of us Christ is … His Church'.[42] Indeed, the relation between Christ and the Church as Christ's body is collapsed so sufficiently by de Lubac that on occasion he can even conceive of the Church as 'the incarnation continued',[43] and thus as 'all-holy and all-sanctifying'.[44] And likewise, Zizioulas and Jenson too – and notwithstanding the explicit pneumatological qualifiers to their ecclesiological accounts – threaten to absorb the social-historical particularity of the Church into the person of Christ, and thereby over-identify the Church as Christ's body with Christ himself. In the Eucharist, Zizioulas argues, Church

---

37. See Nygren, *Christ and His Church*, 96.
38. Ibid., 95–6, emphasis DE.
39. Farrow, *Ascension & Ecclesia*, 3.
40. Nygren, *Christ and His Church*, 32, emphasis altered DE.
41. De Lubac, *The Splendour of the Church*, 112.
42. Ibid., 152 and 153.
43. See ibid., 24.
44. Ibid.

and Christ become 'completely' identified,[45] such that '[a]ll separation between Christology and ecclesiology vanishes in the Spirit.'[46] And notwithstanding a passing reference to the Church's spousal relation and, therefore, distinction to Christ, the Church, argues Jenson, is united so completely to Christ that 'the church is ontologically the risen Christ's human body'.[47] This problematic coinherence of ecclesiology and Christology, and the related over-identification in ecclesiological discourse of the Church as Christ's body with Christ himself, is perhaps best reflected in the recent words of Paul Avis (echoing the claim of Origen): 'If Jesus Christ is *autobasileia*, the kingdom itself, he is also *autoekklēsia*, the church itself.'[48] To suggest such a complete co-inherence between Jesus and the Church, however, as Avis's words seemingly do, or to make Christology the foundational dogmatic *res* of ecclesiology as the over-identification of the Church's being with Christ himself risks doing, not only threatens to collapse the transcendence of the risen and ascended (bodily) Christ into sheer (ecclesiological) immanence, but also is creedally spurious.

III. Locating the Church Pneumatologically?

As I have noted elsewhere, this point is evidenced most clearly by reference to the third article of the Nicene-Constantinopolitan Creed, according to which the doctrine of the Church is located (derivatively) 'under' the doctrine of the Holy Spirit.[49] In terms of creedal sequencing, the creedal sub-clause on ecclesiology emerges from and 'under' the creedal clause on the person and work of the Holy Spirit. The creedal sub-clause on ecclesiology does not arise from the creedal clause on the person and work of Jesus Christ, which would be to coordinate ecclesiology with Christology and thus, creedally speaking, mislocate the doctrine of the Church 'under' the Creed's second article instead of properly 'under' it's third. All this is clear from the Latin rendering of the Creed's third article: *Et in Spiritum Sanctum, Dominum et vivificantem ... Et unam, sanctum, catholicam et apostolicam Ecclesiam ... Et expecto resurrectionem mortuorem, et vitam venturi saeculi* ('And [I believe] in the Holy Spirit, the Lord and giver of Life ... And one holy, catholic and apostolic Church ... And [I] look for the resurrection of the dead,

---

45. John D. Zizioulas, 'Le Mystère de l'Église dans la tradition orthodoxe', in *Irénikon* 60 (1987): 321–35, 328.

46. Zizioulas, *Being as Communion*, 111.

47. Jenson, *Systematic Theology*, vol. 2, 213.

48. Avis, *Theological Foundations of the Christian Church*, vol. 1, 212; see 45: Origin, as Avis notes, first suggested that Jesus is the kingdom itself, or the kingdom in person (*autobasileia*).

49. See David Emerton, *God's Church-Community: The Ecclesiology of Dietrich Bonhoeffer* (London: T&T Clark/Bloomsbury, 2020), 64. See also, Greggs, 'Proportion and Topography in Ecclesiology', 95–100; and Greggs, *Dogmatic Ecclesiology Volume One*, xxx–xxxi.

and the life of the age to come'). Further, and on the basis of this Latin rendering of the Creed's third article it is important to note the theological significance of the absence of the preposition *eis* or *in* before *ecclesiam*. As Calvin argues, 'There is no good reason why many insert the preposition "in"', for as Calvin continues, 'We testify that we believe *in* God because our mind reposes in him as truthful, and our trust rests in him.'[50] Or as Yves Congar puts it: 'It is … possible to believe *in* God, to accept him as the end of one's life, but it is not possible to believe in the same way *in* the Church.'[51] Instead, I believe the Church; and more specifically, as Congar continues, 'I believe in the Holy Spirit … as the one who makes the Church one, holy, catholic and apostolic.'[52] The Church is not – and must never be treated as if it is – 'a fourth article of the creed',[53] independent so-to-speak of the triune life of God, in the sense of having its own dogmatic *res*, and neither must the Church be treated as if it is independent of the life of God the Holy Spirit. As Tom Greggs summarizes aptly: 'The Church is in the creed a mission of the Holy Spirit who is in Himself God and who acts in the economy of salvation to create the church.'[54]

What is more, to condition ecclesiology Christologically – to a point of coinherence or otherwise – is not only creedally spurious, but might be seen to be scripturally spurious as well. As Avis has established, Jesus certainly is – in one sense or another – the *foundation* of the Church,[55] not least because the Church, as the Apostle Paul reminds the Ephesians, has been chosen in Christ from and for all eternity (Eph. 1:4). But as Avis has established equally well, Jesus is not the *founder* of the Church.[56] In Avis' words, 'Jesus had no intention of "founding" a church of any kind', in the sense, that is, of 'intending' or 'foreseeing' the organization or institution of the Church that did in fact come after Jesus had announced the Kingdom (to recall Loisy's sentiment).[57] Rather, and as the narrative of Acts 2 bears witness, the Church (and in whatever organizational or institutional form she orders herself) is founded by the coming of God the Holy Spirit at Pentecost: the founder of the Church is not Jesus but the Holy Spirit of God, and the Church as such is a creature of God the Holy Spirit.

On the basis of both the Creed and the scriptural witness, then, the doctrine of the Church is located most properly subsequent to that of the person and work of the Holy Spirit, and the foundational dogmatic *res* of ecclesiology is not

---

50. John Calvin, *Institutes of the Christian Religion*, vol. 2, ed. John T. McNeill and trans. Ford Lewis Battles (Louisville: Westminster John Knox Press, 2011), 1013.

51. Yves Congar, *I Believe in the Holy Spirit*, vol. 2, trans. David Smith (New York: The Crossroad Publishing Company, 2015), 5.

52. Ibid.

53. Greggs, *Dogmatic Ecclesiology, Volume One*, 13.

54. Greggs, 'Proportion and Topography in Ecclesiology', 100.

55. See Avis, *Theological Foundations of the Christian Church*, vol. 1, 77–80.

56. See ibid., 13–81.

57. Ibid., 77.

Christology but pneumatology.[58] There is thus a need to condition ecclesiology pneumatologically; and this pneumatological conditioning – when best handled – should act to guard ecclesiological speech against succumbing to any problematic coinherence of ecclesiology and Christology, and any related over-identification of the Church as Christ's body with Christ himself. Significantly, the point of creedal sequencing and the force of the scriptural witness – and thus the need to condition ecclesiology *pneumatologically* – is not lost on Bonhoeffer himself. In fact, together, they come to shape foundationally Bonhoeffer's ecclesial thinking. To suggest this is perhaps surprising given the Lutheran theological traditions at play in shaping Bonhoeffer's theology,[59] but also the coinherence of ecclesiology and Christology which Bonhoeffer seemingly suggests by his assertion that the Church is 'Christ existing as church-community', and the frequently rehearsed critique that in Bonhoeffer's theology pneumatology is absent or significantly underdeveloped.[60]

IV. The Church: *Christologically* centred *and pneumatologically* founded

Bonhoeffer's concern, however, with the Creed's third article, and indeed with the relationality of the doctrines of pneumatology and ecclesiology (and for that matter eschatology), came to dominate his theological studies in (and from) the winter

58. Most properly, the foundational dogmatic *res* of ecclesiology is an *eschatologically indexed* pneumatology: in terms of creedal sequencing, the creedal sub-clause on eschatology follows after the creedal sub-clause on ecclesiology, and these both emerge from and 'under' the creedal clause on the person and work of the Holy Spirit. For further discussion of this point (at least in the context of Bonhoeffer's ecclesiology), see Emerton, *God's Church-Community*, 55–68.

59. On the presence of Luther in Bonhoeffer's theological thought, see Michael P. DeJonge, *Bonhoeffer's Reception of Luther* (Oxford: Oxford University Press, 2017).

60. The former critique (of 'absence') is in David A. Höhne, *Spirit and Sonship: Colin Gunton's Theology of Particularity and the Holy Spirit* (Farnham: Routledge, 2016), 23 and the latter (of 'underdevelopment') in Stephen Plant, 'Fresh Treatment of Bonhoeffer', in *Expository Times* 106, no. 6 (1995): 188. Further variations on the same themes include: Farrow, who writes of Bonhoeffer's 'glaring pneumatological deficiency', Farrow, *Ascension and Ecclesia*, 177n43; Ann Nickson, who notes that 'the pneumatological inadequacies of Bonhoeffer's theology are most obvious [in *Sanctorum Communio*], particularly in the concept of "Christ existing as the church", where a greater role of the Spirit seems to be required', Nickson, *Bonhoeffer on Freedom*, 59; and Matt Jenson, who contends that Bonhoeffer lacks 'a robust' and 'proper pneumatology', Matt Jenson, 'Real Presence: Contemporaneity in Bonhoeffer's Christology', in *Scottish Journal of Theology* 58 (2005): 143–60, 158 and 159. Elsewhere I have sought to offer a corrective to this frequently rehearsed critique, at least in the context of Bonhoeffer's ecclesiology, see Emerton, *God's Church-Community*.

semester of 1925-6.⁶¹ This preoccupation is such that, as Hans Pfeifer notes, 'one would not be wrong in placing his [doctoral] dissertation in this context'.⁶² Pfeifer's claim might be said to apply equally well, however, not only to Bonhoeffer's post-doctoral dissertation, but also to his theology as a whole.⁶³ As Bonhoeffer himself describes it, the connection between 'the essence' and 'factual content' of *Act and Being* and *Sanctorum Communio* lies in his understanding both works as being 'basically about nothing other than the church'.⁶⁴ And it is in the context of his doctoral dissertation that Bonhoeffer, of course, writes that the Church is 'Christ existing as church-community'.

The coinherence of ecclesiology and Christology which Bonhoeffer seemingly suggests by this *leitmotif* has subsequently led any number of Bonhoeffer scholars to coordinate his ecclesiology (to one extent or another) with Christology. For instance, John D. Godsey argues that in Bonhoeffer's theology 'Christology includes ecclesiology within itself',⁶⁵ whilst Andreas Pangritz writes of Bonhoeffer's 'almost compulsive identifications' of Christ and the church-community in his early theology.⁶⁶ More recently, this reading has been echoed by Joel Lawrence: 'Bonhoeffer's ecclesiology is simply his Christology placed into the context of community', and as such 'Bonhoeffer's ecclesiology can only be grasped from the perspective of his Christology'.⁶⁷ Or, as Eberhard Bethge puts it, Bonhoeffer 'found ecclesiology on Christology',⁶⁸ such that, for Bonhoeffer, in the words of Dumas, 'Jesus Christ *is himself* the church'.⁶⁹ This tendency to coordinate Bonhoeffer's ecclesiology with Christology, and in doing so, creedally speaking, mislocate his ecclesiology 'under' the Creed's second article, has subsequently led

---

61. See, for example, DBWE 9:285-300, 310-24, 325-70, 370-85, 385-94 and 502-9 (DBW 9:305-24, 335-53, 355-410, 410-30, 430-40 and 449-59).

62. Hans Pfeifer, 'Editor's Afterword', in DBWE 9:574 (DBW 9:628).

63. It is notable in this respect that Sabine Dramm suggests that perhaps the most appropriate way to approximate 'the content and goal' of Bonhoeffer's theology and its 'innermost core' is with reference to the articles of the Apostles' Creed, see Sabine Dramm, *Dietrich Bonhoeffer: An Introduction to His Thought*, trans. Thomas Rice (Peabody: Hendrickson Publishers, 2007), 31-2.

64. DBWE 11:45 (DBW 11:24).

65. John D. Godsey, *The Theology of Dietrich Bonhoeffer* (London: SCM Press, 1960), 264.

66. Andreas Pangritz, 'Who Is Jesus Christ, for Us, Today?', in *The Cambridge Companion to Dietrich Bonhoeffer*, ed. John W. de Gruchy (Cambridge: Cambridge University Press, 1999), 134-53, 151.

67. Joel Lawrence, *Bonhoeffer: A Guide for the Perplexed* (London: T&T Clark, 2010), 49. 37.

68. Eberhard Bethge, *Bonhoeffer: Exile and Martyr*, ed. John W. de Gruchy (New York: The Seabury Press, 1975), 62.

69. Dumas, *Dietrich Bonhoeffer*, 94. 91.

Bonhoeffer – who is often considered to be Christomonist as a theologian more generally[70] – to being described by Jeff Nowers as 'a "Christo-ecclesiologist".'[71] And whilst Nowers is careful to note that pneumatology is 'the bond of Christology and ecclesiology' in Bonhoeffer's theology, he nevertheless considers Bonhoeffer's pneumatology in this regard to be 'latent'.[72] However, a close inspection of how Bonhoeffer understands the coinherence between the Church and Christ which his concept 'Christ existing as church-community' seemingly suggests, might indicate instead that Bonhoeffer's pneumatology is far from 'latent' but in fact deep, and such that it actually conditions his ecclesiology as its most foundational dogmatic *res*.

First, the coinherence of ecclesiology and Christology which the concept 'Christ existing as church-community' suggests is qualified carefully by Bonhoeffer with reference to the doctrine of the ascension. Bonhoeffer writes: 'Christ has ascended into heaven and is now with God, and we still await Christ's coming.'[73] Thus, 'a complete identification between Christ and the church-community cannot be made'.[74] Or as he puts it in his post-doctoral dissertation, 'The tension between "Christ existing as community" and the heavenly Christ, whom we await, persists.'[75] Accordingly, as Michael Mawson notes, reflecting on this tension, 'Even while fully present in the church, Christ himself cannot be reduced to [the church's] presence.'[76] In Bonhoeffer's thought, 'Christ existing as church-community' suggests not, then, that Christ is *only* in the Church – in the sense of his being

---

70. Notwithstanding the divergent hermeneutical keys for reading Bonhoeffer noted above, Christiane Tietz contends that '[i]f there is one consensus in Bonhoeffer studies it is that Bonhoeffer's theology is essentially Christ-oriented', Christiane Tietz, 'The Role of Jesus Christ for Christian Theology', in *Christ, Church and World: New Studies in Bonhoeffer's Theology and Ethics*, ed. Michael Mawson and Philip G. Ziegler (London: T&T Clark/Bloomsbury, 2016), 9–27, 9. This orientation is such that, as Tietz writes elsewhere, 'Christology is the *cantus firmus* of all [Bonhoeffer's] thinking', Christiane Tietz, 'Bonhoeffer's Strong Christology in the Context of Religious Pluralism', in *Interpreting Bonhoeffer: Historical Perspectives, Emerging Issues*, ed. Clifford J. Green and Guy C. Carter (Minneapolis: Fortress Press, 2013), 181–96, 188. Or, in the words of James Woelfel, Christology 'is the golden thread which ties together his works from first to last', James W. Woelfel, *Bonhoeffer's Theology: Classical and Revolutionary* (Nashville: Abingdon Press, 1970), 134.

71. See Jeff Nowers, 'Hegel, Bonhoeffer, and Objective *Geist*: An Architectonic Exegesis of Sanctorum Communio', in *Ontology and Ethics: Bonhoeffer and Contemporary Scholarship*, ed. Adam C. Clark and Michael Mawson (Eugene: Pickwick Publications, 2013), 47–56, 48.

72. See ibid.

73. DBWE 1:140 (DBW 1:86).

74. DBWE 1:140 (DBW 1:86).

75. DBWE 2:112n39 (DBW 2:108n39).

76. Michael Mawson, *Christ Existing as Community: Bonhoeffer's Ecclesiology* (Oxford: Oxford University Press, 2018), 127.

absorbed into it without remainder – but rather that the Church as Christ's body is the form or mode of being which the risen Christ takes in space and time after his ascension.[77] For Bonhoeffer, the events of Christ's ascension and future *parousia* 'categorically rule out any idea of a mystical fusion between church-community and Christ.'[78] Bonhoeffer continues:

> The same Christ who is present in his church-community will return from heaven. In both cases it is the same Lord and it is the same church; in both cases it is the very same body of the one who is present here and now, and the one who will return in the clouds. However, it makes a serious difference whether we are here or there. Thus, both the unity and the distinction are necessary aspects of the same truth.[79]

Critically, and second, in the context of discussing the Church as Christ's body, Bonhoeffer draws specific attention to the pneumatological character of this tensed relation that exists between Christ and the church because of Christ's ascension and future *parousia*: 'Through the Holy Spirit, the crucified and risen Christ exists as the church-community.'[80] Or, as Bonhoeffer writes elsewhere, 'The church-community of Christ is the present Christ *in the Holy Spirit*.'[81] Therefore, with respect to the persistent tension that exists in Bonhoeffer's thought between the heavenly session of Christ and Christ's presence as church-community in space and time, David Höhne's critique that Bonhoeffer 'does not mention how he sees this as being possible'[82] simply will not do. Bonhoeffer is, in fact, clear: in and through God the Holy Spirit, Christ is in heaven even as he exists as church-community in spatio-temporality. The words of Christopher R. J. Holmes are thus apt: 'Jesus' existence as such is pneumatological (spiritual) in nature, meaning his ascended existence is not exhausted in the church.'[83] Whilst Christ *is* wholly present in the Church – the Church is *Christ's* (earthly) body – Christ remains its (heavenly) head, and as such stands over against it.[84] There is, then, according to Bonhoeffer, '[i]dentity and non-identity of the subject [Christ] in connection

---

77. See Tietz, 'The Role of Jesus for Christian Theology', 13; and Christiane Tietz, 'Bonhoeffer and the Ontological Structure of the Church', in *Ontology and Ethics: Bonhoeffer and Contemporary Scholarship*, ed. Adam Clark and Michael Mawson (Eugene, OR: Pickwick Publications, 2013), 44–6, 40–1.
78. DBWE 4:220 (DBW 4:234).
79. DBWE 4:220 (DBW 4:234).
80. DBWE 4:220 (DBW 4:234).
81. DBWE 14:449 (DBW 14:438), emphasis DE.
82. Höhne, *Spirit and Sonship*, 149n43.
83. Christopher R. J. Holmes, 'The Holy Spirit', in *The Oxford Handbook of Dietrich Bonhoeffer*, ed. Philip G. Ziegler and Michael Mawson (Oxford: Oxford University Press, 2019), 168–78, 173.
84. See DBWE 15:422 (DBW 15:413–5) and DBWE 11:302 (DBW 11:272–3).

with the church-community'.[85] Or else, one might say, there is, for Bonhoeffer, a pneumatologically mediated unity-in-distinction by which the risen and ascended Christ exists as church-community.

What is more, for Bonhoeffer, Christ – but critically *only* in virtue of the mediating work of God the Holy Spirit – exists as church-community in a way which accords with Christ's own being. As Bonhoeffer asks in the context of his *Christology* lectures, 'by virtue of what personal ontological structure is Christ present to the church?'[86] Bonhoeffer answers that it is by the *pro-me* (or *pro nobis*) structure of Christ's personal ontology.[87] In other words, the being of Christ's person *is* relatedness; or, put otherwise, Jesus' being is a 'being-for-others'.[88] Pre-eminently, Bonhoeffer see this Christological 'being-for-others' as being displayed in what he describes as the 'vicarious representative action'[89] (*Stellvertretung*) of Jesus Christ in his redemptive history. Here, '[Christ's] death is revealed as the death of death itself, and with this the boundary of history composed by death is abolished, the human body has become the resurrection-body, and the humanity-of-Adam has become the church of Christ.'[90] But what, here, is 'realized' (*realisiert*) in Christ – the possibility, that is, of the creation of new community in Christ in the Church – must yet be 'actualized' in space and time by God the Holy Spirit.[91] That is, the Church is said by Bonhoeffer to be realized or 'chosen' (*erwählt*) in Christ *from* and *for* all eternity: the Church is really and wholly established by God in Christ as an ontological reality, and is – eschatologically speaking – 'already completed'.[92] In this essential sense, the Church (according to Bonhoeffer) is pure and timeless,[93] and Jesus no doubt is '*the foundation* of the church'.[94] At once, however, Bonhoeffer is clear: Jesus is '*not the founder*' of the Church.[95] Indeed, '*the church is to be built within time upon Christ as the firm foundation*.'[96] In this empirical sense, the Church (according to Bonhoeffer) is thus impure and time-bound, and is – eschatologically speaking – 'in the process of growing' towards perfection.[97] It is this actualization of the Church in space and time as the presence or 'body' of Christ – as *Christ's* Church – that Bonhoeffer contends is the work

---

85. DBWE 14:451 (DBW 14:439).
86. DBWE 12:314 (DBW 12:295).
87. See DBWE 12:314 (DBW 12:295).
88. See DBWE 12:314–15 (DBW 12:295–7).
89. DBWE 1:155 (DBW 1:99).
90. DBWE 1:151–2 (DBW 1:95–7).
91. See DBWE 1:145–208 (DBW 1:90–140). For a detailed discussion of Bonhoeffer's 'realization-actualization' paradigm, see Emerton, *God's Church*-Community, 96–109.
92. See DBWE 1:157, 137, 139 (DBW 1:100–101, 85, 85–6).
93. See DBWE 1:153 (DBW 1:97).
94. DBWE 11:301 (DBW 11:271); see DBWE 1:142 (DBW 1:88).
95. See DBWE 11:301 (DBW 11:270–2).
96. DBWE 1:153 (DBW 1:97).
97. See DBWE 1:139, 211 (DBW 1:85–6, 142–3).

of God the Holy Spirit.[98] Bonhoeffer writes: 'In order to build the church as the community-of-God [*Gemeinde Gottes*] in time, God reveals God's own self as *Holy Spirit*. The Holy Spirit is the will of God that gathers individuals together to be the church-community, maintains it, and is at work only within it.'[99] Or, as Bonhoeffer puts it elsewhere: 'It is the Spirit who builds up the church by gathering the individuals, even though in Christ the whole building is already complete. ... The Holy Spirit creates the community ... of the members of the body.'[100] And the Holy Spirit does this (according to Bonhoeffer) by orienting in faith human beings away from themselves and back into community with God and other human beings in (what Bonhoeffer describes as) 'the complete self-forgetfulness of love'.[101] Bonhoeffer continues: 'I and You [now] face each other no longer essentially in a demanding, but in a giving way, revealing their hearts that have been conquered by God's will.'[102] In this 'conquering', the ontic-social relations of the church are rendered unique, Bonhoeffer argues, by the Holy Spirit:[103] the Church is a unique community of love (*Liebegemeinschaft*) because it is the community of the Holy Spirit (*Geistgemeinschaft*),[104] and because the Holy Spirit mediates (to create that community of love as unique) the *Stellvertretung* of Jesus Christ himself.[105]

It is in this way that Bonhoeffer understands the Church's being as being defined by the Church and its members 'being-for-each-other', and necessarily 'with-each-other'.[106] The pneumatologically mediated *Stellvertretung* of Jesus Christ is, therefore, the 'life-principle' (*Lebensprinzip*) both of being in Christ in the Church and of the Church's own corporate relational ontology.[107] As Bonhoeffer writes: 'since the love of God, in Christ's vicarious representative action, restores the community between God and human beings, so the community of human beings

---

98. See DBWE 1:144 (DBW 1:89).

99. DBWE 1:143 (DBW 1:89).

100. DBWE 4:221 (DBW 4:235).

101. See DBWE 1:190 (DBW 1:127–8); see DBWE 14:456 (DBW 14:445): 'The Holy Spirit establishes the relationship between God and human being and between human being and human being.'

102. See DBWE 1:190–1 (DBW 1:127–8).

103. See, for example, DBWE 1:126, and 264 (DBW 1:79–80, and 183).

104. DBWE 1:266 (DBW 1:185).

105. It should be noted that this is a severely truncated and crude over-simplification of the complexities of Bonhoeffer's pneumatological insight into the way in which he sees the Holy Spirit actualizing the being of the Church in space and time and its unique ontic-social relations – not least, because it is silent on how, for Bonhoeffer, the Holy Spirit 'makes use' of the Church's 'objective spirit' as both 'object' and 'means' of its actualizing work (see DBWE 1:208–216, esp. 215 and 216 (DBW 1:140–7, esp 145–7)). For a fuller and more detailed discussion of how I understand Bonhoeffer's pneumatological insight here, see Emerton, *God's Church-Community*, 151–63.

106. See DBWE 1:178 (DBW 1:117).

107. See DBWE 1:143 (DBW 1:88–9).

with each other has also become a reality in love once again.'[108] The vicarious representative action of Jesus Christ makes genuine human community possible, then, as a reality in Christ in the Church – a reality which is actualized, however, only by the Holy Spirit working to create the Church as Christ's body in space and time between Christ's ascension and his future *parousia*. Indeed, the Church *is* Christ's body *only as* the Holy Spirit actualizes in space and time that which is realized in Christ.[109] Or else, one might say, only as the Church is founded on and brought about by the work of the Holy Spirit is the Church continually made manifest as 'Christ existing as church-community'. Holmes echoes this insight thus:

> [T]he Spirit actualizes the new humanity accomplished in Christ and does so in the church, the church being the social and temporal co-ordinate of the Spirit's activity. ... Put differently, the new humanity whose ontological reality is Christ becomes socially and historically real in the community of the church by the work of the Holy Spirit.[110]

Or, as Brendan Leahy comments:

> All the communitarian life of the church is rooted [by Bonhoeffer] in Christ's vicarious action on our behalf. Each person, who is led by the Spirit into actualized ecclesial existence, is enabled to live for and with one another in Christ. The new social sphere that is the church consists in an existence that is not centred on the individual, but rather one that is shared.[111]

What is more, for Bonhoeffer, this shared ecclesial existence is one which is oriented and ordered to live for and with the world: 'The concept of vicarious representative action [*Stellvertretung*] defines this ... relationship most clearly. The Christian community stands in the place in which the world should stand. In this respect it serves the world as vicarious representative; it is there for the world's sake.'[112] And it is this 'worldliness' of the Church, so-to-speak, as a creature of God the Holy Spirit, that Bonhoeffer sees – to recall the force of the scriptural witness noted above – as having its genesis in the event of the church's founding at Pentecost. In the coming of 'the historic [*geschichtliche*] reality of the Holy Spirit', Bonhoeffer argues, and out of the gathered assembly of disciples, the Church is created.[113] Critically, for Bonhoeffer, the gathered assembly of disciples 'itself is not

---

108. DBWE 1:157 (DBW 1:100).
109. See DBWE 11:305 (DBW 11:275–6).
110. Holmes, 'The Holy Spirit', 169.
111. Brendan Leahy, '"Christ Existing as Community": Dietrich Bonhoeffer's Notion of Church', in *Irish Theological Quarterly* 73 (2008): 32–59; 41.
112. DBWE 6:404 (DBW 6:408).
113. See DBWE 14:438 (DBW 14:425–6).

already' the church.[114] The gathered assembly *becomes* the church 'only through the Spirit',[115] for the Holy Spirit constitutes the Church as a new act of creation precisely because 'the Spirit leads the church-community into community with Christ',[116] which necessarily – given the *Stellvertretung* of Christ himself – is community with the world. As Bonhoeffer notes, reflecting on the narrative of Acts 2, the Holy Spirit comes upon the assembly of disciples 'in words comprehensible to *everyone*'[117]; Peter proclaims through the Spirit 'the full and free grace of God, which summons *the people* to action, to repentance, and to new life'[118]; and through the Spirit 'the church-community engages in *missionary* activity.'[119]

In other words, with the coming of the Holy Spirit and the concomitant Spirit-inspired concern for the implementation of the Spirit's act of new creation in the world, the gathered assembly of disciples is turned *outward* – *out* of the house in which they are staying and devoting themselves constantly to building-up a community oriented and ordered, one might say, towards God and itself, and *out towards* the crowd gathered around it.[120] And in this 'turning outward' the gathered assembly of disciples, Bonhoeffer argues, 'breaks into' (*Einbruch*) the world as a missionary *church*-community.[121] Further, in the event of its foundation at Pentecost, and more specifically in the wider articulation of the vocation of this new ecclesial creation in Acts 2.42-47, Bonhoeffer sees 'the beginnings and indications' of the Church's human empirical form and associated vocational function(s):[122] the apostle's teaching is announced; fellowship is created; the breaking of bread and prayers are enabled; wonders and signs are performed; and possessions and goods are shared – and all, according to Bonhoeffer, in and through the Holy Spirit as the establishing subject of the Church and its ministry.[123] The Church, then, as a creature of God the Holy Spirit is, for Bonhoeffer, 'not something unequivocal in the world.'[124] In fact, the Church *is* the Church, argues Bonhoeffer, only when it is with and acts for the world.[125] And the Church is as such precisely because of the structure of Christ's personal ontology in virtue of which Christ exists as church-community by the mediating work of the Holy Spirit. But what, in conclusion,

---

114. DBWE 14:438. (DBW 14:426).
115. DBWE 14:438. (DBW 14:426).
116. DBWE 14:441 (DBW 14:429).
117. DBWE 14:439 (DBW 14:427), emphasis DE.
118. DBWE 14:441 (DBW 14:429), emphasis added and amended DE.
119. DBWE 14:721 (DBW 14:724), emphasis DE.
120. See Acts 1:12-14 and 2:1-2, 6 and 14ff. On the importance of the demarcation between Acts 1 and Acts 2 for ecclesiology, see Greggs, *Dogmatic Ecclesiology Volume One*, li–liii and 12–15.
121. See DBWE 14:724 (DBW 14:726-7).
122. See DBWE 14:443 (DBW 14:430-1).
123. See DBWE 14:331, 443–6, 455–7, 465–6 (DBW 14:312, 430–4, 443–6, 454–6).
124. DBWE 14:439 (DBW 14:427).
125. See DBWE 8:503 (DBW 8:560–1).

might be some of the potential implications of Bonhoeffer's Christologically centred and pneumatologically founded ecclesiology for the Church today?

V. Towards a Christologically Centred and Pneumatologically Founded Ecclesial Reality

Any response to such a question, given the unfinished nature of Bonhoeffer's own theological thinking, can only ever be indicative. That said, three brief points might be ventured if the Church today is to follow the trajectory of Bonhoeffer's Christologically centred and pneumatologically founded ecclesial thinking. First, whenever the Church as 'Christ-existing as church-community' fails to perceive or stand in its place of responsibility for the world, the Church (so-called) ceases to be the Church.[126] This means that the Church must forever be the place in which those outside the Church are summoned to the Church to come under Christ's rule through the Church's unceasing proclamation of God's Word,[127] be it in the Word preached, the Word celebrated in bread broken and wine outpoured, or the Word experienced in proleptic manifestations of new creation in present space and time. But it also means that the Church must become the vicarious burden-bearer of the sins and guilt of the world before God.[128] In this latter sense, and second, the Church as 'Christ existing as church-community' and individual church members must seek to effect in the world Spirit-inspired loving action after the pattern of Christ himself, and thereby become 'a Christ to the other'.[129] As Bonhoeffer extrapolates: 'The hungry person needs bread, the homeless persons need a home, the one deprived of rights needs justice, the lonely person needs community, the undisciplined one needs order, and the slave needs freedom.'[130] To which one could – and indeed should – add: the sins of the Church and its members need bearing and forgiving, and the sins and guilt of the world need taking on by the Church and confessing. Indeed, Bonhoeffer's call to the Church as 'Christ existing as church-community' is to be 'the community of people who, grasped by the power of Christ's grace, acknowledge, confess, and take upon themselves not only their personal sins, but also the Western world's falling away from Jesus Christ'.[131] What might it mean for the Western Church today, then, to understand not only that she is already guilty of her own sins and the sins of the world, but that she must, in fact, actively take on and bear those sins and that guilt? *Metanoia* is perhaps a lost art in today's Church, but for Bonhoeffer it is how one

---

126. See DBWE 16:543 (DBW 16:553–4).
127. See DBWE 16:546 (DBW 16:556–7) and DBWE 6:396 (DBW 6: 399–400).
128. See DBWE 4:88 (DBW 4:81–2); see DBWE 5:100–103 (DBW 5:84–8).
129. DBWE 1:183 (DBW 1:121).
130. DBWE 6:163 (DBW 6:155).
131. DBWE 6:135 (DBW 6:126).

stays awake with Christ in Gethsemane and how one learns to become Christian.[132] Third, and critically, however, if the Church is to stand in its place of responsibility for the world then it must pursue these aspects of its vocation wholly unconcerned for its own self-preservation. As Michael Jinkins notes aptly: 'the church is most attractive when it pursues its vocation unconcerned with its own survival'.[133] This, I think, Bonhoeffer knew well. As the creature of God the Holy Spirit, the Church is 'Christ existing as church-community', and as such must be concerned not with seeking anxiously after its own institutional survival, but with embodying and implementing the form of Christ's body in the world that is the object of Christ's redemptive history.[134] Ultimately, Bonhoeffer's Christologically centred and pneumatologically founded ecclesiology bids the Church to remember that the Church is not an end itself, but a means to an end: and that end is God's will to rule in the world in love.

---

132. See DBWE 8:486 (DBW 8:541–3).
133. Michael Jinkins, *The Church Faces Death: Ecclesiology in a Post-modern Context* (Oxford: Oxford University Press, 1999), 32.
134. See DBWE 6:63 (DBW 6:48).

CUMULATIVE BIBLIOGRAPHY

Bonhoeffer's Works

Bonhoeffer's works [DBWE / DBW] are cited according to the abbreviations introduced at the beginning of this volume. Other editions cited in this volume are listed below for completion:
Bonhoeffer, Dietrich. 'Concerning the Christian Idea of God [CCIG]'. *JR* 12 (1932): 177–85.
Bonhoeffer, Dietrich. *Christology*, translated by John Bowden. London: Collins, 1966.
Bonhoeffer, Dietrich. *Gesammelte Schriften: Band III, Theologie – Gemeinde: Vorlesungen – Briefe – Gespräche, 1927–1944*, edited by Eberhard Bethge. München: Chr. Kaiser Verlag, 1966.
Bonhoeffer, Dietrich. *Zettelnotizen für eine 'Ethik': Ergänzungsband zu DBW 6*, edited by Ilse Tödt. München: Chr. Kaiser Verlag, 1993.

Other Works

Abromeit, Hans-Jürgen. *Das Geheimnis Christi: Dietrich Bonhoeffers erfahrungsbezogene Christologie*. Neukirchen-Vluyn: Neukirchner Verlag, 1991.
Albrecht, Christian and Reiner Anselm. *Öffentlicher Protestantismus zur aktuellen Debatte um gesellschaftliche Präsenz und politische Aufgaben des evangelischen Christentums*. Zürich: Theologischer Verlag Zürich, 2017.
Aquinas, Thomas. *Summa Theologiae*, edited and translated by Thomas Gilby O.P, Cambridge: Eyre and Spottiswoode, 1964.
Avis, Paul. *Jesus and the Church: The Foundation of the Church in the New Testament and Modern Theology*. Theological Foundations of the Christian Church, vol. 1. London: T&T Clark/Bloomsbury, 2021.
Balthasar, Hans Urs von. *Mysterium Paschale*, translated by O. P. Aiden Nichols, Grand Rapids: Eerdmans, 1996.
Barker, H. Gaylon. *The Cross of Reality: Luther's Theologia Crucis and Bonhoeffer's Christology*. Minneapolis: Fortress Press, 2015.
Barreto, Raimundo. 'The Church and Society Movement and the Roots of Public Theology in Brazilian Protestantism'. *International Journal of Public Theology* 6, no. 1 (2012): 70–98.
Barth, Friederike. *Die Wirklichkeit des Guten: Dietrich Bonhoeffers 'Ethik' und ihr philosophischer Hintergrund*. Tübingen: Mohr Siebeck, 2011.
Barth, Heinrich. 'Kierkegaard, der Denker: Vier Vorlesungen'. *Zwischen den Zeiten* 4, no. 3 (1926): 194–234.
Barth, Karl. *Church Dogmatics*. London and New York: T&T Clark International, 1956ff.
Barth, Karl. *Die Christliche Dogmatik im Entwurf: Die Lehre vom Worte Gottes. Prolegomena zur Christlichen Dogmatik*, edited by Gerhard Sauter. Karl Barth Gesamtausgabe. Zürich: Theologischer Verlag Zürich, 1982.

Barth, Karl. *Die Christliche Lehre nach dem Heidelberger Katechismus*. München: Chr. Kaiser Verlag, 1949.
Barth, Karl. *Kirchliche Dogmatik*. Zollikon-Zürich: Evangelischer Verlag A.G., 1932ff.
Bataringaya, Pascal, Traugott Jähnichen, Oliver Munyansanga, and Clemens Wustmans (eds). *Dietrich Bonhoeffer. Life and Legacy*. Zürich: LIT Verlag, 2019.
Bauckham, Richard. '"Only the Suffering God Can Help": Divine Possibility in Modern Theology'. *Themelios* 9, no. 3 (April 1984): 6–12.
Bauke-Ruegg, Jan. *Die Allmacht Gottes: Systematisch-theologische Erwägungen zwischen Metaphysik, Postmoderne und Poesie*. Berlin: De Gruyter, 1998.
Bayer, Oswald. 'Das Wort ward Fleisch'. In *Creator Est Creatura: Luthers Christologie als Lehre von der Idiomenkommunikation*, edited by Oswald Bayer and Benjamin Gleede, 5–34. Berlin: De Gruyter, 2007.
Bayer, Oswald. *Martin Luther's Theology: A Contemporary Interpretation*. Grand Rapids: W. B. Eerdmans, 2008.
Bedford-Strohm, Heinrich. 'Dietrich Bonhoeffer als öffentlicher Theologe'. *Evangelische Theologie* 69, no. 5 (2009): 329–41.
Bell, Daniel M. 'Postliberalism and Radical Orthodoxy'. In *Cambridge Companion to Political Theology*, edited by Craig Hovery and Elizabeth Phillips, 110–32. Cambridge: Cambridge University Press, 2015.
Benjamin, Walter. 'On the Concept of History'. In *Selected Writings: vol. 4: 1938–1940*, edited by Michael W. Jennings and Howard Eiland, 389–400. Cambridge, MA: Harvard University Press, 2006.
Benjamin, Walter. 'One-Way Street'. In *Selected Writings: vol. 1: 1913–1926*, edited by Michael W. Jennings and Howard Eiland, 444–88. Cambridge, MA: Harvard University Press, 2006.
Bethge, Eberhard. 'Bonhoeffer's Christology and His "Religionless Christianity"'. *Union Seminary Quarterly Review* 23, no. 1 (1967): 61–77. Reprinted in *Bonhoeffer in a World Come of Age*, edited by Peter Vorkink II, 46–72. Philadelphia: Fortress Press, 1968.
Bethge, Eberhard. *Bonhoeffer: Exile and Martyr*, edited by John W. de Gruchy. New York: The Seabury Press, 1975.
Bethge, Eberhard. 'The Challenge of Dietrich Bonhoeffer's Life and Theology'. In *World Come of Age: A Symposium on Dietrich Bonhoeffer*, edited by R. Gregor Smith, 22–88. London: Collins, 1967.
Bethge, Eberhard. *Dietrich Bonhoeffer: A Biography*, revised and edited by Victoria Barnett. Minneapolis: Fortress Press, 2000.
Bethge, Eberhard. *Dietrich Bonhoeffer: Theologe – Christ – Zeitgenosse*. München: Chr. Kaiser Verlag, 1967.
Bethge, Eberhard. *Dietrich Bonhoeffer: Eine Biographie*. 8. Auflage. Gütersloh: Kaiser, 1994.
Bindley, Th. Herbert (ed.). *The Oecumenical Documents of the Faith*. Westport: Greenwood Press, 1950.
Bismarck, Ruth-Alice von and Ulrich Kabitz (ed.). *Love Letters from Cell 92: The Correspondence between Dietrich Bonhoeffer and Maria von Wedemeyer 1943–45*. Nashville: Abingdon Press, 1992.
Boniface, Tim. *Jesus, Transcendence, and Generosity: Christology and Transcendence in Hans Frei and Dietrich Bonhoeffer*. Lanham: Lexington Books/Fortress Academic, 2018.
Brunner, Emil. *The Christian Doctrine of the Church, Faith, and the Consummation: Dogmatics Volume III*, translated by David Cairns. London: Lutterworth Press, 1962.
Brunner, Emil. *Der Mittler: Zur Besinnung über den Christusglauben*. Tübingen: Mohr, 1927.

Burtness, James H. 'Als ob es Gott nicht gäbe: Bonhoeffer, Barth und das lutherische finitum capax infiniti'. In *Bonhoeffer und Luther*, edited by Christian Gremmels, 167–83. München: Chr. Kaiser, 1983.
Calvin, John. *Institutes of the Christian Religion*, vol. 2, edited by John T. McNeill and translated by Ford Lewis Battles. Louisville: Westminster John Knox Press, 2011.
Carson, Ronald A. 'The Motifs of "Kenosis" and "Imitatio" in the Work of Dietrich Bonhoeffer, with an Excursus on the "Communicatio Idiomatum"'. *Journal of the American Academy of Religion* 43, no. 3 (1975): 542–53.
Carter, J. Kameron. *Race: A Theological Account*. Oxford/New York: Oxford University Press, 2008.
Clements, Keith W. *The Theology of Ronald Gregor Smith*. Leiden: Brill, 1986.
Chapman, G. Clarke, Jr. 'Hope and the Ethics of Formation: Moltmann as Interpreter of Bonhoeffer'. *Studies in Religion/Sciences Religieuses* 12 (1983): 449–60.
Chul-Han, Byung. *The Burnout Society*. Redwood City, CA: Stanford University Press, 2015.
Coakley, Sarah. *God, Sexuality, and the Self: An Essay 'On the Trinity'*. Cambridge: Cambridge University Press, 2013.
Coakley, Sarah. 'What Does Chalcedon Solve and What Does It Not? Some Reflections on the Status and Meaning of the Chalcedonian "Definition"'. In *The Incarnation: An Interdisciplinary Symposium on the Incarnation of the Son of God*, edited by Stephen T. Davis et al., 143–63. Oxford: Oxford University Press, 2002.
Cockayne, Joshua. *Contemporary with Christ: Kierkegaard and Second-Personal Spirituality*. Waco: Baylor University Press, 2020.
Cone, James H. *The Cross and The Lynching Tree*. New York: Orbis Books, 2011.
Congar, Yves. *I Believe in the Holy Spirit*, vol. 2, translated by David Smith. New York: The Crossroad Publishing Company, 2015.
Dabrock, Peter. 'Responding to "Wirklichkeit": Reclaiming Bonhoeffer's Approach to Theological Ethics between Mystery and the Formation of the World'. In *Mysteries in the Theology of Dietrich Bonhoeffer. A Copenhagen Bonhoeffer Symposium*, edited by Kirsten Busch Nielsen, Ulrik Nissen, and Christiane Tietz, 49–80. Göttingen: Vandenhoeck & Ruprecht, 2007.
Dabrock, Peter. 'Wirklichkeit verantworten: Der responsive Ansatz theologischer Ethik bei Dietrich Bonhoeffer'. In *Verantwortungsethik als Theologie des Wirklichen*, edited by Wolfgang Nethöfel, Peter Dabrock, and Siegfried Keil, 117–58. Göttingen: Vandenhoeck & Ruprecht, 2009.
Dalferth, Ingolf. *Der auferweckte Gekreuzigte: Zur Grammatik der Christologie*. Tübingen: Mohr Siebeck, 1994.
Danz, Christian. *Grundprobleme der Christologie*. Tübingen: Mohr Siebeck, 2013.
DeJonge, Michael P. *Bonhoeffer on Resistance: The Word against the Wheel*. Oxford: Oxford University Press, 2018.
DeJonge, Michael P. *Bonhoeffer's Reception of Luther*. Oxford: Oxford University Press, 2017.
DeJonge, Michael P. *Bonhoeffer's Theological Formation: Berlin, Barth, and Protestant Theology*. Oxford: Oxford University Press, 2012.
De Lange, Frits. 'Aristocratic Christendom: On Bonhoeffer and Nietzsche'. In *Bonhoeffer and Continental Thought: Cruciform Philosophy*, edited by Brian Gregor and Jens Zimmermann, 73–83. Bloomington: Indiana University Press, 2009.
de Lange, Frits. '"Miteinander, Füreinander, Gegeneinander": Bonhoeffers Mandatenlehre in einer pluralistischen Gesellschaft'. *Bonhoeffer Rundbrief: Mitteilungen der internationalen Bonhoeffer-Gesellschaft, Sektion Bundesrepublik Deutschland* 54 (1997): 13–32.

De Lubac, Henri. *The Church: Paradox and Mystery*, translated by James R. Dunne. Shannon: Ecclesia Press, 1969.
De Lubac, Henri. *The Splendour of the Church*. translated by Michael Mason. London: Sheed and Ward, 1956.
Dewey, John. *Logic. The Theory of Inquiry*. New York: Henry Holt and Company, 1938.
Dewey, John. *The Quest for Certainty: A Study of the Relation of Knowledge and Action*. Gifford Lectures 1929. London: George Allen & Unwin Ltd, 1930.
Dodson, Chris. *The God Who Is Given: Dietrich Bonhoeffer's Sacramental Theology and Religionless Christianity*. Lanham: Lexington Books/Fortress Academic, 2021.
Dramm, Sabine. *Dietrich Bonhoeffer: An Introduction to His Thought*, translated by Thomas Rice. Peabody: Hendrickson Publishers, 2007.
Dumas, André. *Dietrich Bonhoeffer: Theologian of Reality*, translated by Robert McAfee Brown. London: SCM Press, 1971.
Ebeling, Gerhard. 'The "Non-Religious Interpretation of Biblical Concepts"'. In *Word and Faith*, ed. Gerhard Ebeling, translated by James W. Leitch, 98–161. London: SCM Press, 1963.
Eco, Umberto. *Die Grenzen der Interpretation*, translated by Günter Memmert. München: Carl Hanser Verlag, 1992.
Emerton, David. *God's Church-Community: The Ecclesiology of Dietrich Bonhoeffer*. London: T&T Clark/Bloomsbury, 2020.
Emery, Gilles. 'The Immutability of the God of Love and the Problem of Language Concerning the "Suffering God"'. In *Divine Impassibility and the Mystery of Human Suffering*, edited by James F. Keating and Joseph Thomas White, 27–76. Grand Rapids: Eerdmans, 2009.
Essen, Georg. 'Geschichte – Metaphysik – Anthropologie: Diskurskonstellationen der Christologie in der Moderne: Eine katholisch-theologische Vergewisserung'. In *Dogmatische Christologie in der Moderne: Problemkonstellationen gegenwärtiger Forschung*, edited by Christian Danz and Georg Essen, 9–18. Regensburg: Pustet, 2019.
Farrow, Douglas. *Ascension & Ecclesia: On the Significance of the Doctrine of the Ascension for Ecclesiology and Christian Cosmology*. Edinburgh: T&T Clark, 1999.
Feil, Ernst. *The Theology of Dietrich Bonhoeffer*, translated by Martin Rumscheidt. Philadelphia: Fortress Press, 1985.
Fiddes, Paul. *The Creative Suffering of God*. Oxford: Oxford University Press, 1988.
Fischer, Johannes. 'Gefahr der Unduldsamkeit: Die "Öffentliche Theologie" der EKD ist problematisch'. *Zeitzeichen* 17, no. 5 (2016): 43–5.
Floyd, Wayne. 'Encounter with an Other: Immanuel Kant and G. W. F. Hegel in the Theology of Dietrich Bonhoeffer'. In *Bonhoeffer's Intellectual Formation*, edited by Peter Frick, 83–120. Tübingen: Mohr Siebeck, 2008.
Floyd, Wayne Whitson. *Theology and the Dialectics of Otherness: On Reading Bonhoeffer and Adorno*. Lanham: University Press of America, 1988.
Frankl, Viktor. *Man's Search for Meaning*. New York: Washington Square Press, 1984.
Frei, Hans. *The Identity of Jesus Christ: The Hermeneutical Bases of Dogmatic Theology*. Philadelphia: Fortress Press, 1975.
Frick, Peter. 'Friedrich Nietzsche's Aphorisms and Dietrich Bonhoeffer's Theology'. In *Bonhoeffer's Intellectual Formation*, edited by Peter Frick, 175–99. Tübingen: Mohr Siebeck, 2008.
Gaine, Simon O.P. *Did the Saviour See the Father?* London: Bloomsbury, 2015.
Galot, Jean. *Dieu Souffre-t-il?* Paris: P. Lethielleux, 1976.

Gavrilyuk, Paul. *The Suffering of the Impassible God: The Dialectics of Patristic Thought.* Oxford: Oxford University Press, 2004.
Godsey, John D. *The Theology of Dietrich Bonhoeffer.* London: SCM Press, 1960.
Goetz, Ronald. 'The Suffering God: The Rise of a New Orthodoxy'. *Christian Century* 103, no. 13 (16 April 1986): 385–9.
Grebe, Matthias. 'Suffering, Sin-bearing, and *Stellvertretung*: Revisiting the Theology of Dietrich Bonhoeffer'. In *Polyphonie der Theologie: Verantwortung und Widerstand in Kirche und Politik*, edited by Matthias Grebe, 175–93. Stuttgart: Kohlhammer, 2019.
Green, Clifford J. *Bonhoeffer: A Theology of Sociality.* Rev. ed. Grand Rapids: Eerdmans, 1999.
Green, Clifford J. 'Editor's Introduction to the English Edition'. In *DBWE* 1: 1–20.
Green, Clifford J. 'Ethical Theology and Contextual Ethics: New Perspectives on Bonhoeffer's Ethics'. In *Religion im Erbe. Dietrich Bonhoeffer und die Zukunftsfähigkeit des Christentums*, edited by Christian Gremmels and Wolfgang Huber, 255–86. Gütersloh: Chr.Kaiser/Gütersloher Verlagshaus, 2022.
Green, Clifford J. and DeJonge, Michael P. (eds). *Theology and Third Reich: The Bonhoeffer Reader*, vol. 4. Philadelphia: Fortress Press, 2013.
Green, Clifford J. and Guy C. Carter (eds). *Interpreting Bonhoeffer: Historical Perspectives, Emerging Issues.* Minneapolis: Fortress Press, 2013.
Greggs, Tom. *Barth and Bonhoeffer as Contributors to a Post-Liberal Ecclesiology: Essays of Hope for a Fallen and Complex World.* London: T&T Clark, 2022.
Greggs, Tom. 'Bearing Sin in the Church: The Ecclesial Hamartiology of Bonhoeffer'. In *Christ, Church and World: New Studies in Bonhoeffer's Theology and Ethics*, edited by Michael Mawson and Philip G. Ziegler, 77–99. London: T&T Clark/Bloomsbury, 2016.
Greggs, Tom. *Dogmatic Ecclesiology Volume One: The Priestly Catholicity of the Church.* Grand Rapids: Baker Academic, 2019.
Greggs, Tom. 'Ecclesiology'. In *The Oxford Handbook of Dietrich Bonhoeffer*, edited by Michael Mawson and Philip Ziegler, 225–40. Oxford: Oxford University Press, 2019.
Greggs, Tom. 'Proportion and Topography in Ecclesiology: A Working Paper on the Dogmatic Location of the Doctrine of the Church'. In *Theological Theology: Essays in Honour of John B. Webster*, edited by R. David Nelson, Darren Sarisky, and Justin Stratis, 89–106. London: T&T Clark/Bloomsbury, 2015.
Greggs, Tom. *Theology against Religion: Constructive Dialogues with Bonhoeffer and Barth.* London: T&T Clark, 2011.
Gregory of Nyssa. *De hominis opificio. Patrologia Graeca* 44, edited by Claude Blume. Paris: Classiques Garnier Numérique, 2006.
Gregory of Nyssa. *Nicene and Post-Nicene Fathers: Second Series Volume V Gregory of Nyssa: Dogmatic Treatises*, edited by Philip Schaff and Rev. Henry Wallace. New York, NY: Cosimo Classics, 2007.
Grillmeier Aloys SJ, in collaboration with Theresia Hainthaler. 'Chapter One: "One of the Trinity Was Crucified"'. In *Christ in Christian Tradition: From the Council of Chalcedon (451) to Gregory the Great (590–604). Part Two: The Church of Constantinople in the Sixth Century*, translated by John Cawte and Pauline Allen, 317–43. Westminster: John Knox, 1975.
Gritsch, Eric W. and Robert W. Jenson. *Lutheranism: The Theological Movement and Its Confessional Writings.* Philadelphia: Fortress, 1976.
Gunton, Colin. *Christ and Creation.* Grand Rapids, MI: Eerdmans, 1992.
Guyer, Paul. *Kant.* London: Taylor & Francis, 2014.

Habermas, Jürgen. 'Religion in der Öffentlichkeit. Kognitive Voraussetzungen für den "öffentlichen Vernunftgebrauch" religiöser und säkularer Bürger'. In *Zwischen Naturalismus und Religion. Philosophische Aufsätze*, 117–84. Frankfurt am Main: Suhrkamp, 2009.

Hamilton, Don. 'When My Dad Killed God'. *The Christian Century*, 15 July 2022, https://www.christiancentury.org/article/first-person/when-my-dad-killed-god, accessed July 2022.

Hamilton, Nadine. *Dietrich Bonhoeffers Hermeneutik der Responsivität: Ein Kapitel Schriftlehre im Anschluss an 'Schöpfung und Fall'*. Göttingen: Vandenhoeck & Ruprecht, 2016.

Hamilton, William. 'The Death of God Theologies Today'. In *Radical Theology and the Death of God*, edited by Thomas J. J. Altizer and William Hamilton, 23–50. Indianapolis: Bobbs-Merrill, 1966.

Hamilton, William. *The New Essence of Christianity*. London: Darton, Longman & Todd, 1961.

Hamilton, William. 'The Shape of Radical Theology'. *The Christian Century*, 82 (6 October 1965): 1219–22.

Hamilton, William. *On Taking God out of the Dictionary*. New York: McGraw-Hill, 1974.

Harasta, Eva. 'Bonhoeffer's Lutheran Ecclesiology and Inter-Religious Dialogue: A Dogmatic Reading of Bonhoeffer'. In *Bonhoeffer and Interpretative Theory: Essays on Methods and Understanding*, edited by Peter Frick, 239–50. Frankfurt am Main: Peter Lang, 2013.

Harnack, Adolf von. *History of Dogma*, vol. 3. New York: Russel; Russell, 1958.

Harnack, Adolf von. *History of Dogma*, vol. 4. New York: Russel; Russell, 1958.

Harnack, Adolf von. *Lehrbuch der Dogmengeschichte: Die Entstehung des kirchlichen Dogmas*. Unveränderter reprografischer Nachdruck der 4., neu durcharbeiteten und vermehrten Auflage, Tübingen 1909. Vol. 1. Darmstadt: Wissenschaftliche Buchgesellschaft, 1980.

Harnack, Adolf von. *Lehrbuch der Dogmengeschichte: Die Entwicklung des kirchlichen Dogmas I*. Unveränderter reprografischer Nachdruck der 4., neu durcharbeiteten und vermehrten Auflage, Tübingen 1909. Vol. 2. Darmstadt: Wissenschaftliche Buchgesellschaft, 1980.

Harnack, Adolf von. *What Is Christianity?*. New York and Evanston: Harper & Row, 1971.

Haußmann, Werner, Andrea Roth, Susanne Schwarz and Christa Tribula (eds). *EinFach Übersetzen: Theologie und Religionspädagogik in der Öffentlichkeit und für die Öffentlichkeit*. Stuttgart: Kohlhammer Verlag, 2019.

Heidegger, Martin. *Being and Time*, translated by Joan Stambaugh. Albany: State University of New York Press, 1996.

Henkys, Jürgen. *Dietrich Bonhoeffers Gefängnisgedichte: Beiträge zu ihrer Interpretation*. Berlin: Evangelische Verlagsanstalt Berlin, 1986.

Herodotus. *Histories: Book 1*, edited by Carolyn Dewald and Rosaria Vignolo Munson. Cambridge: Cambridge University Press, 2022.

Heschel, Abraham J. *The Prophets*. New York: Harper and Row, 1962.

Hick, John (ed.). *The Myth of God Incarnate*. London: SCM Press, 1977.

Hirsch, Emanuel. *Jesus Christus der Herr: Theologische Vorlesungen*. 2. fast unveränd. Aufl. Göttingen: Vandenhoeck & Ruprecht, 1929.

Höhne, David A. *Spirit and Sonship: Colin Gunton's Theology of Particularity and the Holy Spirit*. Farnham: Routledge, 2016.

Hofheinz, Marco. 'Der geistgesalbte Christus. Trinitätstheologische Erwägungen zur umstrittenen Geistchristologie'. *Evangelische Theologie* 72 (2012): 337–56.
Höhne, Florian. *Öffentliche Theologie: Begriffsgeschichte und Grundfragen*. Leipzig: Evangelische Verlagsanstalt, 2015.
Höhne, Florian and Frederike van Oorschot (eds). *Grundtexte der Öffentlichen Theologie*. Leipzig: Evangelisches Verlagsanstalt, 2015.
Holl, Karl. 'Luther'. In *Gesammelte Aufsätze zur Kirchengeschichte*. 6. neu durchges. Aufl. Vol. 1. Tübingen: Mohr, 1932.
Holl, Karl. *What Did Luther Understand by Religion?* Philadelphia: Fortress Press, 1977.
Holmes, Christopher. 'Bonhoeffer and Reformed Christology: Towards a Trinitarian Supplement'. *Theology Today* 71, no. 1 (2014): 28–42.
Holmes, Christopher R. J. 'The Holy Spirit'. In *The Oxford Handbook of Dietrich Bonhoeffer*, edited by Philip G. Ziegler and Michael Mawson, 168–78. Oxford: Oxford University Press, 2019.
Hopper, David H. *A Dissent on Bonhoeffer*. Philadelphia: The Westminster Press, 1975.
Huber, Wolfgang. *Dietrich Bonhoeffer: Auf dem Weg zur Freiheit*. München: C. H. Beck, 2019.
Huber, Wolfgang. *Ethik: Die Grundfragen unseres Lebens von der Geburt bis zum Tod*. München: C. H. Beck, 2013.
Huber, Wolfgang. *Konflikt und Konsens: Studien zur Ethik der Verantwortung*. München: Chr. Kaiser Verlag, 1990.
Hultegren, Arland J. 'The Church as the Body of Christ: Engaging an Image in the New Testament'. *Word & World* 22, no. 2 (2002): 124–32.
Janz, Paul. *God the Mind's Desire*. Cambridge: Cambridge University Press, 2004.
Jenson, Matt. 'Real Presence: Contemporaneity in Bonhoeffer's Christology'. *Scottish Journal of Theology* 58 (2005): 143–60.
Jenson, Robert W. *Systematic Theology, vol. 1. The Triune God*. Oxford: Oxford University Press, 2001.
Jenson, Robert W. *Systematic Theology, vol. 2. The Works of God*. New York: Oxford University Press, 1999.
Jinkins, Michael. *The Church Faces Death: Ecclesiology in a Post-modern Context*. Oxford: Oxford University Press, 1999.
Johnson, Elizabeth. *She Who Is: The Mystery of God in Feminist Theological Discourse*. New York: The Crossroad Publishing Company, 1992.
Jüngel, Eberhard. *God's Being Is in Becoming: The Trinitarian Being of God in the Theology of Karl Barth*, translated by John Webster. Edinburgh: T&T Clark, 2001.
Jüngel, Eberhard. 'Vom Tod des lebendigen Gottes'. *Zeitschrift für Theologie und Kirche* 65 (1968): 93–116.
Karttunen, Tomi. 'Die Bedeutung der Berliner Zeit für das Denkmodell Dietrich Bonhoeffers'. In *Dietrich Bonhoeffer – Orte seiner Theologie*, 45–59. Paderborn et al: Ferdinand Schöningh, 2008.
Karttunen, Tomi. 'Die Luther-Lektüre Bonhoeffers'. In *Bonhoeffer und Luther: Zentrale Themen ihrer Theologie*, edited by Klaus Grünwaldt, 9–31. Hannover: Amt der VELKD, 2007.
Käsemann, Ernst. *Church Conflicts: The Cross, Apocalyptic, and Political Resistance*, edited by Ry O. Siggelkow, translated by Roy A. Harrisville. Grand Rapids: Baker Academic, 2021.
Kelly, Geffrey B. 'Kierkegaard as "Antidote" and as Impact on Dietrich Bonhoeffer's Concept of Christian Discipleship'. In *Bonhoeffer's Intellectual Formation: Theology and Philosophy in His Thought*, edited by Peter Frick, 145–56. Tübingen: Mohr Siebeck, 2008.

Kierkegaard, Søren. *The Book on Adler*, edited by Howard V. Hong and Edna H. Hong. Princeton: Princeton University Press, 1998.
Kierkegaard, Søren. *Gesammelte Werke*, edited by Emanuel Hirsch et al. Düsseldorf: Eugen Dietrichs Verlag, 1986–96.
Kierkegaard, Søren. *Concluding Unscientific Postscript to Philosophical [CUP]*, edited by Howard V. Hong and Edna H. Hong. Princeton: Princeton University Press, 1992.
Kierkegaard, Søren. *Judge for Yourself [JFY]*, edited by Howard V. Hong and Edna H. Hong. Princeton: Princeton University Press, 1990.
Kierkegaard, Søren. *Philosophical Fragments [PF]*, edited by Howard V. Hong and Edna H. Hong. Princeton: Princeton University Press, 1985.
Kierkegaard, Søren. *Practice in Christianity [PC]*, edited by Howard V. Hong and Edna H. Hong. Princeton: Princeton University Press, 1991.
Kierkegaard, Søren. *The Sickness unto Death [SUD]*, edited by Howard V. Hong and Edna H. Hong. Princeton: Princeton University Press, 1980.
Kirkpatrick, Matthew D. *Attacks on Christendom in a World Come of Age: Kierkegaard, Bonhoeffer, and the Question of 'Religionless Christianity'*. Eugene: Pickwick Publications, 2011.
Kitamori, Kazoh. *Theology of the Pain of God*. London: SCM Press, 1966.
Kitamori, Kazoh. *Theology of the Pain of God*, translated by Shinkyo Shuppansha. Richmond: John Knox Press, 1965.
Körtner, Ulrich H. J. *Diakonie und öffentliche Theologie: Diakoniewissenschaftliche Studien*. Göttingen: Vandenhoeck & Ruprecht, 2017.
Koslowski, Jutta (ed.). *Aus dem Leben der Familie Bonhoeffer: Die Aufzeichnungen von Dietrich Bonhoeffers jüngster Schwester Susanne Dreß*. Gütersloh: Gütersloher Verlagshaus, 2018.
Krötke, Wolf. 'Der begegnende Gott und der Glaube: Zum theologischen Schwerpunkt der Christologievorlesung D. Bonhoeffers'. In *Bonhoeffer-Studien: Beiträge zur Theologie und Wirkungsgeschichte Dietrich Bonhoeffers*, edited by Albrecht Schönherr and Wolf Krötke, 25–35. München: Chr. Kaiser, 1985.
Krötke, Wolf. *Karl Barth and Dietrich Bonhoeffer: Theologians for a Post-Christian World*, translated by John P. Burgess. Grand Rapids, MI: Baker Academic, 2019.
LaCugna, Catherine Mowry. *God For Us: The Trinity and the Christian Life*. New York: HarperCollins, 2000.
Law, David R. 'The Existential Chalcedonian Christology of Kierkegaard's Practice in Christianity'. *KSY* (2010): 129–52.
Law, David R. *Kierkegaard's Kenotic Christology*. Oxford: Oxford University Press, 2013.
Lawrence, Joel B. *Bonhoeffer: A Guide for the Perplexed*. London: T&T Clark, 2010.
Leahy, Brendan. '"Christ Existing as Community": Dietrich Bonhoeffer's Notion of Church'. *Irish Theological Quarterly* 73 (2008): 32–59.
Lehmann, Paul L. 'The Concreteness of Theology: Reflections on the Conversation between Barth and Bonhoeffer'. In *Footnotes to a Theology: The Karl Barth Colloquium of 1972*, edited by H. Martin Rumscheidt, 53–76. Halifax, NS: Corporation for the Publication of Academic Studies in Religion in Canada, 1972.
Lehmkühler, Karsten. 'Christologie'. In *Bonhoeffer und Luther: Zentrale Themen ihrer Theologie*, edited by Klaus Grünwaldt, 55–78. Hannover: Amt der VELKD, 2007.
Levering, Matthew. *Did Jesus Rise from the Dead?* Oxford: Oxford University Press, 2019.
Link, Christian. 'Die Entscheidung der Christologie Calvins und ihre theologische Bedeutung: Das sogenannte Extra-Calvinisticum'. *Evangelische Theologie* 47, no. 2 (1987): 97–119.

Loisy, Alfred. *The Gospel and the Church*. New York: Prometheus, 1988.
Luther, Martin. 'Heidelberg Disputation'. In *Luther's Works 31: Career of the Reformer I*, edited by Harold J. Grimm, 39–70. Philadelphia: Fortress, 1957.
Luther, Martin. 'The Heidelberg Disputation'. In *The Selected Writings of Martin Luther, 1517–1520*, edited by Theodore G. Tappert, 61–96. Minneapolis: Fortress, 2007.
Luther, Martin. 'Confession Concerning Christ's Supper (1528)'. In *Luther's Works 37: Word and Sacrament III*, edited and translated by Robert H. Fischer, 151–372. Philadelphia: Muhlenberg Press, 1961.
Luther, Martin. 'On the Councils of the Church'. In *Luther's Works 41: Church and Ministry 3*, edited by Eric W. Gritsch. Minneapolis: Fortress, 1966.
Luther, Martin. 'Disputationen 1539/45'. In *D. Martin Luthers Werke. Kritische Gesamtausgabe*. WA 39.II: Schriften / Werke. Weimar: H. Böhlau Nachfolger, 1883–2009.
Luther, Martin. 'The Disputation Concerning the Passage "the Word Was Made Flesh" (John 1:14) [1539]'. In *Luther's Works 38: Word and Sacrament IV*, translated by Martin E. Lehmann, 235–77. Philadelphia: Fortress Press, 1971.
Mackinnon, Donald. *Borderlands of Theology and Other Essays*. Eugene: Wipf & Stock, 2011.
Maluleke, Tinyiko Sam. 'Reflections and Resources: The Elusive Public of Public Theology: A Response to William Storrar'. *International Journal of Public Theology* 5, no. 1 (March 17, 2011): 79–89.
Markschies, Christoph Johannes. *Hellenisierung des Christentums: Sinn und Unsinn einer historischen Deutungskategorie*. Leipzig: Evangelische Verlagsanstalt, 2021.
Marsh, Charles. *Evangelical Anxiety*. New York: HarperCollins Publishers, 2022.
Marty, Martin E. *Dietrich Bonhoeffer's Letters and Papers from Prison: A Biography*. Princeton: Princeton University Press, 2011.
Mascall, E. L. *Whatever Happened to the Human Mind?* London: SPCK, 1980.
Maurer, Ernstpeter. *Der lebendige Gott: Texte zur Trinitätslehre*. Gütersloh: Gütersloher Verlagshaus, 1999.
Mawson, Michael. *Christ Existing as Community: Bonhoeffer's Ecclesiology*. Oxford: Oxford University Press, 2018.
Mawson, Michael. 'Scripture'. In *The Oxford Handbook of Dietrich Bonhoeffer*, edited by Michael Mawson and Philip Ziegler, 123–36. Oxford: Oxford University Press, 2019.
Mawson, Michael. 'Studying Theology in a Time of Crisis: A Manifesto'. In *Letters to a Young Theologian*, edited by Henco van der Westhuizen, 234–44. Minneapolis: Fortress, 2022.
Mawson, Michael and Philip Ziegler (eds). *Christ, Church and World: New Studies in Bonhoeffer's Theology and Ethics*. London: T&T Clark, 2016.
Maximos the Confessor. 'Ambiguum 7'. In *On the Difficulties in The Church Fathers: The Ambigua*, vol. 1, edited by and translated by Nicholas Constas. Cambridge, MA: Harvard University Press, 2014.
Mayer, Rainer. 'Christology: The Genuine Form of Transcendence'. In *A Bonhoeffer Legacy: Essays in Understanding*, edited by A. J. Klassen, 179–92. Grand Rapids: Eerdmans, 1981.
McCormack, Bruce. 'Grace and Being: The Role of God's Gracious Election in Karl Barth's Theological Ontology'. In *The Cambridge Companion to Karl Barth*, edited by John Webster, 92–110. Cambridge: Cambridge University Press, 2000.

McCormack, Bruce L. *The Humility of the Eternal Son: Reformed Kenoticism and the Repair of Chalcedon*. Cambridge: Cambridge University Press, 2021.
McCormack, Bruce. 'The Person of Christ'. In *Mapping Modern Theology: A Thematic and Historical Introduction*, edited by Kelly M. Kapic and Bruce McCormack, 149-73. Grand Rapids: Baker Academic, 2012.
McCosker, Philip. 'Communicatio idiomatum: Lo scambio delle proprietá: storia, status quaestionis e prospettive'. *Modern Theology* 23 (2007): 298-301.
Menke, Karl-Heinz. *Jesus ist Gott der Sohn: Denkformen und Brennpunkte der Christologie*. Regensburg: Verlag Friedrich Pustet, 2008.
Moltmann, Jürgen. *A Broad Place: An Autobiography*, translated by Margaret Kohl. Minneapolis: Fortress Press, 2009.
Moltmann, Jürgen. *The Crucified God: The Cross of Christ as the Foundation and Criticism of Christian Theology*, translated by R. A. Wilson and John Bowden. Minneapolis: Fortress Press, 1993.
Moltmann, Jürgen. *Ethics of Hope*, translated by Margaret Kohl. Minneapolis: Fortress, 2012.
Moltmann, Jürgen. 'Theologie mit Dietrich Bonhoeffer: Die Gefängnisbriefe'. In *Bonhoeffers Theologie heute: Ein Weg zwischen Fundamentalismus und Säkularismus? Bonhoeffer's Theology Today. A Way between Fundamentalism and Secularism?*, edited by John W. de Gruchy, Stephen Plant, and Christiane Tietz, 17-31. Gütersloh: Gütersloher Verlagshaus, 2009.
Moltmann, Jürgen. *Theology of Hope: On the Ground and Implications of a Christian Eschatology*, translated by James W. Leitch. London: SCM, 1964.
Moltmann, Jürgen. *The Trinity and the Kingdom. The Doctrine of God*, translated by Margaret Kohl. San Francisco: Harper & Row Publishers, 1981.
Morse, Christopher. '"If Johannes Weiss Is Right ...": A Brief Retrospective on Apocalyptic Theology'. In *Apocalyptic and The Future of Theology: With and beyond J. Louis Martyn*, edited by Joshua B. Davis and Douglas Harink, 139-55. Eugene, OR: Cascade, 2012.
Müller, Hanfried. 'The Problem of the Reception and Interpretation of Dietrich Bonhoeffer'. In *World Come of Age: A Symposium on Dietrich Bonhoeffer*, edited by Ronald Gregor Smith, 182-214. London: Collins, 1967.
Müller, Hanfried. *Von der Kirche zur Welt*. Leipzig: Koehler & Amelang, 1960.
Muers, Rachel. *Keeping God's Silence: Towards a Theological Ethics of Communication*. Malden et al.: Blackwell Publishing, 2004.
Newman, John Henry. *Mary: The Virgin Mary in the Writings of John Henry Newman*, edited by Philip Boyce. Leominster: Gracewing, 2001.
Ngien, Dennis. 'Chalcedonian Christology and beyond: Luther's Understanding of the Communicatio Idiomatum'. *Heythrop Journal* 45 (2004): 54-68.
Ngien, Dennis. *The Suffering of God According to Martin Luther's Theologia Crucis*. Vancouver: Regents College Publishing, 2005.
Nickson, Ann L. *Bonhoeffer on Freedom: Courageously Grasping Reality*. Aldershot: Ashgate, 2002.
Nissen, Ulrik. *The Polity of Christ: Studies on Dietrich Bonhoeffer's Chalcedonian Christology and Ethics*. London: T&T Clark, 2020.
Norris, Richard A, Jr (trans. and ed.). *The Christological Controversy: Sources of Early Christian Thought*. Philadelphia: Fortress Press, 1980.
North, Paul. *Bizarre-Privileged Items in the Universe: The Logic of Likeness*. New York: Zone Books, 2021.

Nowers, Jeff. 'Hegel, Bonhoeffer, and Objective Geist: An Architectonic Exegesis of *Sanctorum Communio*'. In *Ontology and Ethics: Bonhoeffer and Contemporary Scholarship*, edited by Adam C. Clark and Michael Mawson, 47–56. Eugene: Pickwick Publications, 2013.

Nygren, Anders. *Christ and His Church*, translated by Alan Carlsten. Philadelphia: The Westminster Press, 1956.

O'Collins, Gerald. *Christology: Origins, Developments, Debates*. Waco: Baylor Press, 2015.

Ott, Heinrich. *Reality and Faith: The Theological Legacy of Dietrich Bonhoeffer*, translated by Alex A. Morrison. Philadelphia: Fortress Press, 1972.

Pangritz, Andreas. 'Dietrich Bonhoeffer: Within, Not Outside, the Barthian Movement'. In *Bonhoeffer's Intellectual Formation: Theology and Philosophy in His Thought*, edited by Peter Frick, 245–82. Tübingen: Mohr Siebeck, 2008.

Pangritz, Andreas. *Karl Barth in der Theologie Dietrich Bonhoeffers: Eine notwendige Klarstellung*. Westberlin: Alektor Verlag, 1989.

Pangritz, Andreas. 'Who Is Jesus Christ, for Us, Today?'. In *The Cambridge Companion to Dietrich Bonhoeffer*, edited by John W. de Gruchy, 134–53. Cambridge: Cambridge University Press, 1999.

Pannenberg, Wolfhart. *Grundzüge der Christologie*, 2nd ed. Gütersloh: Gütersloher Verlagshaus, 1966.

Pius XII, *Sempiternus Rex*. (https://www.vatican.va/content/pius-xii/en/encyclicals/documents/hf_p-xii_enc_08091951_sempiternus-rex-christus.html), accessed July 2022.

Phillips, Jacob. *Human Subjectivity 'in Christ' in Dietrich Bonhoeffer's Theology: Integrating Simplicity and Wisdom*. London: T&T Clark, 2020.

Phillips, John A. *Christ for Us in the Theology of Dietrich Bonhoeffer*. New York: Harper & Row, 1967.

Phillips, John A. *The Form of Christ in the World: A Study of Bonhoeffer's Christology*. London: Collins, 1967.

Phillips, John A. 'Radical Christology: Jesus and the Death of God'. *CrossCurrents* 19, no. 3 (1969): 273–96.

Pinnock, Clark. *Most Moved Mover: A Theology of God's Openness*. Grand Rapids: Baker and Paternoster, 2000.

Placher, William C. *Narratives of a Vulnerable God: Christ, Theology, and Scripture*. Louisville, KY: Westminster John Knox Press, 1994.

Plant, Stephen. '"We Believe in One Lord, Jesus Christ": A Pro-Nicene Revision of Bonhoeffer's 1933 Christology Lectures'. In *Christ, Church and World: New Studies in Bonhoeffer's Theology and Ethics*, edited by Michael Mawson and Philip G. Ziegler, 45–60. London: T&T Clark, 2016.

Plant, Stephen. 'Fresh Treatment of Bonhoeffer'. *Expository Times* 106, no. 6 (1995): 188.

Plotin. *Plotini Opera*, edited by Paul Henry and Hans-Rudolf Schwyzer. 2 volumes. Paris: Desclée de Brouwer et C., 1951.

Pollard, T. E. 'The Impassibility of God'. *Scottish Journal of Theology* 8, no. 4 (1955): 353–64.

Pope Benedict XVI and Seewald, Peter. *Last Testament: In His Own Words*, translated by Jacob Phillips. London: Bloomsbury, 2016.

Prüller-Jagenteufel. *Befreit zur Verantwortung: Sünde und Versöhnung in der Ethik Dietrich Bonhoeffers*. Münster: LIT Verlag, 2004.

Przywara, Erich. *Analogia Entis: Metaphysics: Original Structure and Universal Rhythm*. Grand Rapids: Eerdmans, 2014.

Rahner, Karl. *Theological Investigations I*. Baltimore: Helicon, 1961.
Rahner, Karl. *Theological Investigations V*. Baltimore: Helicon, 1966.
Ramelli, Ilaria. 'Gregorio di Nissa, de hominis opificio 1–13: la natura magnifica della creatura'. *Stylos* 22 (2013): 187–224.
Reed, Esther. *The Limit of Responsibility: Dietrich Bonhoeffer's Ethics for a Globalizing Era*. London: T&T Clark, 2018.
Riches, Aaron. *Ecce Homo: On the Divine Unity in Christ*. Grand Rapids, MA: Eerdmans, 2016.
Robinson, David S. *Christ and Revelatory Community in Bonhoeffer's Reception of Hegel*. Tübingen: Mohr Siebeck, 2018.
Robinson, John T. 'The Debate Continues'. In *The Honest to God Debate*, edited by David L. Edwards, 232–75. London: SCM Press, 1963.
Robinson, John T. *Honest to God*. London: SCM, 1963.
Rohls, Jan. 'Der leidende Gott in der Theologie des 20. Jahrhunderts'. In *Der leidende Gott: Eine philosophische und theologische Kritik*, edited by Peter Koslowski and Friedrich Hermanni, 31–56. München: Wilhelm Fink Verlag, 2001.
Rosenau, Harmut. 'Vom Leid der Nachfolge und der Nachfolge im Leid: Bonhoeffer und die Theodizee-Frage'. In *Interesse am Anderen. Interdisziplinäre Beiträge zum Verhältnis von Religion und Rationalität*, edited by Gerhard Schreiber, 705–22. Berlin: De Gruyter, 2019.
Rumscheidt, Martin. 'The Significance of Adolf von Harnack and Reinhold Seeberg for Dietrich Bonhoeffer'. In *Bonhoeffer's Intellectual Formation: Theology and Philosophy in His Thought*, edited by Peter Frick, 201–24. Tübingen: Mohr Siebeck, 2008.
Saarinen, Risto. *Gottes Wirken auf uns: Die transzendentale Deutung des Gegenwart-Christi-Motivs in der Lutherforschung*. Stuttgart: Franz Steiner Verlag Wiesbaden GmbH, 1989.
Sanders, John. *The God Who Risks: A Theology of Divine Providence*. Downers Grove: InterVarsity Press Academic, 2009.
Schindler, David L. 'The Embodied Person as Gift and the Cultural Task in America: Status Quaestionis'. *Communio: International Catholic Review* 35 (2008): 397–431.
Schlag, Thomas. *Grundtheorien einer praktisch-theologischen Kirchentheorie*. Zürich: Theologischer Verlag Zürich, 2012.
Schlag, Thomas. 'Vom Kopf auf die Füße: Öffentliche Theologie ist nicht nur etwas für Bischöfe und Bischöfinnen'. *Zeitzeichen* 18, no. 3 (2017): 16–18.
Schleiermacher, Friedrich Daniel Ernst. *Der christliche Glaube 1821–1822*, vol. 2. Berlin/New York: De Gruyter, 1984.
Schleiermacher, Friedrich Daniel Ernst. *Der christliche Glaube nach den Grundzügen der Evangelischen Kirche im Zusammenhange dargestellt (1830/31)*, vol. 2. Berlin/New York: De Gruyter, 1999.
Schliesser, Christine. 'Dietrich Bonhoeffer: Ein "Öffentlicher Theologe"?'. *Evangelische Theologie* 78, no. 3 (2018): 180–92.
Schliesser, Christine. '"The First Theological-Ethical Doctrine of Basic Human Rights Developed by a Twentieth-Century German Protestant Theologian": Dietrich Bonhoeffer and Human Rights'. In *A Spoke in the Wheel: Reconsidering the Political in the Theology of Dietrich Bonhoeffer*, edited by Kirsten Busch Nielsen, Ralf K. Wüstenberg, and Jens Zimmermann, 369–84. Gütersloh: Gütersloher Verlagshaus, 2014.
Schlink, Edmund. *The Coming Christ and the Coming Church*. Edinburgh: Oliver & Boyd, 1967.

Schmitz, Florian. '*Nachfolge*': *Zur Theologie Dietrich Bonhoeffers*. Göttingen: Vandenhoeck & Ruprecht, 2013.
Schwöbel, Christoph. 'Christology and Trinitarian Thought'. In *Trinitarian Theology Today: Essays on Divine Being and Act*, edited by Christoph Schwöbel, 113–46. Edinburgh: T&T Clark, 1995.
Schwöbel, Christoph. 'Die Trinitätslehre als Rahmentheorie'. In *Gott in Beziehung: Studien zur Dogmatik*, edited by Christoph Schwöbel, 25–51. Tübingen: Mohr Siebeck, 2002.
Schwöbel, Christoph. 'The Creature of the Word: Recovering the Ecclesiology of the Reformers'. In *On Being the Church: Essays on the Christian Community*, edited by Colin Gunton and Daniel W. Hardy, 110–55. Edinburgh: T&T Clark, 1989.
Schwöbel, Christoph. 'The Generosity of the Triune God and the Humility of the Son'. In *Kenosis: The Self-Emptying of Christ in Scripture and Theology*, edited by Paul T. Nimmo and Keith L. Johnson, 267–88. Grand Rapids: Eerdmans, 2022.
Seeberg, Reinhold. *Christliche Dogmatik*. Erlangen and Wien: A. Deichertsche Verlagsbuchhandlung Dr. Werner Scholl, 1924.
Silcock, Jeffrey G. 'The Truth of Divine Impassibility: A New Look at an Old Argument'. *Lutheran Theological Journal* 45, no. 3 (December 2011): 198–207.
Smit, Dirk J. 'The Paradigm of Public Theology: Origins and Developments'. In *Contextuality and Intercontextuality in Public Theology: Proceedings from the Bamberg Conference 23.-25.06.2011*, edited by Florian Höhne, Heinrich Bedford-Strohm, and Tobias Reitmeier. Zürich, Berlin: LIT Verlag, 2013.
Smith, Ronald Gregor. *The New Man: Christianity and Man's Coming of Age*. London: SCM, 1956.
Smith, Ronald Gregor. *Secular Christianity*. London: Collins, 1966.
Sobrino, John. *Christology at the Crossroads: A Latin American Approach*, translated by John Drury. London: SCM Press, 1978.
Söding, Thomas. 'Gottes Sohn von Anfang an: Zur Präexistenzchristologie bei Paulus und den Deuteropaulinen'. In *Gottes ewiger Sohn: Die Präexistenz Christi*, edited by Rudolf Laufen, 57–93. Paderborn/München et al.: Schöningh, 1997.
Sölle, Dorothee. *Suffering*, translated by Everett Kalin. Minneapolis: Fortress Press, 1984.
Sumner, Darren O. 'The Twofold Life of the Word: Karl Barth's Critical Reception of the Extra Calvinisticum'. *International Journal of Systematic Theology* 15, no. 1 (2013): 42–57.
Surin, Kenneth. 'The Impassibility of God and the Problem of Evil'. *Scottish Journal of Theology* 35 (1982): 97–115.
Tanner, Norman P. *Decrees of the Ecumenical Councils: Volumes 1 and 2: From Nicaea I to Vatican II*. Washington, DC: Georgetown University Press, 1990.
Tietz, Christiane. 'Barth und Bonhoeffer'. In *Barth Handbuch*, edited by Michael Beintker, 111–16. Tübingen: Mohr Siebeck, 2016.
Tietz, Christiane. 'Bonhoeffer's Strong Christology in the Context of Religious Pluralism'. In *Interpreting Bonhoeffer: Historical Perspectives, Emerging Issues*, edited by Clifford J. Green and Guy C. Carter, 181–96. Minneapolis: Fortress Press, 2013.
Tietz, Christiane. 'Bonhoeffer and the Ontological Structure of the Church'. In *Ontology and Ethics: Bonhoeffer and Contemporary Scholarship*, edited by Adam Clark and Michael Mawson, 44–6. Eugene, OR: Pickwick Publications, 2013.
Tietz, Christiane. 'Christology'. In *The Oxford Handbook of Dietrich Bonhoeffer*, edited by Michael Mawson and Philip G. Ziegler, 150–67. Oxford: Oxford University Press, 2019.

Tietz, Christiane. 'Der leidende Gott'. In *Die Spiegelschrift Gottes ist schwer zu lesen: Beiträge zur Theologie Dietrich Bonhoeffers*, 138–40. Gütersloh: Gütersloher Verlagshaus, 2021.
Tietz, Christiane. 'Der leidende Gott'. *Panorama* 23 (2011): 107–20.
Tietz, Christiane. 'The Role of Jesus Christ for Christian Theology'. In *Christ, Church and World: New Studies in Bonhoeffer's Theology and Ethics*, edited by Michael Mawson and Philip G. Ziegler, 9–27. London: T&T Clark/Bloomsbury, 2016.
Tietz, Christiane. *Theologian of Resistance: Life and Thought of Dietrich Bonhoeffer*, translated by Victoria Barnett. Minneapolis: Fortress Press, 2016.
Tietz-Steiding, Christiane. *Bonhoeffers Kritik der verkrümmten Vernunft: Eine erkenntnistheoretische Untersuchung*. Tübingen: Mohr Siebeck, 1999.
Torrance, Thomas. *Incarnation: The Person and Life of Christ*. Downers Grove, IL: IVP Academic, 2008.
Verhagen, Koert. *Being and Action Coram Deo: Bonhoeffer and the Retrieval of Justification's Social Import*. New Studies in Bonhoeffer's Theology and Ethics. London: T&T Clark, 2021.
Wannenwetsch, Bernd. '"Christians and Pagans". Toward a Trans-Religious Second Naïveté or How to Be a Christological Creature'. In *Who Am I? Bonhoeffer's Theology through His Poetry*, edited by Bernd Wannenwetsch, 175–96. London: T&T Clark, 2009.
Webster, John. *God without Measure: Working Papers in Christian Theology, vol. I: God and the Works of God*. London: T&T Clark/Bloomsbury, 2016.
Webster, John. 'Introduction: Systematic Theology'. In *The Oxford Handbook of Systematic Theology*, edited by John Webster, Kathryn Tanner, and Iain Torrance, 1–15. Oxford: Oxford University Press, 2007.
Webster, John. '"In the Society of God": Some Principles of Ecclesiology'. In *Perspectives on Ecclesiology and Ethnography*, edited by Pete Ward, 200–2. Grand Rapids: Eerdmans, 2012.
Weinandy, Thomas. *Does God Suffer?* Edinburgh: T&T Clark, 2000.
Weiss, Johannes. *Jesus Proclamation of the Kingdom of God*, edited and translated by Richard H. Hiers and David L. Holland. London: SCM Press, 1971.
Welker, Christian. *Gottes Offenbarung: Christologie*. Neukirchen-Vluyn: Neukirchner, 2012.
Wenz, Christian. *Christus: Jesus und die Anfänge der Christologie*. Göttingen: Vandenhoeck & Ruprecht, 2011.
Weyl, Dominik. 'Die Verwundbarkeit des Menschen und Gottes: Überlegungen im Anschluss an Dietrich Bonhoeffer'. *Hermeneutische Blätter*, no. 1 (2017): 62–74.
Whitehead, Alfred North. *Process and Reality: An Essay in Cosmology [1929]*. New York: Macmillan Co., 1969.
Whitehead, Alfred N. and David Ray Griffin (eds). *Process and Reality: An Essay in Cosmology*. New York: The Free Press, 1978.
White, Graham. 'Luther's Views on Language'. *Journal of Theology and Literature* 3, no. 2 (1989): 188–218.
White, Thomas Joseph. *The Incarnate Lord: A Thomistic Study in Christology*. Washington: CUA Press, 2017.
Williams, A. N. *The Architecture of Theology: Structure, System, and Ratio*. Oxford: Oxford University Press, 2011.
Williams, Rowan. *Christ the Heart of Creation*. London: Continuum, 2016.

Williams, Rowan. 'Dialectic and Analogy: A Theological Legacy'. In *The Impact of Idealism: The Legacy of Post-Kantian German Thought*. vol. *IV: Religion*, edited by Nicholas Boyle, Liz Disley, and Nicholas Adams, 274–92. Cambridge: Cambridge University Press, 2013.

Woelfel, James W. *Bonhoeffer's Theology: Classical and Revolutionary*. Nashville: Abingdon Press, 1970.

Wüstenberg, Ralf K. 'Religion and Secularity'. In *The Oxford Handbook of Dietrich Bonhoeffer*, edited by Michael Mawson and Philip Ziegler, 321–30. Oxford: Oxford University Press, 2019.

Wüstenberg, Ralf K. *A Theology of Life: Dietrich Bonhoeffer's Religionless Christianity*, translated by Doug Stott. Grand Rapids, MA: Eerdmans 1998.

Wüthrich, Matthias D. 'Ein "theologischer Betriebsunfall"? Erwägungen zum sog. *Extra Calvinisticum* ausgehend vom Heidelberger Katechismus'. *Theologische Zeitschrift* 70, no. 2 (2014): 97–117.

Yeago, David S. 'The New Testament and the Nicene Dogma: A Contribution to the Recovery of Theological Exegesis'. *Pro Ecclesia* 3 (1994): 152–64.

Zachhuber, Johannes: *God, Christ, and Salvation; Topics in 20th Century Christology* (https://users.ox.ac.uk/~trin1631/files/Topics%20in%20Christology%20Lecture.pdf), accessed July 2022.

Zbaraschuk, Michael G. 'God Is Still Dead: Retrieving the Lost Legacy of William Hamilton'. In *Resurrecting the Death of God: The Origins, Influence, and Return of Radical Theology*, edited by Daniel J. Peterson and G. Michael Zharaschuk, 71–82. Albany, NY: SUNY Press, 2014.

Zbaraschuk, Michael G. 'William Hamilton (American, 1924–2012)'. In *The Palgrave Handbook of Radical Theology*, edited by Christopher D. Rodkey and Jordan E. Miller, 241–7. Cham: Palgrave Macmillan, 2018.

Zeyher-Quattlender, Julian. *Du sollst nicht töten (lassen)? Eine Rekonstruktion der Friedensethik Dietrich Bonhoeffers aus der Perspektive Öffentlicher Theologie in aktueller Absicht*. Leipzig: Evangelische Verlagsanstalt, 2021.

Ziegler, Philip G. 'Christ for Us Today: Promeity in the Christologies of Bonhoeffer and Kierkegaard'. *International Journal of Systematic Theology* 15, no. 1 (2013): 25–41.

Ziegler, Philip G. 'God'. In *The Oxford Handbook of Dietrich Bonhoeffer*, edited by Michael Mawson and Philip G. Ziegler, 137–49. Oxford: Oxford University Press, 2019.

Zimmermann, Jens and Brian Gregor (eds). *Being Human, Becoming Human: Dietrich Bonhoeffer and Social Thought*. Eugene: Pickwick Publications, 2010.

Zizioulas, John D. *Being as Communion: Studies in Personhood and the Church*. London: Darton, Longman & Todd, 1985.

Zizioulas, John D. 'Le Mystère de l'Église dans la tradition orthodoxe'. *Irénikon* 60 (1987): 321–35.

INDEX

Abromeit, Hans-Jürgen 45
Act and Being (Bonhoeffer) 3, 15, 21–2, 24–6, 28, 32–3, 35–6, 43, 90, 106 n.60, 118, 127, 173, 247
Adam and Eve 22, 24–9, 32–4, 104–10, 106 n.60, 107 n.62
aesthetic-ontological-dynamic process 7, 210–11, 211 n.4, 212, 214–16, 219, 221–2, 225–6, 228, 231–4
analogia entis 22 n.8
anthropology 32, 39, 76, 78, 88–9, 101 n.40, 106, 168, 175 n.5, 189, 196–7, 200, 204
apatheia 138–42
Avis, Paul 244–5

Balthasar, Hans Urs von 56, 154
Barreto, Raimundo 212
Barth, Friederike 36, 196 n.63
Barth, Heinrich 37
Barth, Karl 5, 56, 66–7, 114, 125–30, 126 n.79, 134, 160 n.39, 180, 183, 187
Bauckham, Richard 138, 139 n.12, 140
Bedford-Strohm, Heinrich 208
being in Christ 24–5, 27, 29, 32–3, 178, 222, 251
Benjamin, Walter 223, 223 n.60, 224 n.66
Bethge, Eberhard 4, 37, 75, 76 n.7, 79, 81–2, 84, 87, 133, 137, 149, 247
Beyond Secular Reason (Milbank) 58
Bleher, Hannah 6, 187–208
Brunner, Emil 14, 241

Calvin, John 125, 245
Carson, Ronald A. 149 n.72
Carter, J. Kameron 183 n.33
Chalcedon
  Christology 1–2, 19, 44, 49, 59, 96, 131, 147, 164, 166
  Creed 122, 133, 135
  Definitio fidei of 61–2
  definition of 12, 12 n.2, 25, 28, 30, 57–8, 69, 82 n.33

  doctrine 99, 110–11, 113–14, 118, 190
  formula 33, 50, 50 n.68, 70, 133, 146, 146 n.43, 156–7
  language 116–18
  metaphysics 143
  negative criteria 17
  sense 89
'Chalcedon: End or Beginning?' (Rahner) 61–2, 64
'Christians and Heathens' (i.e. the poem) 87
Christology 13 nn.3–4
  constructive 94, 105, 110, 112, 117
  contemporary 7, 19, 94, 97, 100
  critical 28
  and ecclesiology 236, 240–2, 244, 246–8
  ethical 55, 65
  existential 49
  godless 77
  and human 38–44
  negative 15, 30, 50, 64, 69–70, 71 n.65, 181–2
  'new' 89–90
  orthodox 12 n.2
  positive 30–1, 33, 71 n.65, 173, 182
  prison 78
Christology lectures 4, 6, 18–19, 25, 28, 32–3, 35, 55, 57, 69–73, 81, 156–9, 167, 169, 173–6, 174 n.2, 181–6, 183 n.32, 212, 250
christ-reality 111 n.82, 133–4, 202–3, 224–8, 224 n.66
Christ, the Heart of Creation (Williams) 1
Church 23–7, 30, 32, 140, 210 n.3, 220 n.45
  Christology 240–4
  community 7, 18, 216 n.25, 218 n.41, 219–20, 220 n.45, 236, 240, 246–50, 252–5
  Confessing 32, 36, 183
  Kirche 210 n.3, 213, 229, 233, 235
  pneumatology/pneumatologically 7, 165, 226, 236–9, 242–55, 251 n.105

Climacus, Johannes (Kierkegaard) 39–41, 45
Coakley, Sarah 95 n.12, 97–9, 111 n.82, 240
Cockayne, Joshua 179–81, 185
commandment 40, 106, 106 n.60, 107–9, 211 n.7, 217
communicatio idiomatum 49, 65, 139, 143–5, 147, 158, 164
Concerning the Christian Idea of God (Bonhoeffer) 42–3, 49, 157 n.21
Cone, James H. 138
Congar, Yves 245
conscience 116, 118
contemporaneity/contemporary 2–4, 7, 11, 19, 27, 38, 46–7, 52–3, 57, 73–4, 79–80, 94, 97, 100, 113, 133, 144, 204, 213, 215, 223, 240–2
Contemporary with Christ (Cockayne) 179–80
cor curvum in se 72, 130
 (cor) incurvatus 109 n.72
counter logos 13, 40, 110, 153, 174–5, 178, 215
creation 3, 5 6, 15–16, 22 n.8, 24, 28 n.29, 35–6, 47–8, 96, 100, 102, 104–6, 108, 110, 133, 138, 142, 150, 152, 154, 157, 175, 181, 203, 213 n.15, 220, 223, 225–6, 230, 232, 234, 242, 250, 253–4
critical theology 158 n.25, 182
cross 13, 26, 48–9, 85–9, 104, 106 n.60, 109, 120–1, 140, 142–5, 149–51, 155, 158, 163–6, 168–9, 191, 197, 216, 219, 222, 229 n.101, 232, 232 nn.110–11
The Crucified God (Moltmann) 143, 148–52, 155, 164
Cyril of Alexandria 59–60, 62, 70, 141, 143 n.28, 145

Dabrock, Peter 189 n.8, 201
Danz, Christian 93–6, 93 n.1, 94 nn.9–10, 95 n.13, 100, 111
Dasein (Heidegger) 21, 24, 122
death 6, 13, 21, 28, 30, 41, 47–8, 51, 71, 77, 83, 86–7, 90, 109–10, 122, 140, 142, 144, 158, 162, 164, 164 n.69, 165–6, 175–8, 197, 199, 216, 219, 223–4, 226 n.75, 230–2, 250

De Lubac, Henri 66–7, 241–3
Der Mittler (Brunner) 14
Deutsche Christen 32–3
Dewey, John 204
Die Grenzen der Interpretation (Eco) 188 n.4
Discipleship (Bonhoeffer) 36–7, 37 n.8, 42, 51, 84, 140, 163, 173–4, 174 nn.3–4, 176–8, 181, 184–6, 186 n.38
divine impassibility *(apatheia)* 138–44, 155, 157
Docetism 15, 28–9
Does God Suffer? (Weinandy) 155
Dramm, Sabine 247 n.63
Dumas, André 237

Ecce homo 113, 123, 135–6, 214
Ecce Homo (Riches) 57–64
ecclesiology 3, 25, 53, 76 n.7, 236–48, 254–5
Eco, Umberto 188, 188 n.4
Eigengesetzlichkeiten 202
Emerton, David 7, 236–55, 244 n.49
enhypostasia 28 n.31, 50, 97, 97 n.20, 99–105, 105 n.56, 106, 124
epistemology/-cal/-cally 14, 24, 26, 45, 56, 58, 66–7, 69, 104, 174
eschatology/eschatological 101 n.38, 133, 166, 217, 223, 246, 246 n.58, 250
'Essence of Christianity' (Harnack) 115
Ethics (Bonhoeffer) 6, 32–3, 72, 85, 88, 109 n.71, 113, 120–3, 130–2, 173, 175 n.7, 186–8, 194, 210, 221 n.51, 225, 238 n.10
etsi deus non daretur 152
Eucharist 125–6, 134 n.126, 242–4
existence/existential 2, 5–6, 11, 13–14, 16–17, 21, 23 n.10, 24, 31, 34, 39–43, 41 n.23, 42 n.30, 43–6, 48–51, 53, 62–3, 65–6, 71, 71 n.65, 83, 85–90, 105, 111, 114, 116, 119–23, 127, 130, 133–4, 140, 159, 167, 167 n.88, 176, 178, 180, 183, 185, 195–6, 211, 211 n.5, 213, 215–16, 219, 220 n.45, 221, 223, 225, 227–8, 230, 232 n.112, 233–4, 242, 249, 252
Extra Calvinisticum 125–6, 126 n.79, 149 n.72

faith 1–2, 4, 13, 13 n.4, 14 n.7, 15–16, 18, 23–4, 35, 37–8, 41–7, 49, 51, 53, 56, 58, 66–7, 72, 79, 82–6, 88–90, 101, 116, 120, 129, 132, 135–6, 159–60, 163, 163 n.60, 167, 178, 178 n.20, 180, 182–3, 193–4, 209, 213, 220 n.45, 222, 222 n.56, 223–4, 224 n.60, 226, 226 n.75, 228, 229 n.101, 232–3, 251
Farrow, Douglas 242
Feil, Ernst 38, 81, 113, 174 n.3
Fiddes, Paul 138, 154–5
finitum capax infiniti 124–30, 147
Floyd, Wayne Whitson 237
form/formation 6–7, 214–25
Frankl, Viktor E. 137, 151 n.83
freedom 24, 30, 34, 40, 42, 83, 85–6, 89–90, 104, 104 n.52, 107 n.65, 108 n.68, 138, 153, 157, 165–6, 193, 195, 199, 199 n.86, 205–6, 254
Frei, Hans 27 n.26, 58

Galot, Jean 154
Gavrilyuk, Paul 141
Gemeinde 210, 210 n.3, 211 n.4, 212, 212 n.8, 213, 217–20, 218 n.41, 220 n.45, 223 n.60, 224, 224 n.66, 225, 229, 229 n.101, 230, 233–4, 234 n.118, 235
Gestaltung 6, 210–11, 211 nn.4–5, 212, 217, 218 n.41, 219–20, 221 n.49, 222, 227, 227 n.83, 228, 231, 233, 235
Girard, René 55
God-human 4–5, 17–18, 30, 38–41, 43–54, 46 n.48, 71, 85, 93–4, 96–7, 103–10, 145, 159, 167, 176, 214
Godsey, John D. 247
God-world reality 228
'Going ahead' 211 n.6, 230–4
good and evil 52, 195, 205
gospels 30, 79, 81, 88–9, 100, 102, 104 n.52, 105 n.59, 115, 117, 140, 149, 159, 161, 224, 232, 232 n.109
grace 15, 24, 29, 32, 37, 37 n.8, 40, 66, 68, 84, 104 n.52, 105, 177, 189–90, 192–3, 201, 217, 219, 220 n.45, 227 n.83, 253–4
Grebe, Matthias 5, 137–53, 146 n.49

Greggs, Tom 213, 213 n.15, 220 n.45
Gregory of Nyssa 34
Gunton, Colin 100–2, 102 n.43, 103, 105, 109

Habilitationsschrift (Bonhoeffer). See *Act and Being* (Bonhoeffer)
Hamilton, Nadine 4–5, 93–112, 119 n.39, 124 n.73, 190, 190 nn.18–20, 191 n.21, 200 n.90
Hamilton, William 77, 77 n.11, 78, 190
Harnack, Adolf von 3, 5, 31, 35, 45, 65, 93 n.1, 113–15, 115 n.11, 116, 119, 122
Hegel, Georg W. F. 28, 43, 115, 128 n.93, 129
Heidegger, Martin 21, 24, 122, 234 n.118
Hellenization thesis 5, 114, 118
Heschel, Abraham 148
Hick, John 12 n.1, 55
Hirsch, Emanuel 114, 117–19, 122
historical materialism 224 n.60
Höhne, David A. 249
Holl, Karl 5, 113–20, 122, 147 n.53
Holmes, Christopher R. J. 158 n.24, 249, 252
Holy Spirit 7, 19, 101–2, 105, 165, 220 n.45, 226, 229, 236, 242, 244–5, 246 n.58, 249–55, 251 n.105
Hopper, David H. 237
horizon 15, 25, 98–9, 111, 111 n.82, 132–3, 135–6, 202
humanity 1, 5, 12–13, 15–16, 18, 20 n.20, 23–5, 30–4, 40–1, 44, 48–9, 53, 58–63, 70–1, 73, 77–8, 80, 83–90, 94–7, 99–119, 121–6, 128, 130, 133–6, 146–7, 151–3, 156, 158–9, 164, 175, 190–1, 191 n.21, 192 n.37, 201, 204, 211, 213–14, 216, 218–20, 231, 252
human logos 13–14, 25–8, 28 n.29, 33, 109–10, 174–5, 215–16
human nature 24, 29, 34, 53, 58–9, 62, 62 n.29, 63, 65–7, 70, 86, 94–5, 100, 101 n.40, 107, 119–20, 122–3, 125, 134, 141–7, 157–8, 164, 190
humiliation 17–18, 26, 30, 44–5, 76, 85, 147, 159, 164, 169, 192, 218 n.38

hypostasis 4, 30, 59–63, 65, 67, 69–71, 93, 98–100, 102–3, 103 n.50, 105, 108
hypostatic union 57, 59–60, 65, 67, 125, 145

Ideologiekritik 33
imago Dei 107, 210
impassibility 5–6, 59, 138–44, 148, 151, 154–5, 157, 159
The Incarnate Lord (White) 57, 64–9, 71–2
Incarnation 17, 28–30, 35–6, 39, 41, 43–9, 53, 67–9, 85, 93, 96, 102, 104–5, 118, 121, 123, 129–31, 135–6, 164, 184, 191, 198

Jenson, Matt 246
Jenson, Robert 154, 243–4
Jesus Christ 1, 3–7, 13–18, 20, 26–7, 30, 32, 36, 38, 40–1, 44–5, 47, 49–54, 69–70, 76–7, 80–9, 86 n.45, 93–106, 105 n.59, 106 n.60, 108–12, 112 n.85, 113–14, 116, 118–19, 121–6, 132, 134–6, 139 n.12, 143, 143 n.28, 145–6, 146 n.45, 147 n.56, 151, 153, 156–7, 158 n.25, 160 n.39, 161, 167, 173–6, 181–4, 190–4, 197–201, 205, 211 n.4, 213–14, 218, 218 n.38, 219, 220 n.45, 221 n.52, 226, 228–9, 229 n.101, 234, 241, 244, 247, 248 n.70, 250–2, 254
Jesus Christ and the Essence of Christianity (Bonhoeffer) 38
Jesus of history 18, 27
Jesus of Nazareth 45–6, 60, 89, 100, 111, 118–20
Jinkins, Michael 255
Jüngel, Eberhard 138, 154
justification 6, 15, 48, 116–17, 120, 133, 136, 160, 177–8, 189–93, 197, 199–200, 202, 205, 224

Kant, Immanuel 57, 63–4, 64 n.34, 68–9, 73
Kelly, Geffrey B. 36
kenoticism/*kenosis* 30, 86, 147 n.53, 149 n.72
Kierkegaard, Søren 3–4, 36–54, 37 n.8, 39 n.13, 43 n.33, 43 n.36, 46 n.48, 114, 123, 128–32, 128 n.393, 129 n.102

kingdom (of God) 226–7
Kirkpatrick, Matthew D. 36–7, 37 n.5
Kitamori, Kazoh 138
Krötke, Wolf 53, 78

Lawrence, Joel B. 247
Leahy, Brendan 209–10 n.2, 252
Lectures on Christology (Bonhoeffer) 5–6, 13, 13 n.3, 15, 27 n.27, 40, 43, 43 n.36, 44, 49, 52, 79, 118, 126–7, 129, 129 n.102, 130–5, 135 n.132, 138, 145, 147, 149, 156, 161
Letters and Papers from Prison (Bonhoeffer) 4, 12, 55–6, 75, 76 n.7, 77–8, 81–9, 82 n.33, 137, 159 n.31, 160–3, 204, 206
life 194–8, 201–2
  Christ 46, 52, 187, 189, 191, 194
  new 84, 191, 198, 212 n.9, 230, 234, 253
  philosophy of 196
Life Together (Bonhoeffer) 173
logos 13–14, 13 n.4, 16, 25–8, 28 n.29, 30, 33, 40–2, 109–10, 157, 174–5, 178, 215–16, 223, 227 n.83, 233
Logos of God 13–14, 16, 60, 63, 67, 71–2, 99–100, 102, 105–6, 108–11, 115, 125–6, 135, 141, 145, 153, 174, 178, 215
Loisy, Alfred 236
love 22, 35–6, 51, 84, 90, 102, 106 n.60, 122, 133, 135–6, 142, 148–9, 152, 152 n.93, 153, 155, 165, 165 nn.77–8, 166, 168–9, 194, 227 n.83, 229 n.101, 251–2, 255
Lutheran 16–17, 29, 48, 50, 87, 121, 124–7, 130, 134, 134 n.126, 135, 138, 147, 147 n.54, 147 n.56, 149 n.72, 176, 187, 202, 206 n.129, 220 n.45, 241–2, 246
Luther, Martin 16–17, 29, 35, 46–50, 66, 78, 87, 109 n.72, 116–17, 120–1, 124–7, 130, 134, 134 n.126, 135, 138–9, 143–7, 147 n.54, 147 n.56, 150, 158, 158 n.26, 163 n.62, 164, 166, 176, 187, 202, 241–2, 246

McCosker, Philip 59, 59 n.17
Maluleke, Tinyiko 207

mandates 33, 52, 202–3
Markschies, Christoph 114
Marty, Martin E. 206
Mawson, Michael 6, 78 n.16, 80 n.22,
    149 nn.69–70, 161 n.45, 168 n.93,
    173 n.1, 183 n.32, 190 n.17,
    210 n.2, 211 n.5, 213 n.11,
    233 n.116, 237 n.5, 248, 248 n.70,
    248 n.76, 249 n.77, 249 n.83
Mayer, Rainer 84
metaphysics/metaphysical 1, 4–5, 14, 14
    n.7, 15, 18, 21, 22 n.8, 31, 35, 56–60,
    62–5, 64 n.34, 65, 67–70, 72–4, 85,
    90, 93, 98, 112–14, 116–19, 130,
    135–6, 141, 143, 151–2, 160, 160
    n.39, 196
Metz, Johann Baptist 138
mia physis 60, 70
Milbank, John 58
Moltmann, Jürgen 6, 55–6, 137–8, 141–2,
    148, 153, 155, 159 n.34, 163–9, 164
    nn.68–9, 165 n.74, 165 nn.77–8,
    168 n.94, 169 n.95
monophysitism 15, 29, 60–2, 70, 116, 156
Müller, Hanfried 76–7
mystery 17, 41, 45, 49, 53, 67–70, 72, 74,
    86, 90, 127, 136, 155, 183, 183 n.34,
    184, 189 n.8, 215, 241
The Myth of God Incarnate (Hick) 12 n.1,
    55

neighbour 41, 84, 133, 162, 189, 199, 204
Nestorianism 15, 29, 57–64, 67, 69–71, 71
    n.65, 73–4, 145, 156, 156 n.17
Newman, John Henry 73
New Testament 14, 65–6, 87, 101, 105–6,
    143, 228, 240 n.20
new theology 4, 75, 75 n.2, 79
Nicene Creed 66, 140
Nickson, Ann 246
Nissen, Ulrik 1 n.1, 2, 3 n.5, 189 n.8, 210
    n.2
Nowers, Jeff 248
Nygren, Anders 241, 243

O'Collins, Gerald 56
ontology/ontological 4, 7, 14–19, 20 n.20,
    21–2, 22 n.8, 23–8, 31, 33–4, 58–60,
    65, 67, 72–4, 82, 85, 95, 98, 103,
    108, 111, 116, 118, 122, 142, 176,
    191 n.21, 200, 210, 210 n.3, 211,
    211 n.5, 214–16, 218, 218 n.41, 219,
    221–2, 225–6, 228, 231–4, 242, 244,
    250–3
'Outline for a Book' (Bonhoeffer) 76, 80,
    82, 161–2

Pangritz, Andreas 126–7, 147 n.56, 149
    n.72, 174, 247
paradox 1–3, 18, 24, 38, 41, 41 n.25,
    44–54, 63, 69–71, 73, 81–2, 89, 98,
    104, 109 n.72, 129, 133, 135, 141,
    149, 164, 164 n.68, 166–7, 178, 184,
    237
Paul, Apostle 240, 245
penultimate. *See* ultimate and penultimate
person 5–7, 13, 13 n.4, 14, 24, 26–7, 29–
    30, 39–40, 42, 45–54, 57, 59–60, 65,
    67, 70, 85, 89, 93–5, 95 nn.11–12,
    96–100, 110–12, 115–16, 133, 135,
    144–8, 156–7, 158 n.26, 174–85,
    195, 205, 211 n.7, 216–19, 232, 238
    n.8, 244–6, 250, 254
person of Christ 13 n.4, 15–19, 45, 49, 53,
    65, 115 n.11, 143, 153, 158–9, 167,
    177, 180, 183–4, 216, 218–19, 232,
    243
Pfeifer, Hans 247
phenomenology 14, 63
Phillips, Jacob 4, 56 n.9, 71 n.65, 212 n.7
Phillips, John A. 75–6
Philosophical Fragments (Kierkegaard) 39,
    46, 53, 128
philosophy/philosophical 2, 11, 21, 24,
    37–8, 43, 60, 65–8, 73, 93, 97, 103,
    105, 115, 117–18, 121, 132–5,
    139–41, 143, 143 n.28, 144, 148,
    156, 195–6, 196 n.63, 198 n.77, 218
    n.41, 224
physis 59–60, 63, 93, 95, 95 n.12, 98
Pilate, Pontius 119, 136
pneumatology 7, 165, 226, 236–8, 242–55
political ethics 6, 188, 201–6
potential/potentiality 1, 4, 6, 15, 31, 40,
    75, 108, 122, 128, 152 n.94, 187–8,
    201–7, 227, 227 n.83, 239–40, 254
Practice in Christianity (Kierkegaard) 39,
    44, 46

prayer 72, 253
preaching/preached word 16, 31, 193, 218, 222, 224 n.60, 254
'preparing the way' 6, 187–208
pro nobis/pro me/promeity 16, 18–20, 20 n.20, 24–7, 46–9, 53, 82, 85, 132, 134, 145–6, 146 n.50, 149–50, 153, 167, 183, 216 n.25, 219–25, 250
The Prophets (Heschel) 148
prosopon 59–64, 70–1
Przywara, Erich 21–2, 22 n.8
public theology 6–7, 187 n.1, 188, 206–8, 206 n.129, 207–8

Rahner, Karl 61–5, 61 n.22, 62 n.29, 69–71, 71 n.65
Ratzinger, Joseph 56
reality
 divine 35, 68
 ecclesial 7, 236, 242, 246, 252–5
 finite 21
 infinite 21, 23, 129
 ultimate 211, 218–19, 222 n.56, 223, 225–30
reconciliation 101, 136, 175, 198, 229
Reed, Esther 221 n.51
Reformation 104, 107 n.65, 112 n.85, 220 n.45
religion 38, 68, 77–81, 84–5, 88, 115, 123, 137, 160, 160 n.35, 160 n.39, 162–3, 212, 212 n.8, 213 n.15, 218 n.41, 222–4, 229–30, 233, 235
religionless Christianity 80, 139, 149, 160–1, 160 n.35, 163, 212, 233
responsibility 6, 16, 21, 25, 33, 52, 132, 191–2, 194, 199–206, 221 n.51, 254–5
revelation 4–5, 14, 16, 20–1, 23, 31, 33, 36, 38, 41–51, 53, 67–8, 72, 77–8, 89, 114, 125, 128–31, 136, 150, 153, 179, 183, 191, 215, 222 n.56, 228
Riches, Aaron 56–65, 61 n.22, 62 n.29, 69–71, 71 n.65
Robinson, John T. 76, 80
Rosenau, Harmut 153 n.95

salvation 3, 13, 17, 29, 31–2, 32 n.46, 93, 95–6, 102, 132, 142, 144, 149 n.72, 229, 233, 233 n.117, 242, 245

sanctification 160
Sanctorum Communio (Bonhoeffer) 15, 25, 36, 118, 173, 210 n.3, 219 n.41, 236, 246 n.60, 247
Schindler, David L. 58
Schleiermacher, Friedrich Daniel Ernst 59, 67, 93 n.1
Schlenker, Christian 5, 113–36, 211 n.4
Schwöbel, Christoph 3, 11, 13 n.3, 20 n.20, 89, 89 n.56, 89 n.58, 93, 93 n.1, 97 n.19, 102 n.47, 105 n.56
Scripture 65–7, 90, 95, 140–1, 161, 161 n.45, 163, 180, 182
secular/-isation 4–5, 58, 63, 76–80, 88–9, 132, 152, 160, 207, 213, 213 n.15, 227
Seeberg, Reinhold 45, 113–14, 118–19, 122–3
Sickness Unto Death (Kierkegaard) 37
simplicity 212 n.7, 220
Smith, Ronald Gregor 75–6, 78
Sobrino, Jon 55–6, 74
Söding, Thomas 105
Sölle, Dorothee 138
soteriology/-cally 4–5, 13 n.4, 17, 49, 100, 144, 217, 232
Stellvertretung 17–18, 36, 250–3
suffering God 5–6, 20, 137–8, 139 n.12, 140–1, 143–4, 147, 147 n.54, 149, 151–3, 155–6, 160–2, 164, 166, 168–9, 176
sui juris 62–3, 71

temptation 61, 101, 109, 222
theologia crucis 48, 48 n.63, 49, 76, 81, 81 n.27, 87, 121 n.51, 143, 163–6, 168
theology 1–7, 11–12, 14, 17, 20, 23–8, 30, 32–8, 42–3, 46, 49–52, 55–8, 66, 72–7, 79, 86, 93–4, 96–100, 110, 111 n.82, 113–14, 138–9, 142–5, 148, 150, 155–6, 158, 158 n.24, 159–64, 166–9, 173, 178, 182–4, 187–8, 206–8, 213 n.15, 222–3, 232 n.110, 237, 239–40, 247
Theotokos 60, 63
Tillich, Paul 17, 55–6
Torrance, Thomas F. 138
Torres, Samuel Murillo 6–7, 209–35

transcendence 12–14, 17, 21–4, 30, 35, 41–2, 58, 68, 73, 78, 80–1, 83–6, 88–9, 132, 142, 149, 155, 162, 244
Trinity 17, 67, 135, 145, 158 n.24, 164–7, 184, 215, 241–2
The Trinity and the Kingdom of God (Moltmann) 155
two-nature doctrine 1–2, 4–5, 15, 19, 50, 60, 69–70, 82, 86, 90, 93–4, 96–7, 99–100, 102–3, 110–11, 113–15, 133, 144–7, 146 n.43, 147 n.56, 156

ubiquity 16, 53, 125–6, 128, 134
ultimate and penultimate 6, 25–6, 36, 41, 43, 71–2, 120, 133–4, 184, 187–94, 192 n.37, 197, 200–2, 204, 211, 211 n.6, 214–16, 218–19, 222 n.56, 223, 225–30, 227 n.85, 232 n.112

Verhagen, Koert 6, 173–86, 175 n.5
von Wedemeyer, Maria 37

Weber, Lea 3–4, 36–54, 128 n.94
Weinandy, T. 139, 155, 168 n.94
Welker, Christian 111 n.82
White, Thomas Joseph 57, 62–9

'Who Is Jesus Christ, for Us, Today?' (Pangritz) 13–18, 36, 149 n.72, 150 n.75
who question 5, 13–14, 14 n.7, 40–1, 79, 86, 97, 111, 129, 133, 135, 146–7, 167 n.88, 174–5, 177–8, 180–2, 185–6, 211 n.7, 214–19
Widerstand und Ergebung 55 n.2
Williams, Anna 238–9
Williams, Rowan 1, 3, 97 n.20, 98 n.24, 112 n.85, 129, 131, 135 n.132, 186 n.38, 192 n.37
word (of God) 28, 120, 124, 141, 168 n.93, 189–91, 208, 216, 216 n.25, 217, 222
'world come of age' 2, 7, 77–8, 80–1, 88, 139, 149–50, 152, 160–1, 163, 212

Yeago, David S. 66

Zachhuber, Johannes 55
Ziegler, Phil 4, 47 n.52, 78 n.16, 80 n.22, 82 n.34, 149, 149 nn.69–71, 152 n.88, 161 n.45, 167 n.87, 173 n.1, 183 n.32, 190 n.17, 211 n.5, 213 n.11, 233 n.116, 237 n.5, 248 n.70, 249 n.83
Zimmermann, Jens 191, 192 n.37
Zizioulas, John 242–3

www.ingramcontent.com/pod-product-compliance
Lightning Source LLC
Chambersburg PA
CBHW071933240426
43668CB00038B/1527